D1228584

GOVERNING THE ENVIRONMENT

Persistent Challenges, Uncertain Innovations

Edited by Edward A. Parson

UNIVERSITY OF TORONTO PRESS
Toronto Buffalo London

© University of Toronto Press Incorporated 2001
Toronto Buffalo London
Printed in Canada

ISBN 0-8020-8406-0

Printed on acid-free paper

National Library of Canada Cataloguing in Publication Data

Main entry under title:

Governing the environment : persistent challenges, uncertain innovations

(Trends series)
Includes bibliographical references.
ISBN 0-8020-8406-0

1. Environmental policy – Canada.   I. Parson, Edward Anthony.
II. Series: Trends series (Toronto, Ont.).

GE190.C3G68 2001   333.7'2'0971   C00-933122-0

The University of Toronto Press acknowledges the financial assistance to its publishing program of the Canada Council for the Arts and the Ontario Arts Council.

University of Toronto Press acknowledges the financial support for its publishing activities of the Government of Canada through the Book Publishing Industry Development Program (BPIDP).

Contents

Preface

Exchanging ideas, perspectives, frameworks and data between academics and government is, at once, necessary for the development of innovative and effective public policy and increasingly difficult in times of constant change. The Trends Project, a collaborative effort of the Policy Research Initiative and the Social Sciences and Humanities Research Council, was conceived as a means of addressing this difficulty by providing a new model for academics and government to collaborate on research that informs the policy-development process.

Three goals lie at the heart of the Policy Research Initiative and the Trends Project:

• Supporting the creation, sharing, and use of policy research knowledge;
• Strengthening departments by recruitment, development, and retention of people; and
• Building a policy research community through networks and concrete vehicles and venues.

This volume represents the work of the Environment team, one of eight in the Trends Project. In the past, relations between government and the research community have typically taken one of two forms: either the government has commissioned research to address knowledge needs that it has identified; or the federal granting councils have funded research on questions identified and proposed by academic researchers. Under the Trends Project, academics, think tanks, and government officials collaborated to identify priority areas for research. This collaboration sought to identify opportunities for research and scholarship to inform longer-term policy and societal choice.

The make-up of the teams themselves was unique. Led by some of Canada's leading academics, the project's eight teams involved more than fifty researchers from universities across the country, chosen through a call for proposals administered by the Social Sciences and Humanities Research Council. These multidisciplinary teams of participants from across Canada brought people together who would not normally have the opportunity to collaborate.

The Trends Project was also innovative because it provided a means for academics to have their ideas and research circulated widely throughout government. The project was not only concerned with producing papers, but also with the continued process of dialog and collaboration between thoughtful people engaged in these issues from multiple disciplines and professions, and from the university, government, private, and non-profit sectors. To this end, drafts of the papers prepared by the Environment team were discussed at a workshop, held at Green College in the University of British Columbia on April 23 and 24, 1999. In addition, the second annual National Policy Research Conference in November 1999 offered an opportunity for researchers on the Environment and other Trends Project teams to showcase their work to more than 800 experts and policy-makers in the federal and provincial governments. Commentaries and research excerpts have also been featured regularly in *Horizons*, the Policy Research Initiative's newsletter. *Horizons* targets a broad policy audience from throughout the Canadian policy research community, both inside and outside of government, reaching more than 8100 people.

By bringing government and academic communities together on an ongoing basis, the Trends Project exposed these groups to each other's research needs, perspectives, and constraints. The Trends Project has been one part of a larger effort to build a Canada-wide policy research capacity. It is a model on which we would like to build in the future.

Laura A. Chapman
Executive Director
Policy Research Initiative
August 2000

Acknowledgments

This project has benefited from the contributions of many people in addition to the members of the Environment team. I gratefully acknowledge the contributions of Allen Sutherland, Laura Chapman, Daniel Wolfish, and Michael Carley of the Policy Research Secretariat; the oversight provided by the Trends Project steering committee, chaired by Norman Riddell; valuable discussions with leaders of other teams, especially George Hoberg and Neil Nevitte; all participants in the Green College workshop, in particular discussants Jennifer Clapp, Linda Coady, Elizabeth Dowdeswell, Robert Gibson, George Hoberg, Gordon McBean, June McCue, William Rees, and Harry Swain; and research assistance from Victoria Chow.

Contributors

Edward A. Parson is Associate Professor of Public Policy, John F. Kennedy School of Government, Harvard University, and Faculty Associate in Harvard's Belfer Center for Science and International Affairs.

Fay Cohen is Professor in the School for Resource and Environmental Studies, and Assistant Dean for Interdisciplinary Studies of the Faculty of Graduate Studies, Dalhousie University.

Anthony H.J. (Tony) Dorcey is Professor and Director of the School of Community and Regional Planning, University of British Columbia.

Patricia Doyle-Bedwell is Assistant Professor of Law and Director of the Indigenous Black and Mi'kmaq Programme, Dalhousie University Law School. She is also the chair of the Nova Scotia Advisory Council on the Status of Women.

Kathryn Harrison is Associate Professor of Political Science, University of British Columbia.

Michael Howlett is Professor of Political Science, Simon Fraser University.

Luc Juillet is Assistant Professor of Political Science and Senior Fellow in the Centre on Governance, University of Ottawa.

Timothy McDaniels is Professor, Institute of Resources and Environment and School of Community and Regional Planning, University of British Columbia.

Robert Paehlke is Professor of Political Studies and Environmental and Resource Studies at Trent University.

Ted Schrecker is an Associate Member of the Centre for Medicine, Ethics and Law at McGill University.

GOVERNING THE ENVIRONMENT:

PERSISTENT CHALLENGES, UNCERTAIN INNOVATIONS

1. Environmental Trends: A Challenge to Canadian Governance

Edward A. Parson

Environmental protection is the most prominent new domain of politics and public policy to arise over the past few decades, in Canada and internationally. Though the roots of environmentalism can be traced to the turn-of-the-century conservation movement, or still further to English reformers' revulsion at the 'dark satanic mills' of the early industrial revolution, the modern environmental movement arose in the 1960s, driven first by concern about radioactive contamination from atmospheric nuclear tests and, subsequently, by concerns about toxic pesticides and air and water pollution. In the early 1970s widespread environmental concern, both popular and elite, spurred a new wave of activist environmental groups and the establishment of environment agencies in all major industrialized countries. While the elaboration of domestic environmental protection has continued since then, in the 1980s and 1990s the centre of environmental policy-making has progressively shifted to the international level, with the increasing prominence of issues that cross borders and so cannot adequately be managed by nations acting alone.

This volume considers prominent current trends in governing the natural environment, and its human implications, with a focus on two aspects: key challenges that evolving environmental issues pose for governance; and significant innovations that have been proposed to address these challenges. The volume reviews prominent environmental trends, speculates on their potential development over the next few decades, identifies some of the prominent challenges they pose for Canadian society (including but not limited to public policy), and discusses the highest-priority knowledge needs that they imply.

This introductory chapter briefly provides background information, of several types, that is necessary to frame the discussions that follow. It opens with a short sketch of the Canadian institutional context for environmental protection. It then turns to an overview of the major biophysical trends in the Canadian and world environments – for instance, trends in pollutant burdens and emissions, ecosystems protected or degraded, resources depleted or conserved – and summarizes the associated policy issues. Such biophysical trends underlie environmental issues, and must inform discussions of the policy and governance questions that are the volume's primary focus. The chapter closes with brief previews of the chapters that follow.

The Canadian Institutional Context for Environmental Governance

The broad shape of Canada's environmental institutions was established in the early 1970s, with the foundation of Canada's first national environmental advocacy organizations in 1970 and of environment ministries in the federal and all provincial governments over the next few years. Environment Canada, established in 1971, combined and expanded the mandates of existing weather, wildlife, and parks services, and added a new Environmental Protection Service. Although predominantly a scientific organization, Environment Canada also held some regulatory authority, articulated in a set of basic environmental laws and regulations enacted through the 1970s, governing air and water pollution, hazardous chemicals and wastes, and requirements for environmental assessment. Because of substantive linkages between environmental issues and other ministries' mandates, as well as the provisions of particular statutes, there is substantial sharing of environmental responsibility between Environment Canada and other federal ministries.

The late 1980s and early 1990s saw a second period of creating new institutions for the environment, less rapid but more sustained than that of the 1970s. Canada joined, and played an active role in negotiating, several major international environmental treaties, including the first emission-reduction protocols to the Convention on Long-Range Transboundary Air Pollution (LRTAP), the Montreal Protocol on ozone-depleting substances (1987), and the conventions on climate change and biodiversity (1992). The Canadian Environmental Protection Act was enacted in 1988, consolidating five previous statues authorizing regulation to control air and water pollution, acid rain,

ozone depletion, toxic substances, and ocean dumping. Other significant initiatives of the late 1980s included the establishment of multi-
sector consultative Roundtables on Environment and the Economy at
both national and provincial levels, and the subsequent proliferation of
many consultative processes nationwide; and the 1988 establishment
of the Commons Standing Committee on the Environment.[1] Although
holding no formal legislative authority, the committee took effective
advantage of 1986 parliamentary rule changes that increased the
autonomy and resources of committees, holding prominent public
hearings and coming to exercise substantial influence on the government's environmental agenda. In December 1990, following more than
a year of intensive negotiations, the federal government adopted the
Green Plan, a comprehensive 'policy framework and action plan for
sustainable development,' whose concrete implications for policy and
expenditures have been substantially less dramatic than was originally
envisioned. A new federal office, the Commissioner for Environment
and Sustainable Development, was established in 1995 within the
auditor general's office. The commissioner is an independent monitor
of federal departments' progress toward their required sustainable
development plans.

   Coordination of environmental protection between federal and provincial governments is a continual challenge in Canada. The constitution does not explicitly assign authority for environmental protection,
and the division of related authorities is rather complex, creating
ample opportunities for ambiguity, redundancy, conflict, and evasion
of responsibility.[2] The provinces own and control public lands and natural resources, and have authority over 'local works and undertakings'
and 'property and civil rights,' each of which areas confers broad regulatory authority.[3] The federal government has authority over coasts
and fisheries, navigable waters, criminal law, emergencies affecting
health or safety, trade (both interprovincial and international), and the
negotiation of international treaties. The implications of this treaty-
making power are contentious, however, because in the absence of
future court decisions to the contrary, it is the provinces that hold the
power to *implement* treaty commitments in matters of their authority.
Both levels of government can tax, while the federal government holds
residual powers.[4] In practice, the provinces have exercised the greater
share of environmental authority, and in most cases have full authority
over land, water, and stationary-source air pollution. The federal government has asserted its authority in some matters with salient extra-

provincial or international implications, such as protecting migratory wildlife and setting new automobile emissions standards,[5] and has regulated emissions of air pollutants with the most acute health effects, including mercury, lead, asbestos, and vinyl chloride. The federal government has, however, been consistently unwilling to press for broad interpretations of its powers, such as the potentially expansive authority available under the residual 'peace, order, and good government' clause of the constitution.[6] Indeed, as Harrison and Paehlke point out in this volume and elsewhere, the federal government has often even avoided exercising environmental authority it clearly does possess. It more frequently attempts to influence provincial conduct by conducting and disseminating environmental research and analysis (only the largest provinces have comparable research capacity), or by using its spending power to defray the costs of environmental protection and thereby influence provincial governments on matters within their jurisdiction.

Federal, provincial, and territorial environment ministries attempt to coordinate their activities through the Canadian Council of Ministers of the Environment (CCME), a consultative body organized as a nongovernmental organization in which all are equal members, with a hierarchical structure of committees of ministers, deputy ministers, and lower-level officials. Following a few years of remarkable effectiveness around 1990, this process became less so after 1992, when federal-provincial conflict mounted over the climate and biodiversity treaties, and when an ambitious attempt to explicitly harmonize environmental protection overreached and failed, ultimately yielding a limited, face-saving agreement.

Three other aspects of the institutional setting for environmental governance in Canada are prominent. First, as in many domains, much Canadian policy must be coordinated with the United States, either because disparities would disrupt trade (e.g., auto emission standards), or because environmental resources are shared and can only be managed cooperatively (e.g., Great Lakes pollution or long-range air pollution). Obligations under the North American Free Trade Agreement (NAFTA) intensify this long-standing need for coordination, and provide a means for firms or governments to challenge differences in regulations. Second, as in many policy domains, Canada exhibits a general preference for managing environmental problems through multilateral institutions, in part to diffuse the potentially overwhelming power of the United States in bilateral interactions. Finally, non-governmental organizations (NGOs), including environmental activist groups, have become increasingly central to Canadian environmental governance in the 1990s. Although Canadian NGOs had little policy influence in the 1970s and 1980s, their position strengthened markedly following the increasing emphasis on consultative processes inspired by the Brundtland Commission, which reached a peak in the preparation for the 1992 Earth Summit in Rio.

Describing and Interpreting Environmental Trends

The need for more comprehensive and useful information on the environment's status and trends has been identified repeatedly since the 1970s. The Brundtland Commission and the 1989 G-7 Summit in Paris both called for the development of environment or sustainable-development indicators. Canada and the OECD began indicator programs soon thereafter, with a few other nations following in the 1990s. Describing the state of the environment, its salient trends, and human stresses on it might initially appear a straightforward task, but in fact poses substantial difficulties. In some cases, the importance of a particular measure is obvious, and the associated challenges are primarily the operational ones of ensuring sufficiently accurate and stable measurement, at appropriate frequency and spatial scale, sustained for long enough to establish baselines and trends. In other cases, even deciding what environmental characteristics to measure is surprisingly problematic. Interpreting environmental measures and using them to guide policy and management pose additional challenges. Because of these challenges, the data available to assess the aggregate environmental state and trends remain quite limited in their comprehensiveness, quality, comparability, and utility, despite substantial efforts.

What should we measure to describe the status and trends of the environment? The environment is a vast domain, plausibly comprising all characteristics of the natural world that provide context and support for human activities. But while the environment's contribution to human well-being is enormous, it is also imperfectly known and usually taken for granted. We rarely attend to how some aspect of the environment matters to us until it is damaged or threatened. Some such neglect clearly has a rational foundation in the economic insight that goods' value is defined according to scarcity at the margin, not their absolute worth or necessity (so water is cheap and diamonds expensive). But it also no doubt reflects a less rational but widespread human predilection, described for nature and other things of value by Joni Mitchell: 'You don't know what you've got till it's gone.'

The attempt to assess status and trends in the environment must also confront the diversity of ways that people value and depend on the environment. What aspects of the environment you care about depends on where and how you live, how you make your livelihood, your beliefs and values, and your wealth. Poor or vulnerable communities, or those deriving most of their livelihood from a single resource, may be severely threatened by a single dimension of environmental change, such as rising sea level or depletion of a fishery, whose impact on a richer or more diversified community would be insignificant. People's different values and ways of life also shape the relative priority they accord to protecting different aspects of the environment, such as environmental quality in cities (where most people live), versus protecting wild places, species, and ecosystems. Environmental concerns consequently reflect a blending of imperfectly understood dynamics of biophysical systems and people's reliance on them; and of human conceptions, individual and collective, of what things are sacred or valued, and what changes are feared.[7]

Supposing that a reasonable set of environmental measures is chosen, interpreting their meaning is also not obvious. Some measures – perhaps the size of a fish stock or the rate of conversion of agricultural or forest land – may have direct meaning to those who depend on them for specific benefits such as livelihood or recreation. But most environmental measures – a pollutant's emissions or its concentration in the air, a lake, or a seal's fat; production of a hazardous substance or waste; changes in the area or species mix of a particular ecosystem – only derive meaning indirectly. Their meaning will most often reflect some conception of a limit to acceptable environmental perturbations, or some measure of human-relevant impacts. When some environmental measure is subject to agreements or regulations, its meaning might also be defined by comparison with a target value, or with levels required or achieved in other nations. One would hope, however – granted, sometimes in vain – that the level of such regulations would in turn be grounded in a conception of either environmental limits or human impacts.

The simplest of these notions, fixed environmental limits, is deeply problematic if applied to human activities themselves, rather than to associated environmental perturbations. Claims of absolute limits to human numbers or well-being have been advanced repeatedly since their statement by Malthus in the eighteenth century. Never either fully verified or fully refuted, they recur periodically in new forms, in which both the hypothesized environmental limit and the human pressure threatening to violate it continually change.[8] Attempts to identify a fixed 'carrying capacity' of the earth for humans have been repeatedly frustrated, not just by our ignorance of the dynamics of natural systems and the limits to their stability domains, but also by the fundamental dependence of the question upon how we live, our affluence and technology, and what conditions we are willing to endure.[9]

It is more persuasive to suggest that there exist limits to anthropogenic flows of materials and energy (as opposed to human numbers or affluence) beyond which disruptions of natural systems would mount sharply. At local and regional scales, such limits have often been experienced by being exceeded; at a global scale, the single such experience to date remains the appearance of the Antarctic ozone hole in the early 1980s, but the case for the existence of more general and more consequential limits remains strong. The more that human perturbations approach the order of magnitude of the corresponding natural processes, the greater the risk of large-scale system disruption. In some cases, we appear already to be close.

Measurements of particular environmental characteristics can be useful, but forming a holistic view of the status of the environment requires some way of integrating measures of many diverse characteristics, and aggregating from measures made at local or regional scale to a national or global synthesis. Environmental reporting programs typically aspire to present such a holistic view of environmental health: for example, the goal of Environment Canada's indicators program is to present 'a picture of ecosystem integrity, human health and well-being, and sustainability of natural resources.' But the challenge of coherently aggregating environmental indicators is extreme. No current program attempts it, and some observers declare the attempt to be inappropriate. At a minimum, such an integrated view would require much greater knowledge than we now possess of dynamic interactions among different environmental components, and better understanding of how society values various environmental characteristics, relative to each other and to other values.

Instead, attempts to integrate environmental indicators have typically been limited to accounting frameworks or taxonomies. One such approach, the 'PSR' framework, sorts indicators into measures of human *pressure* on some aspect of the environment (e.g., emissions of some pollutant); the associated *state* of that aspect of the environment (e.g., the pollutant's build-up in some environmental reservoir); and human *responses* to mitigate the pressure.[10] An alternative approach, called 'IPAT,' separates measures of human pressures on the environment into factors that reflect population, economic affluence, and technology. For example, total Canadian emissions of CO_2 can be represented as the product of Canada's population, GDP per capita, and emissions of CO_2 per dollar of GDP.[11] Such approaches provide coherent organization of environmental measurements, and may also serve to highlight important points. For example, the IPAT framework forcefully illustrates the magnitude of the challenge posed by continued population and economic growth. If population and incomes are assumed – or required – to continue growing, then limiting environmental harm is a race between this growth and technological progress that reduces the energy and materials intensity of economic output. These accounting frameworks can also easily mislead if they are taken to imply simple causal relations between the components that may not in fact be present.[12]

More ambitious attempts are periodically made to subsume all aspects of the environment into an economic accounting, by identifying and valuing ecosystem services or tabulating people's willingness to pay to protect specific environmental amenities.[13] While these approaches have theoretical potential, their methodological difficulties are severe and they do not overcome the fundamental obstacles of uncertainty, unknown degrees of substitutability, and disparate environmental valuations that afflict any attempt to condense the aggregate state of the environment into a single metric. The even more ambitious attempt to construct aggregate indices of sustainable development, by embedding environmental measures in a broader structure that includes measures of social development and human well-being, has also proved profoundly resistant to specification.[14] The notion of sustainable development poses important and fundamental questions – for instance, what social and political factors shape human development or its stagnation? how much, in what ways, and with what possibilities for substitution does human welfare depend on the natural environment – but thus far (other than through its substantial value as a symbol of political aspiration) has been of little help in answering them.

In sum, our ability to describe and understand the aggregate state of the natural environment, and its consequences for people, are limited by imperfect knowledge of natural systems, perceptual habits and biases, and disparate bases for valuing environmental attributes. Striking examples of these limits arise when new, previously unsuspected mechanisms of potential environmental damage are identified, revealing that activities or emissions previously thought benign can be harmful. Examples include the bioaccumulation of persistent organic pollutants in the 1960s, the destruction of stratospheric ozone in the 1970s and 1980s, and the potential endocrine disruption from synthetic chemicals in the 1990s.

For practical purposes, however, existing programs of environmental measurement and assessment usually avoid addressing these conceptual difficulties. Rather, they simply report long lists of environmental measures that meet a few reasonable criteria of practicality and potential usefulness. Such criteria include, for example, adequate measurability at low cost, widely accepted relevance to prominent environmental concerns, and seeming correlation with other environmental characteristics of concern.[15] Existing programs typically avoid any explicit interpretation, aggregation across locations, or integration into comprehensive measures of environmental quality. With a few exceptions, environmental measures are thus far little used in developing or evaluating policy or management decisions. Indeed, in a forthcoming critique of the roughly parallel state of ecosystem indicators in the United States, an expert group commented that 'it is as though we would seek to develop sound economic policy without having reliable measures of the nation's GDP, unemployment, or inflation rate, relying instead on idiosyncratic reports from individual firms, sectors, and local chambers of commerce.'[16]

Status and Trends of the Environment, in Canada and Worldwide: An Overview

These conceptual problems must be borne in mind, but many specific measures are of clear relevance to the state of the environment and aggregate human pressures on it, even if the precise details of their influence are not known. Such clearly important measures are of several types. They would include major drivers of human environmental impacts such as population and economic output, emissions or concentrations of major pollutants, waste quantities of various types produced, and indicators of stresses on species and ecosystems such as population counts, identification of species at risk, or measures of habitat loss. This section provides a brief review of measures and trends from each of these categories.

Canada's population of thirty-one million constitutes about 0.5 per cent of the world's six billion. Recent population growth has been slightly over 1 per cent annually, of which somewhat more than half is due to net immigration.[17] Canada's GDP is $22,480 per capita, ranked thirteenth in the world, with average real GDP growth of nearly 3 per cent through the 1980s and 1990s.[18] Total 1997 primary energy consumption was 11 exajoules (EJ), which came (in approximate proportions) from oil (34%), gas (32%), hydroelectricity (12%), nuclear (11%) and coal (10%); this represented about 350 gigajoules (GJ) per person – among the highest rates of per capita energy consumption in the world – or 19 megajoules (MJ) per dollar of GDP.[19] With its high per capita income, low infant mortality, life expectancy over seventy-nine years, and adult literacy rate over 99 per cent, Canada consistently ranks first in the world in UNDP's Human Development Index.[20]

Just as where and how you live determine what aspects of the environment you care about, they also determine the environmental stresses you impose. The status and trends of the environment in Canada reflect the character of the Canadian landscape, society, and economy. Canada is a large, lightly populated, wealthy country, with a temperate to cold climate, in which most people live in cities and close to the American border, and whose economy is highly diversified at the national level but includes many regions dependent on particular natural resources. The major environmental stresses are consequently those of the rich, associated with high levels of consumption, transport, and energy use. Aggregate environmental stresses are comparatively low for a major industrialized nation, although the major metropolitan areas face the universal problems of air pollution, noise, congestion, and waste. Central Canada's proximity to the U.S. industrial heartland exposes it to long-range oxidizing air pollution and to acid deposition, to which the lakes and forests of the boreal shield are especially sensitive because of their low buffering capacity. Sensitive Arctic ecosystems, and the subsistence livelihoods and cultures that depend on them, are increasingly recognized to be vulnerable to both global climate change and long-range transport of persistent organic pollutants. The regional concentration of resource industries creates a highly variable pattern of sometimes extreme local and regional environmental stresses, including loss of old-growth forest and habitat, disruption of fish stocks and marine ecosystems, and local air and water pollution. Moreover, the political power of industries that dominate local economies has in some cases allowed scandalous environmental abuses, of which perhaps the most extreme examples have been the mercury poisoning of the Grassy Narrows Band in Northwestern Ontario by paper-mill effluent and the intensely contaminated tidewater area in Nova Scotia known as the Sydney tar ponds, the largest toxic waste site in North America.

Since the 1960s, the broad character of major environmental stresses in Canada has shifted, roughly in parallel to those in all rich industrialized countries. The acute environmental stresses that provoked the emergence of modern environmentalism are mostly resolved or improving, largely due to technological changes and investment in pollution controls that have allowed production to continue growing with reduced environmental insult. Even without counting the benefits of the resultant environmental improvement, the cost of these measures has been very modest, in the order of 1 to 2 per cent of GNP.[21] But as these stresses have been relieved and economies have continued to grow, other more complex and recalcitrant stresses have arisen that pose greater challenges to processes of assessment, decision-making, and implementation. This broad pattern is replicated in examples as diverse as water and air pollution, the conservation of natural resources, and the appearance of novel global-scale issues such as ozone depletion, global climate change, and the preservation of global biodiversity.

For example, acute pollution of major eastern Canadian freshwater bodies has declined markedly, if unevenly, since the 1970s thanks to reductions in toxic emissions, pulp-mill and other industrial effluents, and expanded construction of municipal wastewater treatment plants. Growing population and industrial output and continuing needs for more wastewater treatment, however, maintain continuing pressure on these waters. At present, while about 80 per cent of Ontario's municipal population has tertiary wastewater treatment, nearly one million in Quebec and half a million in the Atlantic provinces have none.[22] Moreover, even remote waters are increasingly suffering from long-range transport of both acidifying and toxic pollutants.

The story is similar for air pollution. The major contributors to local and regional air pollution include particulates (smoke, dust, and soot), tropospheric ozone (the principal component of smog), and ozone's chemical precursors, volatile organic compounds (VOCs) and oxides of nitrogen (NOx). Canada has made strong progress in controlling particulate pollution, with concentrations falling nearly half between 1980 and 1996,[23] but much weaker progress in controlling ozone precursors.[24] These precursors are transported hundreds of kilometres, however, so Canadian air quality depends on both Canadian and U.S. emissions. American emissions are roughly ten times higher than Canadian emissions, but have been more effectively controlled in recent decades.[25] For Canada, the combined effect has been a large reduction in the frequency of extreme summer urban air-pollution episodes, but a continuing increase in average pollution levels.[26]

Acid deposition is caused by emissions of NOx and sulfur dioxide (SO_2), both of which can be transported hundreds of kilometres. Of these pollutants, sulfur has been controlled first. Canada reduced SO_2 emissions by more than 40 per cent from 1980 to 1994,[27] but since more than half the sulfur deposited in central and eastern Canada originates in the United States, U.S. reductions were also required to reduce deposition in Canada. These were finally achieved in the 1990s after more than ten years of struggle, following enactment of the 1990 U.S. Clean Air Act amendments, including their SO_2 trading program, and the Canada-U.S. Air Quality Agreement that followed. These cuts have markedly reduced sulfate deposition,[28] but have brought little change in overall lake acidity, principally because NOx reductions have been so much less successful in both countries.[29] It is projected that even with complete implementation of the reductions in the Canada-U.S. agreement, more than 800,000 square kilometres in eastern Canada will still be receiving harmful levels of acid deposition.

Because regional transport of air pollution is increasingly important, air pollutants are now managed at three levels: domestically, under bilateral agreements with the United States, and under the multilateral Convention on Long-Range Transboundary Air Pollution (LRTAP), which includes nearly all European nations as well as Canada and the United and States. Separate Protocols under this convention have controlled SO_2, NOx, VOCs, persistent organic pollutants (POPs), and heavy metals, while a novel 'multi-pollutant, multi-effect' Protocol adopted in late 1999 (but not yet ratified) will jointly control emissions of sulphates, NOx, ammonia, and VOCs to limit acidification, photochemical smog, and eutrophication. Canada is a signatory to all completed Protocols, has ratified all except the VOC and multi-pollutant Protocols, and was the first nation to ratify the 1998 POPs and heavy metal Protocols.[30]

Most of the environmental issues prominent on the current Canadian policy agenda are global in scale, and are principally being driven by international policy. These include climate change, stratospheric ozone depletion, protection of biodiversity, and, most recently, international control of POPs. Of these, global climate change is the issue that evolves the most slowly, and whose potential long-term significance is the greatest. Anthropogenic climate change arises from emissions of several 'greenhouse gases' that absorb the infrared radiation that cools the earth to maintain its temperature, thereby changing the heat structure of the atmosphere and the climate. The most important anthropogenic greenhouse gas is carbon dioxide (CO_2), which contributes about two-thirds of present warming and which we mainly emit by burning fossil fuels. The past two centuries of fossil-fuel use have increased the atmospheric concentration of CO_2 from its pre-industrial level of about 280 parts per million (ppm) to about 370 ppm, while present world emissions, about 22 billion tonnes (Gt) of CO_2 per year, are causing a continuing increase of 1.5 ppm per year.[31]

In 1997, Canada's emission of greenhouse gases was 682 million tonnes (Mt) of CO_2-equivalent, about 2 per cent of the world total and a 13 per cent increase over 1990. This figure represented about 22.5 tonnes per person, a per capita emissions rate second only to the USA among major nations, or about 1.2 kilograms per dollar of GDP.[32] Other major greenhouse gases include methane (CH_4) and nitrous oxide (N_2O), which are both increasing in the atmosphere[33] but have more complex budgets that include both natural and anthropogenic sources, as does the contribution of net CO_2 emissions from land-use change.

While the scientific basis for projecting substantial future climate change from these changes is very strong, whether or not a definitive signal of global anthropogenic climate change can already be seen remains controversial enough to provide minimal – and declining – support for skepticism. The world has warmed about 0.5 degrees Centigrade over the twentieth century, with the 1990s being the warmest decade on record. Canada has warmed 0.4°C since good nationwide record-keeping began in the 1940s, reflecting a combination of a 1°C warming in western and northern Canada, a small cooling in the Great Lakes–St Lawrence region, and a 0.5°C cooling in Atlantic Canada. The evidence for climate change and its impacts is strongest in the circumpolar Arctic, where strong warming, retreat and thinning of sea ice, and thawing of discontinuous permafrost have been observed over the past few decades.[34]

Climate change is addressed in two international treaties, the 1992

Framework Convention on Climate Change and its 1997 Kyoto Protocol. While these provide a minimal institutional framework to address the issue, they lack any effective or coherent approach to emission controls. There have been two attempts to limit emissions. The first, the hortatory emission stabilization commitment in the 1992 Convention, has already failed, while a second, the Kyoto Protocol's binding commitments to a 6 to 8 per cent reduction from 1990 emissions in a control period around 2010, is unratified by all major emitters and on its way to probable failure. Beyond being rushed and half-hearted, both attempts were arguably misconceived in their focus on marginal near-term emission reductions, rather than putting in place early policies, technology development, and investments to effect the required larger shift of the global energy system over a period of several decades. The basic mechanisms and political will to manage this gravest of environmental challenges largely remain to be developed.

While climate change is essentially a problem of human disruption of the global carbon cycle, large human disruptions of other global biogeochemical cycles have not yet gained similar levels of popular and policy attention. The largest human perturbation of all is to the nitrogen cycle: global human nitrogen fixation through fertilizer manufacture, legume cultivation, and combustion is presently about 160 million tonnes of nitrogen per year, which more than doubles the natural rate of about 140 MtN/year.[35] This disruption is implicated in multiple environmental changes including acidification, eutrophication of waterways, and smog, but has only recently begun to receive policy attention, in particular through the recently negotiated 'multi-pollutant, multi-effect' Protocol under the LRTAP Convention. Similar but smaller human perturbations are occurring in other global biogeochemical cycles, including those of phosphorus and sulphur.

In contrast to climate, there has been great progress in managing the other truly global-scale issue, depletion of the stratospheric ozone layer. Ozone depletion is principally caused by various industrial chemicals containing chlorine or bromine, whose extreme chemical stability and desirable thermodynamic properties made them highly valuable as refrigerants, solvents, foaming agents, aerosol propellants, and fire extinguishers. Treaty commitments implemented under the 1987 Montreal Protocol and its amendments have reduced global emissions of these ozone-depleting substances by about 80 per cent since 1986, through production phase-outs in industrial countries that will soon be extended to developing countries.[36] Canada, like all OECD countries, phased out all but a few small essential uses of these chemicals by the end of 1996, reducing its consumption by 97 per cent, from 1987 to 1998.[37]

The beginning of environmental recovery is now observable in the cessation of growth in atmospheric concentration of chlorine and bromine, and the beginning of a decline. This decline is expected to eliminate the Antarctic ozone hole by about 2050. Ozone depletion closely follows stratospheric chlorine, and so is now near its maximum, with about a 3 to 6 per cent loss in northern mid-latitudes and a 15 per cent loss in the Arctic spring.[38] Important challenges remain, such as ensuring that developing countries are able to achieve their promised phase-outs and controlling the black market in ozone-depleting chemicals. If nations stay the course they have begun, however, ozone depletion will likely be the first global environmental problem to be solved.

Loss of biological diversity has emerged as a third prominent environmental issue of global concern, although most threats to species, ecosystems, and biodiversity act at local or regional scales. Biodiversity has become the primary modern label for the 'nature' agenda, subsuming all concerns for protection of species, ecosystems, and wilderness. The Convention on Biodiversity was signed in 1992, but subsequent negotiations under the Convention have strayed from the mission of protecting ecosystems and habitats, into tangentially related matters of ownership of biological resources and sharing of the proceeds from their exploitation, and of safety from genetically modified organisms.

Moreover, basic aspects of the meaning and measurement of biodiversity remain unspecified, with consequent confusion about what people value about biodiversity and how it can best be protected.[39] Different views of what is valued and why would imply assessing biodiversity by measures of particular familiar species, total species, higher taxa, remote taxa, complete ecosystems, or genetically based measures of diversity. Because the extent of biodiversity and the mechanisms by which it is threatened are not well known, various imperfect proxy measures of human pressures on ecosystems and biodiversity are used.

The most widely used proxies are species counts. While it is widely believed that extinctions are occurring at an unprecedented rate, neither total numbers nor the rate of loss is known with any precision. Worldwide, about 1.7 million species have been identified. A recent assessment puts the true total at 14 million, while other estimates range from 4 to more than 100 million. Species diversity is highly uneven across taxa and locations: a third of all identified species are beetles, while many regions are extremely diverse in particular taxa and not in others. Worldwide, the present extinction rate is estimated at 100 to 1000 species per year, compared to a natural rate of about one per year. More than 30,000 species have been identified as being at risk of extinction worldwide, while estimates of the true number at risk range as high as 20 per cent of all species. In Canada, about 71,000 species have been identified and a further 66,000 are suspected to exist.[40] Of these, 340 are deemed to be 'at risk,' including about 10 per cent of known mammal species, 5 per cent of birds, and 8 per cent of reptiles and amphibians.[41] Two ongoing expert committees address threats to species under a 1996 federal-provincial accord, one that determines endangerment status and one that prepares non-binding recovery plans for species judged to be endangered.[42] Most provinces and territories now have endangered-species legislation. Federal legislation was introduced in 1995 but not enacted, and a new federal Species at Risk Act was introduced in April 2000.

Inadequate as they may be as measures of diversity, species counts can also be difficult to obtain. Other proxies include measures of areal loss of particular ecosystem types such as forests, wetlands, or coral reefs; road access as a measure of likely human intrusion; and the extent of protected areas. Some such proxies make striking statements about the scale of human pressure on the global environment. One-third to one-half of the earth's land surface has been transformed by human action,[43] while the fraction of global potential net primary productivity that is appropriated or modified by humans has been estimated as 40 per cent.[44] In Canada, the rate of land-use conversion is a small fraction of the total: of 418 million hectares (ha) of Canadian forest, about 0.02 per cent (90–800 thousand ha) is converted to non-forest use annually. More detailed measures of forest trends are required to assess Canada's forest carbon budget, or the long-term sustainability of forest biodiversity and timber supply. These are presently unavailable due to limitations of data at finer than provincial scale, but are under development. The federal government and most provinces have committed to increase the present 6.3 per cent of land area that is protected to 12 per cent, in line with recommendations from the Brundtland Commission and the United Nations Environment Programme (UNEP).

Although the convention on biodiversity has achieved no concrete protection commitments, it has supported valuable assessment exercises. Perhaps most importantly, its general non-operational commitments have exercised some influence on national policy debates about protected areas, endangered species, forest management, coastal zones, and assessment, in Canada as in many other countries.

The newest environmental issue now prominent on the international agenda concerns a group of long-lived chemicals known as 'persistent organic pollutants' (POPs), principally organochlorine pesticides, whose risk of bioaccumulation in wildlife played a strong role in the 1960s arousal of environmentalism. Through domestic regulation in Canada and elsewhere, recently supplemented by voluntary programs, environmental burdens of these chemicals declined sharply from the 1970s to the early 1990s.[45] Recently, however, three new factors have brought these chemicals to prominence on the international policy agenda: a levelling off in concentration declines in the 1990s; increasing evidence of long-range transport and accumulation in seemingly pristine environments like the Arctic; and the recent hypothesis that concentrations of certain POPs previously thought benign can disrupt endocrine function in humans and animals. Several international initiatives to restrict a dozen of the most persistent, toxic, and accumulating POPs are under way, including the recently concluded Protocol under the LRTAP Convention.

These are the substantive issues that are most prominent on the Canadian environmental-policy agenda at the turn of the millennium. Other prominent current issues principally concern process and institutions. They include, for example, harmonization of environmental protection in the context of evolving Canadian federalism; integrating environmental protection and NAFTA; coordinating environment and natural-resource management under the rapidly evolving status of First Nations in Canada; and the amendment of the principal authorizing statute for Environment Canada, the Canadian Environmental Protection Act (CEPA), which was proclaimed into law in March 2000 after a five-year review process. Each of these issues is discussed in the chapters that follow.

In sum, for environmental policy in Canada the past few decades have been a period of substantial but mixed progress against persistent, uncertain, and shifting environmental problems. Canada, like most of the rich world, has thus far largely succeeded at deflecting its environmental challenges at very modest cost to income growth. Environmental problems rarely disappear, however. As the scale of human activities continues to grow, old problems re-emerge in new forms, and new ones appear. They require continued monitoring, an increasing capacity for far-sighted and integrated understanding, and commitments to sustained yet adaptable management. Moreover, as human society expands, the trade-offs between the environment and economic growth are likely to grow sharper and clearer. Although the environment may be the most important long-term social problem, however, it is rarely the most urgent one. Personal and national security, and jobs and incomes, remain persistently at the top of policy agendas, certainly when they are perceived to be in any way threatened. In contrast, clear environmental threats that compel action are rare, making the challenge of effective and timely response all the greater.

Moreover, this story of progress leading to subtler and harder challenges applies principally to wealthy nations like Canada. In much of the developing world the most urgent environmental problems remain acute local air and water pollution. Diarrhoeal diseases from contaminated water remain among the leading killers of children worldwide, responsible for more than 2 million deaths per year.[46] Historical development patterns suggest that different environmental stresses are most acute at different income levels: unsafe drinking water and exposure to particulate pollution (especially indoors) are worst at lowest incomes; exposure to sulfur dioxide is worst at intermediate incomes; emissions of greenhouse gases are highest at high incomes. While much of the world desperately needs to develop and raise consumption levels, such progress will likely increase their contribution to those environmental stresses that rise with income. The magnitude of the increase in global material and energy flows necessary to meet the development imperative, and the degree of disruption this increase would imply for global-scale processes, remain profoundly contested questions.[47]

Preview of the Volume

Against this backdrop of substantial but mixed progress against persistent, uncertain, and shifting environmental problems, the Environmental Trends project considered the social and political problem of governing the environment to manage these trends. Some papers primarily consider persistent challenges that environmental trends pose to effective management; others primarily consider innovations of governance, involving both public and private decision-making, that have been proposed to help enhance effective management environmental trends.

Each author was charged to cut a broad swath through an important question, to review and synthesize current knowledge, to identify major implications for policy and decision-making; and to identify critical gaps in knowledge. Authors were encouraged to be provocative, and were instructed to speak to a broad audience of professionals and academics, avoiding arcane disciplinary jargon and controversies without sacrificing precision. This section previews the major arguments of each author.

In chapter 2, Ted Schrecker examines the challenges that scientific uncertainty poses to environmental decision-making, and the two needs that follow from it: for processes that synthesize the best available scientific knowledge to inform rational and legitimate policy deliberations; and for a capacity to make policy and management decisions under uncertainty about their consequences. As cautionary examples, he reviews several recent Canadian controversies in the use of scientific information for environmental decision-making, and proposes three specific reforms to promote more responsible science-based policy. His first proposal seeks to protect scientists doing policy-relevant research who are employed or funded by government from suppression or manipulation of their results, or from professional retaliation, by establishing stronger organizational barriers between senior policy-making and the management and support of research. His second and third proposals both seek to increase the transparency of policy-making, by requiring both disclosure of the relevant evidence and analysis supporting major policy decisions and explicit articulation of the general principles employed to evaluate evidence and draw conclusions from uncertain scientific evidence.

Recognizing how acute a challenge such innovations would pose to ministerial discretion, and to the presumption that accountability to the public is adequately ensured by ministers' responsibility to Parliament, Schrecker is not optimistic about the likelihood of realizing such reforms. He concludes that prospects for more responsible use of scientific knowledge in Canadian environmental policy are likely to be limited.

In chapter 3, Robert Paehlke examines the challenges that arise from the complex mixture of local, regional, and global-scale dynamics that characterize environmental stresses, and the resultant difficulties of even approximately matching the primary scale of a problem with the primary scale of authority to manage it. The appropriate division of small-scale and large-scale environmental authority has been particularly contentious in Canada, where decision-making is simultaneously pulled both outward and inward: outward, toward environmental management through international treaties and institutions; and inward, toward increasing decentralization of policy authority to the provinces.

Arguing both against those environmentalists who advocate decentralized environmental authority along bioregional divisions such as watersheds and against provincial aspirations, Paehlke argues that persistent structural factors favour locating the bulk of environmental authority at higher spatial scales, at the national or international level. Biophysically, these factors include the increasing predominance of long spatial scales in current and emerging issues, through such factors as long-range transport of pollutants or long-range migration that links wildlife and habitat protection over continental scales. Politically, they include the dominance of smaller jurisdictions by single industries, often resource-based; and the risk that increasingly global mobility of capital may promote a 'race to the bottom' in environmental protection, which only national governments possess the authority to avoid through international treaty-making. Looking beyond the national level, Paehlke argues that an environmentally benign globalism is possible, though it would require a more equal balancing of principles and authority at the international level between the goals of economic liberalization and environmental protection. He concludes by sketching the outline of such an environmentally benign globalism.

Where Paehlke examines overlap of authority across spatial scales, Luc Juillet in chapter 4 examines its overlap across substantive policy domains. He considers the challenges posed to environmental management by the increasing internationalization of economic power and authority, arguing that the rules and organizations of international economic regimes are increasingly shaping and constraining domestic environmental policy-making. He argues that the experiences of North America under NAFTA, and of Europe under the European Union, offer distinct models for integrating markets while reconciling trade and environmental imperatives. NAFTA, he contends, does not adequately balance trade and environmental concerns, as a consequence of several normative and organizational factors: its greater deference to national sovereignty; the predominant status it grants to free-trade principles; and its secretive and unbalanced dispute-resolution process. The EU, in contrast, better respects the principles of sustainable development in its integration of markets, through its emphasis on flexible forms of harmonization, its provision of financial assistance to lagging countries, and its more open dispute-resolution process. Juillet concludes with some proposals to improve the reconciliation of economic and environmental governance in the context of increasing North American market integration.

In chapter 5 Patricia Doyle-Bedwell and Fay Cohen explore the rapidly evolving role of Aboriginal peoples in managing the environment and natural resources in Canada. They argue that the evolving constitutional, legal, and policy framework in Canada is in the midst of a historic recognition of First Nations' rights concerning lands, resources, and the environment, and consequently that First Nations will be central participants in future Canadian environmental and resource policy. Drawing on historical evidence, traditional and contemporary teachings on stewardship, and three current cases, the authors consider the potential implications and challenges that this empowerment of Aboriginal peoples and perspectives will pose for environmental policy and practice.

The papers by Kathryn Harrison (chapter 6) and by Anthony Dorcey and Timothy McDaniels (chapter 7) examine two prominent innovations in environmental governance that are widely proposed to ease some of its intractable difficulties. Harrison examines the increasing interest of industrialized states in voluntary approaches to implementing environmental policy, such as eco-labelling, voluntary agreements, and non-binding codes of practice, as alternatives both to traditional 'command-and-control' regulation and to the market-based mechanisms that have been widely proposed but as yet little adopted outside the United States. This trend is associated with a blurring of roles and authority between state and non-state actors, with states increasingly pursuing their objectives as private actors do, and non-governmental organizations increasingly assuming governance functions traditionally within the domain of the state. Harrison considers both the causes and the consequences of this trend, and argues that these are coupled. Regarding causes, policy-makers may favour voluntary approaches out of either of two conflicting motivations: because they believe such measures hold the potential to protect the environment at reduced cost to both government and business; or because such measures can assuage public environmental concern, while accommodating business opposition to regulation. Causes and consequences are coupled because the first motivation suggests that voluntary approaches will be chosen when they are likely to be effective in changing industry behaviour, the second that they will be chosen when they are not.

Turning to the effectiveness of these approaches in practice, Harrison finds that the question cannot be answered, because evaluations of voluntary programs have been conducted infrequently and inadequately, such that the few evaluations that are available have clearly overstated benefits. Voluntary programs tend to have unclear targets and inadequate requirements for monitoring, verification, and reporting of performance, which systematically thwart attempts at evaluation; they are also frequently enacted in parallel with regulatory requirements or market incentives, confounding attempts to attribute observed changes to the voluntary program. After surveying several voluntary programs, Harrison also identifies a particular weakness in the limited opportunities they grant non-business actors to receive information and participate in decision-making.

Dorcey and McDaniels examine a parallel trend in the development of environmental policy: direct citizen involvement through consultative processes. They argue that the last three decades have seen two waves of expansion and innovation in citizen involvement (CI) in Canadian environmental governance, the first in the early 1970s and the second in the early 1990s. Both waves receded after a few years, due to overreaching in the ambitions and claims of CI and a return of economic priorities to the predominant place on the political agenda. The authors contend that present trends toward a reduced role for government in society and expanded roles for business and civil society make a third wave of CI likely. This new wave, they argue, should be more selective and targeted than the previous ones, should judiciously employ effective practices increasingly recognized from assessments of the increasing body of CI experience, and should involve more clearly specified responsibilities for sponsors and facilitators to ensure the process's competence and fairness.

In chapter 8 Michael Howlett places these policy trends in a broader context. The increasing use both of voluntarism in implementation and of consultative processes in policy formation represent a reduction in the exclusivity of state authority and action. Howlett argues that a broader diminution of state authority is making traditional coercive policy instruments less viable, and indirect, procedural instruments more prevalent. In this context, he examines the prospects for major change in Canadian environmental policy. He argues that the rate and character of policy change are governed by the presence or absence of new actors and new ideas in policy systems. While forces promoting both policy change and policy stability are present, he contends that those promoting change – internationalization of environmental management efforts, ecological crises, economic globalization and restructuring, and domestic social and political changes including evolving federalism and evolving relationships with First Nations – are likely to predominate, promoting rapid and fundamental policy change. Such change can, however, be facilitated, channelled, or resisted by various procedural policy tools employed by Canadian governments.

In the concluding synthesis chapter, I discuss the major cross-cutting themes and insights that emerge from the other papers, and identify the priorities for research and policy that they imply. The chapter first discusses some of the requirements for realizing the often articulated vision of 'adaptive management.' Realizing this vision will impose demanding conditions both on the institutions that advance scientific knowledge of natural systems and synthesize it to inform policy, and on the institutions responsible for public and private decision-making. Second, the chapter discusses the need for substantially increased institutional capacity to protect the environment at the international level, to counterbalance the present predominance of principles of free trade and investment. This shift of authority must, however, allow room for some degree of inter-jurisdictional diversity in environmental standards and measures, and in the specific aspects of the environment chosen for protection. Third, the chapter discusses the need to construct networks to negotiate shared responsibilities, in order to reconcile inevitable areas of overlapping capacity and authority between levels of government, and between various state and non-state actors. Managing the environment over the medium term involves sufficient uncertainties that precise and static division of responsibilities is unlikely to be viable. Finally, the chapter discusses the likely adequacy of major innovations proposed for environmental governance, noting the apparent paradox that the most salient proposed innovations – the voluntary measures and citizen involvement discussed in the Harrison and Dorcey/McDaniels papers, as well as market-based measures – amount to a giving up of state authority. There is a near-unanimous consensus that conventional command-and-control regulation is an inadequate response to environmental challenges, because it is too short term in scope, because it provides inadequate incentives for innovation, and because, as a consequence of its high cost, it is unlikely to be politically feasible. Still, the adequacy of these alternative measures remains undemonstrated. At first glance they appear unlikely to achieve the behaviour shifts required, but this view may understate their cumulative influence over several decades, particularly in conjunction with other policy measures and medium-term technological change. Still, how radical a challenge the environment poses to governance remains fundamentally unknown. Over the coming few decades, neither of the extreme views of the severity of this challenge – that modest revision of the policy environment to price externalities appropriately is adequate or that we are within sight of a global environmental catastrophe – can be rejected from the available evidence.

NOTES

1 Since renamed the Committee on Environment and Sustainable Development.
2 K. Harrison, *Passing the Buck: Federalism and Canadian Environmental Policy* (Vancouver: UBC Press, 1996).
3 Constitution Act, 1867, section 92. The provinces' control of public lands includes authority over mining and forestry (s.92(5)); their power over property and civil rights allows them to regulate land use, as well as many aspects of business, industry, and mining (s.92(13); *R. v. Lake Ontario Cement* [1973] 2 O.R. 247 (Ont. H.C.)).
4 Constitution Act 1867, section 91.
5 D. VanderZwaag and L. Duncan, 'Canada and Environmental Protection: Confident Political Faces, Uncertain Legal Hands,' in R. Boardman, ed., *Canadian Environmental Policy: Ecosystems, Politics, and Process* (Toronto: Oxford University Press, 1992); G. Skogstad and P. Kopas, 'Environmental Policy in a Federal System: Ottawa and the Provinces,' in R. Boardman, ed., *Canadian Environmental Policy.* New automobile emission standards have been set by Memorandum of Understanding (MOU) between the federal government and the automakers, in effect adopting U.S. standards for Canada with a regulatory lag.
6 Constitution Act, 1867, section 91.
7 M. Douglas and A. Wildavsky, *Risk and Culture: An Essay on the Selection of Technological and Environmental Dangers* (Los Angeles: University of California Press, 1982); B. Fischhoff, P. Slovic, and S. Lichtenstein, 'Knowing What You Want: Measuring Labile Values,' in T. Wallsten, ed., *Cognitive Processes in Choice and Decision Behavior* (Hillsdale, NJ: Erlbaum, 1979).
8 See, e.g., T.R. Malthus, *An Essay on the Principle of Population and a Summary View of the Principle of Population,* ed. & intro. A. Flew, reprint, 1798 (Harmondsworth, Middlesex: Penguin, 1970); D.H. Meadows, D.L. Meadows,

and J. Randers, *Beyond the Limits: Confronting Global Collapse, Envisioning a Sustainable Future* (Post Mills, VT: Chelsea Green Publishing, 1992); W.C. Clark, 'Sustainable Development of the Biosphere: Themes for a Research Program,' in W.C. Clark and R.E. Munn, eds, *Sustainable Development of the Biosphere* (Cambridge: Cambridge University Press, 1986); and C.S. Holling, 'An Ecologist's View of the Malthusian Conflict,' paper presented at the Population-Environment-Development Lecture Series (Royal Swedish Academy of Sciences, 1993).

9 See, e.g., C. Marchetti, '10^{12}: A Check on the Earth Carrying Capacity for Man,' *Energy* 4 (1979): 1107–17; and J.E. Cohen, *How Many People Can the Earth Support?* (New York: Norton, 1995).

10 See, e.g., United Nations, Dept. of Policy Coordination and Sustainable Development, *Critical Trends: Global Chanage and Sustainable Development* (New York, 1997).

11 P.R. Ehrlich and J.P. Holdren, 'Impact of Population Growth,' *Science* 171 (1971): 1212–17. 'IPAT' is an acronym for 'Impact = population * affluence * technology.'

12 E.g., the PSR framework is sometimes taken to state a one-to-one relationship between single pressures and single environmental states.

13 E.g., R. Costanza et al., 'The Value of the World's Ecosystem Services and Natural Capital,' *Nature* 387, no. 6630 (1997): 253–60.

14 The concept of sustainable development, popularized by the Brundtland Commission, was defined ambiguously as development that 'meets the needs of the present without compromising the ability of future generations to meet their own needs.' United Nations World Commission on Environment and Development, *Our Common Future* (New York: Oxford University Press, 1987).

15 Such correlation is assumed, for example, when measures of one or two indicator species are used as surrogates for the state of an ecosystem.

16 The Heinz Center, 'Designing a Report on the State of the Nation's Ecosystems' (Washington: H. John Heinz III Center, 1999). www.us-ecosystems.org.

17 1999 figures, Statistics Canada. http://www.statcan.ca/english/Pgdb/People/Population/demo02.htm.

18 UNDP, Human Development, *Indicators 1999* (New York, 1999), 134. GDP expressed in 1997 US$.

19 'Canada's Emissions Outlook: An Update,' Analysis and Modelling Group, Natural Resources Canada, December 1999. http://www.nrcan.gc.ca/es/ceo/update.htm.

20 UNDP, Human Development, *Indicators 1999*.

21 J.R. Markusen, E.R. Morey, and N. Olewiler, 'Competition in Regional Environmental Policies When Plant Locations Are Endogenous,' *Journal of Public Economics* 56, no. 1 (1995): 55–78.

22 Environment Canada, 'Municipal Population Served by Wastewater Treatment,' National Environmental Indicator Series, http://www3.ec.gc.ca, Spring 1998.

23 Over this period, average concentrations of 10-micron particles fell from 29 to 17 micrograms/m^2, while concentration of the more harmful 2.5-micron particles dropped from 15.6 to 8.7 micrograms/m^2. National Environmental Indicator Series, http://www3.ec.gc.ca, Spring 1998.

24 Canadian VOC emissions grew 40% from 1980 to their 1988 peak of 3 million tonnes, and have since dropped about 8%. Canadian NOx emissions have changed little since 1980, increasing from 2.0 Mt to 2.1 Mt in 1990, then dropping back to 2.0 Mt in 1994 (LRTAP emission data at http://www.unece.org).

25 American VOC emissions declined about 20% from their 1980 peak to about 18 Mt at present, while NOx emissions decreased a few per cent in the early 1980s and have remained relatively constant since then, around 21 Mt (LRTAP emission data at http://www.unece.org).

26 The ozone objective (0.82 ppm for 1 hour) was exceeded 5.35 days in summer 1980, 1.55 days in summer 1996. Over the same period, annual average ozone increased 37 per cent (National Environmental Indicator Series).

27 The reduction was from 4.7 Mt in 1980 to 2.7 Mt in 1994, under a domestic plan to reduce emissions by 40% in the seven eastern provinces.

28 The area of eastern Canada receiving more than 20 kg of wet sulphate per hectare per year, the politically agreed 'target load' intended to protect moderately sensitive ecosystems, dropped from 708,000 km^2 in 1980 to 290,000 in 1993.

29 J.L. Stoddard et al., 'Regional Trends in Aquatic Recovery from Acidification in North America and Europe,' *Nature* 401, no. 6753 (7 Oct. 1999): 571.

30 LRTAP ratification-status data, at http://www.unece.org.

31 J.T. Houghton et al., eds, *Climate Change 1995: The Science of Climate Change* (Cambridge: Cambridge University Press, 1995), 15.

32 'Canada's Emissions Outlook: An Update,' Analysis and Modelling Group, Natural Resources Canada, December 1999. http://www.nrcan.gc.ca/es/ceo/update.htm.

33 Atmospheric concentration of methane increased by 4% from 1987 to 1996, concentration of nitrous oxide by 2.2%.

34 G.A. Weller and M. Lange, eds, *Impacts of Global Change in the Arctic Regions,*

report from a workshop, 25–6 Apr. 1999 (Tromso, Norway: International Arctic Science Committee, 1999).

35 Robert Socolow, 'Nitrogen Management and the Future of Food,' *Proceedings of the National Academy of Sciences* 96 (May 1999): 6001–8.

36 World emissions of all ozone-depleting chemicals controlled by the Protocol, with each chemical weighted by its ozone-depleting potential, declined from 1.4 Mt in 1986 to 0.3 Mt in 1996. Montreal Protocol Technology and Economics Assessment Panel, *1998 Assessment.*

37 Environment Canada, 'Ozone-depleting Substances,' National Environmental Indicator Series, www3.ec.gc.ca/ind/english/ozone/bulletin/ stind1_e.cfm.

38 Montreal Protocol Science Assessment Panel, *Scientific Assessment of Ozone Depletion: 1998* (Geneva: World Meteorological Organization, 1999).

39 P.F. Steinberg, 'Setting Global Conservation Priorities: The Political Economy of Noah's Ark,' *Society and Natural Resources* 9, no. 5 (July 1996): 322–38.

40 Environment Canada, *The State of Canada's Environment 1996* (Ottawa: Environment Canada, 1996), tables 14.3, 14.11 (available at http:// www1.ncr.ec.gc.ca/~soer/SOE).

41 Ibid.

42 The Committee on the Status of Endangered Wildlife in Canada (COSEWIC), and the Committee on the Recovery of Nationally Endangered Wildlife (RENEW).

43 P.M. Vitousek, H.A. Mooney, et al., 'Human Domination of Earth's Ecosystems,' *Science* 277, no. 5325 (25 July 1997): 494–9.

44 P. Vitousek et al., 'Human Appropriation of the Products of Photosynthesis,' *Bioscience* 36 (6 June 1986): 368. Progressively narrower definitions of human modification in the same study gave estimates of 31% and 3%.

45 For example, concentrations of two monitored POPs in double-crested cormorant eggs at four sites across Canada declined 70 to 90% from the 1970s to the 1990s, but levelled off or reversed in the 1990s (National Environmental Indicator Series, at http:/www3.ec.gc.ca /~ind/english/toxic/ bulletin).

46 World Health Organization, 'Improving Child Health.' http:// www.who.int/chd/publications/cdd/meded/1med.htm.

47 E. von Weizsäcker, A.B. Lovins, and L.H. Lovins, *Factor Four: Doubling Wealth, Halving Resource Use*, New Report to the Club of Rome (London: Earthscan, 1998).

2. Using Science in Environmental Policy: Can Canada Do Better?

Ted Schrecker

1. Introduction: Learning from the Headlines

In the summer of 1997, Canadians were offered an unusually candid examination of how our government uses science in making environmental policy. Three respected scientists, one of whom had only recently left the Department of Fisheries and Oceans (DFO), published a stinging article in which they argued that 'bureaucratic influence' had seriously compromised the scientific basis for fisheries management.[1] To support this claim, they cited the history of overly optimistic stock assessments that contributed to the eventual collapse of the north Atlantic cod fishery in 1992, and the questionable scientific basis for DFO's position on the minimum water flows from Alcan's hydroelectric facilities on British Columbia's Nechako River that were consistent with the protection of salmon habitat.

By the time the article appeared, it was clear that grotesque mistakes had been made in the management of the cod fishery, leading to its collapse and the subsequent closure of the fishery by DFO.[2] The article described a process in which the raw data for fisheries stock assessments originated with DFO scientists in their roles as members of various subcommittees of the Canadian Atlantic Fisheries Scientific Advisory Committee (CAFSAC). Subcommittee reports, in turn, 'constituted the primary source of information for the CAFSAC Steering Committee,' but 'were not available to the public. Following its vetting of these reports, the Steering Committee prepared Advisory Documents which formed the primary source of scientific information for the Atlantic Groundfish Advisory Committee (AGAC), the committee of industry and government (federal and provincial) representatives that provided recommendations to the senior managers and planners within the management structure of the DFO.'[3] I suggest later in the chapter that the channels of power and influence that led to the perpetuation of fisheries mismanagement can only be understood with reference to the broader political economy of fisheries management in Atlantic Canada.

By 1997, much of the history of the BC case had been well documented, because a newly elected BC government had directed the BC Utilities Commission (BCUC) in 1993 to conduct an environmental review of Alcan's current operations and of proposals to expand Alcan's hydroelectric facilities (the Kemano completion proposals). Before that review, the federal government had gone to extraordinary lengths to avoid a publicly visible examination of the environmental impacts of Alcan's operations. Its strategy included convening an ad hoc working group under the chairmanship of David Strangway, then president of the University of British Columbia, with instructions to take the flow rates that Alcan considered essential to its expansion plans and work around them. The four days of closed meetings held by the working group did not include the DFO scientists who had previously been most directly involved in assessing the environmental impacts of the proposed smelter expansion.[4] At the end of the BCUC's lengthy hearings, an environmentalist coalition (the Rivers Defence Coalition, or RDC) was moved to ask, 'How is it possible that new information arose in the Strangway Working Group negotiations in four days that satisfied the DFO members that the salmon would be protected under the Alcan flows when the best scientists in the DFO had insisted it was impossible for the better part of a decade?'[5] This seems like a reasonable question. It is also a question of the kind that outsiders to the process of decision-making in Canadian environmental policy do not usually get to ask, and indeed in this case did not get to ask until well after the fact. As if to underscore this point, the federal government subsequently exempted the Kemano completion by Cabinet order from the application of the federal Environmental Assessment and Review Process Guidelines Order as it then existed. The legality of the exemption was challenged in the courts, but ultimately upheld.

Nothing about the fisheries science example is unique. Canadian studies have consistently identified a pattern of environmental policymaking that is secretive and opaque, organized around negotiations that involve only a limited number of parties and are insulated from public scrutiny.[6] This pattern is not confined to environmental policy;

regulatory decision-making in other areas related to public health like-wise remains a 'black box.'[7] For example, the Canadian government has successfully argued before panels of the World Trade Organization that the European Union's ban on imports of beef from cattle to which certain growth hormones have been administered constitutes an impermissible protectionist measure. However, the scientific assess-ments on the basis of which Health Canada approved the same sub-stances for domestic use are not routinely available to the public.[8]

This situation creates formidable barriers to social-scientific re-search. Incidents like the mismanagement and subsequent collapse of the Atlantic fishery and the failure of regulatory authorities to prevent viral contamination of the Canadian blood supply (which on the best available evidence directly resulted in the premature death of more than a thousand people and perhaps many times that number),[9] clearly constitute 'policy disasters.'[10] It is impossible to tell whether these were extraordinary and pathological malfunctions of the policy pro-cess, or whether such incidents are routinely repeated on a smaller scale in policy choices whose individual impacts may be far less conspicuous, but whose cumulative consequences may be equally destructive. We do know that despite increasingly severe resource con-straints, the malfunctions are accompanied by some remarkably com-prehensive governmental efforts to compile and disseminate scientific information on environmental impacts that are profoundly disturbing, at least to those of us who care about such things. Environment Can-ada's *Canada Country Study* of climate-change impacts and the British Columbia government's biennial *Environmental Trends* report are two conspicuous examples.[11]

A brief flurry of publicity followed the publication of the 1997 article on fisheries science. David Schindler, a biologist who had left DFO for a university career, was one of thirty-six scientists who called for a 'long overdue debate on how to ensure the integrity of government-administered science.'[12] Around the same time, Schindler described the pattern identified by the 1997 article's authors as 'generic. It's almost a tradition in the Canadian civil service to act this way. Every environmental organization in the federal government ought to be scrutinized for the way these suppression and intimidation matters are handled.'[13] That debate was indeed long overdue; it has yet to occur in the public domain, although various internal government exercises (briefly discussed in section 6 of this chapter) have aimed at improving the use of science in public policy. I argue here that although a number of ways to improve the use of science for purposes of environmental policy-making can be identified, they are unlikely to be implemented in the absence of an environmental or public-health crisis larger than any in recent memory. This is partly because of a combination of factors related to political institutions, political economy, and a highly imperfect understanding of the way intellectual and institutional commitments affect the resolution of scientific uncertainty. More fundamentally, to define 'improving' the use of science in environmental policy-making is to enter contested terrain, and to confront a range of underlying assumptions about the relative priority that public policy should assign to environmental conservation and to such objectives as facilitating capital accumulation or protecting jobs in particular firms, industries, and regions.

2. Elements of Context: Market Economy and Organizational Structure

Understanding the place of science in environmental policy requires reference both to the characteristics of industrialized market economies and to the organizational setting within which scientists work. Under each of these headings, many elements are common across national cultures and political institutions, but some are distinctive to the Canadian context.

Environmental policy in any market economy must be analysed with reference to the distinctive power of business,[14] and specifically to investors' 'power to define reality' by way of their investment or disinvestment choices.[15] Most environmental policy initiatives directly or indirectly imply some erosion of property rights, at least in situations where those rights are exercised for income-generating purposes. The qualifier is important because the history of Canadian environmental law provides a number of examples in which property rights (for example, riparian rights) established under common law were circumscribed by legislation in order to improve the prospects for industrial enterprise.[16] In any market economy, and especially given today's hypermobility of capital both within and among national jurisdictions, academic cant about the compatibility between environment and development ('jobs') is supremely irrelevant. The primacy of investors' property rights gives them a unique ability to involve third parties in contests about the appropriate balance among the competing values of economic return and environmental protection: to practise 'job blackmail.'[17] Advocates for environmental conservation normally lack comparable resources, and both industry and government routinely oppose legislative changes that would create judicially enforceable environmental rights. Such rights would give litigants outside government the ability to involve third parties, with or without their agreement,[18] just as investors have always been able to do by way of the simple threat to close the mine or locate the new plant elsewhere. Even though environmental rights could never realistically compete for primacy with property rights over the long term, they might decisively alter the terms of specific conflicts.

Who are the environmentalists? The term is convenient, but also problematic from the perspective of political economy. At the personal level, they may be people who can take for granted a level of material security that much of the rest of the population cannot. Whether experiences of affluence are individual or shared, they may help to account for the spread of what Ronald Inglehart has called post-materialist values.[19] On the other hand, commitments to environmental conservation, however intense they are, may or may not motivate the politically effective segments of the public[20] to make investments of time, money, and other political resources comparable to those that may be mobilized with respect to such issues as local property values, cable rates, or the taxation of investment income. Another way of stating this point is that support for environmental conservation is often a mile wide, but only a few inches deep. The distinction is normally well understood by political elites; thus, polls like the one that found that '94% of Canadians from coast to coast would support a federal endangered species act'[21] are likely to be taken with a grain of salt, and addressed by way of responses that are largely symbolic.

Canada's economic mix introduces a further dimension to the analysis because Canada, although highly urbanized,[22] remains heavily reliant on non-urban resource industries and the export revenues they generate. This dependence is clear at the national level[23] and even more dramatic at the regional level. 'Natural resources, including agricultural products, make up 79 percent of Atlantic Canada's merchandise exports, 80 percent of Alberta's, 74 percent of Saskatchewan's, and 77 percent of B.C.'s.'[24] The one-industry town, usually reliant on a resource industry, remains a fundamental feature of the Canadian social and political landscape. It is only a slight exaggeration to say that if resource-based industries (including agriculture) were to disappear, there would be little economic rationale for the continued human habitation of large sections of Canada outside the Quebec-Windsor corridor beyond the levels sufficient to sustain subsistence production and an overwhelmingly export-oriented tourism and entertainment industry.

These facts of economic and political life can lead governments to permit (or require) the public to absorb extraordinarily high costs associated with environmental damage in situations where the economic future of a community dependent on a particular resource industry is at stake.[25] Kathryn Harrison has persuasively identified 'blame avoidance' as a central issue in environmental policy with reference to the relations among levels of government.[26] Blame avoidance is also relevant in other senses, and would be even if Canada were a unitary state. To paraphrase Tip O'Neil, all politics is regional politics. The incentives for short-termism in resource management, which is another way of describing the socialization of environmental costs, are immense. Few governments will risk policies that would have the effect of shutting down a town, or an industry, in the interests of environmental conservation. This is true *even if* the result of failure to do so is, as in the case of the Atlantic fishery, the eventual destruction of the resource base itself.[27] It is preferable, from a political point of view, for governments to permit continued exploitation until a moratorium is decided on by the fish,[28] or by the trees and the international trading regime.[29] The dynamic here is the same one encountered in policy toward industries that are declining for other reasons: they are allowed to struggle on, often with substantial public subsidy (including environmental subsidy in the form of unregulated and uncompensated environmental damage) until their demise can credibly be ascribed to market conditions in a way that minimizes the attribution of responsibility to governments.[30]

Prescriptions for improving the use of science in environmental policy must be cognizant of these elements of political economy. They must also incorporate an awareness of the organizational context within which scientists work, and within which scientific information is used by governments. Perhaps the most significant element of this context is hierarchy: few outsiders understand the intensely hierarchical structure of Canadian departments of government. Backbench Members of Parliament routinely misidentify the locus of decision-making authority by referring to mid-level managers in departments like Environment Canada or Health Canada as 'regulators.' Such individuals normally do not make binding decisions on their own, either in Canada or elsewhere, about the content or the implementation of regulations. Furthermore, their career paths may depend on the extent to which their findings and recommendations, as transmitted up the departmental or agency food chain, are viewed as congruent with or troublesome for the government's objectives – including concern with matters that are unmentioned in the relevant enabling legislation, such as regional economic development and trade policy, but are very much part of the policy context.

Hutchings and his colleagues may therefore have erred in emphasizing the 'bureaucratic' influence on science. Most people who work as scientists in government, and for that matter outside it, are also bureaucrats in the Weberian sense. They work in a context of fairly clear reporting relationships, in terms of both superiors and subordinates, and their work is structured in a way that would make them relatively easy to replace without extensive disruption of the organization's functioning. The reference to bureaucracy is highly relevant, however, with respect to the process by which scientific findings are communicated to senior management, ministers, and ultimately those outside government. In a delightful article on how resource-management agencies produce environmental-impact statements that support the objectives of their leaders, David Bella points out that routes of information transmission, and the process of converting scientific findings into policy advice and recommendations, are critically important for understanding how and why 'systemic distortion arises through the behaviors of ordinary people doing what is commonly expected of them within organizational systems.'[31] The nature of information flow, and the hierarchical and lateral division of labour within the organization, make it almost impossible to assign individual responsibility for such distortions. In Bella's hypothetical, the occupants of four roles – a high-level manager, a mid-level manager, a professional technologist, and a 'troublemaker' – have explanations that show each did his or her job as defined with reference to the organization's internal structure.

Bella's analysis suggests the value of understanding the role of scientists in government by way of the complementary concepts of filters and reinforcements. Philosopher of science Jon Elster notes the importance for social science of filter explanations, which involve choices made by a particular actor with a stake in the results. 'Military financed research may be analyzed by a filter-explanation. If academic personnel apply for military funds in order to be able to conduct the research that they would have done in any case ... the Department of Defence may serve as a filter that selects some applications and rejects

others. The resulting composition of research will be beneficial to the
military interests, while wholly unintended by the individual scientist,
who can argue truthfully that no one has told him what to do.'[32] Filters
may operate in another way as well. Staying with the example of
academic scientists for the moment, one can argue that if attracting
substantial research funding from external sources is a significant
determinant of promotion and tenure decisions within the academic
world, then the composition of academic departments will shift over
time to emphasize specialties and normative orientations that are compatible with the priorities of external sponsors.

The operation of filters depends, however, on the availability of a
highly receptive audience for the selective provision of reinforcements.
Competition for income, promotion, and security within any organization demands the ability to learn fast, and the successful adapt with
striking facility to the moving target represented by changing objectives and changing requirements for success within the institution. In a
particularly eloquent illustration, Cheryl Payer has described the
World Bank as 'a cage with glass walls. Within this barrier the bureaucrats and technocrats work, argue, debate, cooperate or fall out with
one another, attempting to aggrandize their own position or to defeat
opponents. They have the illusion of freedom because the barrier is
invisible. The smart or ambitious ones, having once experienced or
observed such a collision, remember where the barrier is and avoid it
thereafter; those who are slower, stubborn, or angry continue to beat
their heads against it until they are bloody. The recruitment and promotion practices naturally favor the smart ones who don't have bloody
heads.'[33] In other words, individual self-interest, which must always
be a central element of social-scientific explanation, leads those who
work within an organization to alter their behaviour in response to
organizational priorities as they are reflected in the filtering process.
Often, scientists and people working at the science/policy interface
within government are not cynical or careerist; indeed, some have
gone to extraordinary lengths to demonstrate their commitment both
to sound science and to environmental conservation. The organizational context does, however, determine the price of that commitment,
which can be very high.[34]

Some such limits on what scientists and other professionals in
government can say or do are generic, while others are specific to
Canada's political institutions. The latter include the extraordinary
concentration of power in the hands of the political executive (Cabinet)

and, within Cabinet, in the hands of the prime minister or premier and his entourage.[35] 'It is hardly possible to overemphasize the fact that the Canadian prime minister has no outer limits defining his political authority within the government.'[36] An organizational point of particular significance is that deputy ministers (the senior civil servants within any given department) normally control the flow of information, advice, and recommendations to ministers. They also have substantial political responsibilities, which are reflected in the fact that they are chosen not by the minister whom they serve but rather by the prime minister or premier.[37] '[B]oth Prime Ministers Mulroney and Chrétien reminded' deputy ministers 'from time to time ... that deputy ministers work for the prime minister.'[38] They would in any event not have risen so far in the bureaucratic ranks without demonstrating a substantial ability to adapt to the changing political agenda as defined from above: what the Privy Council Office calls 'being corporate.'[39]

Ethnographies of the policy and implementation process that document the effect of Cabinet and prime ministerial priorities on science-based policy, and the differential effects on individual careers of responsiveness to those priorities, would be as useful as they are be difficult to conduct.[40] Even case studies of specific policy choices without reference to such micro-level organizational dynamics are few and far between, because of the secretive character of the Canadian policy process. (William Leiss has referred to the model in question as 'science in the (secret) service of policy.')[41] Such ethnographies and case studies would be useful in identifying not only the factors that lead to policy failures or disasters, but also – perhaps even more importantly – the preconditions for establishing institutional routines that conform to the criteria identified in sections 3 and 4 of this chapter. It is nevertheless possible to draw clear distinctions between Canada's Westminster-style political institutions and some other actual and potential models.

The organizational factors that give Canadian political executives a remarkable degree of control over the environmental policy and implementation agenda[42] are magnified by full line forcing. The term refers to the ability of political candidates or parties to define electoral competition in terms of a choice among a limited number of 'full lines' of policies, and it is central to understanding policy outcomes in all parliamentary systems because of the strength of party discipline. Students to whom this process is explained by analogy to a town with three or four supermarkets, each of which offers only one basket of groceries, are thereafter notably more sceptical about the rhetoric of democracy. They begin to understand the importance for political analysis of asking who has, and who does not have, the resources needed to convince the supermarket manager, or regional purchasing agent, to change the contents of the market basket.

The U.S. congressional system, by contrast, offers at least the potential for multiple reporting channels. Although the heads of executive-branch agencies like the United States Environmental Protection Agency (EPA) are appointed by the president, subject to congressional confirmation, the potential exists for congressional oversight with respect not only to annual appropriations, but also to the fit between agency policies and the stated goals of the legislation under which agencies operate. Such oversight can be initiated independently of the executive branch, and sometimes even in direct opposition to it. Neither executive-branch agencies like EPA nor legislative-branch agencies like the Congressional Budget Office or the now-deceased Office of Technology Assessment (OTA) are shielded from the demands of political expediency. This became particularly clear at EPA during the first Reagan administration;[43] the elimination of OTA by the Republican congressional majority shortly after the 1994 elections is another case in point. However, the complicated institutional connections among weak party discipline, the separation of powers, the fixed interval between elections, and the accessibility of judicial review of many regulatory decisions probably make it easier for U.S. agencies with environmental responsibilities to cultivate clienteles outside government than for their Canadian departmental counterparts. This fact is important because departments or agencies whose statutory mandates emphasize environmental conservation or protection of public health lack an obvious clientele, apart from an amorphous and geographically diffuse 'public.' By contrast, departments of agriculture, industry, or natural resources (to give but a few examples) define their roles with reference to the economic prospects of specific client industries and, at least by implication, of the regions that rely on those industries for jobs and tax revenues.[44]

3. Science and Uncertainty: Neither Science Nor Policy Is 'Value-Free'

One set of problems at the interface of science and policy involves situations in which scientists working for government agencies, or interacting with them in other capacities (for example, as contractors or grant recipients) are directed to lie, to reinterpret findings in ways that support a policy position that has already been decided upon, or not to disclose findings that might be politically inconvenient. Such situations represent relatively straightforward confrontations between truth and power, to use Wildavsky's famous categories. The preceding discussion of filters and reinforcements suggests that a more common situation is likely to be the one in which scientists, especially those with administrative responsibilities, understand the context well enough to anticipate the reactions a particular set of findings will elicit, and to create the spin that corresponds to organizational priorities or promises to expand their own career horizons. As noted, the institutional characteristics of Canadian environmental policy make it very difficult even to identify the frequency with which each kind of situation occurs, much less to study individual cases in adequate detail.

A separate area of study, which raises a distinct set of substantive questions, involves the conceptually complicated set of problems associated with uncertainty and ambiguity in scientific findings. The most familiar examples of such uncertainty arise in the field of toxic-substances control. At first glance such questions as 'Will a particular chemical cause cancer or birth defects in human beings when they are exposed to it in the environment?' appear straightforward. However, even a strictly provisional answer to this question means resolving conflicts associated with pathways of exposure and uptake; dose-response relations; and the appropriate basis, if any, for extrapolating from toxicological findings in non-human species.[45] Although perhaps less familiar, the uncertainties in some other areas of science are if anything even more pervasive. For example: what is the minimum contiguous area of undisturbed habitat necessary to prevent the extinction of a particular wildlife population? Based on that conclusion, will a contemplated program of habitat protection prevent the extinction of a species like the Florida panther, the Sonora tiger salamander, or the northern spotted owl?[46]

These questions are deliberately stated in a naive and oversimplified manner in order to highlight the contrast between the view of science as an enterprise capable of delivering 'just the facts, ma'am' (what one might call *Dragnet* epistemology) and the multiple levels of inference and methodological choice that normally characterize the scientific research on which environmental policy depends. One of the most fundamental methodological choices involves the appropriate standard of proof. In 1978, Talbot Page[47] identified the regulation of toxic chemicals as exemplifying a class of 'environmental risks' that present challenges different from those associated with 'the more familiar pollution and resource depletion problems.' Central to Page's analysis, which has now been incorporated into numerous studies of regulatory policy, was the distinction between false positives and false negatives, or Type I and Type II errors. The scientific enterprise, very much like an idealized version of the criminal-justice system, is organized around minimizing the occurrence of false positives – that is, incorrect rejections of the null hypothesis. (The null hypothesis is that a particular chemical does not cause the harmful effect of concern in human beings who are exposed to it in the natural environment, or that the defendant did not commit the crime with which she is charged.) Indeed the process of scientific peer review often consists primarily of identifying all the possible methodological shortcomings of a study that might cause its authors incorrectly to have rejected the null hypothesis. One often-used illustration is the demand for statistical significance at the 95 per cent confidence level – corresponding to only one chance in 20 that the observed effect occurred by chance – before positive findings are considered sufficiently robust for publication.

Good reasons exist for conducting scientific research in this way, but many problems can arise when results of scientific research are used as a basis for public policy without an adequate understanding of uncertainty. For instance, the costs of acting on false negatives and false positives may be highly 'asymmetrical,' in Page's words. The consequences of adopting as the basis for public policy the same standards of proof that would be used by scientists may be catastrophic – for example, if discharges of an environmental contaminant that subsequently turns out to cause birth defects are permitted because the evidence of harm is unclear or equivocal. When the stakes are high enough, it is surprisingly easy to make the evidence appear unclear or equivocal, as economist Thomas Crocker suggests in his reference to a 'cigarette company standard of proof,' invoking the tobacco industry's long-standing claim that 'the etiology of cigarette smoking and lung cancer has not been "scientifically demonstrated."' Like the tobacco industry, generators of environmental impacts will clearly 'wish to minimize the probability of the policymaker treating as true some hypothesized environmental impact source that really is not true,' even when the evidence of harm is overwhelming.[48]

The choice to study a particular set of hypothetical cause-effect relations further before acting is unexceptionable in the laboratory context, where the stakes are limited to delays in publishing the next article or submitting the next grant application. The same may not be true in the policy context, where such choices may imply accepting a particular set of potential consequences on behalf of a large number of third parties.[49] Consequently 'a risk/benefit assessment,' which may be implicit or even intuitive, 'is part of every public policy action which is based upon the interpretation of the results of a scientific investigation.'[50] In the words of a former EPA official:

> The regulator's every action – or inaction – represents a decision of some kind. For example, postponing action on some chemical until there is better information is a decision; taking precautionary action in the meantime is a decision; delaying action for the time being because of limited resources or other priorities is a decision.
>
> There is no way to escape this difficulty. A regulator may say that he is postponing a decision, but this is just another way of saying that he has decided to postpone action. Whichever way he goes, he runs the risk of making the wrong decision in the midst of pervasive uncertainty. The law of averages says that he will not be right every time. Therein lies the inevitability of being wrong.[51]

The task of those who make and implement environmental policy is best described in terms of integrating: the best available scientific evidence; the costs of obtaining additional evidence, recognizing that sometimes such evidence is simply impossible to obtain; and the potential consequences, which may themselves be highly uncertain, of being wrong in different kinds of ways.[52]

Science, qua science, simply cannot answer questions about the appropriate standard of proof in such contexts. The choices must be based on considerations of policy, or values, or ethics. Scientists have no special competence when it comes to making such choices. The choice of a threshold of statistical significance, for instance, is 'an issue of pure policy'; in other words, there is no reason a priori to demand a 95 per cent confidence level for policy purposes rather than 90 per cent, or 80 per cent, or even 51 per cent.[53] The appropriate basis for the choice involves the anticipated consequences, keeping in mind again the warning that one cannot always be right.

It may help here to return to the example of the legal system. In criminal cases, at least in theory, every element of an offence must normally be proved beyond a reasonable doubt before the defendant is found guilty. The underlying presumption is that allowing a few guilty defendants to go free is less objectionable than convicting innocent ones.[54] In civil cases, a defendant may be found liable for damages on the balance of probabilities, which is a considerably less demanding standard. This state of affairs reflects the belief, whether or not it is an accurate belief, that undeserved loss in a lawsuit is a less objectionable outcome than undeserved conviction on criminal charges, and therefore need not be guarded against with the same determination.

Meaningful questions that are relevant to environmental policy can seldom be resolved in the simple, dichotomous fashion that might be inferred from the preceding discussion. It is therefore particularly important for scientists and non-scientists alike to recognize and communicate the importance of what Shrader-Frechette and McCoy have called methodological value judgments.[55] Such judgments are in no way unscientific, and the phrase does not imply a criticism of scientists who make them. Indeed, 'scientists make methodological value judgments whenever they follow one methodological rule, rather than another. For example, whenever one uses a particular research design because of available computer software, one is making a methodological value judgment that the research design is adequate ... Even collecting data requires use of methodological value judgments because one must make evaluative assumptions about what data to collect and what to ignore, how to interpret the data, and how to avoid erroneous interpretations. For example, one must always simplify any scientific problem, in order to make it tractable.'[56] There is no hard and fast line between such methodological value judgments and what McGarity has called 'science policy' decisions in situations of incomplete or ambiguous evidence. The best one can do is to indicate that choices of the former kind usually occur, chronologically and institutionally, before scientific researchers present results or findings: for example, when study designs are being selected, standards of proof defined, or study populations chosen.

To use an example from outside the environmental field, a quantitative questionnaire survey for purposes of studying the relation between homelessness and serious mental illness is likely to yield quite a different *kind* of result from that obtainable by way of a longitudinal ethnography, even if the study populations are identical. Each methodology may be subject to criticism on its own terms, but neither is prima facie inaccurate, much less unscientific, and the difference will persist even if each study is a paragon of methodological virtue. The use of the theory of island biogeography as the basis for estimating the minimum appropriate size of nature reserves, according to Shrader-Frechette and McCoy, exemplifies the need for multiple methodological value judgments. With respect to the health effects of toxic substances, methodological value judgments are incorporated in choices about (for example) the appropriate basis for extrapolating from high to low exposures, and the relative weight accorded to various forms of evidence from non-human species and to human evidence from epidemiological studies.[57] A common methodological value judgment in environmental-impact statements, especially when they are prepared by or for project proponents, involves identifying and quantifying the impacts of the development in question in isolation. Like the hypothetical studies of mental illness referred to above, each study that results may be a masterpiece, yet even taken together they will provide a fatally incomplete account of the project's effects on the environment. An alternative approach would instead consider those impacts in combination with those of other undertakings that are proceeding simultaneously, or that are actually required by the project.[58] Thus, value judgments are integral not only to the evaluation of scientific evidence for purposes of public policy, but also to the research enterprise itself.

Analysts of environmental policy therefore need to concentrate attention not only on 'better science,' but also on defining the appropriate values for environmental policy. We can draw important lessons from a real-world example: Cancer researcher Beverley Paigen was actively critical of governments' slow response to the health concerns of Love Canal area residents, who discovered in the late 1970s they were living on top of a disused chemical waste dump. She describes a conversation she had

> with a Health Department epidemiologist concerning the data on adverse pregnancy outcomes at Love Canal. We both agreed that we should take the conservative approach only to find that in every case we disagreed over what the conservative approach was. To him 'conservative' meant that we must be very cautious about concluding that Love Canal was an *unsafe* place to live. The evidence had to be compelling because substantial financial resources were needed to correct the problem. To me 'conservative' meant that we must be very cautious about concluding that Love canal was a *safe* place to live. The evidence had to be compelling because the public health consequences of an error were considerable. And so we disagreed on specific detail after specific detail.

This is not a scientific issue, nor can it be resolved by scientific methods. The issue is ethical, for it is a value judgement to decide whether to make errors on the side of protecting human health or on the side of conserving state resources.[59]

In ecosystem management more broadly, the kinds and sources of scientific uncertainty are somewhat different,[60] but competing ideas of conservatism could be identified with respect, for example, to decisions about the maximum permissible harvest of a variety of renewable resources.

Cases like the one described by Paigen account for the growing appeal of the precautionary principle. The principle was apparently first articulated in the context of regulating toxic pollution of the North Sea, and with specific reference to the possible consequences of failing to take regulatory action in the absence of conclusive scientific evidence.[61] It has since been articulated in numerous other forms, some of which make explicit reference to 'the scientist's need for 95% certainty.'[62] A lukewarm version was also incorporated into *Agenda 21*, the document that emerged from the United Nations Conference on Environment and Development (the Earth Summit).[63] More expansive, even extravagant notions of the precautionary principle involve both standards of proof and the burden of proof. In one version, 'the precautionary principle ... presumes that any regulatory procedure should begin with a presumption against the discharge of wastes unless the proponent can adequately demonstrate that harm is not likely to occur.'[64] (But what should constitute an adequate demonstration that harm is not likely to occur? This formulation simply ignores the values embodied in the choice of a standard of proof.) Another author wonders: 'What if the burden of proof was [sic] on the other side? If chemical manufacturers or developers had to 'prove' with 95% certainty that a particular substance or activity did not cause an adverse effect on the environment ...'[65]

The short answer is that any jurisdiction that imposed such a test on all pollutant discharges or industrial activities, unless it were imposed in a strictly rhetorical way – like the provisions on human rights in the old Soviet constitution – would rapidly cease to have an industrial economy. Such an economic cataclysm would have its own, highly destructive, consequences for public health. On a less apocalyptic scale, Leiss points out that applying such a test only to new technologies, chemical compounds, or industrial undertakings is likely actually to be counterproductive by slowing the replacement of old processes and products by new, more technologically sophisticated (and less environmentally destructive) ones.[66] So the precautionary principle must itself be treated with caution when it incorporates reference to the burden of proof, as well as the standard of proof. The principle is, indeed, best described as (a) a commitment to acknowledging that values judgments are unavoidable when choosing a standard of proof for purposes of environmental management, and (b) an explicit rejection of unreflective 'conservatism' oriented toward minimizing false positives in the manner of laboratory science, without regard to the potential consequences.

4. Evaluating the Use of Science in Environmental Policy

In some respects, then, concern about the infusion of political (or, more broadly, non-scientific) considerations into environmental management is misplaced. Such considerations will *always* be involved, in the sense that governments must resolve tensions or conflicts among competing values and the scientific enterprise itself is not value-free. Some explicitly normative framework is needed to evaluate the way science is used in environmental policy. Such a framework is needed for another reason, as well. When governments make decisions about acceptable levels of harm, to their subjects and arguably to the natural environment as well, even rudimentary democratic principles dictate the importance of process and informed consent. 'An acceptable decision process reflects a political philosophy, that is, the principles that govern the interaction between different groups.'[67]

One line of argument, which is frequently invoked by politicians and senior managers in environmental departments, both defines and infers accountability with reference to the existing structure of political institutions. 'The rigid, linear top-down Westminster model of governance is still regarded by a large majority of public servants as the only model that has any legitimacy in Ottawa.' Furthermore, 'the very protocol used to select the new cohort of pre-approved assistant deputy ministers ... has made it very unlikely that the emerging bureaucratic elite might see the world differently from the old.'[68] According to this model, ministers are accountable to Parliament for the operations of their department; the accountability of government is ensured by the prospect that it might be replaced at the next election. The appropriateness of any use of science in environmental policy is demonstrated if the minister or government in question survives these tests. Q.E.D.

On its own terms this line of reasoning, or defence, is circular and irrefutable. If a minister continues in her portfolio or a government survives at the polls, the system works; if a minister is shifted or demoted, or a governing party is defeated, the system also works. Further, it is not clear what the accountability of ministers to Parliament actually means, in practice, except that when a department's acts or omissions cause sufficient political embarrassment the minister may be dropped from Cabinet or moved to another portfolio.[69] Indeed, this tactic can be used by prime ministers and premiers to create the appearance of change without the substance.

More basic problems with this notion of accountability are suggested by Robert Dahl's warning that 'in no large nation state can elections tell us much about the preferences of majorities and minorities, beyond the bare fact that among those who went to the polls a majority, plurality or minority indicated their first choices for some particular candidate or group of candidates.[70] Dahl's observation is especially applicable to Westminster-style political systems like Canada's, because of the prevalence of full line forcing. Voters are forced to balance their preferences in any one policy field against what may be a strong aversion to other policies in the political market basket. Agenda-setting (determining the contents of the market basket) thus emerges as especially significant. In that process, producer interests that tend to generate environmental damage possess a number of advantages, including not only organization and money but also, in many cases, the implicit or explicit threat of disinvestment.

Even if public outrage in the aftermath of events such as the collapse of the Atlantic fishery or the viral contamination of the blood supply were sufficiently widespread to outweigh all other policy preferences, voters might regard punishing the government responsible after the fact by removing it from office as an exercise in retribution with limited practical effectiveness. They might well be correct. If voters had instead been asked ahead of time whether they would prefer to avoid the policy disaster, or even to avoid a very low probability of the disaster's occurrence, a clear majority might have answered affirmatively. The same critique applies to less conspicuous policy outcomes that many voters might nevertheless regard as strongly objectionable, such as the extirpation of a particular species or the continued release of a particular environmental contaminant while debate continues about its effects on human health. The category of contaminants variously referred to as endocrine disruptors or as hormonally active agents, discussed briefly in the next section of the chapter, may constitute a relevant example in this latter category.[71]

The preceding considerations suggest the value of assessing the use of scientific evidence in environmental policy with reference to criteria that have to do with fairness and the nature of political obligation, but that are exogenous to any particular set of political institutions. Such an approach is exemplified by Elisabeth Paté's thoughtful and much-neglected effort to set out eight principles for the acceptability of risk-related decision processes:

- A sound legal basis with clear understanding of individual and societal rights, burden of proof, and treatment of economic effects.
- An information system (risks, costs, benefits, redistribution, etc.) with appropriate expression of uncertainties and assumptions.
- A communication system such that this information can circulate among concerned individuals and organizations and be fully understood.
- A good criterion for selection of experts and a mechanism of aggregation of experts' opinions that reflects the characteristics of the problem.
- A public review process in which the information used can be examined and criticized by intervenors, industry, etc.
- A clear but flexible set of decision criteria that reflect public preferences given the nature of the hazard, the state of information, and the economic implication of the considered regulations.
- An appropriate conflict-resolution mechanism (mediation, arbitration, etc.).
- A feedback mechanism gathered and used in an appropriate and predictable way to measure the regulatory effects a posteriori, including those that had escaped initial policy analysis.[72]

These criteria stand in dramatic contrast not only to the inference that risks are acceptable because formal mechanisms of accountability exist, but also to much of the contemporary literature on risk communication and risk management. I have drawn on Paté's work in order to identify three core institutional prerequisites for the responsible use of scientific evidence in Canadian environmental policy.

First, sound firewalls[73] must be constructed between the scientific inquiry that provides inputs for public policy and the process of evaluating those inputs. Scientific researchers working in or for government must be unrestricted in their ability to publicize their findings, without having to take into account considerations of political advantage or expediency. This is clearly what Hutchings and colleagues had in mind when they recommended that 'the science and stock assessments conducted for government be provided by a publicly funded, but politically independent, institution (somewhat analogous to the Canadian judiciary)' one perhaps modelled on the Fisheries Research Board of Canada, which was absorbed into DFO in 1979.[74] It also appears to be what Leiss has in mind in suggesting the potential usefulness of independent, issue-specific expert panels under the auspices of the Royal Society of Canada.[75] The depth of the chasm between this ideal and recent practice is evident from DFO's own media-relations guidelines (as of 1997), described by DFO authors as 'similar to those of other government departments': 'Public servants should be prepared to openly provide *factual information* to the public and the media within their areas of responsibility *that describes or explains programs or policies that have been announced or implemented by this government* ... Public servants should not go beyond this discussion of factual information.'[76] A more thoroughly Orwellian notion of what constitutes factual information, or full disclosure, is hard to imagine.[77]

Second, because of the pervasiveness of scientific uncertainty and because waiting for that uncertainty to be resolved itself represents a significant policy decision, the relevant decision-makers must articulate the principles on which they resolve scientific uncertainty in situations where the evidence is incomplete or inconclusive. These principles must include explicit reference to the values that guide the choice of a standard of proof. On this point the precautionary principle is genuinely significant, even though it does not represent a decision rule but rather a guide to choosing among competing decision rules. Principles for resolving scientific uncertainty must also include what Vern Walker has called 'a default rule for making a finding when the weight of evidence is in "equipoise" – that is, when it appears ... that the evidence for a proposition seems equal in weight to the evidence for its negation.'[78] In practice, such situations are relatively infrequent. Decision-makers often think such a situation exists when it does not, because of conceptual confusion about such issues as the distinction between failure to find an effect and a finding of 'no effect.'[79] However, unless decision-makers are required to articulate such a 'tie-breaking rule,'[80] they are unlikely to come to grips with such conceptual issues, since there are few rewards for doing so.

Third, and perhaps most importantly, the evidentiary basis for all environmental policy and management decisions must be publicly disclosed in enough detail to enable outsiders to identify each step in the decision-making process. This disclosure should include an identification of *all* the evidence, whether generated within government or outside it, that has been considered, and should contain enough detail to enable the outsider to identify methodological value judgments that have been incorporated in what might otherwise be opaque scientific 'findings.' This point is especially important with respect to unpublished studies, and to assessments of scientific evidence that have been conducted within government.[81] Ideally, academic researchers whose work is used for purposes of governmental decision-making would further be required to disclose the sources and amounts of all their grant and contract support; in practice, this requirement is probably impossible to implement, since no scientific journal requires a comparable level of disclosure. The general principle here is that a comprehensive, publicly accessible record should document the evidence for governments' environmental policy and management decisions – including, crucially, the decision not to begin new policy initiatives or to change existing operational routines.

This third criterion is essential to ensuring the implementation of the first two. Without requirements for such extensive disclosure, governments with the best intentions in the world will find that existing patterns of accommodation, bargaining, and blackmail quickly reassert themselves. For better or for worse, openness or transparency with respect to the evidentiary basis for decisions need not entail transparency with respect to the decision-making process itself. 'The basic premise is simply increased transparency in the scientific advice used. Plainly decision makers may well still not act on such advice, but openness would assure that they could no longer claim to have done so, and their incorporation of other considerations would be more explicit.'[82]

Various actors may have a stake in confusing the conceptual issues I have identified, and consequently in opposing the disclosure that might aid in their clarification. For example, the federally appointed task force that surveyed the socio-economic wreckage created by the collapse of the cod fishery belatedly pointed out that evidence of overcapacity and overcapitalization in the fishing and fish-processing industries had been ignored for more than a decade.[83] This oversight may be attributable to federal efforts to 'restructure' the industry that actually intensified the economic pressure to catch more fish.[84] Under the circumstances, it was hardly to be expected that ensuring the long-term viability of the resource base would be a priority. Control over scientific information can also be used to forestall the development of potentially intractable conflicts between economic activity and environmental conservation.[85] Especially in Canada, governments play a crucial role in financing scientific research, and they may simply decline to support a particular line of inquiry that promises to be politically troublesome, unless they can exert strict control over both the research design and the dissemination of findings. As Leiss and Chociolko point out, in such situations, 'Quite simply, *it is preferable not to know.*'[86]

For this reason among others, further research is needed into the conditions under which government departments or agencies are most likely to conduct or support, and to disseminate, research on environmental quality that is likely to generate demands for substantive policy responses. One hypothesis is that departments without a clearly defined commercial clientele, like environment departments, are more likely to do so than are departments, such as agriculture or health, that have environmental policy and regulatory responsibilities but also well-defined relations with industrial client groups.

Firms or industries that view environmental conservation initiatives as an economic threat are likely to contend that all policy and regulatory decisions should be 'purely science-based,' or to use some similar phrase. They invoke the cognitive authority of science (who, after all, can be against science?) for strategic purposes, in order to avoid discussing concepts like standards of proof in the terms that are appropriate. Governments may pursue the same course of action in order to defend decisions that have been reached primarily on grounds unrelated to either science or the environment, such as trade-policy implications or the avoidance of major economic disruptions.[87] Thus, the idea of science-based environmental policy is superficially attractive, yet ultimately pernicious. The next section of the chapter explores and critiques its appeal.

5. The Seductive Appeal of 'Science-Based' Environmental Policy

Canada has no comprehensive national legislation to protect endangered species. A government proposal for such legislation (Bill C-65) was first introduced in Parliament in 1995.[88] After extensive committee hearings and numerous proposed amendments, the bill died on the order paper in 1997. Endangered-species legislation continued to be the topic of consultations initiated by the federal government, and in April 2000 draft legislation (the Species at Risk Act, SARA, or Bill C-33) was reintroduced.[89]

Several aspects of the use of science are relevant to the legislative proposal, but the one of primary concern here is the process by which species are to be designated as endangered. Since 1977, such identifications have been made on a strictly advisory basis by the Committee on the Status of Endangered Wildlife in Canada (COSEWIC), which operates under an agreement among the federal, provincial, and territorial governments. Bills C-65 and C-33 both incorporated some version of this role. As of early 2000, COSEWIC consisted of 'representatives from each provincial and territorial government wildlife agency, four federal agencies (Canadian Wildlife Service, Parks Canada, Fisheries and Oceans, Canadian Museum of Nature) and three national non-government organizations (Canadian Nature Federation, Canadian Wildlife Federation, World Wildlife Fund Canada).'[90] Beyond its core membership, subcommittees known as Species Specialist Groups involve additional scientists from outside government. Despite the fact that its core membership is determined largely on the basis of affiliation with a government agency, conservation groups and the scientific community often describe COSEWIC and its decision processes, in approving terms, as 'science-based.' However, COSEWIC's status designations currently 'have no legal standing. This means that no legal consequences flow from COSEWIC designations.'[91]

In September 1998 the federal minister of the environment, with the agreement of her provincial counterparts, changed COSEWIC's terms of reference by removing the voting rights of many of the non-governmental scientists. Critics quickly charged that the change would seriously undermine COSEWIC's insulation from political considerations, and the move was sharply criticized in an open letter sent to the prime minister by more than 600 Canadian scientists in February 1999.[92] The minister subsequently declared that the voting rights of subcommittee chairs would be restored,[93] but controversy continued about the role of COSEWIC. Bill C-33 would have enabled Cabinet to establish or amend the list of species at risk in Canada by regulation, just as Bill C-65 would have done. Numerous critics of the two bills have argued that, instead, COSEWIC's designations should be transformed directly into an official and legally binding list of species at risk.[94] In the words of the February

1999 letter: 'It is scientific findings – and scientific findings alone – that should determine if a species needs to be listed as endangered.'

The idea is intuitively appealing, but consider what might happen if COSEWIC's listings were automatically to generate legal consequences. Pressure on COSEWIC members not to list species as endangered in situations where such a listing might carry inconvenient political consequences would be immense. To some degree, this could be guarded against by requiring – as did some proposed amendments to Bill C-65 – that a majority of voting COSEWIC members not be named by government agencies. However, non-governmental members may not be isolated from political pressures, and the paradoxical effect of giving COSEWIC's listings legal status might be to make the politics of endangered-species designation *less* rather than more visible. The arena of conflict would shift to the internal deliberations of COSEWIC, political pressure on its members would intensify, and governments might be able to avoid identification with the politically contentious choice not to protect an identified species. After all, being able to announce that a particular species is not actually at risk is almost certainly preferable, from a political point of view, to announcing that a species identified as being at risk based on the best available scientific evidence will receive only limited protection in deference to other priorities.

Let us heroically assume, for purposes of argument, that a regime for giving COSEWIC designations legal status were put in place without seriously compromising the process of arriving at such a designation. Discretionary (non-)enforcement is a familiar feature of the Canadian environmental-policy landscape,[95] and indeed has been identified as a problem in the four provinces that have enacted their own endangered-species legislation.[96] If the scope for discretionary action on the part of the political executive were reduced at the level of designating species for protection, discretion might instead be exercised at the level of enforcement, potentially turning the designation of a species as endangered under federal law into a form of symbolic legislation. Perhaps in anticipation of such an outcome, proposals by some conservation organizations to allow for private enforcement of endangered-species legislation by way of civil suits 'generated considerable controversy' during hearings on Bill C-65,[97] as such proposals almost always do. However, it is hard to see how effective protection of endangered species and their habitat[98] could be provided in the face of local political and economic pressures if discretion were not also limited at the level of implementation and enforcement.

Thus, both practical considerations and the discussion of the nature of scientific evidence in previous sections of this chapter suggest that advocates of environmental conservation might do well to rethink the idea of science-based policy. This suggestion is strongly reinforced by brief examination of two other case studies.

First, as noted earlier, the dispute-resolution mechanism of the WTO has recently supported the claim of Canada and the United States that the European Union's ban on imports of beef from cattle treated with certain growth hormones could not be justified on scientific grounds and therefore violated the Sanitary and Phytosanitary Standards (SPS) Agreement, which is part of the WTO agreement. Vern Walker, who served as a consultant to the European Commission (roughly speaking, the executive branch of the EU) in the hormones dispute, argues persuasively that the WTO panels retreated uncritically into the conservatism that equates science-based decision-making with the scientist's strategy of minimizing false positives.[99] Since the EU did not claim to have evidence of danger to health, and admitted that its stance was precautionary in nature, it could not produce the 'sufficient scientific evidence' needed in order to demonstrate the legitimacy of an import restriction for purposes of the SPS.[100] Walker's analysis of the dispute suggests that national governments seeking to defend environmental standards against the charge that they are merely protectionist measures will need, at the very least, to do so in terms that reflect a clear understanding of the kinds of questions that can, and cannot, be resolved by science. Whether they will be able to do so successfully, or whether they will even try, remains an open question.[101] Since the mandate of the WTO incorporates a strong presumption against restrictions on international trade, its institutions are unlikely to be receptive to precautionary approaches when precaution is defined with reference to avoiding public health or environmental consequences with admittedly uncertain probability and magnitude. Science-based policy, in the WTO context, is likely to recall Page's observation that '[i]n its extreme, the approach of limiting false positives requires positive evidence of "dead bodies" before acting.'[102]

Second, consider the case of endocrine disruptors. The possibility that environmental contaminants may be damaging the health of wildlife and human beings by disrupting the operation of hormonal systems first came to widespread public attention in 1996 when Thea Colborn and two colleagues published a book entitled *Our Stolen Future*.[103] (An intriguing parallel exists with the public awareness of pesticide effects that followed the 1962 publication of Rachel Carson's *Silent Spring*.) 'These chemicals have been called endocrine disruptors because they are thought to mimic natural hormones, inhibit the action of hormones, or alter the normal regulatory function of the immune, nervous, and endocrine systems. Possible human health end points affected by these agents include breast cancer and endometriosis in women, testicular and prostate cancers in men, abnormal sexual development, reduced male fertility, alteration in pituitary and thyroid gland functions, immune suppression, and neurobehavioural effects.'[104] The chemicals that may be involved include not only pesticides, but also a variety of industrial chemicals often found at waste-disposal sites.[105] Even before the book appeared, the U.S. National Research Council (USNRC) had appointed a committee to evaluate the scientific evidence on this topic.[106] The work of the USNRC committee proceeded concurrently with a review of the evidence by a team of scientists from within the EPA, whose findings were published in 1998.[107]

Scientific uncertainty pervades the study of endocrine disruptors. One of many unanswered questions is whether, and to what extent, effects on wildlife populations can be used as the basis for predicting potential hazards for human health. Disagreement on this and a range of other points among the members of the USNRC panel was deep enough to lead them, in the interests of consensus, to abandon the term 'endocrine disruptors' in favour of the alternative 'hormonally active agents in the environment.'[108] To the credit of its members, the panel devoted considerably more attention than is usual in such cases to identifying the epistemological bases for disagreement among its members.[109] The EPA panel, by contrast, began the report on its activities with the following comment: 'Based on the current state of the science, the Agency does not consider endocrine disruption to be an adverse end point per se, but rather to be a mode or mechanism of action potentially leading to other outcomes, for example, carcinogenic, reproductive, or developmental effects.'[110] It is hard to see how the current, or any, state of the science can be invoked to justify such a basic implied judgment about the acceptability of a particular category of risks against a background of pervasive uncertainty.[111]

6. Conclusion: *Plus ça change ...*

The preceding examples show that 'science-based' environmental policy is neither a practical nor a conceptually coherent goal. Needed instead is a framework for making environmental policy decisions that is sensitive to the kinds of questions that can be answered by science, and the kinds that cannot – in other words, that incorporates the requisites identified in section 4 of this chapter.

Little evidence suggests that Canadian public policy at the national level is moving in this direction. The federal departments most directly responsible for protecting public health and the environment, Health Canada's Health Protection Branch (HPB) and Environment Canada, have suffered major cuts in their research budgets and complements of scientific personnel over the past few years. Whether or not the result was intended, the cuts have probably compromised both basic research and the ability to evaluate scientific research done by others.[112] Meanwhile three internal government initiatives have addressed the uses of science in policy: the Council of Science and Technology Advisors (CSTA), which reports to the Cabinet Committee on Economic Union and 'is composed of representatives of external advisory boards which report to Ministers of federal science-based departments and agencies';[113] the Committee of Science Assistant Deputy Ministers (ADMs); and the so-called 5NR group, which involves the five departments with natural-resource management responsibilities: Agriculture and Agri-Food, Environment, Fisheries and Oceans, Health, and Natural Resources.[114] However, few substantive statutory or organizational changes relevant to the use of scientific evidence in environmental policy have been implemented.

Consider, first, issues of transparency and accountability. As part of its activities, the Committee of Science ADMs established a Best Practices Initiative, led by Health Canada. A January 1999 presentation on the initiative's conclusions to Health Canada's Science Advisory Board included the following conclusions:

- Federal scientists are public servants subject to organizational accountabilities.
- Primary accountability is to supervisor.
- Accountability of scientist to Canadians is through superiors to Deputy Minister and through DM to Minister who is accountable to Parliament.[115]

A clearer prescription for perpetuating 'the (secret) service of science to policy,' in Leiss's words, is hard to imagine.

Since 1996, a number of science-based departments have established

Science Advisory Boards (SABs). Environment Canada's 12-member SAB, which reports to (and is appointed by) the deputy minister, is charged with 'provid[ing] the Deputy Minister with broad, strategic advice on the relevance of the Department's entire R&D portfolio.'[116] The board is chaired by the director of international business development of the Alliance of Manufactures and Exporters of Canada, and at least three other members (as of October 1999) identified themselves with reference to present or former corporate affiliations. Not a single member was identified with reference to scientific, rather than managerial, duties in government or the academic world. Nevertheless, the board's October 1999 report on its 'achievements to date' invoked the need 'to maintain its current broad-based composition.'[117]

The terms of reference for the SAB that advises Health Canada's HPB indicate that the board 'provides independent advice to the Minister of Health on how best to position the scientific, technical and policy aspects of HPB programs now and in the future.' The board's role includes 'advising on ongoing measures required to ensure HPB science retains the confidence of the public,' but surely a more appropriate starting point for any Science Advisory Board worthy of the name would involve determining whether such public confidence is deserved. The terms of reference further state that the board will consist of 'independent scientists, health professionals, consumer advocates, business people and social scientists.' (Why should business people have any role whatsoever on a science advisory board?) Of its sixteen members as of August 1999, eleven were physicians and/or research scientists; not a single member held an academic appointment in the social sciences.[118] Research conducted for the Council of Science and Technology Advisors identifies the same industry orientation in the membership of advisory bodies to Agriculture and Agri-Food Canada.[119]

The membership of CSTA itself reflects a strikingly similar pattern. Of its twenty-one members as of May 1999, nine were identified with reference to current or former corporate affiliations, and a further three with reference to university administrative posts (vice-presidencies for research) that imply a close and cooperative relationship with the business community. Only one member was identified with reference to a current university academic appointment. Such compromises may be good politics, driven by the laudable objective of avoiding even more direct assaults by business on the remnants of Canadian social regulation and social provision, but they are hardly good public policy.

Indeed, if one had tried to design an advisory-board structure around the primary objective of preventing environmental conservation from creating substantial impediments to capital accumulation, this is probably what it would look like.

Research conducted for CSTA indicates that publications by DFO scientists receive internal peer review both by other scientists and by departmental management,[120] and that HPB 'science is vetted within the unit' (on what basis, one wonders) 'prior to submission to a journal.'[121] Thus, although the value of increased openness and transparency has received rhetorical acknowledgment, for instance in CSTA's report on *Science Advice for Government Effectiveness* (the SAGE Report),[122] this recognition has not been accompanied by significant operational change. At best, progress has been incremental: for example, HPB's Science Advisory Board now posts summary meeting minutes and presentations on Health Canada's web site, but the presentations tend to consist simply of PowerPoint slide decks. This approach must be contrasted with practices like those of the U.S. National Bioethics Advisory Commission (NBAC), whose meetings are open to the public and whose web site provides not only meeting agendas and (in some cases) briefing books, but also – after the fact – verbatim transcripts of meetings.[123]

We come back to the tensions between formal and substantive notions of accountability, and between economic power and meaningful public involvement in policy choices that affect environmental quality and public health. In 1979, two early students of the role of public inquiries in scientific and technological decision-making concluded that '[m]ost of them are simply structured discussions, over predetermined policy, with few real options. The financial and administrative investments involved in specific technologies are simply too profound to allow a real margin of choice.'[124] Their data were drawn from inquiry processes related to the construction or expansion of nuclear generating plants. However, the observation may be relevant to many other policy choices in an era of national competition for capital, where almost every decision about public health and environmental quality is likely to have not only direct effects on business profitability, but also ramifications for subsequent disputes about trade and investment, if only in terms of precedential value.[125] Parliamentary institutions give the Canadian political executive an extraordinary degree of autonomy, and a corresponding range of strategic options. Recent experience provides little basis for believing that Canadian political leaders will accept the limits to those options that would go along with the recommendations made in this chapter, except in response to a catastrophe sufficiently dramatic to create a genuine crisis of confidence in the institutions of government themselves.

NOTES

Edward Parson's comments resulted in major improvements to earlier drafts; Stewart Elgie, the Hon. John Fraser, Janet Halliwell, David Schindler, and Risa Smith provided useful suggestions for further research. None of them should be blamed for any of the ideas or conclusions in this chapter.

1 J.A. Hutchings, C. Walters and R.L. Haedrich, 'Is Scientific Inquiry Incompatible with Government Information Control?' *Canadian Journal of Fisheries and Aquatic Sciences* 54 (1997): 1198–1210.
2 J.A. Hutchings and R.A. Myers, 'What Can Be Learned from the Collapse of a Renewable Resource? Atlantic Cod, *Gadus morhua*, of Newfoundland and Labrador,' *Canadian Journal of Fisheries and Aquatic Sciences* 51 (1994): 2126–46; J.A. Hutchings, 'The Biological Collapse of Newfoundland's Northern Cod,' in D. Newell and R.E. Ommer, eds, *Fishing Places, Fishing People: Traditions and Issues in Canadian Small-Scale Fisheries* (Toronto: University of Toronto Press, 1999), 260–75.
3 Hutchings, Walters, and Haedrich, 'Scientific Inquiry,' 1199.
4 Ibid., 1204–5; B. Christensen, *Too Good to Be True: Alcan's Kemano Completion Project* (Vancouver: Talonbooks, 1995), 147–57; A. Thompson et al., 'Rivers Defence Coalition Final Argument, Phase V, Kemano Completion Project Review,' BC Utilities Commission (Vancouver, mimeo, 1993; on file with West Coast Environmental Law Association and author), 11–20.
5 Thompson et al., 'Final Argument,' 18.
6 J.F. Castrilli and C.C. Lax, 'Environmental Regulation-Making in Canada: Towards a More Open Process,' in J. Swaigen, ed., *Environmental Rights in Canada* (Toronto: Butterworth, 1981), 334–95; M. Rankin, 'Information and the Environment: The Struggle for Access,' in ibid., 285–333; T. Schrecker, *Political Economy of Environmental Hazards*, Study paper, Protection of Life, Health and the Environment Project (Ottawa: Law Reform Commission of Canada, 1984), 17–20, 34–7; K. Harrison and G. Hoberg, *Risk, Science and Politics: Regulating Toxic Substances in Canada and the United States* (Montreal: McGill-Queen's University Press, 1994), 52–4, 62–3, 176–9; G. Hoberg, 'Governing the Environment: Comparing Canada and the United States,' in

K. Banting, G. Hoberg, and R. Simeon, eds, *Degrees of Freedom: Canada and the United States in a Changing World* (Montreal: McGill-Queen's University Press, 1997), 350–6; W. Leiss, 'Between Expertise and Bureaucracy: Risk Management Trapped at the Science/Policy Interface,' in G.B. Doern and T. Reed, eds, *Risky Business: Canada's Changing Science-Based Policy and Regulatory Regime* (Toronto: University of Toronto Press, forthcoming).

7 T. Schrecker et al., 'Biotechnology, Ethics and Government: Report to the Interdepartmental Working Group on Ethics in Biotechnology,' in *Renewal of the Canadian Biotechnology Strategy, Resource Document 3.4.1: Ethics* (Ottawa: Industry Canada, 1998; <http://strategis.ic.gc.ca/ssg/bh00195e.html>), 220–9 (discussing the regulation of biotechnology by Health Canada's Health Protection Branch). The same phrase was used to describe the operation of the agency by David Dodge, then the recently appointed deputy minister of Health Canada, in Standing Senate Committee on Agriculture and Forestry, *Evidence*, 29 Oct. 1998.

8 Telephone interview with Dr André Lachance, Director, Bureau of Veterinary Drugs, Health Canada, August 1999.

9 Mr Justice H. Krever, *Commission of Inquiry on the Blood System in Canada: Final Report*, 3 vols. (Ottawa: Public Works and Government Services Canada, 1997), 708–18. For a thorough summary of the contaminated-blood saga in Canada see M.A. Somerville and N. Gilmore, 'From Trust tô Tragedy: HIV/AIDS and the Canadian Blood System,' in E.A. Feldman and R. Bayer, eds, *Blood Feuds: AIDS, Blood, and the Politics of Medical Disaster* (New York: Oxford University Press, 1999), 127–59.

10 The term is borrowed from P. Gray, 'Policy Disasters in Europe: An Introduction,' in P. Gray and P. 't Hart, eds, *Public Policy Disasters in Western Europe* (London: Routledge, 1998), 3–20. Among the case studies in the volume, the example most closely comparable to those discussed in the present chapter, and the only one that involves the use of scientific evidence, is discussed by B. Baggott, 'The BSE Crisis: Public Health and the "Risk Society,"' in ibid., 61–78. The known, documented health impacts of contamination of the Canadian blood supply are far more extensive than those of BSE (bovine spongiform encephalopathy, or mad cow disease). A generation later, when the collapse of the Atlantic fishery has worked its way through the social fabric by way of such variables as impoverishment and community disorganization, the same may prove to be true in that case as well.

11 B.C. Ministry of Environment, Lands and Parks, *Environmental Trends in British Columbia 2000* (Victoria, BC Ministry of Environment, 2000; <http://www.elp.gov.bc.ca/sppl/soerpt>); Environment Canada, *Canada Country*

Study: Climate Impacts and Adaptation, 8 vols. (Downsview, ON: Atmospheric Environment Service, Environment Canada, 1997; <http://www.ec.gc.ca/climate/ccs/>).

12 Quoted in C. Enman, '36 scientists: End the suppression,' *Ottawa Citizen*, 4 July 1997: A1, A4.

13 Quoted in C. Enman, 'DFO officials threaten to sue Citizen,' *Ottawa Citizen*, 3 July 1997: A1, A2.

14 C. Lindblom, *Politics and Markets* (New York: Basic Books, 1977), 170–221; Schrecker, *Political Economy of Environmental Hazards*, 16–23; T. Schrecker, 'Resisting Environmental Regulation: The Cryptic Pattern of Business-Government Relations,' in R. Paehlke and D. Torgerson, eds, *Managing Leviathan: Environmental Politics and the Administrative State* (Peterborough, ON: Broadview, 1989), 165–99.

15 C. Offe, *Contradictions of the Welfare State*, ed. John Keane (Cambridge, MA: MIT Press, 1984), 151.

16 T. Schrecker, 'Of Invisible Beasts and the Public Interest: Environmental Cases and the Judicial System,' in R. Boardman, ed., *Canadian Environmental Policy* (Toronto: Oxford University Press Canada, 1992), 83–8.

17 R. Kazis and R. Grossman, *Fear at Work: Job Blackmail, Labor, and the Environment* (New York: Pilgrim Press, 1982). In a relatively simple illustration, an Ontario Ministry of the Environment spokesperson explained the province's choice of permissible effluent levels for the chemical industry in 1994 by saying: 'We could say zero discharge but they would all close their plants and move to Mexico'; quoted in D. Westell, 'New rules to cut toxic wastes 47%,' *Globe and Mail*, 14 Sept. 1994: B2. As this example illustrates, the threat of disinvestment need not be explicit to be effective; it can operate instead by way of the mechanism of anticipated reaction.

18 S. Jasanoff, 'Acceptable Evidence in a Pluralistic Society,' in D.G. Mayo and R.D. Hollander, eds, *Acceptable Evidence: Science and Values in Risk Management* (New York: Oxford University Press, 1991), 29–47; T. Schrecker, 'Environmental Law and the Greening of Government: A Cynical Guide,' in G. Thompson, M. McConnell and L. Huestis, eds, *Environmental Law and Business in Canada* (Aurora, ON: Canada Law Book, 1993), 164–8; Hoberg, 'Governing the Environment,' 355–6.

19 R. Inglehart, *Culture Shift in Advanced Industrial Society* (Princeton, NJ: Princeton University Press, 1990).

20 A category that is by no means coextensive with the entire electorate: cf. the observations of E.E. Schattschneider that '[p]robably about 90 percent of the people cannot get into the pressure system' so crucial not only to setting the electoral agenda but also to the political exchanges that occur during

the period between elections, and of Lynton Caldwell to the effect that even in formally democratic states, '[p]oliticians generally know whom they must regard as important and whom they can afford to neglect.' Schatt-schneider, *The Semisovereign People: A Realist's View of Democracy in America* (Hinsdale, IL: Dryden Press, [1960] 1975), 34–5, see generally 30–45; Caldwell, *Between Two Worlds: Science, the Environmental Movement, and Policy Choice* (Cambridge: Cambridge University Press, 1990), 88.

21 Canadian Endangered Species Coalition, 'Federal Endangered Species Legislation – Background' [handout] (Ottawa, 8 Aug. 1997).

22 Because of that high level of urbanization, an intriguing area for future research, which unfortunately is outside the scope of this chapter, involves the effects on environmental policy of the consistent overrepresentation of the rural electorate in parliament and in provincial legislatures.

23 A. Eadie, 'On the grid: Net balances for Canada's exports and imports,' *Globe and Mail*, 17 Sept. 1998: B15.

24 N. Klein, 'The Real APEC Scandal,' *Saturday Night*, February 1999: 48.

25 For example, in August 1999 the governments of Canada and the Northwest Territories jointly agreed to assume liability for disposal of toxic tailings generated by the operation of the Giant gold mine, in order to facilitate the mine's sale to a new operator following the bankruptcy of its current owner, Royal Oak Mines Inc. Cost was estimated at $250 million. A. Robinson, 'Ottawa, NWT to pay for Giant cleanup,' *Globe and Mail*, 28 Aug. 1999.

26 K. Harrison, *Passing the Buck: Federalism and Canadian Environmental Policy* (Vancouver: UBC Press, 1996).

27 Patricia Marchak has suggested that a similar outcome may be in store for the forest-products industry in British Columbia: see her *Logging the Globe* (Montreal: McGill-Queen's University Press, 1995). Such an outcome would be in keeping with the historical pattern of exhaustion of renewable resources documented in H. Regier and G.L. Baskerville, 'Sustainable Redevelopment of Regional Ecosystems Degraded by Exploitive Development,' in W. Clark and R.E. Munn, eds, *Sustainable Development of the Biosphere* (Cambridge: Cambridge University Press, 1986), 75–100.

28 In the words of a fishery industry executive quoted by S. Feschuk, 'Only one big processor ready for cod clobbering,' *Globe and Mail*, 3 July 1992.

29 Some time before the last merchantable tree is cut down in British Columbia, the provincial government will probably end up paying forest-product firms to harvest trees for export. The strategy will in turn probably be frustrated, at least as it applies to the U.S. market, by understandable protests from competitors in the Pacific northwest. Meanwhile, the Japanese will be

quite happy to have Canadian taxpayers continue to help finance their imports of forest products from both BC and Alberta.

30 M. Trebilcock, *The Political Economy of Economic Adjustment: The Case of Declining Sectors*, Royal Commission on the Economic Union and Development Prospects for Canada, Collected Research Studies Series vol. 8 (Toronto: University of Toronto Press, 1986), 24–5, 34.

31 D.A. Bella, 'The Pressures of Organizations and the Responsibilities of University Professors,' *BioScience* 46 (1996): 772.

32 J. Elster, *Ulysses and the Sirens: Studies in Rationality and Irrationality* (Cambridge: Cambridge University Press, rev. ed., 1984), 30.

33 C. Payer, *The World Bank: A Critical Analysis* (New York: Monthly Review Press, 1982), 353.

34 D.J. Mattson, 'Ethics and Science in Natural Resource Agencies,' *BioScience* 46 (1996): 767–71.

35 See generally D.J. Savoie, *Governing from the Centre: The Concentration of Power in Canadian Politics* (Toronto: University of Toronto Press, 1999). The 1996 report of a task force on the federal government's policy capacity similarly noted that line departments 'rarely control the interdepartmental allocation of resources, so they are lacking a key lever – and when a line department does lead in the allocation of resources, as happened under the Green Plan, other departments can challenge its objectivity. Typically lead departments also have only weak levers in relation to the process of decision making and they have none of the broader influence that comes from the Prime Minister's and the Clerk's [i.e., the Clerk of the Privy Council's] role in Ministerial and deputy ministerial appointments.' I. Fellegi (chair), *Strengthening Our Policy Capacity: Task Force Report* (Ottawa: Privy Council Office, December 1996), 18.

36 Savoie, *Governing from the Centre*, 108; see generally 71–108.

37 On the role of deputy ministers see ibid., 248–59, 275–81, 314–17.

38 Ibid., 277.

39 Ibid., 255; see also 275–6, 315 and G.B. Doern, *The Peripheral Nature of Scientific and Technological Controversy in Federal Policy Formulation*, Background study no. 46 (Ottawa: Science Council of Canada, 1981).

40 Indeed, I know of only one such Canadian study: Paul Rock's *A View from the Shadows: The Ministry of the Solicitor General of Canada and the Making of the Justice for Victims of Crime Initiative* (Oxford: Clarendon Press, 1986) dealt with the evolution of federal policy toward victims of crime during the Trudeau era.

41 Leiss, 'Between Expertise and Bureaucracy.'

42 Schrecker, 'Invisible Beasts' and 'The Greening of Government.'

43 E. Silbergeld, 'Risk Assessment and Risk Management: An Uneasy Divorce,' in Mayo and Hollander, eds, *Acceptable Evidence*, 99–114.

44 The classic discussion of the internal structure of interest representation within the Canadian state remains R. Mahon, 'Canadian Public Policy: The Unequal Structure of Representation,' in L. Panitch , ed., *The Canadian State: Political Economy and Political Power* (Toronto: University of Toronto Press, 1977), 165–98. The continuing importance of Mahon's analysis for environmental policy was illustrated by the first report of the Commissioner of the Environment and Sustainable Development to Parliament. The report noted that the approach taken by Industry Canada and Natural Resources Canada to regulation of industrial chemicals tends to be quite different from that taken by Health Canada, Environment Canada, and DFO. In specific cases, such as those involving regulation of aquatic herbicides and activities that may result in increased discharges of mercury into the aquatic environment, the effect of such disagreements has been a policy impasse. This amounts, of course, to a tacit endorsement of the status quo, which may be precisely what the development-oriented departments and their clients had in mind. See Commissioner of the Environment and Sustainable Development, *Report to the House of Commons* (Ottawa: Public Works and Government Services Canada, 1999), chap. 3.

45 T. Page, 'A Generic View of Toxic Chemicals and Similar Risks,' *Ecology Law Quarterly* 7 (1978): 207–44; Schrecker, *Political Economy of Environmental Hazards*, 25–37; Harrison and Hoberg, *Risk, Science and Politics*, 20–7.

46 J. Maienschein, J.P. Collins, and D.S. Strouse, 'Biology and Law: Challenges of Adjudicating Competing Claims in a Democracy,' *Jurimetrics Journal* 38 (1998): 153–4, 159–65; K.S. Shrader-Frechette and E.D. McCoy, *Method in Ecology: Strategies for Conservation* (Cambridge: Cambridge University Press, 1993), 86–92, 198–239; B.L. Taylor and T. Gerrodette, 'The Uses of Statistical Power in Conservation Biology: The Vaquita and Northern Spotted Owl,' *Conservation Biology* 7 (1993): 489–500.

47 Page, 'Generic View.'

48 T.D. Crocker, 'Scientific Truths and Policy Truths in Acid Deposition Research,' in T. Crocker, ed., *Economic Perspectives on Acid Deposition Control*, Ann Arbor Science Acid Precipitation Series (Boston: Butterworth, 1984), 8: 66–7.

49 J.S. Weis, 'Scientific Uncertainty and Environmental Policy: Four Pollution Case Studies,' in J. Lemons, ed., *Scientific Uncertainty and Environmental Problem Solving* (Cambridge, MA: Blackwell Science, 1996), 169.

50 W. Darby, 'An Example of Decision-Making on Environmental Carcinogens: The Delaney Clause,' *Journal of Environmental Systems* 9 (1979): 116.

51 S.D. Jellinek, 'On the Inevitability of Being Wrong,' *Annals of the New York Academy of Science* 363 (1981): 43–4.
52 Maienschein et al., 'Biology and Law,' 156–8; T.O. McGarity, 'Substantive and Procedural Discretion in Administrative Resolution of Science Policy Questions,' *Georgetown Law Journal* 67 (1979): 732–40.
53 McGarity, 'Substantive and Procedural Discretion,' 748–9; Stewart Cohen et al., 'Climate Change and Sustainable Development: Towards Dialogue,' *Global Environmental Change* 8 (1998): 360–2.
54 Page, 'Generic View,' 233–4.
55 Shrader-Frechette and McCoy, *Method in Ecology,* 84–101. Their discussion relies on a more extensive, if somewhat impenetrable, treatment of the issues by Helen Longino, *Science as Social Knowledge: Values and Objectivity in Scientific Inquiry* (Princeton: Princeton University Press, 1990).
56 Shrader-Frechette and McCoy, *Method in Ecology,* 84.
57 Such methodological value judgments, and the inability of science to provide resolution of the disagreements that result, are discussed at length in a detailed case study of Canadian decision-making concerning two particular herbicides: C. Brunk, L. Haworth, and B. Lee, *Value Assumptions in Risk Assessment: A Case Study of the Alachlor Controversy* (Waterloo, ON: Wilfrid Laurier University Press, 1991).
58 The importance of such judgments is evident in the report of a panel that considered the impact of a proposed pulp mill in northern Alberta, under the terms of an agreement between the federal and Alberta governments. The members of the panel insisted on considering the impact of discharges from the proposed mill in combination with those from other existing or anticipated industrial developments, and on that basis recommended that the mill not be approved pending the completion of additional environmental-impact studies. However, they were instructed in their terms of reference, which were drafted jointly by the federal and Alberta governments, not to address the environmental impacts of the forest harvesting without which the proposed mill would lack a supply of fibre. The panel identified this limitation as 'a serious shortcoming in the process': Alberta-Pacific Environmental Impact Assessment Review Board, 'The Proposed Alberta-Pacific Pulp Mill: Report of the EIA Review Board' (Edmonton: Alberta Environment, March 1990). On the history of the panel report, and subsequent developments, see L. Pratt and I. Urquhart, *The Last Great Forest: Japanese Multinationals and Alberta's Northern Forests* (Edmonton: NeWest Press, 1994), 135–200.
59 B. Paigen, 'Controversy at Love Canal,' *Hastings Center Report* 12 (June 1982): 32.
60 See, e.g., R.A. Carpenter, 'Uncertainty in Managing Ecosystems Sustain-

ably,' in J. Lemons, ed., *Scientific Uncertainty and Environmental Problem Solving*, 118–59; J. Lemons, 'The Conservation of Biodiversity: Scientific Uncertainty and the Burden of Proof,' in ibid., 206–32.

61 R.M. M'Gonigle et al., 'Taking Uncertainty Seriously: From Permissive Regulation to Preventive Design in Environmental Decision Making,' *Osgoode Hall Law Journal* 32 (1994): 158.

62 R.C. Earll, 'Commonsense and the Precautionary Principle – An Environmentalist's Viewpoint,' *Marine Pollution Bulletin* 24 (1992): 184; see also R.M. Peterman and M. M'Gonigle, 'Statistical Power Analysis and the Precautionary Principle,' *Marine Pollution Bulletin* 24 (1982): 231–4.

63 'In the face of threats of irreversible environmental damage, lack of full scientific understanding should not be an excuse for postponing actions which are justified in their own right. The precautionary approach could provide a basis for policies relating to complex systems that are not yet fully understood and whose consequences of disturbances [sic] cannot yet be predicted.' UN Conference on Environment and Development [UNCED], 'Agenda 21,' in J. Quarrie, ed., *Earth Summit '92* (London: Regency Press, 1992), chap. 35.

64 M'Gonigle et al., 'Taking Uncertainty Seriously,' 161.

65 Weis, 'Scientific Uncertainty,' 161.

66 W. Leiss, *Governance and the Environment*, Working Paper Series 96-1 (Kingston, ON: Environmental Policy Unit, School of Policy Studies, Queen's University, 1996), 19–20.

67 M.E. Paté, 'Acceptable Decision Processes and Acceptable Risks in Public Sector Regulation,' *IEEE Transactions on Systems, Man, and Cybernetics* 13 (March/April 1983): 114; see also D. MacLean, 'Risk and Consent: Philosophical Issues for Centralized Decisions,' *Risk Analysis* 2, no. 2 (1982): 59–67; K.S. Shrader-Frechette, *Risk and Rationality: Philosophical Foundations for Populist Reforms* (Berkeley: University of California Press, 1991).

68 G. Paquet, 'Tectonic Changes in Canadian Governance,' in L.A. Pal, ed., *How Ottawa Spends, 1999–2000: Shape Shifting – Canadian Governance toward the 21st Century* (Toronto: Oxford University Press, 1999), 101.

69 In *Governing from the Centre* Savoie quotes 'a former senior Privy Council Office official' to the effect that '"Parliament is about assigning blame and not much else"' (340–1).

70 R.A. Dahl, *A Preface to Democratic Theory* (Chicago: University of Chicago Press, 1956), 129–30.

71 D.L. Davis et al., 'Rethinking Breast Cancer Risk and the Environment: The Case for the Precautionary Principle,' *Environmental Health Perspectives* 106 (September 1998): 523–9.

72 Paté, 'Acceptable Decision Processes,' 120.
73 The idea of a firewall is borrowed from the financial-services sector, where there are clear synergies among (for example) investment banking, brokerage, and other business lines. At the same time, it is imperative that firms operating in several such areas have some level of credibility with respect to the effective segregation of each operation; otherwise, there would be grounds for suspicion that they were favouring their own interests at the expense of their clients'. Since governments often have a stake, both financial and political, in the extractive or industrial activities whose environmental impacts they are simultaneously charged with managing, the term is uniquely apposite here.
74 Hutchings, Walters, and Haedrich, 'Scientific Inquiry,' 1206–8.
75 W. Leiss, 'The Trouble with Science: Public Controversy over Genetically-Modified Foods,' paper presented at eastern regional meetings of Canadian Society of Plant Physiologists, Queen's University, 12 Dec. 1999; <http://www.ucalgary/ca/~wleiss/news/trouble_with_science.htm>.
76 Quoted in W.G. Doubleday, D.B. Atkinson, and J. Baird, 'Comment: Scientific Inquiry and Fish Stock Assessment in the Canadian Department of Fisheries and Oceans,' *Canadian Journal of Fisheries and Aquatic Sciences* 54 (1997): 1424; emphases added.
77 See also J.E. Halliwell and W. Smith, *Scientific Advice in Government Decision-Making: The Canadian Experience*, report to Council of Science and Technology Advisors (Gloucester, ON: JEH Associates Inc., March 1999), app. I, 14 on the perceived need at the Canadian Food Inspection Agency 'to develop a clear code on what scientists can and should say in public to ensure balance of openness and respect for Cabinet solidarity.'
78 V.R. Walker, 'Keeping the WTO from Becoming the "World Trans-science Organization": Scientific Uncertainty, Science Policy, and Factfinding in the Growth Hormones Dispute,' *Cornell International Law Journal* 31 (1998): 291.
79 'There is literally no information content in a negative finding unless there is an analysis of ... the probability of a false negative.' T. Page, 'A Framework for Unreasonable Risk in the Toxic Substances Control Act (TSCA),' *Annals of the New York Academy of Sciences* 363 (1981): 162; see also Page, 'Generic View,' 231.
80 Walker, 'Keeping the WTO,' 291.
81 In a number of situations, the secrecy of Canadian regulatory procedures has been defended with reference to the proprietary nature of the data submitted in support of applications for product approval, such as those involving pesticides or veterinary biologicals; see Schrecker et al., 'Biotechnology, Ethics and Government,' 226–7. However, such information as a list

of study titles and topics cannot reasonably be considered proprietary, and both the extent of regulatory reliance on such studies and the fact that they cannot have undergone the usual process of scientific peer review are important items of information in themselves.

82 W. Smith and J. Halliwell, *Principles and Practices for Using Scientific Advice in Government Decision Making: International Best Practices*, report to the Science and Technology Strategy Directorate (Ottawa: Industry Canada, January 1999), 14.

83 Task Force on Incomes and Adjustment in the Atlantic Fishery, *Charting a New Course: Towards the Fishery of the Future* (Ottawa: Communications Directorate, Dept. of Fisheries and Oceans, 1993); see also R. Ommer, 'Deep Water Fisheries, Policy and Management Issues, and the Sustainability of Fishing Communities,' in A.G. Hopper, ed., *Deep Water Fisheries of the North Atlantic Slope*, Proceedings of the NATO Advanced Research Workshop (Dordrecht: Kluwer, 1995), 307–322.

84 M. Trebilcock et al., *The Political Economy of Business Bailouts* (Toronto: Ontario Economic Council, 1985), 276–93.

85 On the strategic significance of the ability to define the scope and terms of political conflict, see Schattschneider, *The Semisovereign People*, 60–75.

86 W. Leiss and C. Chociolko, *Risk and Responsibility* (Montreal: McGill-Queen's University Press, 1994), 54.

87 Two examples will suffice. First, at least as of the late 1990s one of the objectives of Health Canada's Health Protection Branch, as part of its overall policy framework, was 'to maintain an effective and efficient regulatory system that is in balance with those of competitor nations so Canada is not economically disadvantaged.' Halliwell and Smith, *Scientific Advice in Government Decision-Making*, app. I, 46.

Second, an exhaustive study of Canada's re-evaluation of the herbicide Alachlor, after its original registration turned out to have relied on fraudulent safety data (Brunk, Haworth, and Lee, *Value Assumptions in Risk Assessment*), pointed out that no regulatory decision-makers took seriously the option of cancelling the registrations both of Alachlor and a substitute herbicide produced by a competing agrochemical firm. The clear inference is of an a priori conclusion that the economic disruption of corn and soybean farming associated with cancelling both registrations would be politically unacceptable – a conclusion that turned the review process into a purely scholastic exercise in risk comparison.

88 Principal sources for the discussion that follows are COSEWIC, 'FAQs' [Frequently Asked Questions] (Ottawa: COSEWIC, 2000; <http://www.cosewic.gc.ca/cosewic/faq_e.htm>; J.V. DeMarco, A.C. Bell, and

S. Elgie, 'The Bear Necessities,' *Alternatives* 23, no. 4 (Fall 1997): 22–7; H. Versteeg, ed., 'Workshop Proceedings: Environmental Canada Workshop to Obtain Advice on Essential Elements for Federal Endangered Species Legislation' (Ottawa: Environment Canada, 1998; <http://www1.ec.gc.ca/~cws/endangered/work10/eng/index.html>).

89 Bill C-33, the Species at Risk Act, 2nd session, 36th Parliament, 11 April 2000. The bill died on the order paper when a federal election was called in late 2000.

90 COSEWIC, 'FAQs.'

91 COSEWIC, 'A Brief History' (Ottawa: COSEWIC, 2000; <http://www.cosewic.gc.ca/cosewic/history.cfm>; this statement appears entirely in capitals in the original).

92 Mark Abrahams et al. (640 signers), 'Endangered Species Protection,' letter to Rt. Hon. Jean Chrétien, Prime Minister of Canada (Vancouver: BC Endangered Species Coalition, 24 Feb. 1999); <http://www.bcendangeredspecies.org/inforesources/scientists.html>.

93 A. McIlroy, 'Wildlife panel scientists to get vote, Stuart says,' *Globe and Mail*, 23 March 1999: A2.

94 See e.g. Sierra Club of Canada, 'Action Alert! SARA Is Weak and Ineffective' (Toronto: Sierra Club of Canada, 2000; <http://www.sierraclub.ca/national/es>).

95 Schrecker, 'Invisible Beasts,' 88–93; K. Webb, 'Between Rocks and Hard Places: Bureaucrats, Law and Pollution Control,' in Paehlke and Torgerson, eds, *Managing Leviathan*, 201–28.

96 DeMarco et al., 'Bear Necessities,' 24.

97 Versteeg, ed., 'Workshop Proceedings,' app. 3.3.

98 Although Bill C-65 did not contain provisions for habitat protection, it is highly improbable that any effort to protect endangered species can succeed without enforceable requirements for habitat protection. This, in turn, implies direct confrontation with the provinces over land-use planning jurisdiction, and with any number of locally powerful economic interests such as farmers and woodlot owners as well as industrial firms operating on a larger scale. Bill C-33 did not fully resolve these problems, leaving the prospect that effective protection for endangered species on a national scale may simply be incompatible with Canadian federalism.

99 Walker, 'Keeping the WTO.'

100 Ibid., 257.

101 So, too, does the question of whether governments will ever try to defend regulations aimed at protecting public health or environmental quality in the WTO arena unless a substantial commercial interest is also at stake – as

was clearly the case in the beef hormones dispute. This should not vitiate the issues of science policy that arose. If noble motives were a precondition for attaining desirable policy outcomes, democracy would not stand much of a chance. Neither would any other set of political arrangements.

102 Page, 'Generic View,' 237.

103 T. Colborn, D. Dumanoski, and J.P. Myers, *Our Stolen Future: Are We Threatening Our Fertility, Intelligence, and Survival?* (New York: Dutton, 1996).

104 T.M. Crisp et al., 'Environmental Endocrine Disruption: An Effects Assessment and Analysis,' *Environmental Health Perspectives* 106 (Suppl. 1, 1998), 11.

105 C. De Rosa et al., 'Environmental Exposures That Affect the Endocrine System: Public Health Implications,' *Journal of Toxicology and Environmental Health, Part B* 1 (1998): 5–6.

106 The U.S. National Research Council, unlike the Canadian organization with a similar name, is not a government agency but rather a non-profit society that receives funding from government and whose mandate explicitly includes providing scientific advice to government. The study of endocrine disruptors was funded by contracts from EPA; the Centers for Disease Control and Prevention, another federal-government agency; and the Department of the Interior.

107 Crisp et al., 'Environmental Endocrine Disruption.'

108 U.S. National Research Council, *Hormonally Active Agents in the Environment* (Washington: National Academy Press, 1999), 15.

109 Ibid., 13–23.

110 Crisp et al., 'Environment Endocrine Disruption,' 12.

111 Cf. Davis et al., 'Rethinking Breast Cancer Risk.'

112 See e.g. Council of Science and Technology Advisors, *Building Excellence in Science and Technology (BEST): The Federal Roles in Performing Science and Technology* (Ottawa: Industry Canada, 1999), 31–3; Commissioner of the Environment and Sustainable Development, *Report to the House of Commons* (1999), chaps 3 and 4; G.B. Doern, '"Patient Science" versus "Science on Demand": The Stretching of Green Science at Environment Canada,' paper prepared for Conference on Science, Government and Global Markets (Ottawa: Carleton Research Unit on Innovation, Science and Environment [CRUISE]), 20 Sept. 1998: 2; and M. Wiktorowicz, 'Shifting Priorities at the Health Protection Branch: Challenges to the Regulatory Process,' *Canadian Public Administration* 43 (2000): 1–22.

113 Impact Group, 'The Roles of the Federal Government in Performing Science and Technology: The Canadian Context and Major Forces,' report prepared for Council of Science and Technology Advisors (Ottawa: Industry Canada, 1999), 1.

114 G.B. Doern, 'Science and Scientists in Federal Policy and Decision Making,' paper prepared for Policy Research Secretariat, Government of Canada (Ottawa: Carleton Research Unit on Innovation, Science and Environment [CRUISE]), 1999, part I; Halliwell and Smith, *Scientific Advice*, 8, 32.

115 'The Best Practices: The Conduct, Management and Use of Science in Government,' app. C to Health Canada, Science Advisory Board, 'Meeting Report – January 19–20, 1999' (Ottawa: Health Canada, 15 May 1999); <http://www.hc-sc.gc.ca/hpb/science/jan99.html>.

116 Environment Canada, Science and Technology Advisory Board, *Achievements to Date, Recommendations for Future Action* (Ottawa: Environment Canada, October 1999), 10.

117 Ibid., 6, 11.

118 Health Canada, Science Advisory Board, 'Terms of Reference' (Ottawa: Health Canada, 1998; <http://www.hc-sc.gc.ca/hpb/science/mandat .html>).

119 Halliwell and Smith, *Scientific Advice*, app. I, 2–3.

120 Ibid., app. 1, 30.

121 Ibid., 42.

122 Council of Science and Technology Advisors, *Science Advice for Government Effectiveness (SAGE)* (Ottawa: Industry Canada, 1999), 7–8.

123 See the NBAC web site at <http://www.bioethics.gov>.

124 D. Nelkin and M. Pollak, 'Public Participation in Technological Decisions: Reality or Grand Illusion?' *Technology Review* 82 (Aug./Sept. 1979), 55–64.

125 On the merging of trade policy and foreign policy and the integration of trade-policy concerns into superficially unrelated domestic-policy fields see C.T. Sjolander, 'International Trade as Foreign Policy: "Anything for a Buck,"' in G. Swimmer, ed., *Seeing Red: How Ottawa Spends, 1997–98* (Ottawa: School of Public Administration, Carleton University, 1997), 111–34.

3. Spatial Proportionality: Right-Sizing Environmental Decision-Making

Robert Paehlke

The appropriate jurisdictional level for environmental policy decision-making has long been widely contested and discussed. The open-endedness of this discussion is based in part on the fact that most national constitutions and jurisdictional arrangements pre-date the era of strong political support for environmental concerns, which some analysts date from 1960 and others, more loosely, from the period following the Second World War.[1] Jurisdictional uncertainty also derives from the advantages in terms of effectiveness that can be argued for each and every jurisdictional level from local to global. It is worth noting that historically the strongest environmental-policy initiatives have most often come at the national level, even within federal systems such as Canada, Australia, the United States, and Germany. The reasons for this will be discussed throughout this paper.

In recent years, however, there are indications that all prior arrangements and patterns are under considerable pressure – with jurisdictional shifts taking place both 'upwards' to the international level and 'downwards' to the provincial, state, or even local level. As Holtzinger put it: 'Since the end of the Cold War, our collective political vision has globalized and become one with a world-wide-angle lens. At the same time, however, American political constituencies are becoming narrower and more discrete, as power devolves from the national to the state level. Thus, ironically, the American political system is becoming less and less equipped to deal with the globalizing political arena.'[2] Or, in the words of Holgate, in identifying a global pattern: 'Today, the nation-state that has been the dominant unit of government for centuries is being challenged by two forces: decentralization and supra-nationalism ... And internationally, governments are being held accountable for actions arising within their jurisdictions which affect the well-being of others.'[3]

Some international-relations theorists speak now of a new medievalism, a world with multiple and competing, nested, power centres – a world no longer dominated by nation-state actors.[4] Some post–cold war political economists link the simultaneous upwards and downwards pressures on national governments as part of a 'hollowing out of the state.' That is, this trend is seen as coincident with, and related to, such contemporary policy trends as privatization, public-sector downsizing, reductions in taxation and public spending, and the outsourcing of public services. All of these changes weaken government relative to the private sector, increasing the opportunities for capital accumulation through lower taxation on private market activities and through expansion of that realm. These analysts would add that any decentring of authority makes it more difficult to assign political responsibility and may thereby undermine the effectiveness of democratic practice.

Canada, for a number of reasons, is particularly susceptible to this dual upwards and downwards jurisdictional pull. Policy-making in Canada is pulled outwards into the global realm because Canada is perhaps the most trade-oriented of the advanced economies. Trading nations, particularly those trading heavily in resources and commodities, are especially vulnerable to international economic cycles and competitive pressures. Their power to make autonomous domestic policy decisions is continuously subject to the habits, intentions, decisions, preferences, and inclinations of their competitors, customers, and trading partners – and the multinational firms that operate within their borders and without. Canada also reaches outwards as a nation, rightly or wrongly believing itself to be a positive moral force in the world. Reaching out is a two-way street, national political influence being now more and more conditioned by international economic success.[5]

The jurisdictional authority of the Canadian national government is pulled inwards first and foremost by the decades-long threat of Quebec independence. There would appear to be no limit to the decentralization of power and authority that many French-speaking Quebeckers would seem to prefer. This intense decentralizing pressure is complemented by attitudes in several western Canadian provinces that are also strongly inclined to decentralization for at least three reasons: (1) they wish to protect and expand a near-exclusive jurisdiction over resource wealth; (2) the more politically conservative elements within all four western provinces wish to weaken rules and minima mandated by Ottawa regarding social programs; and (3) the wealthy provinces resist national spending and equalization (interprovincial transfer) payments and programs that provide a net benefit to Canada's poorer provinces (at the expense of British Columbia, Alberta, and Ontario).

Many environmental-policy analysts are concerned about this complex international trend, which sees the simultaneous upwards and downwards shifting of authority. This analysis includes, but is not limited to, the literature regarding globalization, which raises questions and concerns regarding declines in both social equity and environmental protection. As will be discussed below, as early as 1989 Daly and Cobb, for example, opposed heavy dependence on 'free trade' on both social and environmental grounds. However, these environmentalist concerns are compounded, and perhaps compromised, by a historic inclination to local decision-making, and a general distrust of centralization to the national level, especially amoung U.S. environmental advocates. It is with a closer look at these environmentalist inclinations to decentralization that I begin this inquiry.

The Myth of Locally-based Environmental Protection

From early in the development of environmental thought there has been a significant decentralist orientation rooted in part in anti-urban sentiment. This should not be surprising – many of the nineteenth-century giants of environmental thinking were oriented first and foremost to wilderness and nature. Muir and Thoreau revelled in a spiritual communion in isolation from urban life, hiking alone in vast wilderness or resting on mountaintops. Wilderness was linked by many environmentalists with purity, goodness, beauty, healthfulness, and spirituality.[6] Nineteenth-century cities were generally not pleasant places to be – open sewers and back-alley trash disposal prevailed, the roads were unpaved, the principal means of transportation defecated in them, and early factories had no pollution abatement whatever – often not even smokestacks. Human settlement was thus seen as an imposition and these sentiments remain today, long after many excesses have been at least partially remedied. For some, it was not a large step from such sentiments to preferring rural life to urban, geographic dispersion to urbanization, and, in a largely unconscious leap, decentralized decision-making.

This anti-urban view was often implicit among 1960s and 1970s environmentalists, and was manifest in a short-lived back-to-the-land trend. Some analysts were explicit in their anti-urban views, few moreso than Roszak, who asserted: 'To call for the deurbanization of the world is only to recognize the historical truth that city life has never suited more than a strict minority of mankind – mainly merchants and intellectuals.'[7] This broad sentiment was also implicit in Schumacher's widely influential *Small Is Beautiful*, in the writings of the economist Mishan, and in Bookchin's eco-anarchism, which rejected large-scale governance altogether.[8] Lovins's *Soft Energy Paths* added technological depth to the inclination and, in combination with his other work, provides at least an implicit technological and political case for the decentralization of settlement and smaller-scale decision-making.[9] Lovins's rejection of nuclear power arises in large part out his fear of the centralized political power of a 'nuclear priesthood,' and his comfort with dispersed, renewable energy sources is not unrelated to his preference for a restoration of Jeffersonian democracy within a political economy altogether different from that within which it originally thrived.

This current of political decentralization and distrust of large-scale governance has been strong throughout modern environmentalism. The slogan 'think globally, act locally' captures this viewpoint well and seems to imply that acting nationally, regionally, or globally is either futile or somehow beyond human capacities. Such a decentralist view is explicit within the literature of bioregionalism. Mander and Goldsmith (1996) describe bioregionalism as 'watershed economics,' a viewpoint that 'advocates economies of self-sufficiency within naturally articulated "bioregional" boundaries.'[10] As Sale puts it: '[F]ar from being deprived, even the most unendowed bioregion can in the long run gain economic health with a careful, deliberate policy of self-sufficiency.'[11] The organization of economic and political activity within biologically and geophysically determined local jurisdictions is also in keeping with Lovins's decentralized energy visions.

Bioregionalism, an important subtheme within contemporary environmentalism, stresses the importance of rootedness and of knowing the subtleties of, and lovingly caring for, one particular place, learning about that place over a lifetime and through the generations. This 'sense of place' is seen to be threatened by industrial society and globalization. Bioregional literature also praises 'traditional knowledge,' seeing it as at least equal to scientific knowledge. Others have also noted the importance of a sense of known landscapes and criticize as environmentally doubtful architectural norms whereby office towers are designed without adequate consideration of climate, positioning and movement of the sun, temperature, or winds – all is overwhelmed by engineering and cheap (non-sustainable) supplies of energy and (construction) materials. Many humans, indeed, come to lose all awareness of nature in the conduct of everyday modern lives lived in air-conditioned cars, residences, and office towers.

Bioregionalism and decentralization do have three particular strengths. One is the relative political accessibility of, and relative lack of inertia within, local government – political efficacy, accordingly, is potentially higher. Second, bioregionalism itself advances a great potential strength of local jurisdictions as a seat of environmental protection in particular – detailed knowledge, including multigenerational traditional knowledge, building to a sense of what truly is or is not important within any region. This strength lies at the heart of environmentalist inclinations to the local and suggests to any analysis that local authority has a place within environmental decision-making. We humans care most for that which we know and love. As will be seen below, however, creating local structures that are not consistently overwhelmed by external political and economic forces is no small task. The third strength of bioregionalism, however, speaks to this challenge – bioregionalists advocate local self-sufficiency and economic decentralization. Even selectively more self-sustaining local economies would command greater political autonomy. A clearer sense of how to counterbalance economies organized wholly 'at the other end of the scale' – globally – is urgently needed, but remains a weakness within both bioregionalist literature and contemporary society.

Environmentalist critiques of the costs of globalism are more effective. Morris, in opposing free trade, argues that it separates authority from responsibility for environmental and social costs and trades sovereignty over our affairs for a promise of more jobs, more goods, and a higher standard of living.[12] Daly argues that long-distance trade is too energy-intensive, proceeding apace in part because the costs of energy and, in California export-agriculture, the cost of water are heavily subsidized.[13] Daly and Cobb, while accepting the logic of comparative economic advantage also assert that Smith and Ricardo 'would have found compelling' the case against free trade 'in a world of free capital mobility, demographic explosion, ecological distress, and nation-states unwilling to cede any sovereignty to a world government.'[14] Daly's criticism of overdependence on comparative advantage is also telling: 'Uruguay has a clear comparative advantage in raising cattle and sheep. If it adhered strictly to the rule of specialization and trade, it would afford its citizens only the choice of being either cowboys or shepherds.'[15] Curiously, neither Morris nor Daly make the case that economic overspecialization imposes environmental costs through the excessive concentration of extractions from nature and emissions to it. Nature's reproductive and absorptive capacities might well cope better with small, widely dispersed sawmill or hog operations, for example.

Sale integrates many of the political and policy themes of environmentalism and political decentralization within a quintessentially American distrust of government. What is striking is the extent to which environmentalist decentralism, 1960s New Left thinking (Sale's roots), and neo-conservatism have a common language. The cover of Sale's *Human Scale* states: 'Big government, big business, big *everything* – how the crises that imperil modern America are the inevitable result of giantism grown out of control – and what can be done about it ... Sale examines a nation in the grips of growthmania and presents the ways to shape a more efficient and livable society built to the Human Scale.'[16] Sale speaks of a crisis in capitalism and advocates educational decentralization, organic agriculture, workplace democracy, worker and community ownership of industry, solar energy, recycling, public transportation, enhanced democracy, and restraints on city size. Yet he quotes arch-anti-environmentalist, then candidate, Ronald Reagan prominently sounding very much like the cover quotation above in saying: 'I am calling ... for an end to giantism, for a return to the human scale – the scale that human beings can understand and cope with ... It is within this activity on a small, human scale that creates the fabric of community, a framework for the creation of abundance and liberty.'[17]

The one difference between the two quotations is telling: Sale speaks of growthmania, where Reagan speaks of the creation of abundance. Sale sees 'human scale' as a means of achieving environmental protection and the restraint of overconsumption; Reagan saw it, and then used it, to achieve the exact opposite – ever more concentrated wealth and less environmental protection. What is also telling is how the New Left emphasis on participatory democracy, the New Right rejection of 'big' government, and environmentalist regulatory openness and public hearings all proffer increased citizen participation and a limiting of the power of 'faceless bureaucracies.' All instinctively distrust the structures of government and none thinks very clearly about how local-scale governance can contend with global-scale economic institutions. The preference for pastoral and wilderness settings and the distrust of government, so seamlessly blended by Sale and within environmentalism, are quintessentially American notions dating to the federalist papers, the power-checking provisions of the U.S. constitution, and America's long affinity for acadianism and bucolic mythology.[18]

Opinion polling bears out the same reality: Americans consistently stand out in their distrust of government – at the point of constitutional origin and yet today. This is not to say that these cultural traits are not historically admirable, only that they are culturally distinctive and possibly problematic with regard to environmental protection within a globalizing economy. Traditions of unitary government (rather than federalism) and 'responsible' parliamentary government, wherein majoritarian rule is constitutionally promoted rather than discouraged, constitute the more widely adopted constitutional approach. The contemporary trend to rising distrust of government, while most dramatic in the United States, where voter turnouts are notoriously low and declining, is, however, widespread. It is important to appreciate that this trend is related to the increasing mismatch between economic and political scales associated with globalization. Both citizens and governments defer to the leaders of global corporations, especially those who can believably claim to deliver the fruits of global economic organization.

Where yearning for Jeffersonian democracy, and assuming that 'human scale' will result in the demise of growthmania or the radical advance of environmental protection, miss the mark is in a failure to recognize the extent to which political power is inherent in, and all but synonymous with, economic scale. Within bioregionalism and much early environmentalist literature, it seems as if policy and political decision-making were more about ideas than about power. Marx perhaps overstated economic determinism, and underestimated the power of ideas (as Gramsci and other Marxists soon realized), but in stark contrast green decentralists seem simply to underestimate the power inherent in the scale of contemporary economic decisions and the new speed with which such decisions can alter the social and economic fate of nations (not to mention communities, states, and provinces). Small-scale, decentralized, 'Jeffersonian' democracy works best when political jurisdictions contain within their borders most (and roughly equal) economic actors.

The power to shift investment, employment opportunities, taxable income, and assets from one jurisdiction to another (or simply to forgo expanding or producing within a jurisdiction) is the power to affect, if not determine, policy outcomes. The larger the scale of economic organizations and the smaller the scale of political decisions (and the less diverse the economic options within the jurisdiction), the greater the power mismatch. The power of economic organizations is not, of course, always fully exercised – the full political resources of even the most powerful can only be used selectively. Environmental-protection initiatives thus gained ground in the 1970s, even enjoying for a time a 'motherhood' status, but during the late 1980s economic actors began to take environmental issues more seriously – taking some positive actions, but mounting a sophisticated political resistance to further change.[19] Environmental-protection expenditures were rolled back in most jurisdictions despite the considerable organizational sophistication of environmental NGOs.

It is not always fully understood within political jurisdictions when power has fundamentally shifted. The local government participants in the classic community study *Small Town in Mass Society* had little sense of how constrained and trivial their public agendas had become – they continued to revel in the virtues of small town life and local governance.[20] Increasingly, however, the decisions that most affected their community were made elsewhere. The effective analysis of power requires seeing which issues either never arise or do not find their way onto the public agenda. As we will see below, in the contemporary setting domestic economic considerations overwhelm international treaty obligations, but international trade regimes override domestic environmental legislation. Within contemporary environmental policy-making, the challenges of getting and keeping environmental issues on the public agenda are compounded by global 'realities.' Issues often cannot be resolved at the levels where they can effectively be raised by local or provincial environmental organizations.

As well, a compounding factor at the local level is often overlooked. Local governments almost always depend on a revenue stream dominated by property taxes. Too great a dependence on property taxes undermines municipal autonomy with regard to the most environmentally important aspect of municipal policy jurisdiction – planning decisions (the other principal environmentally relevant areas being water, sewers, and waste disposal). Planning decisions determine urban form – the shape of the municipality and the 'mix' of buildings, which in turn contributes powerfully to choices regarding transportation mode and intra-city distances travelled (and thereby to virtually all aspects of environmental protection). The initiative and dominant voice in planning decisions frequently falls to developers, given that it is politically easier to permit expansion of the tax base on developers' terms than to raise property tax rates. The shape of whole urban regions are often, thus, determined by small municipal governments at the periphery who are in turn dominated by builders seeking a combination of low-cost land and easy acceptance of high-profit single-family dwellings.

At the other end of the scale spectrum, almost all environmental issues have been complicated by economic globalization. Global trade expansion and global trade regimes have rushed to fill the post–cold war vacuum, seeking to secure the world for mobile capital investment. In this new context, global investors can bring enormous pressures to bear on national governments regarding environmental regulations by even implicitly threatening to withhold or transfer investment. Governments have learned to anticipate investor antipathies (or even to imagine them) and accordingly voluntarily roll back (or, as in Ontario in the early days of the Harris government, signal a disinclination to enforce) environmental regulations. Such actions are seen by governments (and many citizens) as part and parcel of 'remaining competitive.' This new reality thus suggests some need for more centralized environmental protection.

In general, one might hypothesize that the smaller the unit of governance and the less economically diverse the political jurisdiction, and the higher the local unemployment rate, the greater the relative power of globally mobile corporations. In the 1990s environmental-protection rollbacks were widespread despite the fact that much environmental politics and decision-making had at the same time moved to an international, treaty-based, level. In theory movement to this higher jurisdictional level should lessen tendencies to 'race to the bottom,' and perhaps such treaties have slowed the race with regard to some environmental issues. In practice, few treaties are enforced at the international level and environmental agencies, even in environmentally progressive jurisdictions, have reduced enforcement staffs and expenditures.[21] For want of effective enforcement, the potentially positive impacts of the internationalization of environmental policy-making have thus far been limited. One result is a new dimension for the passing of the environmental buck – upwards from the national level as well as downwards to the provincial and local.

A distinction might also be drawn here between increased global economic integration and negotiated trade regimes, such as the North American Free Trade Agreement (NAFTA) or the General Agreement on Tariffs and Trade (GATT). When firms pay skilled manufacturing workers a dollar or two a day in Indonesia, China, or Mexico, they can afford the tariffs necessary to sell into the United States, Japan, or Europe. The ability to pay tariffs (or to direct ever higher proportions of corporate income to marketing and profits) is also aided by the common absence of legal protections for trade unions, workplace health and safety, and the environment. Trade treaties, in and of themselves, do not cause these problems, though they do accelerate trade growth. Trade treaties and enforcement regimes have the potential to harmonize upwards, as is sometimes the case within the European Union. The NAFTA Side Agreement on Labor and the Environment also shows that in principle there is no technical (as distinct from political) reason why trade treaties could not incorporate strong and positive social and environmental provisions.[22] A first step toward harmonization upwards might involve changes to the notorious chapter 11 of NAFTA, which opens the way to polluters suing (and threatening) governments for attempting (or contemplating) domestic environmental protection.

The new realities of global corporate and investment mobility, and of widespread employment vulnerability, have enormous implications for environmental politics. Even in the richest nations, in government circles at every level and among both public- and private-sector employees, there has been a thoroughgoing political timidity throughout the 1990s. Every government fears losing employment, investment, and tax revenues. Almost any social behaviour – even child labour – is now justified somewhere in terms of global competitiveness. Employees and firms throughout the world compete within these 'new' standards (though obviously all need not adopt any particular practice). Further, what would be seen in Europe or North America as environmentally intolerable, even outrageous, behaviour is almost expected in Nigeria, Indonesia, or Guyana, even when far less problematic corporate environmental citizenship is the norm for the same firms when operating in the Netherlands, Canada, or the United States.

The 1970s notion that local governments can protect local environments, when national governments frequently can no longer do so, now seems quite spectacularly naive. One reason that many environmentalists cling to this localist hope is the realization of how little influence humans of ordinary means have at the global level – and how different are our everyday experiences, sensibilities, and priorities from those who ordinarily have such influence. In this regard, even the notion of sustainable development is distrusted by Wolfgang Sachs as being too far removed from people whose lives are affected by such global ecological planning: 'It is inevitable that the claims of global management are in conflict with the aspirations for cultural rights, democracy, and self-determination. Indeed, it is easy for an ecocracy that acts in the name of "one earth" to become a threat to local communities and their life-styles. After all, has there ever, in the history of colonialism, been a more powerful motive for streamlining the world than the call to save the planet?'[23]

This caution is not unwarranted, but may also serve as a rationalization for unecological local practices (such as slash-and-burn agriculture, perhaps appropriate at lower population densities, but altogether inappropriate now). The challenge in all this is to establish new trade rules, structures, and patterns that at once encourage democracy, diversity, and economic equity, as well as sustainability and environmental protection. What is needed is an international and national context that opens, rather than forecloses, the possibility of local environmental initiatives. Internationally, this context might include deliberately setting commodity prices on a gradual upward trajectory and finding the means to enforce environmental protection treaties. I will return to this issue, following a look at the legal and biophysical factors relevant to appropriate environmental jurisdiction.

The Constitutional and Legal Context

Too little has been made of the fact that in Canada there is no direct and clear constitutional assignment of jurisdiction over environmental matters to either the federal or the provincial governments. Neither the British North America Act, nor any succeeding constitutionally relevant document, is clear on this point, nor has there yet been any definitive legal or political clarification of environmental jurisdiction. The resulting ambiguity carries many risks: chiefly an on-going 'passing of the buck' whereby each level casts blame on the other and neither is held fully responsible, or assumes responsibility for acting effectively. The resulting ambiguity may also carry an advantage for environmental advocates: when frustrated with one level of government they can direct their attention to the other. But it remains the case that there has

TABLE 3.1
Canadian constitutional provisions relevant to federalism and environmental protection

---

Exclusive relevant federal powers
- Regulation of international and interprovincial trade and commerce
- Regulation of navigation and shipping
- Regulation of seacoast and inland fisheries
- Broad taxing and spending powers
- Criminal law (can be interpreted to include protection of public health)
- Regulation of undertakings that are international or interprovincial in nature (e.g., rail-roads and airlines) or of works within one province declared by Parliament to be for the general advantage of Canada as a whole (e.g., grain elevators, nuclear power)
- Peace, order, and good government (the residual-powers clause)

Exclusive provincial jurisdiction
- Control of natural resources (except uranium)
- Management and sale of provincial public lands (including timber rights)
- Establishment and control of municipalities
- Property and civil rights
- Generally, all matters of a private or local nature

---

been even less clarification of environmental than social policy responsibilities in Canada. The 1999 signing of the 'social union' agreement only reinforces this conclusion.

There are constitutional provisions that can be seen as pertinent to environmental protection. Table 3.1 lists environmentally relevant powers that are distributed by the BNA Act between the provinces and the federal government.[24] Though even collectively the listed powers are not definitive, they do provide a partial basis for resolution. Nonconstitutional factors may be more important, however, given the mixed and inconclusive answer that the constitution itself provides.

As well, some areas of overlapping and shared jurisdiction, such as agriculture, have turned out to be highly relevant to environmental-policy jurisdiction. Most shared jurisdiction in Canada regarding environmental matters, however, has evolved politically or been derived in judicial interpretation. Generally, when the courts consider jurisdiction over matters (such as environment) that were not widely considered or well known at the time of Confederation they begin by inquiring as to whether or not the power existed at the time. If it did not, the power is usually taken to be a matter of shared or overlapping jurisdiction. Thus, the host of contemporary confusions in the realm of environmental policy and, arguably, a need for a constitutional update in this regard (through, for example, the addition of a right to clean air and water, and the protection of the natural world that we as Canadians share, to Canada's Bill of Rights).

Two other forms of jurisdictional adjustment – the delegation of powers and the spending power – have also been used in ways important to environmental protection. Delegation of powers allows one level of government to cede jurisdiction to another. The Canada Fisheries Act, for example, delegates enforcement to the provinces. On the other hand, it has been determined that while the federal government cannot regulate within areas of provincial jurisdiction, they can spend money on research, on pilot projects (such as the federal Model Forests program), and on draft or 'model' laws (such as one concerning leaking underground storage tanks) that can then be adopted within any or all provinces. On the whole, though, the Canadian federal government has, it is fair to say, been at the very least tentative and restrained in asserting constitutional authority regarding the environment. The one notable exception to this pattern is with regard to uranium mining and processing and nuclear power, where the federal government, citing international treaty obligations, invoked its 'declaratory power' and assumed control for all aspects of the industry very early in its history.[25]

Federal jurisdiction regarding environmental protection has also been an ongoing issue in the United States, Australia, and Germany. To compare Canadian federalism with that in the United States, for example, it must first be recalled that Canada's basic constitutional documents are comparatively more federally oriented. That is, residual powers lean more to the central government in Canada than in the United States. One reason for this is that the Canadian constitution was developed immediately after, and in many ways in response to, the civil war in the United States. However, political history and the courts in both nations have altered historic intentions in many matters, including the environment, in a patterned way. Canada has become more decentralized than the text of its constitution might suggest, and the United States has become more centralized. In environmental policy there is a less consistent pattern, but Hoberg, comparing environmental policy in Canada and the United States, concludes that the Canadian system is 'both more decentralized and discretionary.'[26] Overall, Canada is now widely seen to be perhaps the most decentralized federal system in the world, with the possible exception of Switzerland.

The principal reason for this evolution, as noted above, is the continuous strong desire for more provincial powers in both Quebec and western Canada, but there are other reasons. Canada has fewer provinces, larger, on average, than the individual states in the United States. Economic 'spillovers' between states came sooner and more frequently in the United States, in terms both of interstate commerce (a key U.S. constitutional basis for policy centralization through time) and of urbanization (parts of Connecticut and New Jersey were within the New York City metropolitan area by early in this century). Environmentally, there are surprisingly few cross-border issues among Canadian provinces; there are more among and between U.S. states and even between states and provinces. Thus, even without linguistic and cultural differences, the evolutionary patterns on the two sides of the border might well have been very similar.

There are, however, two good arguments to be made against provincial jurisdiction over matters environmental and only one good one in favour. Both arguments against have been noted above. The first is that several Canadian provinces have been (and arguably remain) dominated by the interests and desires of environmentally significant industries to a greater extent than Canada as a whole has been. The British Columbia forest industry is politically predominant, as is the oil industry in Alberta. Provincially, these industries usually get what they want, but on a national scale their power is more diluted. The second argument against is that particular interests can play multiple jurisdictions off against each other by threatening to relocate or to reduce investment if rules are, or are not, changed. If rules apply across the country, this is harder to do – though since NAFTA this factor is less determining as investment shifts are more likely to be made to the United States or Mexico than to another province.

In favour of decentralization, it is argued that provincial and local governments are closer to problems and can thereby protect environments more effectively. Provinces can, for example, develop expertise in relation to particular industries in a more concentrated fashion. They can pay special attention without having to face 'diluted' public concern in locations distant from problems. There is thus some truth on either side of this debate and reason to think that multilevel jurisdiction and shared powers regarding the environment could be for the best despite the seemingly inevitable carping, contestation, and lack of clear responsibility. The challenge is to involve all levels in ways wherein the lines of responsibility remain clear. Arguably, there have been points in time where the provinces and Ottawa, through a strong Canadian Council of Ministers of the Environment (CCME) worked in

a spirit of equal-partnered cooperation. In recent years, however, neither level of government is willing to advance power-challenging environmental initiatives and the CCME itself has languished.

In contrast to the U.S. states, Canadian provinces have extensive
authority, both in general and within the realms of environmental and
social policy. This result has come about through political and administrative practice and through interpretation of the natons' two constitutions by their courts. Where the U.S. government induces conformance
of the states with national objectives by various means, Canada con-
ducts negotiations between equal federal and provincial partners.
Where U.S. states submit plans to the (U.S.) Environmental Protection
Agency for approval, the provinces in Canada hold an ever more
prominent and independent role in environmental matters. In contrast,
the Canadian government has coordinated some research regarding
common national standards, but the provinces have held sway in the
key role: enforcement. Since 1987, however, several disputes have
ended up in Canadian courts and the courts have favoured federal
powers. Some of these cases are discussed shortly below. However,
most recently there have been political efforts in both Canada and the
United States to further decentralize environmental administration.

The case of Australia is also instructive here. As in Canada (and contrary to the United States) the Australian constitution (of 1901) grants
Australian states dominant decision powers regarding resources. Australia's Commonwealth government can, however, use several constitutional provisions to override the powers of states with regard to
environment. Most notably, the national government of Robert Hawke
overturned a decision by Tasmania to dam the Lower Gordon River
within a World Heritage wilderness site. The Franklin dam was a for-
mative issue in the development of environmental politics in Australia.
Other national governments, and indeed the Hawke government on
other occasions, have been much more hesitant to intervene in environmental policy controversies. Legal bases for Commonwealth intervention include national environmental-impact assessment legislation
(the Environmental Assessment [Impact of Proposals] Act of 1974), the
power to enforce international treaties to which Australia is a signator,
and the protection of the land rights of aboriginal peoples (following
the landmark 1992 decision *Mabo v. Queensland*).

Returning to Canada, the courts have ruled variably on the authority
of provincial and national governments with regard to their respective
parks. Questions considered have been, Are parks a property held in

trust by government? And if so, can governments be required to prevent self-interested economic activities within those parks? In *Green v. the Queen in Right of the Province of Ontario* (1972) the courts ruled that the Ontario government could not be forced to prevent the commercial use of sand from Sandbanks Provincial Park, that it can decide when it will and will not prevent or permit such activities. However, in a more recent case involving the federal government (*Canadian Parks and Wilderness Society v. the Queen*) it was allowed that the National Parks Act provides protections that were not being adequately enforced and that logging in Wood Buffalo National Park was therefore illegal. It should be noted here that neither level of government sought to prevent commercial exploitation within its parks. Provincial governments have more often been deemed to have the discretion to allow such actions.

In the noted *Crown Zellerbach* case (1988) the peace, order, and good government clause of the BNA Act was the basis for allowing that the federal government can act within a largely provincial area of jurisdiction (resources management) and that the federal Ocean Dumping Control Act applied in British Columbia. As well, in a 1982 case, the Manitoba Queen's Bench upheld federal air-pollution regulations, arguing that, in Harrison's words, 'because air contaminants do not respect provincial boundaries, control of air quality clearly is a matter beyond private or local concern. It is noteworthy that the court did not demand proof that individual sources affected by the regulations had interprovincial impacts; rather, the court found the entire subject of air pollution control to be within federal jurisdiction under "Peace, Order, and Good Government."'[27] Interestingly, Harrison also notes that the federal government had 'studiously avoided' relying on this clause when drafting the federal Clean Air Act. Such behaviour is in keeping with a long-standing federal environmental policy hesitancy.

Regarding inland water pollution the courts have struck down provincial jurisdiction over pollution originating in another province (in this case, Manitoba legislation establishing liability for water pollution originating in Saskatchewan and Ontario). Again, in Harrison's view federal jurisdiction expanded despite great reluctance: 'The willingness of these ... judges to confer such broad authority on the federal government is striking; the argument of exclusive federal jurisdiction was not advanced by either side in the dispute, nor any of the intervenors, including the federal government itself. In fact, the federal government joined Ontario and Quebec in arguing in favour of provincial jurisdiction.'[28] It is difficult to imagine a greater hesitation to assume power or to accept responsibility. Ronald Reagan, who was as hostile to environmental protection as any leader elected since the rise of the environmental movement, shifted some federal environmental powers to the states, but in this only lessened a very strong federal dominance. In contrast, a Canadian federal government that at the time purported to be strongly in favour of environmental protection seemingly sought to divest itself altogether of jurisdictional responsibilities.

Two recent Canadian cases have added to federal environmental rights and duties, specifically with regard to environmental-impact assessment. In the Rafferty-Alameda case the courts ruled that federal Environmental Assessment and Review Process (EARP) guidelines do apply to a provincially approved dam in Saskatchewan because the federal government must license provincial irrigation projects. The federal government would rather not have been involved, as was the case with the Oldman dam in Alberta. There, again, the courts ruled that the federal government could have halted a provincial project under the Navigable Waters Protection Act (though it was too late to effectively do so by the time the courts made their ruling). Again, one notes here that the courts were obliging a federal government to enforce its own laws and procedures when it was loath to do so.[29]

Thus, it has been politically, not constitutionally or even legislatively, that the Canadian government is most restricted in terms of national environmental-policy initiatives. As Harrison notes, when (as in the mid-1980s) there is a very strong surge of pro-environmental public opinion, both the federal and provincial governments increase their environmental activity level.[30] When this happens, conflicts arise. However, it is perhaps more normal that both levels are hesitant. It might also be argued that the Rafferty-Alameda and Oldman cases arose when the federal government avoided challenging dam construction in jurisdictionally touchy western provinces, in large part owing to worries regarding the potential for extreme conflict – at a time when a second referendum on Québec sovereignty was looming – over the then-active second stage of the James Bay (Quebec) hydro-electric project.

James Bay II did not become a point of federal-provincial conflict, arguably because the separatist government of Quebec did not want a confrontation that placed them on the side of environmental damage and the federal government in the role of protector. Thus, the federal government was again more cautious than it need have been. The James Bay II issue was overridden when the Cree peoples of the region, and to a lesser extent environmentalists, successfully lobbied within New England and New York to block U.S. purchases of additional James Bay power. The need for the electricity from this source had also been lessened by technical and policy successes in improving the efficiency of electricity use. The important point here is that a major environmental issue was resolved at the international level that could not have been effectively resolved at the provincial level. Without international pressure we might well have also seen the Canadian federal government backing away from tough environmental action in the name of higher political priorities (in this case, a combination of national unity and economic growth). Constitutional and legal authority are important, but do not determine outcomes when governments are unwilling to accept authority.

The contrast here between Canada and the United States is again striking. In the United States there have been complaints about 'unfunded mandates' with regard to drinking-water quality, for example. Unfunded mandates are regulatory requirements imposed by the federal government on state and local authorities without commensurate federal funding. States in some cases have sought the opportunity for input into the decisions about which chemicals would be monitored and tested in the hopes of lowering treatment costs.[31] In other cases, there have been legal actions taken by state governments against pollution originating in facilities owned and operated by the U.S. federal government (usually military or energy installations), as in the case of weapons production and testing facilities in Colorado. In both of these situations the two levels of government in the United States are acting to force (without always being willing to pay for) additional environmental protection activity. In Canada, the federal government has more typically sought to avoid assuming responsibility, while some provincial governments, as we will see, are increasingly reluctant, recently, to establish or enforce environmental regulations.

Ecological and Biophysical Factors and Appropriate Jurisdictional Scale

Bioregionalists argue that jurisdiction should be determined, at least in part, by biophysical factors. It does not take long to realize, however, that ecologically and geophysically demarcated borders are often rather complex and inexact. Sale, for example, discusses ecoregions (based on native vegetation and soil types such as those within the

Great Plains of North America), georegions (e.g., watersheds), mor-
phoregions (subsets of watersheds based on many factors including
settlement and economic patterns), and biotic communities.[32] He
acknowledges that bioregions (including watersheds, for example)
vary enormously in size. However, he underplays the fact that they frequently cross and compound historic and legal, national and state, borders. Few bioregionalists have dealt extensively with cultural and
linguistic factors, other than perhaps to note that culturally and linguistically distinctive native peoples in pre-European North America
followed bioregional settlement patterns.

Within his identification of ecoregions Sale makes this assertion:
'Ultimately, the task of determining the appropriate bioregional
boundaries – and how seriously to take them – will always be left up to
the inhabitants of the area.'[33] This, again, shows the political innocence
of bioregionalism. Neighbouring bioregions and 'old' political–legal
(or cultural–linguistic) jurisdictions (especially sovereign nations)
might well differ regarding bioregional borders, rights, and responsibilities. It is often unclear as to whether bioregionalism is intended to
serve as a basis for governance or is simply an educational tool meant
to encourage individuals to be more mindful of the ecology and geo-
morphology of their area. Bioregionalists are clear, however, that much
is intended in terms of the decentralization of economic activity.

Bioregionalism, as noted above, usually focuses on watersheds, but
ecological and environmental governance is concerned with much more
than water quality and quantity or even ecology. Environmental politics
and policy has operated within three broad realms: (1) ecology, habitat
and wilderness conservation, preservation, and protection; (2) pollution
abatement and environmental health; and (3) resource conservation and
sustainability. Each of these realms would lead one to different bases for,
and patterns of, appropriate jurisdiction. Bioregionalism's watershed
orientation provides a focus for dealing with some ecological matters,
some resource issues, and water pollution abatement, but nothing like
the full range of environmental concerns. Consideration of the full
range of environmental issues complicates appropriate jurisdiction considerably. Let us consider further, then, the jurisdictional logic of each of
the three realms of environmental policy-making.

Some Ecological Determinants of Appropriate Jurisdiction

Many animal species, during the lifetimes of each individual animal, transverse numerous bioregions (however determined) and frequently occupy territories that transcend two or more bioregions. 'Canada's' loon population is susceptible to mercury pollution from agricultural run-off within its wintering habitat in Florida. 'North American' songbirds and monarch butterflies are at risk from habitat loss within the tropical forests and other bioregions of Latin America. The endangered whooping cranes, which reproduce in Canada, are most vulnerable in their travels and stays across a broad band of U.S. states. Numerous bird, predator, and other species move across, and require for healthy survival, corridors that stretch from Yellowstone National Park to the Yukon (though arguably in this case virtually all of the territory in question may lie within a Rocky Mountain bioregion). The broad point here is that animal habitat frequently exceeds both historical–legal boundaries and bioregionally determined territories.

It is thus difficult, if not impossible, to achieve effective ecological management within discrete bioregions, however much the human citizens of each region come to know, and identify with, the 'web of life' within that region. Human technologies and economic activities, as well as animal habits, now assure this. Chernobyl fallout affected lichen and reindeer in Sweden, as well as migratory birds in Afghanistan. Much of the lumber from the rainforests of Southeast Asia and British Columbia is consumed in Japan. Air quality (and ecological health) in Australia is affected by Asean haze generated primarily within Indonesia. Coral bleaching in the Caribbean and the Pacific are accelerated by climate warming, to which all human communities contribute. Further, examples abound of ecological disruption caused by exotic species hitch-hiking on the ever-accelerating movement of human goods – one need only mention here zebra mussels, purple loosestrife, and blackthorn. No ecosystem is, any longer, an island and the most serious ecological problems are perhaps those that transverse bioregional boundaries.

Rykiel correctly sees habitat loss and related biodiversity problems as the result of very long-term trends. 'This transition from a wilderness planet to a tame planet started about 10,000 years ago with the rise of agriculture, and the magnitude of change mirrors the growth of the human population. Human habitations are no longer islands in a sea of wilderness; instead, wilderness islands float in a sea of humanity.'[34] Many non-human species do not fare well in fragmented patches of habitat and even on protected territory are – without corridors for movement to feed, breed, or escape predators – vulnerable. Peterson and Parker show that this reality is abundantly the case on both small and large scales.[35] The solution is at least two-fold: habitat protection within all scales of governance and, as well, an end to the growth of human populations. The latter challenge, arguably, can only be achieved in the context of significant social and economic gains within the poorest nations.[36] This in turn implies that a 'simple' slowing of, or stop to, economic growth is not (as was imagined by some) an adequate solution. Nor, of course, is unlimited economic growth. As impossible as it sounds, human population stabilization may well require at least a partial resolution of North–South inequities – no challenge could be more global than that.

Pollution and Jurisdiction

As the case of Chernobyl suggests, the movement of pollutants has especially complex implications for environmental jurisdiction. Humans have been known to consciously foul their own nests – little wonder that jurisdictions are often little concerned with fouling others. Pollution movement is far from a 'simple' matter of upstream and downstream – toxics move by air, water, and food chain as well as across media. Airsheds and even atypical air movement patterns, for example, greatly influence water quality. The Great Lakes have been measurably affected by airborne toxaphene emissions from Texas petrochemical plants moving northwards against prevailing winds. Numerous other examples of toxic-chemical mobility are well known.[37]

The long-range transport of air pollutants (LRTAP) is perhaps most often associated with acid deposition from coal-fired power plants and metal smelters. Oxides of nitrogen and sulfur move from Britain to Sweden and from Ohio, Indiana, and Illinois into Ontario, Quebec, Nova Scotia, New York, and New England. Less well-known is movement from the Inco high stack in Sudbury to the forests and streams of Maine. Moreover, a wide variety of pollutants, both air- and sea-borne, are channelled to the ecologically vulnerable high Arctic – the best known example here being the contamination of polar bear livers by DDT (long after, and thousands of miles from where, the pesticide was produced or used). The patterned flow of toxics into the Arctic demonstrates that Canada cannot, on its own, resolve the environmental problems within its national territory and, more important, that environmental problems are irretrievably international and therefore, within Canada, irretrievably more national than provincial.

In the late 1980s it was determined that Inuit women in northern Labrador had in excess of five times more pesticides in their breast milk than did women within industrialized countries in general. The chemicals in question had not been used within the Arctic, or indeed anywhere near to where the women lived. As well, one of the pesticides found to still contaminate the Arctic, DDT, was banned by thirty-four countries more than twenty years ago. While DDT levels are now (in 1999) beginning to slowly drop within Arctic ecosystems, new inputs from tropical countries (which still use the pesticide to combat malarial mosquitoes) continue to arrive.[38] The flow of pesticides and PCBs to the Arctic involves complex processes. One geophysical determinant of toxic accumulation in the far north is the fact that such chemicals evaporate readily in warmer climes, travel to the Arctic on air currents, fall as snow or rain, but do not re-evaporate so rapidly at lower temperatures. As well, chemicals that make their way to the oceans are absorbed by plankton and move northwards on ocean currents. The plankton are consumed by fish and the chemicals in turn end up in the fatty tissue of seals, a prime food source of human Arctic inhabitants (and polar bears).

The complex and continuous movement of pollutants is one of the core reasons why exclusively local environmental governance, or even exclusively national governance, is insufficient. It has long been known that acid deposition and LRTAP issues, where consistently there is no territorial match of benefits and costs, can only be resolved at higher jurisdictional levels. Otherwise one jurisdiction gains the economic benefits of non-abatement while other jurisdictions suffer virtually all of the environmental consequences. The number of such cases would be all the greater within any system of relatively smaller environmental-policy jurisdictions. This is a different argument from one which notes that subnational jurisdictional entities have no significant presence within international decision-making. It is an assertion that the best prospect for effective protection exists when territories of impact and responsibility coincide. Another (third) argument is that many provincial (or other subnational) governments do not have the institutional and scientific capacity to deal with a full array of environmental problems – especially those that do not originate within their territory. For all three of these reasons, the far north of Canada and many other parts of the nation cannot deal effectively with the LRTAP problems they face. In many cases the problems would not have been (or for that matter have not been) detected in the first place (by local governments).

This conclusion is reinforced if one considers the patterned outcome in large multi-jurisdictional common-property resource situations such as ocean fisheries, the Great Lakes, or large, multi-jurisdictional river systems, such as the St Lawrence or the Rhine. Smaller environmental-policy jurisdictions (perhaps especially at a scale larger than face-to-face communities) in effect render the passage of a larger proportion of environmental problems to the level of a multi-jurisdictional commons and create a greater potential for tragedies thereof.

This is not to say that enduring resolutions of common-property resource problems are not possible – Ostrom and others have studied cases of successful resolution of such problems at the village and community level. However, beyond this scale (and often within it) management successes are rare.[39] Ostrom argues that village-level resource management works better (and discusses Canada's east-coast fishery in this regard), but does not seem prepared to consider the significance of the entry of greater-than-village-scale technologies (and markets) into the situation. Could local jurisdictions resist the entrance of for-eign (or Canadian) radar-equipped factory ships or whole-tree logging machines? Even if they could, could they compete with them for markets?

Suffice it to say as regards pollution that there have been many issue-by-issue attempts to match the jurisdiction with the scale of envi-ronmental determinants. One relatively successful multi-jurisdictional initiative is the Fraser River Management Board (discused elsewhere in this volume), another is the effort to improve water quality in the Great Lakes and the St Lawrence. Initiatives in the latter case have come pri-marily from an international body – the International Joint Commis-sion (IJC), established in 1909 by the Canada-U.S. Boundary Waters Treaty. A high proportion of the IJC's work has always been oriented to the Great Lakes, at least two of which (Erie and Ontario) are severely degraded by pollution.[40] The most important recent initiative consists of some fifty remedial action plans (RAPs) to deal with the worst pol-lution hotspots, such as Hamilton Harbour and several points on the Ohio side of Lake Erie. These RAPs are developed multi-jurisdiction-ally with grassroots involvement (of widely varying levels of success) in the hopes of overcoming decades of bureaucratic inertia and buck-passing.

The failure to protect Great Lakes water quality has been in part a failure of jurisdictional right-sizing, a tragedy of the commons prob-lem. The IJC has documented water-quality problems, but too many

TABLE 3.2

Tangled jurisdictions in the Cornwall/Akwesasne/Massena segment of the St Lawrence

---

International Joint Commission (IJC)
United States government
Government of Canada
Environment Canada
United States Environmental Protection Agency
Government of the State of New York
New York State Department of Environmental Conservation
Government of Ontario
Ontario Ministry of Natural Resources
Ontario Ministry of Environment and Energy
Ontario Hydro (public utility that controls water flows on this segment of the river)
Government of Quebec
Cornwall Remedial Action Plan (RAP)
Massena RAP
St Lawrence PASL-ZIP (Plan d'action Saint-Laurent zone d'intervention prioritaire)
St Lawrence SSL-ZIP (Stratégies Saint-Laurent zone d'intervention prioritaire)
Mohawk government of Akwesasne
City of Cornwall
City of Massena
Numerous smaller local governments
Several county governments in Ontario and New York
Conservation councils (in Ontario), e.g., the Raisin River Conservation Authority
St Lawrence Seaway Authority

---

pollution sources in too many jurisdictions contribute (including industrial sources in numerous jurisdictions; municipal storm sewer run-off; agricultural run-off; road salt; household detergent use; inadequate municipal-sewage treatment; individual residences on rivers, shorelines, and islands; abandoned hazardous-chemical dumps; mine tailings; shipping discharges; exotic plants and animals on recreational vehicles; and many other insults, each subject to varying jurisdictional authority). For decades effective action was delayed by the sheer inertia of jurisdictional complexity. RAPs may be a means of overcoming this problem, but that is far from certain. Some argue that the effort has shown signs of success, but there are also signs that not all RAPs are effective and the Ontario government has now severely cut funding for these initiatives.[41]

The problem in the Great Lakes and St Lawrence remains one of tangled jurisdictions. Table 3.2 (adapted from Paehlke 1996) identifies some of the jurisdictional authorities involved in environmental decisions regarding one ecologically defined segment of the St Lawrence River near Cornwall, Ontario, and Massena, New York, that reaches also just into the province of Quebec (and includes the Akwesasne territory of the Mohawk nation). The array of entities suggests some of the administrative, political, and legal challenges involved in creating effective RAPs.

Despite tangled jurisdictions, the best hope for resolving pollution problems lies in establishing responsibility within jurisdictions large enough to encompass both sources and impacts. In the case of the Great Lakes, Canada must take responsibility for acting (and seeing that the provinces act) at least as effectively as does the United States. Greenhouse gases and ozone are global concerns that can only be resolved globally. Acid deposition and LRTAP issues could be encompassed, with exceptions, within continental frameworks. In effect, many large watersheds like the Great Lakes and some large river systems require continental jurisdictions (though some are sufficiently contained within single nations). All of these issues, however, require jurisdictions much larger than discreet bioregions and often larger than nations. In Canada, interestingly in this regard, more pollution issues transcend the national border than transcend provincial boundaries. This reality all the more thrusts the burden to the federal government.

Sustainability and Jurisdiction

Sustainability has jurisdictional implications different from those of either ecology or pollution. Sustainability shortfalls (resource failures) are felt immediately at the local level, but commodity production is generally organized globally. For a number of reasons there is declining local influence on decisions related to the sustainability of locally produced resources – few commodity-producing localities are in any position to withhold production or even to influence price (and thereby demand). Yet at the local level the interconnection between economy and environment is palpable with regard to sustainability – when the ore is exhausted, the forest cut, or the wildlife or fish stocks depleted local extractive-oriented economies are devastated. In economic terms, the local effects of moderate levels of ecological damage or pollution may be far less dramatic. Yet the decisions that govern sustainability outcomes are largely global and private.

Most resources are extracted within localities that have few alternative ways to participate in the global economy. Local authorities have little room for manoeuvre with regard to, for example, restraining the rate of extraction via export controls or taxation. The rectification of sustainability problems, then, most often rests at a great distance from production, at the point of resource use, not extraction. There is, thus, an almost complete jurisdictional mismatch with regard to sustainability and the result is a world where non-sustainability on the local level is the norm. Threatened fisheries are typically only shut down near to, or past, the point of exhaustion. Forest industries only rarely have been operated on a sustained-yield basis, despite the rhetoric of forestry and forest-policy discourse. (The one or two exceptions here may be Scandinavia and some locations in the southern United States.) Mining and fossil fuels are inevitably non-sustainable (though some minerals are in themselves abundant). Energy availability and prices largely determine the reserve levels of minerals (lower-grade ores can be extracted so long as low-cost energy supplies are available). Most commodity production is exported from the nation where extraction takes place, and much is exported in raw form from the particular location where it is extracted.

Sustainability initiatives are, unfortunately, often seen as threats within producer locales. That is, enhanced recycling, for example, benefits (makes less import-dependent) the consuming locale, but may threaten the economy of the extracting locale. Mining jurisdictions are not in the vanguard of recycling technologies and energy-producing regions are not noted for energy-efficiency policies and practices. Indeed, more-sustainable consumption introduces a double threat – export sales decline *and* commodity prices may be pressured downwards when demand is restrained. There are, of course, long-term economic benefits to producer locales as the life of resource supplies is extended. This, alas, provides only minimal consolation to producers who are desperate today.

Despite sustainability problems consistent upward price movement for commodities is far from certain, as the famous wager between Paul Ehrlich and Julian Simon made clear and the recent events following the economic turmoil in Southeast Asia have reaffirmed. Commodity prices remain on a long-term downward trajectory, the many reasons for which must be understood if we are to draw valid conclusions regarding sustainability and jurisdiction. One important reason that commodity prices trend downwards is that most commodities are extracted predominantly within nations with few economic options – economies where wages are extremely low and prone to falling further, and/or where public subsidies to commodity production are routine.[42] Canada is partially exceptional in this regard (being a relatively developed commodity producer). Moreover, extractive processes are highly prone to automation and economies of scale – whole-tree cutters, mega-scale power shovels, and monster coal trucks come to mind. Another reason for declining commodity prices is a century-long (but extremely slow) trend to increased economic output per unit of energy and materials. Acceleration of this established 'dematerialization' of economies is at the heart of sustainability advocacy.[43] The effect of accelerated dematerialization on commodity prices is, however, complex – its successes tend to frustrate future successes, as was the case following the OPEC price increases of the 1970s.

Rapidly rising demand for oil, and for oil importation in particular, combined with war in the Middle East, created the conditions necessary for the oil price increases of 1973 and 1979. There was, however, a five-fold response to this change: (1) demand from poor and economically marginal individuals and firms fell immediately (people went cold, some energy-dependent businesses contracted); (2) oil supply sources outside the control of OPEC were developed (enhanced extraction techniques and North Sea oil being the most notable); (3) energy-efficiency investments were made (in fuel-efficient cars, added insulation, energy-efficient appliances, and recycling – all sustainability-enhancing changes); (4) some fuel substitutions took place (especially to domestically sourced natural gas); and, crucially, (5) emergency reserves were increased to provide insurance against future supply disruptions (thereby preventing new price increases). These efforts caused oil prices to fall sharply by 1985; they did not return to 1980 levels until 2000. This fifteen-year delay has in turn discouraged necessary investments in alternative energy sources and energy efficiency – sustainability was again deferred.

In broad terms, it is arguable that the time horizons of markets are in this crucial case, far too short. Without intervention by governments now or in the near future, there is a real chance that future generations will have too little time to avoid extremely negative environmental, economic, and social consequences. There is no certainty of this outcome, but prudence would suggest that greater efforts be undertaken to at least understand the multidimentional possibilities and risks involved.

Enhanced sustainability depends not only on current commodity prices, but on anticipated commodity prices, and especially on current and anticipated energy prices. The fundamental problem is that markets focus on the momentary, whereas sustainability is dependent on decisions that have a time horizon of years, decades, and even centuries. For example, while energy efficiency in buildings can be improved after construction, we do not and cannot sharply improve energy efficiency of our whole building stock in less than twenty or thirty years. Buildings can last for centuries (and if they do not they are wasting construction materials – and forests), whereas markets rarely operate within a time horizon suited to the achievement of sustainability. Even major appliances have a lifespan of several decades and are not often replaced simply to improve operating efficiency. Moreover, modal choices in transportation are determined by urban density and design, factors determined in turn over even longer spans of time. In sum, energy prices should lead supply changes by at least several decades, but likely do not.

The broad point here is a crucial one – markets will force changes toward sustainability as and when fossil-fuel prices rise, but would force radically different (and altogether less socially disruptive and environmentally problematic) change over longer time spans. There is, however, little evidence to suggest that (without political intervention) energy prices will rise in timely fashion, gradually and evenly over a long period of time. The bottom line regarding sustainability policy is that there is no basis for *assuming* that there is, or ever will be, a viable and equivalent alternative to fossil fuels. There could be, but it would seem prudent to assume that the inevitable decline of fossil fuels will ultimately restrain total global energy use. Such limits argue for energy-price intervention (possibly through taxation), intervention that is only achievable through wide international agreement and coordination.

Intergenerational considerations and prudence are the core of both sustainability and environmental policy. The analysis here, however, suggests that markets alone will not arrive at the long, slow adjustment that can be accommodated within human capacities for democratic (or any other form of orderly) governance. Under duress human institutions may be incapable of rational decisions about environmental tolerance for whatever energy alternatives are available at the time of the future crisis that present prices all but guarantee. Nor are we humans necessarily capable of avoiding wars over scarce energy resources in the midst of extreme pressures. Over and above such bleak futures, today's risks of climate warming reinforce the prudential case for gradually reducing fossil-fuel use.

Analysis in *Scientific American* early in 1999 suggested that energy prices would again rise, and this seems to have been borne out in the short term, but the durability of the current increase is still uncertain. Moreover, the technical-scientific 'solutions' offered within this analysis are generally temporary – primarily more advanced oil and gas extraction techniques. As Campbell and Laherrère put it: 'From an economic perspective, when the world runs completely out of oil is ... not directly relevant: what matters is when production begins to taper off. Beyond that point, prices will rise unless demand declines commensurately. Using several different techniques to estimate current reserves of conventional oil and the amount still left to be discovered, we conclude that the decline will begin before 2010.'[44] The only hedge these authors seem to allow, other than a (presumably efficiency-based) 'commensurate decline in demand' is that a global recession could delay the anticipated price rise. Anderson points to good prospects for advanced drilling techniques (steerable drilling, underground imaging, and deep-water production), Fouda to other fossil fuels, especially natural gas, and George to the oil sands of Alberta.[45]

It would appear, then, that over and above the Kyoto obligations, Canada may see another complex round of provincial/federal struggles over energy – this time complicated by NAFTA. We, as a nation, should consider now several important questions. Should Canada export all the oil-sands output that it can sell? What are the environmental and sustainability implications of such a course? Is there not some way to achieve a North American Kyoto-related tax on fossil-fuel consumption in order to anticipate and smooth future disruptions associated with slowing fossil-fuel output? It must be recalled here that North American carbon-dioxide output per capita is twice that of Europe and that North American energy demand per dollar of GDP is also sharply higher than that of either Europe or Japan.[46] In the United States such matters are clearly a matter of national (as opposed to state-level) policy, but such national dominance is far from clear within a Canadian context.

What follows more broadly for jurisdictional matters from the limits to fossil fuels? First, sustainability concerns have a mismatch in time, much as other environmental concerns are mismatched in terms of spatiality and jurisdiction. Second, sustainability concerns are the ultimate mismatch in terms of jurisdiction – they run counter to trends within an increasingly competitive and global economic system. Building sustainability arguably requires a global commitment to a continuing long-term gradual adjustment in energy prices – at a rate of increase that might even restrain economic growth in the short term (though this is far from certain and depends very much on the distribution and use of the enhanced fossil-fuel revenues and the rate at which fossil-fuel prices rise). A broader global redistribution of funds might be achieved from an agreement on commodity (as opposed to only energy) extraction. The overall objective, again, is a gradual acceleration of 'economic dematerialization' – increased investment in such things as telecommunications, recycling, public transportation, and energy efficiency.

Needless to say there is as yet little, if any, return to a broad public or governmental concern with resource sustainability, especially in North America – though recent European environmental-policy literature is clearly moving in this direction.[47] Early in the Clinton years there was some consideration of energy taxes (in the face of huge governmental deficits), but the administration was easily beaten back politically by oil companies and energy-producing states. Within Canada any such initiative would be compounded by the even greater power of our energy-producing provinces, and by easy access to cross-border gas stations for a significant proportion of Canadians. Despite these challenges Canada is well positioned to advocate change regarding sustainability. Culturally and ideologically we bridge Europe and North America in many ways and, while we are high per capita consumers of energy, we might well benefit economically from a long-term rise in energy (and thus commodity) prices.

The mismatches in space and time do not bode well for significant policy advances regarding sustainability. Today's global investment climate sees things in seconds and minutes, not decades and centuries. Achieving sustainability may require nothing less than a reversal of some of the trends linked with globalization (though perhaps the acceleration of others). Ironically, the necessary political agreements imply more, not less, globalization – but a politically led globalization guided by values that go beyond the acceleration of trade, economic growth, and profits as a sole guiding objective. Only OPEC has ever successfully imposed higher commodity prices for any extended period, and even then only temporarily within a unique context (war). It is yet to be seen if recent increases will hold. One reason that even some success has been achieved by OPEC is that as a commodity oil is less prone to substitutions than are many others.

In general, nations that are net importers of commodities externalize both environmental costs and the costs of future sustainability short-falls (both are borne locally). They will continue to do so as long as they can expect falling commodity prices and continue to stockpile reserves, and have multiple supplier and substitution options. Neither exporters nor importers would seem likely to initiate change. While import dependency carries some risks, the 'tax shift' envisioned by the Worldwatch Institute and others is necessary to sustainability, and will not be achieved without the international leadership necessary to effect jurisdictional and political change.

In sum, ecological and biophysical factors suggest a need for larger jurisdictional structures and arrangements, at the least layered (some-times called nested), issue-specific approaches. Some factors, most notably concerning sustainability, point to a need for larger, even global, management. Different factors point toward varying jurisdictional patterns, but unique jurisdictions for each issue would seem inappropriate and unwieldy. Arrangements should seek to minimize the risks of tangled jurisdictions and to assure relatively clear lines of political responsibility. There is also a need to avoid approaches (such as too-pure forms of bioregionalism) that are not sufficiently mindful of polit-ical, historic, and related considerations. One might then assume that global environmental governance, given its challenges, should be reserved for a small number of issues such as sustainability and issues with irreversible global-level lock-in effects (such as biodiversity and climate warming). That said, in many ways most environmental prob-lems, from a biophysical perspective, would seem suited to large regions of perhaps continental proportions – big enough to incorporate migratory animals, large river systems, and airsheds and containing markets large enough to be essential to even the largest of corporations.

Economic and Political Factors in Appropriate Environmental Jurisdiction

New communications and transportation capabilities continuously transform political economy and the organizational structure of human productive activities. At the close of the Middle Ages the beginnings of industrial production burst through the feudal organi-zation of social, economic, and political life. Productive capacities overwhelmed earlier arrangements and made possible, and all but required, political and economic (market) structures on the scale of the nation-state. The contemporary process of globalization parallels this transformation and, many argue, threatens to overwhelm governance within nation-states.[48] The imminent demise of the nation-state may be exaggerated, but there is little doubt that finance and production are increasingly organized on a global scale. Technological determinism, as well, overstates the technological basis for the new economic realities, but computers, telecommunications, low-cost air travel, computer-tracking, and containerized shipping have rendered actual what, in terms of economic structures and patterns, was barely imaginable but a few decades ago.

I will not review these issues here in detail, but rather offer only a few observations by way of a context for assessing the implications of globalization for environmental governance. I begin with the recent observations of two wealthy participants in the process of globalization. George Soros wrote: 'Laissez-faire capitalism holds that the common good is best served by the uninhibited pursuit of self-interest. Unless it is tempered by the recognition of a common interest that ought to take precedence over particular interests, our present system is liable to break down.'[49] James Goldsmith, the late British/French billionaire was more direct: '[F]orty-seven Vietnamese or forty-seven Filipinos can be employed for the cost of one person in a developed country, such as France. Until recently, ... 4 billion people were separated from our economy by their political systems, primarily communist or socialist, and because of a lack of technology and of capital. Today all that has changed. Their political systems have been transformed, technology can be transferred instantaneously anywhere in the world on a microchip, and capital is free to be invested anywhere the anticipated yields are highest.'[50]

Others have documented the rapidly rising significance of 'offshore' tax havens, suggesting that governments, individually or collectively, are now challenged to collect full taxation from either corporations or wealthy individuals.[51] Tax rates on mobile personal and corporate income have been in rapid decline in every jurisdiction throughout the 1980s and 1990s. In Germany, for example, total taxation of corporate profits fell by 40 per cent between 1980 and 1995 – much of the difference being accounted for by 'transfer pricing,' which allows global corporate profits to emerge within the nations with the lowest tax rates. At the same time, in most wealthy nations, the proportion of individual earnings attributable to wages has significantly declined relative to earnings from investment income and stock-market speculation. With few exceptions, the overall distribution of wealth has become more skewed. Most nations have responded to these new realities with reductions in public expenditures and contractions in the size of their public service, cuts that usually include, and sometimes (as in Ontario and Canada) are led by, the resource-management and environmental ministries.

Some environmental advocates have concluded that global economics requires global environmental and social standards – that is, that an economically integrated globe needs more political integration, not less. They might argue, on apprehending Goldsmith's figures, that if Southeast Asian forest workers earned even half the wages of those in the Pacific northwest, the rate of destruction of tropical rainforests might slow considerably. Similarly, if Caribbean bauxite miners were paid half what a miner earns in Germany, there would be less aluminum that was not recycled.

There is now broad agreement among environmental advocates that the economic, the social, and the environmental are thoroughly linked. Employment and economic insecurity (often associated with the global-scale rationalization of production), it is agreed, lessen environmental concern and the prospects for new environmental initiatives. Debt levels in poor nations, especially in combination with currency collapses, all but assure the non-sustainable exploitation of resources and reduce concern regarding biodiversity and habitat. As well, there is a wide recognition of the potential for a 'race to the bottom' in terms of environmental protection as all governments seek to curry favour with corporations and investors and to gain competitive advantage and access to markets. Thus, there is a recent tendency within environmental NGOs to internationalize their organizations and to seek treaty-based environmental initiatives, but successes thus far are very limited and globalization is generally feared and distrusted by environmentalists.

In North America strong opposition to NAFTA and the proposed Multilateral Agreement on Investment (MAI) has come from moderate environmental and conservation organizations that previously would have consistently steered clear of economic and social-policy issues. It is not insignificant that Mander and Goldsmith's *The Case against the Global Economy*, as well as Karliner's *The Corporate Planet: Ecology and Politics in the Age of Globalization* (1997), were published by Sierra Club Books. This opposition and distrust has risen in the face of GATT/WTO panel decisions, such as the dolphin-tuna case.[52] Distrust has not been lessened by private standard-setting initiatives such as ISO 14000, which have been seen by some as an attempt to undermine state-based regulation without providing a substantive replacement. Academic assessments of ISO 14000 are also wary. Clapp concludes that 'it is not clear that the ISO 14000 series of environmental management standards will help to meet environmental goals for industry ... particularly those that are most urgent for developing countries ... Yet the ISO 14000 series is rapidly becoming accepted as the international environmental 'standard,' even though it is now widely seen by critics as well as some industry experts as being weak in terms of its requirements.'[53]

The focus of environmentalists is thus being drawn to the international level. McCormick now makes an analytic distinction between environmental NGOs with international interests (such as World Resources Institute and Worldwatch Institute) and international NGOs, or INGOs.[54] INGOs operate on a day-to-day basis in two or more nations, often as globally as multinational corporations. Greenpeace and the World Wide Fund for Nature (WWF) panda symbol are recognized globally. These organizations, as well as International Union for the Conservation of Nature and Natural Resources (IUCN), Friends of the Earth (FOE), and several other groups, including the Rainforest Action Network coalition, operate on a global basis. Other organizations have a continental, often European, focus and structure.

Numerous multilateral and bilateral environmental treaties have recently been signed – indeed, since the late 1970s environmental politics seems to be as often conducted at the diplomatic level as at the national level. Major treaties include CITES, the Convention on International Trade in Endangered Species of Wild Flora and Fauna (1973, 1979, 1983); the Montreal Protocol on Substances That Deplete the Ozone Layer (1987); the Basel Convention on the Control of Transboundary Movements of Hazardous Wastes and Their Disposal (1989); the United Nations Biodiversity Convention (1992) and the UN Framework Convention on Climate Change (1992, followed up by the Kyoto agreement in late 1997). It is thus widely acknowledged that many environmental problems are global in scale and can only be resolved with the active participation of many, if not most, nations. The question that remains is, How meaningful are international environmental agreements when there are as yet few effective enforcement mechanisms?

While environmental agreements are frequently unenforced, in Canada both trade and strategic international agreements have, at times, overwhelmed domestic environmental policy. One example is of particular note: the case of low-level NATO military overflights of Innu territory in Quebec and Labrador. These sometimes frequent training flights threaten a variety of animal species, including the 600,000 caribou in the George River herd, and disrupt Innu hunting and trapping. A federal environmental assessment (EA) of the issue simply would not consider the question of discontinuing the flights and this 'pre-decision' resulted in the Innu withdrawing their participation. Regarding discontinuation the EA report stated: '[B]ecause of commitments to its allies, the Government of Canada could not accept such a recommendation at this time ... It follows that those participating in the review ought not to think that the work of the Panel could reasonably result in such a termination.'[55] This overpowering of domestic decision processes and politics by international obligations stands in marked contrast to the frequent weakening of international environmental agreements in Canada and elsewhere by domestic political considerations .

Particularly notable as enforcement failures are the pre-Kyoto climate-warming agreements and the biodiversity convention. Germany and Europe achieved reductions in greenhouse-gas emissions through the 1990s, in part as a result of the modernization of East Germany and Eastern Europe. In North America, reductions were agreed to in 1992, but greenhouse outputs have not only not been stabilized and restored to 1990 levels, but have risen throughout the 1990s, by double-digit amounts in both Canada and the United States.[56] New reductions were then agreed to in Kyoto (6% below 1990 levels by 2012). The Biodiversity Convention of 1992 has not slowed the destruction of tropical forests, nor has it had political influence in Canada (one of its strongest promoters at Rio). Canada still, in 2001, has not produced legislation to protect endangered species. Continuing federal caution regarding habitat protection, ongoing overcutting in British Columbia, new pulp and paper development across the north of the prairie provinces, and (though the election-focused outcome was somewhat better than might have been expected) the Orwellian style of, and limited protection offered by, Ontario's 'Lands for Life' process, all suggest significant future species losses in Canada.

Even relatively successful treaty initiatives have had flawed results. The Basel Convention is sometimes avoided under the guise of recycling, and significant quantities of CFCs are illegally imported into the United States for use in automobile air conditioners.[57] Overfishing remains the norm globally, with fifteen of seventeen major ocean fisheries suffering from overfishing despite numerous treaties and enforcement regimes such as the North West Atlantic Fisheries Organization (NAFO).[58] Moreover, international environmental bodies, such as the

United Nations Environment Program (UNEP) are desperately weak. As McCormick put it: 'The UN system ... is regarded by INGOs as having only limited influence and power, mainly because its decisions are not binding on member states, but partly because of funding and personnel problems.'[59] Again, in contrast, prohibitions against trade dumping and cross-subsidization are overseen and enforced rather more systematically.

Overall, economic interests have more power than do environmental-protection interests, especially at the global level. That power prevents effective enforcement. One can, however, better understand the weakness of international environmental protection by taking a closer look at the need for expanded (supranational and global) environmental jurisdiction. There are many reasons for this expanded jurisdiction, including (1) the hemispheric or global nature of ecological and/or biophysical factors in some cases; (2) the race to the bottom in environmental regulation; (3) environmental problems resulting from impoverishment associated with global currency speculation, the race to the bottom in wages, or falling commodity prices; (4) impacts resulting directly from the global scale of production; (5) environmental protection itself being taken to be a restraint of trade within trade regimes, even to the point where foreign firms can sue governments over en-vironmental regulation; and (6) the nature of sustainability dilemmas that may require concerted and cooperative, global-scale, economic intervention.

At present only trade treaties and trade regimes provide effective international enforcement, save for military and strategic agreements. There have been tentative attempts to incorporate environmental and social considerations into such treaties (as in the NAFTA side agreement), but even these steps are often resisted by participating governments and may be more than offset by powers granted to corporations to sue signatory governments over national environmental-protection initiatives.[60] There are three distinct challenges here: (1) the incorporation of meaningful, openly reviewed, and enforceable social and environmental minima within trade treaties; (2) some means to link global commodity prices (especially for energy and other overexploited commodities such as fish and forests) to global GDP growth in order to gradually accelerate the de-materialization of economic outputs; and (3) an international fund (perhaps based on a Tobin tax and/or non-compliance penalties) to provide monetary aid to poorer nations for environmental retrofits.

The overarching objective here is to establish a minimum national environmental performance – to globalize environmental protection at least as much as we have globalized economic activity. In a new context some nations might develop the courage to act effectively. Canada would no longer be so obviously rent by both centrifugal and centripetal forces, and might even lead such an effort, rather than being overwhelmed by its own provincial governments.

Decentralization, Disentanglement, and Downloading

The long-standing pattern in Canada is for a generally reluctant federal government to accept environmental-policy jurisdiction only when pro-environmental public opinion is at its strongest. I have noted elsewhere that there have been two such waves of environmental concern – 1968–75 and 1987–94.[61] Harrison describes three periods of alternating federal environmental-policy assertiveness and retreat: 1969–72, the emergence of environmental action; 1972–85, a federal retreat; and 1985–95, a 'second wave' re-emergence of federal assertiveness.[62] Inertia would seem in this case to have explanatory power – the Canadian government is an entity at rest environmentally, unless forced into action by strong public pressure. Environment Canada was created in 1971, Canada's Green Plan was approved by the federal cabinet in 1989, both mid-points in waves of environmental activism. As well, in 1992, Canada took an assertive and visible role at the Rio conference, but since then the federal government has been all but invisible environmentally.

Thus, no sooner has Canada acted environmentally than it has retreated. By the mid-1970s budgets for the new Environment Canada were shrinking and the ministry's mandate never lived up to Prime Minister Trudeau's initial description.[63] By the mid-1990s the green plan was effectively dead in a wave of widespread federal cutbacks that hit environmental protection harder than almost any other sector of government activity. Much of the 1990s retreat in federal funding for environmental protection (32 per cent between 1994–5 and 1997–8) was accompanied by rhetoric about eliminating duplication through federal-provincial 'harmonization.' Unspoken was the irony that many provincial governments, most dramatically Ontario, were cutting environmental activities at the same time (rather than picking up the slack). Missing as well has been any contrarian view that 'provincialization' can replicate in miniature the global 'race to the bottom.'

There has been some debate within U.S. legal journals regarding the race to the bottom in environmental policy at the state level. Revesz argues that there should be no presumption that such a race is always problematic.[64] Engel, Esty, Sarnoff, and Swire all argue that the potential for a race to the bottom at this level justifies continued (or increased) action at the federal level.[65] Revesz largely ignores both global-level competition and international-scale environmental problems. He also is overly concerned with federal responsiveness to variations in local conditions and preferences, as if stiff prevailing winds were nothing but a local economic advantage and 'preferences' were never arrived at out of desperation (and always somehow shared by all local residents). He is highly tuned to firm- and plant-specific costs as if all threats to move would only be made if the actual move were cost-effective. Finally, Revesz assumes that there is an 'optimal' level of pollution at which economic 'systems' will naturally arrive (one that presumably has something to do with health-care costs and foregone earnings of the deceased, as if public decisions either were, or should be, made on such a basis).

Decentralization of environmental authority has been prominent in the United States,[66] where it has raised concern regarding disparities in institutional capacities among states. While many U.S. states have a stronger capacity to form environmental policy than they once did, a substantial variation among the fifty states remains.[67] Some states, usually the larger and wealthier ones, are far better equipped to handle the new responsibilities in term of funding, staffing, and implementation (monitoring and enforcement). The variability in capacity in environmental matters may be even greater among the Canadian provinces and is, ironically, only rendered nearer to equal by recent capacity reductions in Ontario, once the clear Canadian leader in environmental protection.

Ontario, since the June 1995 election, has reduced environmental protection to the point where prosecutions of polluters have been all but halted. This turn followed a February 1994 reduction in funding for the Alberta Ministry of the Environment of 30 per cent. Later that same year the Klein government passed its Government Organization Act, which allowed ministers to delegate 'any power, duty or function' except the power to make regulations to any legal person. Responsibility for the registration and inspection of underground storage tanks was delegated to the Petroleum Tank Management Association. In April 1995 the Alberta government established a Regulatory Reform Task Force, which was mandated, for example, to ensure that all regulations were 'cost-effective,' contained a sunset clause, enhanced 'economic values,' and were the only way to achieve their objective. The intent was to transform many environmental regulations into non-binding codes of practice or guidelines, delegate them to non-governmental enforcement, or both.

All provincial governments have been under political pressure from industry, as has the federal government, but Ontario is the Canadian jurisdiction where there has been a particularly dramatic rollback of environmental protection. From the outset the Harris government made it clear that it opposed all regulation and intended to shrink the size of government. The 1995 Ontario election followed immediately on the economic fallout of the NAFTA treaty that saw the loss of hundreds of thousands of industrial jobs in the province and the closure of numerous branch operations, especially between 1991 and 1993. On election the Harris government launched a very public assault on minor regulations. An interim report of the province's Red Tape Review Commission recommended elimination of more than one thousand minor regulations in a variety of (predominantly non-environmental) areas. This relatively non-controversial housecleaning set a public tone for more significant forthcoming actions, but the removal of regulations did not come. Instead, in the tradition and style of the Reagan administration in the United States, the Harris government cut the budgets of environmental agencies (in the 30–40% range) and reduced the enforcement of anti-pollution regulations. In 1996, the first full year of the Harris government, only three of 1024 water-pollution violations were prosecuted and fines were slashed by two-thirds from the average of the previous four years.[68] Headlines about regulatory rollbacks were largely avoided and non-enforcement mostly lost within the budgetary reductions.

Environmental initiatives in Harris's first year included (1) elimination of provincial support for municipal recycling; (2) repeal on an 'emergency basis' of a law requiring mine owners to obtain government approval of mine closure plans and to set aside funds in advance for cleaning up mine sites; (3) reduction by 70 per cent of funding for conservation authorities and by amounts that led to 50 per cent lay-offs by the Niagara Escarpment Commission, which protects this internationally significant land form; (4) elimination of the Environmental Assessment Advisory Committee, all intervenor funding for citizens participating in public hearings, and all provincial support for the network of community-based energy-efficiency and waste-reduction initiatives; (5) formal removal of a standing ban on incineration of municipal solid waste; (6) radical reductions in provincial subsidies for public transit and elimination of funds for the protection of sensitive farm lands; (7) approval of additional logging and mining in the Temagami region, the locus of the strongest pro-environment demonstrations of the past decade; and (8) reduced minimum requirements for insulation in building construction. (On this latter item recall the discussion of time and sustainability above.)

One of the most fundamental changes to environmental governance in Ontario has been in municipal planning. Here change was more subtle, but no less significant or revealing of the link between jurisdictional scale and protection. A multi-year review of the Ontario Planning Act conducted by the previous government resulted in provincial–level environmental guidelines for planning decisions – including the protection of wetlands, prime farmland, and significant topographical features, such as the highly contested Niagara Escarpment (sought for gravel) and Oak Ridges Moraine (sought for near-Toronto development). Developers participated in the process and in a consensus on increased municipal approval powers within the confines of the new environmental guidelines. The new guidelines were crucial given the pro-development proclivities of municipalities and a frequent lack of environmental expertise at that level. On election, the Harris government changed the wording regarding the guidelines such that municipalities must be 'aware of,' rather than 'in conformity with,' provincial–level rules. This change was well understood by all concerned – municipalities were now free to approve any and every form of development; the protective guidelines were not so much abolished as 'archived' within a tacit provincial promotion of all development (up until early 2000, when the government did act in response to widespread public pressures to protect some of the Oak Ridges Moraine).

The one area that saw additional funding in Ontario in the early years of the Harris government was highway construction – while subsidies to public transit were lowered to the point that the Toronto Transit Commission earns a higher percentage of its revenues from the farebox (about 80%) than does any major urban jurisdiction in North America. Outside Toronto's downtown core – in the province's fastest-growing municipal jurisdictions – public transit carries a very small, and declining, proportion of passengers. At the same time, the government's 'disentanglement' process has shifted, in net terms, additional functions to municipalities and to the property-tax base (away from income tax). In combination with the tacit elimination of environmental planning, the long-term effects of all this are clear. Few municipalities are able to fully fund public transportation (other than through higher fares) and few will be in any position to reject any (or any but the most disastrous) proposals from property developers – sprawl at below-transit densities and in transit-poor locales is the likely outcome of this array of changes.

Other Canadian provincial governments, even those lacking the Harris/Klein ideological bent, have also been challenged in their ability to stringently protect the environment as and when such action affects industries with particular local strength. A recent study of forest policy by Wilson bears out this trend in the case of British Columbia.[69] While gains in protected areas have been made overall, the province's original forest, one of the world's great ecological treasures – and the core of British Columbia's prosperity – will be cut before significant second growth is available. Wilson documents meticulously the ways in which both right- and left-leaning governments have been fundamentally powerless to alter this future – a future that has been seen to be coming for years and about which many yet remain in denial.

These provincial environmental limitations and recent deregulatory inclinations must be seen within the overall Canadian pattern of federal reluctance and 'federal-provincial harmonization.' Even where the federal government has sought to act, as in the case of endangered species legislation, it has thus far been either unwilling or politically unable to do so, or both.[70] After nearly a decade of delay it appears that there will be no federal, or joint federal-provincial protection, of habitat – nor any process that avoids dominance of scientific judgments regarding endangered status by closed political decision-making. As well, there has been a further devolution of responsibility from the provincial to the municipal level – where, however uneven are provincial environmental-policy capacities, capabilities vary enormously and the tax base is dependent on the one industry (property development) that municipal governments are asked to regulate through the planning, zoning, and approvals processes. The best hope at the municipal level is that planning education has recently become more environmentally oriented and there has been some increase in municipally oriented environmental activism.[71]

Decentralization in the United States shows a contrast to Canada in that there the federal government retains important controls. For example, most U.S. public lands are federal lands, whereas in Canada such lands are predominantly provincial. As well, many state environmental activities, including state-based comparative-risk assessment and risk-reduction projects and some twenty other EPA programs, involve federal funding or technical assistance. While overall only 20 per cent of state environmental spending comes from federal sources, some states receive as much as 30 to 40 per cent of their environmental funding from Washington. In Canada virtually all federal-provincial funding transfers are in the form of ever more delicately conditioned educational and social transfers and unconditional equalization transfers. While U.S. federal environmental grants to states declined significantly during the Reagan administration, they recovered after 1989 and reached new levels by the mid-1990s, rising sharply at the very time that Canadian environmental funding was in radical decline.

Decentralization also, however, has important positive dimensions. Multiple jurisdictions offer considerable potential for policy innovation. Wisconsin, for example, imposed tough rules on proposed mining initiatives, New Jersey initiated multi-media pollution prevention, and California requires that 10 per cent of motor vehicles sold in the state have 'zero emission' by the year 2003. California, of course, is unique among state and provincial jurisdictions in that its market is large, easily the equal of Canada's. Before NAFTA economic restructuring and the Harris government, Ontario, under the Liberals, showed superior initiative on recycling and the Rae NDP government initiated an innovative Environmental Bill of Rights. Many Canadian municipalities were highly innovative in the early 1990s (during the second wave of environmentalism), providing, for example, a right to refuse unsolicited flyers or preventing the sale of newspapers without recycled content on municipal sidewalks. As well, the U.S.-wide NGO negotiations with McDonald's over excessive packaging (which eliminated the 'clamshell') were sparked in part by new municipal ordinances in Berkeley, California. Such innovations can spread through intergovernmental communications or NGO campaigns. Thus, the challenge is, simultaneously, to recognize the political limits of smaller jurisdictions while not discouraging innovative actions. Innovation in smaller jurisdictions would seem more likely, however, if the global race to the bottom could be offset by treaty regimes, national regulatory minima, and the use of market-based tools at national and international levels.

From Local to Global – Right-Sizing Environmental Policy

How, then, can environmental affairs be conducted within sufficiently large jurisdictions when warranted by biophysical and/or political factors without seeking politically unachievable, and possibly undesirable, levels of global governance? Is treaty-based environmental-policy 'adhocery' likely to be sufficient as globalization continues to advance? Where is it insufficient? Within Canada, can provinces rise to the challenges of environmental decision-making? Is there any hope of federal assertiveness? What positive can be extracted from bioregional advocacy? What is an appropriate environmental role for municipalities? Is an environmentally benign globalism possible? Such questions cannot be resolved definitively, but some tentative conclusions and speculative policy suggestions can be offered.

All levels of governance from global to local have a role in environmental policy-making. In determining dominant and specialized roles we must be mindful of history and culture. To strengthen democracy, we must protect sovereign, responsible, accountable national governments. This is not to say that biophysical realities do not need to be trusted to ad hoc treaties and other international arrangements. How but through international cooperation could climate warming, ozone depletion, acid deposition, LRTAP, or many habitat-loss questions be resolved? Quite impressive progress has been made at times in this way – humankind has moved with considerable dispatch in some cases, allowing for the complexities involved. Though world conferences and unenforced multilateral treaties are far from sufficient, it is not impossible that a growing array of ad hoc treaties could eventually build to an integrated global arrangement with sufficient teeth.

The problem has not been one of reaching wide agreement; rather, of achieving effective enforcement of the agreements reached (partly of course a function of the lack of specificity within agreements necessary to obtain some signatures). The first climate-warming treaty was blatantly ignored, especially by Canada and the United States and to date there is little evidence that the Kyoto provisions will be met (new investments in automobile energy-efficiency research and high-speed-rail development in the United States are encouraging, but are not sufficient given continuously rising truck and sport-utility vehicle sales even in the face of rising gasoline prices). What is necessary is likely some form of economic sanction for national environmental non-compliance and some economic assistance in achieving compliance. One possibility is an international taxation regime (such as a Tobin tax), with the distribution of funds used to aid low-income nations in the achievement of compliance with important environmental treaties. The wealthiest nations might also pay penalties for any failure to meet their obligations.

Another global-scale policy option is linked to the inevitably global question of sustainability. Here one needs first to recognize both the environmental risks and the human moral imperative of achieving an additional increment of global economic output. It is often asserted by advocates of global 'free' trade that economic growth is the only hope for the poor in poorer nations. It is simultaneously asserted by unequivocal opponents of globalization that globalization all but assures both growing income inequities and environmental disaster. It is possible that both of these views are correct, but one might ask what it would take politically to see a larger proportion of the next increments of global growth redistributed downwards? How else, if sustainable behaviours require some minimum of economic well-being (as all sustainable development advocates assert) and we are already near to the limits of total energy-production capabilities (and perhaps beyond sustainable capabilities), is sustainability ever to be achieved? It costs far more environmentally to add a third car for a North American family than it does to provide a bushel of cell phones and a dozen bicycles in poorer nations.

Almost no one seriously advances appropriate environmental and social terms and conditions for accelerated globalization and growth. Advocates of globalization assume (or at least assert) that all ships will rise; opponents assume that globalization can only proceed on the terms of its corporate advocates. National governments do still exist and collectively have the capability to establish appropriate terms and conditions. Two such conditions (at the considerable risk of oversimplification) might be (1) a global minimum wage proportional to national GDP per capita (perhaps combined with some 'universal' declaration of labour rights) and (2) a common introduction of a standard energy (or energy and materials) extraction tax (or a global price regime for key commodities). Universal here is in quotations to indicate that these conditions are only relevant to those nations participating in the trade and investment agreement(s) within which these conditions might be incorporated.

These two conditions in combination could alter the basic structure of globalization. They would move a greater proportion of the benefits of globalization from North to South and West to East. How great a shift resulted would depend on the levels set. The trade-off, obviously, is the capital guarantee sought within the failed MAI treaty. Were the second condition not in the form of a tax, it could involve pegging

commodity prices to global GDP growth (or to price increases sufficient to slowly accelerate the de-materialization of economic growth
and to adequately advance sustainability investments). I would not
pretend to be able at this point to attach numbers to these conditions,
but the broad point is what is important – without incorporating significant social and environmental conditions economic globalization
will debase environmental and social realities. The conditions proposed here will not resolve all concerns, or centrally govern the world.
The objective is an overarching context within which environmental
protection would more likely be attained at all levels of governance.
Clearly, on the international level, supplementary treaties on climate
warming and biodiversity would remain necessary (and to work effectively would require economic incentives such as those mentioned
above). In combination, these international measures would encourage
national governments to take some of the right steps.

Obviously, no 'transformation of the structure of globalization' is
easily achieved, to say the least. The one hope is that further steps to
'protect investment' will otherwise continue to be successfully resisted
within several important nations or groups of nations. Global economic turmoil associated with global speculation, and the anti-
democratic nature of imposed cures, might also increase international
openness to revised approaches. But even with every effort a changed
approach to globalization will not come without some nations shifting
their views considerably. Canada, arguably, is well placed to advocate
adjustments in the evolution of a global economy. We understand, for
example, what it means to have a culture vulnerable to homogeniza-
tion. We are both a commodity producer and a rich nation. We are also
stewards of a significant proportion of the world's wild lands and fresh
water. If it is not Canada that shifts ground, who will?

What of environmental policy jurisdiction within Canada? The case
has been made throughout this chapter that effective environmental
management requires the courage to be a nation. Few Canadian provinces have sufficiently diversified economies and Ontario, the most
diversified, is highly vulnerable to the pressures of a globalizing economy and, though the third most polluted of the sixty jurisdictions in
North America, has sharply curtailed the enforcement of environmental legislation.

Federal environmental primacy must also be seen in the context of
the recent resolution of social and health jurisdiction in favour of the

provinces (with an absolute minimum of national standards). So long as there are federal social-policy standards this devolution may be warranted, but environmental policy is different from social policy. As we have seen, there is a biophysical and a political logic to resolving environmental problems within a hemispheric or global context. Only a national government can participate effectively on the international stage where many, perhaps now most, environmental problems must be resolved. Decentralization of environmental authority to the provincial level, especially with several provinces economically (and therefore politically) dominated by single (environmentally problematic) industries, only lessens the prospect for transforming global environmental decision-making. Moreover, only a market at least the size of Canada can command the attention of global-scale corporations (and through them their suppliers).

In the Canadian constitution and the law, pollution lies substantially within federal jurisdiction. Pollution and the protection of habitat are very much a part of providing peace, order, and good government (and therefore within the purview of criminal law). There is a basis for increased federal assertiveness regarding environmental regulation. Even with federal assertiveness, however, much scope would remain for provincial and municipal environmental initiatives. The global initiatives suggested above, in combination with national regulatory assertiveness, would encourage provinces and municipalities, perhaps with federal fiscal support, to develop the opportunity structures to foster compliance and to accelerate fulfilment of national and global objectives.

Significant and consistent local and provincial initiatives are unlikely without an end of the race to the regulatory bottom and without continued downwards pressure on commodity prices. But, even with only a global climate-warming treaty in place, there is scope now for concerted provincial and local actions, if only there is some clear sign that national governments are serious this time about what they have signed. Alternatively, a continuation of higher oil prices may advance the prospect for public transportation initiatives. Also important, and clearly within provincial jurisdiction, are the practices of electrical utilities, as well as education, and thereby environmental education. Further, additional municipal initiatives on recycling and land-use planning are essential to environmental protection. At the moment, however, little, if any, of this will happen without a demonstration of environmental seriousness on the part of the Canadian government.

NOTES

1 R. Paehlke, *Environmentalism and the Future of Progressive Politics* (New Haven: Yale University Press, 1989) and S.P. Hays, *Beauty, Health and Permanence: Environmental Politics in the United States, 1955–1985* (Cambridge: Cambridge University Press, 1987).

2 B.E. Holtzinger, 'Rethinking American Public Policy: The Environment, Federalism, States, and Supranational Influences,' *Policy Studies Journal* 26, no. 3 (Autumn 1998): 505.

3 M.W. Holgate, 'Pathways to Sustainability: The Evolving Role of Transnational Institutions,' *Environment* 37, no. 9 (November 1995): 39.

4 R. Diebert, *Parchment, Printing, and Hypertext* (New York: Columbia University Press, 1998).

5 S. Strange, *States and Markets* (London: Pinter, 1988) and K. Ohmae, *The End of the Nation State* (New York: Free Press, 1995).

6 W. Cronan, ed., *Uncommon Ground: Toward Reinventing Nature* (New York: Norton, 1995).

7 T. Roszak, *Where the Wasteland Ends* (Garden City, NJ: Doubleday, 1973), 382.

8 E.F. Schumacher, *Small Is Beautiful* (New York: Harper & Row, 1973); E.J. Mishan, *The Costs of Economic Growth* (London: Staples Press, 1967); and M. Bookchin, *Post-Scarcity Anarchism* (Berkeley, CA: Ramparts Press, 1971).

9 A. Lovins, *Soft Energy Paths* (Cambridge, MA: Ballinger, 1977).

10 J. Mander and E. Goldsmith, eds, *The Case against the Global Economy and for a Turn toward the Local* (San Francisco: Sierra Club Books, 1996), 471.

11 K. Sale, 'Principles of Bioregionalism,' in Mander and Goldsmith, eds, *The Case against the Global Economy*, 34.

12 D. Morris, 'Free Trade: The Great Destroyer,' in Mander and Goldsmith, *The Case against the Global Economy*, 218–28.

13 H.E. Daly, 'Free Trade: The Perils of Deregulation,' in Mander and Goldsmith, *The Case against the Global Economy*, 229–38.

14 H.E. Daly and J.B. Cobb, Jr, *For the Common Good* (Boston: Beacon Press, 1989).

15 Daly in Mander and Goldsmith, *The Case against the Global Economy*, 231.

16 K. Sale, *Human Scale* (New York: Coward, McCann & Geoghegan, 1980), front cover.

17 Ibid., 417.

18 R. Nash, *Wilderness and the American Mind* (New Haven: Yale University Press, 1973).

19 R.B. Gibson, ed., *Voluntary Initiatives and the New Politics of Corporate Greening* (Peterborough, ON: Broadview Press, 1999) and T. Boston, 'Greenwash-

ing in America: An Ideological Analysis of Corporate Front Groups,' paper presented to Environmental Studies Association of Canada, Ottawa, June 1998.

20 A. Vidich and J. Bensman, *Small Town in Mass Society* (Garden City, NJ: Doubleday, 1960).

21 B.G. Rabe, 'State Policy Innovations as Models for Sustainable Development,' forthcoming (author: brabe@umich.edu); M.E. Kraft, *Environmental Politics and Policy* (New York: HarperCollins, 1996); B. McAndrew, 'Politicians flout deal on lakes, report says,' *Toronto Star*, 8 March 1999: A6 and 'Water pollution violations ignored,' *Toronto Star*, 1 March 1999), A1, A13.

22 R. Kiy and J.D. Wirth, eds, *Environmental Management on North America's Borders* (College Station: Texas A & M University Press, 1998).

23 W. Sachs, 'Neo-Development,' in Mander and Goldsmith, *The Case against the Global Economy*, 251.

24 Sources for table include D. VanderZwaag and L. Duncan, 'Canada and Environmental Protection: Confident Political Faces, Uncertain Legal Hands,' in R. Boardman, ed., *Canadian Environmental Policy: Ecosystems, Politics, and Process* (Toronto: Oxford University Press, 1992), 3–23.

25 M. Hessing and M. Howlett, *Canadian Natural Resource and Environmental Policy: Political Economy and Public Policy* (Vancouver: University of British Columbia Press, 1997), 55.

26 George Hoberg, 'Comparing Canadian Performance in Environmental Policy,' in Boardman, ed., *Canadian Environmental Policy*, 260.

27 K. Harrison, *Passing the Buck: Federalism and Canadian Environmental Policy* (Vancouver: UBC Press, 1996), 45.

28 Ibid., 46.

29 D. Estrin, and J. Swaigen, eds, *Environment on Trial*, 3rd ed. (Toronto: Emond & Montgomery, 1993); P. Emond, 'Environmental Case Law: Canada,' in R. Paehlke, ed., *Conservation and Environmentalism: An Encyclopedia* (New York: Garland, 1995), 225–8; and VandenZwaag and Duncan, 'Canada and Environmental Protection,' in Boardman, *Canadian Environmental Policy*.

30 K. Harrison, 'Federalism and Environmental Protection: Canada,' in Paehlke, ed., *Conservation and Environmentalism*, 274–5.

31 Kraft, *Environmental Politics and Policy*, 92.

32 Sale, 'Priciples of Bioregionalism,' in Mander and Goldsmith, *The Case against the Global Economy*.

33 Sale, *Human Scale*, 477.

34 E. Rykiel, Jr, 'Relationships of Scale to Policy and Decision Making,' in D.L. Peterson and V.T. Parker, eds, *Ecological Scale* (New York: Columbia University Press, 1998), 494.

35 Peterson and Parker, *Ecological Scale.*

36 Paehlke, *Environmentalism and the Future.*

37 M. Mellon, *The Regulation of Toxic and Oxidant Air Pollution in North America* (Don Mills, ON: CCH Canadian, 1996).

38 K. Toughill, 'Pesticide levels dropping in Arctic,' *Toronto Star,* 5 March 1999: A6.

39 E. Ostrom, *Governing the Commons* (New York: Cambridge University Press, 1990) and D.W. Bromley, *Making the Commons Work* (San Francisco: Institute for Contemporary Studies, 1992).

40 J.E. Carroll, 'International Joint Commission,' and H.A. Regier, 'Great Lakes,' in Paehlke, *Conservation and Environmentalism,* 367 and 309–12.

41 J. Hartig, *Under RAPs: Towards Grassroots Ecological Democracy in the Great Lakes Basin* (Ann Arbor: University of Michigan Press, 1993) and McAndrew, 'Politicians flout.'

42 J. MacNeill, P. Winsemius, and T. Yakushiji, *Beyond Interdependence* (New York: Oxford University Press, 1991) and D.M. Roodman, *Paying the Piper: Subsidies, Politics, and the Environment* (Washington: Worldwatch, 1996).

43 T. Schrecker, *Surviving Globalization: The Social and Environmental Challenges* (London: Macmillan, 1997) and E. von Weizsäcker, A.B. Lovins, and L.H. Lovins, *Factor Four: Doubling Wealth, Halving Resource Use* (London: Earthscan, 1998).

44 C.J. Campbell and J.H. Laherrère, 'The End of Cheap Oil,' *Scientific American* 278, no. 3 (March 1999): 78–9.

45 R.N. Anderson, 'Oil Production in the 21st Century,' S.A. Fouda, 'Liquid Fuels from Natural Gas,' and R.L. George, 'Mining for Oil,' *Scientific American* 278, no. 3 (March 1999): 86–91, 92–5, and 84–5.

46 M. Carley and P. Spapens, *Sharing the World* (London: Earthscan, 1998), 43.

47 C. Jeanrenaud, ed., *Environmental Policy: Between Regulation and Market* (Basel: Birkhäuser, 1997); T. O'Riordan, ed., *Ecotaxation* (London: Earthscan, 1997); and Carley and Spapens, *Sharing the World.*

48 M. Dobbin, *The Myth of the Good Corporate Citizen: Democracy under the Rule of Big Business* (Toronto: Stoddart, 1998); W. Greider, *One World, Ready or Not* (New York: Simon & Schuster, 1997); and H.P. Martin and H. Schumann, *The Global Trap* (Montreal: Black Rose Books, 1997).

49 G. Soros, 'The Capitalist Threat,' *The Atlantic Monthly* 279, no. 2 (Februrary 1997): 47.

50 J. Goldsmith, *The Trap* (London: Macmillan, 1994), 17.

51 Martin and Schumann, *The Global Trap.*

52 T. Andersson, C. Folke, and S. Nyström, *Trading with the Environment* (London: Earthscan, 1995).

53 J. Clapp, 'The Privatization of Global Environmental Governance: ISO 14000 and the Developing World,' *Global Governance* 4, no. 3 (1998): 312.

54 J. McCormick, 'International Nongovernmental Organizations: Prospects for a Global Environmental Movement,' in S. Kamieniecki, ed., *Environmental Politics in the International Arena* (Albany: SUNY Press, 1993), 132.

55 Canadian Environmental Assessment Agency, *Military Flying Activities in Labrador and Quebec: Report of the Environmental Assessment Panel* (Ottawa: Minister of Supply and Services, 1995), 79.

56 Gibson, ed., *Voluntary Initiatives*, 134 and G. Toner, 'Environment Canada's Continuing Roller Coaster Ride,' in G. Swimmer, ed., *How Ottawa Spends, 1996–97: Life under the Knife* (Ottawa: Carleton University Press, 1996).

57 J. Clapp, 'The Illicit Trade in Hazardous Wastes and CFCs: International Responses to Environmental "Bads,"' in R. Friman and P. Andreas, eds, *The Illicit Global Economy and State Power* (Lanham, MD: Rowman & Littlefield, 1999), 91–123.

58 P.W. Birnie, 'Fisheries Conservation,' in Paehlke, ed., *Conservation and Environmentalism*, 278–82 and R.A. Rogers, *Solving History: The Challenge of Environmental Activism* (Montreal: Black Rose Books, 1998).

59 McCormick, 'International Nongovernmental Organizations,' 140.

60 It has been suggested by a coalition of environmental NGOs that the strongest resistance within NAFTA has come from the Canadian government. See P. Knox and B. McKenna, 'NAFTA partners' environmental deal at risk, groups say,' *Globe and Mail* (April 27, 2000): A9.

61 R. Paehlke, 'Eco-History: Two Waves in the Evolution of Environmentalism,' *Alternatives: Perspectives on Society, Technology and Environment* 19, no. 1 (September/October 1992): 18–23.

62 Harrison, *Passing the Buck*.

63 Toner, 'Roller Coaster,' and G.B. Doern and T. Conway, *The Greening of Canada* (Toronto: University of Toronto Press, 1994).

64 R.L. Revesz, 'The Race to the Bottom and Federal Environmental Regulation: A Response to Critics,' *Minnesota Law Review* 82, no. 2 (December 1997): 535–64 and 'Rehabilitating Interstate Competition: Rethinking the "Race-to-the-Bottom" Rationale for Federal Environmental Regulation,' *New York University Law Review* 67, no. 4 (December 1992): 1210–54.

65 Cited in Ravetz, 'The Race to the Bottom.'

66 Kiy and Wirth, *Environmental Management*, 250.

67 J. Lester, 'A New Federalism? Environmental Policy in the States,' in N. Vig and M. Kraft, eds, *Environmental Policy in the 1990s*, 2nd ed. (Washington: CQ Press, 1994), 51–68.

68 McAndrew, 'Water pollution.'

69 J. Wilson, *Talk and Log: Wilderness Politics in British Columbia* (Vancouver: UBC Press, 1998).
70 Rogers, *Solving History*, 149–73.
71 M. Roseland, *Eco-city Dimensions: Healthy Communities, Healthy Planet* (Gabriola Island, BC: New Society Books, 1997).

4. Regional Models of Environmental Governance in the Context of Market Integration

Luc Juillet

In the current context of the globalization of economic and social relations, regional and international governance regimes are influencing the way we govern ourselves and our relationship to the natural world. Post-national governance regimes, like the World Trade Organization (WTO), the European Community (EC), and the North American Free Trade Agreement (NAFTA), are playing a significant role in defining the relationship between international trade rules and environmental-protection measures. Their approach to integrating environmental concerns with trade-liberalization objectives will have important implications for the management of the conflicts emerging between free trade and environmental protection.

This paper examines the institutional arrangements governing the trade-environment nexus in two of these international governance regimes. I argue that the NAFTA and the European Community offer two distinctive models for reconciling trade and environmental imperatives. I further argue that the approach allows for a more complete integration of environmental and trade objectives as well as for a more balanced resolution of the tensions between trade agreements and domestic environmental measures. As such, it appears to better embody the principles of sustainable development. In contrast, the NAFTA's normative and organizational frameworks, characterized by the predominance of national sovereignties and the prevalence of free-trade principles, seem less poised to bring lasting resolution to these tensions by providing for a consistent and balanced consideration of trade and environmental imperatives.

The argument unfolds through five sections. The first section briefly states the importance of examining post-national, multilevel regimes of governance for understanding the emerging context of national policy-making. The second section offers a background to the paper by reviewing some of the main issues raised by the interaction between free trade and environmental-protection policies. The third section offers an analysis of the models offered by the European Community and the NAFTA (and its environmental side deal) for dealing with environmental policies in the context of market integration. An examination of both the normative frameworks and the organizational features of each regime is offered. The fourth section, drawing on the preceding analysis, makes the case that the EC and the NAFTA illustrate two fundamentally distinctive models for addressing trade and environment conflicts. It attempts to show that the European Community's approach appears better suited to an effective and more balanced integration of economic, social, and environmental imperatives and, as such, more likely to provide the means to reach sustainable development as a policy objective. The paper then concludes by drawing some insights and lessons from the analysis that may help in enriching the debate in North America.

1. Economic Integration and Post-National Governance Regimes

As citizens and corporations struggle to adapt to the new social, economic, and political conditions created by a higher level of economic integration, national states find themselves confronted with the task of rethinking models of social and economic governance in a world where national rules and institutions appear increasingly inapt at dealing with many important social problems. In economic and social areas, global problems and globalization processes are forcing a complex displacement of powers from national states to other levels of governance – local, regional or global.[1] Progressively, complex multi-level forms of post-national governance, constituted by rules, norms, and actors emerging at different levels and interacting on the same issues, are becoming increasingly important in many sectors. These emerging post-national forms of governance do not necessarily represent the marginalization of national states, but they announce at least a re-articulation of political and policy capacities that will give greater weight to the incentives provided by international institutions. In particular, more than ever, international trade regimes are playing a pivotal role in domestic policy-making and local behaviour. In this context, the World Trade Organization (WTO), the North American

Free Trade Agreement (NAFTA), and the European Community (EC) can all be conceived as experiments in post-national governance.[2]

The nexus between trade and environmental rules constitutes an important test for emerging post-national governance regimes. Current industrial practices are damaging to the health of our collective environment and, across the world, the resilience of many ecosystems is threatened by human activities. In response to these trends, international policy-making has extended to foster collaborative regimes designed to tackle shared environmental problems. While the multiplication of multilateral environmental agreements should be looked upon favourably, as Richard Falk observed, the process of globalization also appears to have detrimental effects on the ability of public institutions to effectively curtail environmentally damaging activities.[3] Long-standing concerns about the collective-action problems faced by national states in solving disputes over the over-exploitation of the commons have now been joined by growing worries that existing post-national governance regimes might impose (culturally as much as legally) a set of global economic and political disciplines that could prevent states from appropriately protecting environmental resources within and outside their borders.

The relationship between international trade regimes and environmental-protection measures constitutes an interesting example of these new sets of governance concerns over the impact of globalization on the protection of the environment. International rules about free trade have been portrayed as bearing the potential to undermine national governments' pursuit of solutions to domestic and international environmental problems. And, both at the international and regional levels, some efforts have already been made to 'integrate' environmental protection with trade-liberalization objectives, that is, to agree on common judgments about the proper balance to assign to these respective objectives and on rules to resolve inevitable conflicts between policies pursuing them.

2. Free Trade and the Natural Environment: An Overview of Contentious Issues

Over the years, conflicts between the liberalization of trade and the protection of the environment have focused on a number of different issues. From questions about the legitimacy of American and Austrian unilateral trade sanctions to protect the world's natural heritage to the more arcane debates about the GATT compatibility of the Ontario beer levy system or the American gasoline border-tax adjustment programs, the debate about the compatibility between trade and environmental policies has regrouped a wide range of issues, which, although related, are difficult to apprehend as a whole. In order to clarify some of these issues and to provide an adequate backdrop for the following analysis, it is worth disaggregating the debate into a set of four distinctive issues:

1 Free trade causes environmental destruction by expanding the scope of economic activities.
2 Trade sanctions used by countries in order to promote compliance to a number of multilateral environmental agreements (MEAs) conflict with the goals and terms of trade liberalization regimes.
3 A free-trade environment, in the absence of the harmonization of standards or the permissible use of countervailing duties against lax environmental standards by trading partners, creates a 'race to the bottom' in environmental standards.
4 Trade rules contained in market access agreements can be used to invalidate or trump legitimate domestic environmental regulations.

Cutting through the heart of post-national governance, the third and fourth issues emphasize the potential tensions between domestic environmental policies and international trade rules. Leaving aside the first two sets of issues,[4] this paper essentially focuses on the latter two. Concerns about the detrimental effects of one set of policies on the other have been expressed by both trade advocates and environmentalists. Many environmentalists argue that trade agreements already place undue constraints on the capacity of national-governments to set their own levels of environmental standards; while many trade advocates worry that environmental policies will be increasingly used to justify protectionist measures detrimental to the current multilateral trade regime. These issues raise important questions about how political trade-offs are made between competing, legitimate social objectives in a post-national-governance context. They cut to the heart of the relationship between national policy-making and supranational institutions and rules of decision-making.

Responding to these challenges in a manner that will be satisfactory to both trade advocates and environmentalists is not going to be easy. It seems undeniable that the use of trade-restrictive measures for environmental reasons bears the potential of introducing unwarranted protectionist measures into the multilateral trade regime. However, dismissing any environmental-protection measures that may lead to trade restrictions on the basis that they might constitute first steps on a slippery slope toward a protectionist nightmare shows a bias in favour of trade objectives that is equally unwarranted at a time when the world is facing growing environmental problems. Environmental protection and freer trade may not necessarily be incompatible. But from a sustainable-development perspective, one objective should not be considered or assumed to be predominant over the other; the decisions required for their reconciliation or the necessary trade-offs between them should always be the object of a democratic value judgment where both imperatives are duly considered.

The GATT's approach for dealing with aspects of this third dimension of the trade and environment nexus reflects its general focus on reducing restrictive border measures. In general, GATT rules purport to allow trading partners to set their own level of environmental protection within their borders. However, domestic environmental measures are nevertheless circumscribed by a number of principles requiring, in particular, that they do not discriminate between foreign states (article I) or favour domestic producers (article III). In fact, with very few exceptions (e.g., article XX), the GATT does not contain any explicit rules about environmental policies and environmental-protection measures are judged according to the general principles at the heart of the multilateral trade regime. In other words, according to GATT rules, environmental policies with trade effects must pass the test of trade rules and principles.

While this general focus on assuring the non-discriminatory character of environmental policies seems imminently reasonable, the application of general principles to specific cases dealing with the trade-restrictive effects of environmental policies led trade-dispute panels to render some decisions that have irritated many actors in the environmental-policy community. At least three interrelated outstanding issues seem to have emerged as points of contention and will demand some form of resolution if further disputes and controversies are to be avoided.

Extraterritoriality and the Process/Product Controversy

Several rulings by GATT panels, especially the two tuna-dolphin rulings against the United States, have shown that unilateral trade sanctions against foreign producers who do not respect the importer's environmental standards in their production processes are incompatible with international trade laws. In other words, national states are prohibited from using trade restrictions aimed at applying their own environmental standards to the production processes of other countries who wish to export into their markets.

This rule has emerged due to a restrictive interpretation of the national-treatment principle (art. III) of the GATT by dispute-resolution panels. National-treatment obligations prohibit GATT members from discriminating between like products sold by domestic firms and foreign exporters in the domestic market. In this context, one of the key issues becomes the determination of what constitute 'like products.' In the Tuna-Dolphin I case, the dispute-resolution panel found that the United States could not discriminate between Mexican tuna caught with fishing gear that threatens dolphin populations and other tuna caught with fishing gear likely to minimize the incidental killing of dolphins. Once processed for sale in the U.S. market, a can of tuna was a can of tuna and any trade discrimination was incompatible with GATT obligations. The decision declared the trade provisions of the U.S. Marine Mammal Protection Act, which sought to protect dolphin populations in international waters, to be GATT-inconsistent.

Trade advocates generally support this reading of the GATT rules. For example, Jagdish Bhagwati, a leading trade economist, portrays the use of import restrictions based on process characteristics as the practical equivalent of 'eco-imperialism,' that is, as the equivalent of one country (usually in the North) imposing its own priorities and values on another (usually in the South). Bhagwati's argument indicates that the process/product dispute really hides an ethical dilemma rather than a fundamental breach of international trade principles. In discussing the social and environmental challenges to the GATT, Bhagwati concedes that some exceptions, like the trade of goods produced by slaves, would warrant the use of extraterritorial measures.[5] In sum, some objectives (e.g., the fight against slavery) are sufficiently universally shared to excuse the application of extraterritorial measures. But if we accept this to be the case, surely the determination of which objectives are sufficiently important to justify extraterritorial measures must remain in the realm of politics and democratic choices. Whether the survival of threatened species or the protection of the commons constitute such valued and shared objectives are matters for democratic debate. It should not be left to trade experts to decide strictly on the basis of legal rules written years ago in an entirely different context.

In this era of globalization and in the face of alarming depletion rates of our commons resources (e.g., migratory fish stocks), the concept of extraterritoriality increasingly appears inappropriate for dealing with the big problems of the world. Although it might have been in correspondence with a world of sovereign states attempting to manage their relations, this concept seems increasingly ill adapted for a world that is growing ever more concerned with the protection of our common heritage. Moreover, the prohibition to discriminate on the basis of production processes seems in direct conflict with a sustainable-development perspective that calls for the transformation of production processes to improve both the economic and environmental performance of firms. Without the ability to make the distinction, in a competitive international economic context, between firms that produce the same products in environmentally friendly ways and those that do not, environmental agencies are deprived of an essential policy tool to further sustainable production at home.

Overly Restrictive Interpretations of Article XX Exceptions

The only significant environmental exception in the GATT is found in article XX, which allows the infringement of trade obligations when necessary for the conservation of exhaustible natural resources and for the protection of the life and health of humans, animals, and plants. However, environmentalists have generally found panel interpretations of this exception to be too restrictive to allow sufficient leeway for environmental policies. In particular, the interpretative requirements that the contested measures be 'primarily aimed at' conservation or that the policy instrument chosen be the 'least trade-restrictive' one available for achieving the environmental objective in order to fall within the scope of article XX exceptions have raised some concerns that GATT rules would make it too easy for foreign governments to challenge domestic environmental policy choices as discriminatory.

The controversy surrounding Ontario's environmental levy on beer cans illustrates this point. While the issue has temporarily been resolved outside the dispute-resolution process, American arguments about the discriminatory nature of this environmental tax on non-refillable containers have heightened environmentalists' concerns that trade rules will be used to undermine domestic environmental measures. By introducing a 10-cent levy on non-refillable alcoholic-beverage containers, the Ontario government succeeded between 1992 and 1994 in raising significantly the proportion of Ontario beer sold in refillable bottles and, as such, the levy was considered an effective environmental policy. The U.S. trade representative, under pressures from the U.S. beer and aluminum industries, argued however that, because U.S. beer is exported to Canada in cans and Canadian beer primarily sold in bottles, the levy amounted to a protectionist measure *in practice* and was therefore inconsistent with GATT rules, even if, *technically*, it was applied equally to domestic and foreign producers. Moreover, U.S. representatives claimed that life-cycle analysis did not always support the environmental superiority of refillable bottles over aluminum cans and that, therefore, the measures were not 'primarily aimed at' conservation, and hence did not fall within the scope of article XX exceptions.[6]

While the issue was resolved through negotiation in the context of a larger dispute over beer trade, this dispute served to demonstrate the potential vulnerability of domestic environmental policies to trade challenges. While environmentalists worried that trade rules could be used to invalidate effective environmental policies, they were also concerned that the threat of easy challenges under trade regimes (especially from the United States) would lead to 'regulatory chill' and hinder further development of environmental policies. According to this view, the perspective of having to go through expensive and costly dispute processes to prove the legitimacy of one's policy choices would serve as a deterrent.

The Marrakesh agreement, which concluded the GATT 1994 negotiations, has attempted to address these issues in part. The parallel agreements on the application of sanitary and phytosanitary standards (SPS) and on technical barriers to trade (TBT), in particular, contain a loose call for the harmonization of national norms to international-standards levels. At the same time, both agreements recognize that countries can set national norms that are more stringent than international ones, but stipulate some conditions for doing so. The TBT agreement calls for 'legitimate reasons' for adopting more stringent standards. The SPS agreement permits them, provided that the measures used for their implementation are justified by scientific evidence and based on proper risk assessment. Contracting parties are also required to select policy instruments that are the 'least trade restrictive' for attaining their stated objectives.[7] Overall, these measures still suggest a somewhat ambiguous position by the WTO (standards should be harmonized but higher norms are allowed under some conditions) and there remain uncertainties about the exact meaning of several of the key provisions, such as what constitutes sufficient 'scientific evidence' or 'legitimate objectives.'[8] Unless further progress is made in the near future through the WTO, and its Committee on Trade and the Environment, clarification will come once more through dispute-resolution panels.

The Dynamics of International Competition

Finally, notwithstanding the legal constraints on domestic environmental legislation, the existence of differentials in national environmental standards might lead to a competitive race to the bottom in environmental standards. In order to ensure the competitive advantage of domestic firms in the global market, governments will be less inclined to enact stringent domestic environmental regulations for fear that they may be more costly for domestic producers. As a result of a competitive dynamic, the liberalization of trade could prove detrimental to environmental protection.

This argument has typically been dismissed by trade advocates on the basis of empirical studies showing that environmental-abatement costs usually constitute only a small fraction of the production costs of industries and that, consequently, environmental standards should not be a significant drag on the price competitiveness of industries. This predominant view has recently been challenged by some authors. For example, Jennifer Clapp points out that, in fact, many of the early empirical studies underpinning the common wisdom found such a pattern of relocation for environmental reasons in the most hazardous industries. Moreover, she points out that current economic conditions justify a revision of the cost argument. Since the mid-1980s, the costs for handling and disposing of hazardous waste in industrialized countries have been increased significantly due to new international and national regulations. Further, the early studies on abatement costs neglected to take into account important costs associated with liability insurance, legal fees, public relations, and dealing with regulatory and impact-assessment procedures (including delays associated with these processes).[9]

Moreover, even if the low-abatement-cost argument were to be empirically valid, the recent Canadian trend in environmental deregulation in the name of competitiveness, especially in Ontario and Quebec, suggests another dynamic may be at play. Despite studies showing otherwise, environmentalists point out, producers and governments still perceive environmental regulation as detrimental to growth and success in international markets and the discourse of international competition is amply used to justify a slashing of standards. In practice, it is clear that the credibility of relocation threats made by corporations (or claims about the detrimental impacts of environmental costs on location decisions) varies and depends on specific circumstances. However, there may also be broader factors that make politicians and bureaucrats particularly receptive to such claims, such as an ideological bias toward neo-liberal market values, regulators' desire to avoid conflicts, or the usefulness of such claims for politicians who wish avoid making difficult political judgments in sensitive situations.[10]

The potentially perverse effect of political and economic competition on environmental standards have led many environmentalists to call either for the harmonization of standards as a way to prevent a race to the bottom or for the possible use of antidumping duties against countries with standards that fail to fully internalize the environmental costs of production. The harmonization of standards across jurisdictions raises difficult dilemmas from a policy standpoint. There are strong economic, political, and ecological arguments justifying variations in standards across jurisdictions, most of them based on the fact that collective preferences and environmental conditions vary significantly across regions. Yet, there appear to be few methods other than harmonization that are likely to prevent the competitive dynamic that encourages the adoption of suboptimal standards by competing jurisdictions. For this reason, coupled with the fact that business interests see it as a way to prevent non-tariff barriers to trade, harmonization seems to be gaining in popularity and trade agreements are somewhat encouraging it.

In contrast, the use of antidumping duties to counter 'unfair competition' by countries with lower standards has received a less enthusiastic response from trade advocates. Theoretically, suboptimal environmental standards, because they fail to properly internalize all social costs of production, can be considered hidden subsidies to producers. In virtue of this fact, some environmentalists argue that they should be treated as subsidies by the multilateral trade regime and that countervailing measures should be permitted to offset this form of government assistance to foreign competitors.

Leaving aside the technical difficulties that would have to be over-come (e.g., the determination of appropriate levels for standards in the exporting country and the corresponding levels of duties to be imposed) to make such a system work in practice, trade advocates and governments have rejected outright the use of such measures because of the obvious potential for protectionist abuse. Still, theoretically, it is not as easy to dismiss the legitimacy of such measures. To praise the virtue of free international markets for the allocation of resources in defence of trade agreements while glossing over the possibility that inadequate domestic policies fail to internalize the environmental costs of products in many countries, hence distorting resource allocation, seems to reveal a bias in favour of current free-trade rules that is unjustified in theoretical terms.

This brief discussion of issues serves to illustrate the complexity of the current debates about the interplay between international trade and domestic environmental policies. Although many actors in the trade-policy community argue that the two policy fields are better left on separate tracks and that trade laws have nothing to do with environ-mental policies, the issue of integration has remained on the agenda. Trade and environment conflicts have become more frequent in the dispute-resolution process. The last round of GATT negotiations has resulted in the inclusion of sustainable development as one of the objectives of the WTO. In March 1999, the WTO held its first high-level symposium on trade and the environment, in anticipation of the issue's importance in the next round of multilateral negotiations. The organization's Committee on Trade and the Environment has been formalized and is slowly proceeding with its work program. In sum, the issue has become sufficiently contentious to force trade regimes to address it and to pledge to account for it in their evolution.

3. NAFTA and the European Community

The prospects for achieving significant institutional innovation within the World Trade Organization appear to remain limited, at least in the near future.[11] Despite the rhetoric about a coming 'green round' of talks, there remain serious doubts among many trade specialists and contracting parties about the necessity or the desirability of developing new GATT rules about environmental-protection measures. Moreover, the institutional and political contexts of the WTO suggest that, even in the presence of political will, reforming GATT 1994 in any significant way to deal with environmental concerns would entail an extremely long and treacherous process that would yield uncertain results. The decision rules structuring the amendment process, the disparity of views about acceptable changes, and the North-South divide on the issue could combine to create insurmountable obstacles to change. At the global level, we will likely have to live with the results of the Marrakesh agreement for some time to come.

In this context, regional agreements might turn out to be more promising avenues of progress for their member countries. Regional governance regimes might indeed, as Richard Falk hypothesized in a 1993 paper,[12] represent some of the most promising forums to give some credibility to national governments' rhetorical commitment to sustainable-development policies in the context of a globalized economy. It is to the examination of the experiences of two of these regional regimes that we now turn.

The North American Free Trade Agreement and Its Side Agreement

The 1994 North American Free Trade Agreement has been widely trumpeted as the 'greenest trade agreement' ever signed.[13] Finalized in the midst of a heated debate where environmental concerns played a significant role, NAFTA explicitly incorporated a number of provisions meant to alleviate some of the negative impacts of greater continental economic integration. Its main text has made sustainable development one of its primary objectives; but its 'environmental friendliness' is more generally attributed to the existence of an associated 'side agreement' on environmental cooperation designed to assist the member states in moving toward sustainability in the context of an integrating continental market. In particular, the side deal and the Commission on Environmental Cooperation it created were the main reasons that some key American environmental organizations supported the ratification of NAFTA.[14]

However, despite some favourable assessments of the environmental provisions of NAFTA, a closer examination suggests a rather timid attempt at integrating trade and environmental imperatives. More importantly, it reveals an approach in dealing with the convergence of trade and environmental policies that, despite a formal recognition of the importance of sustainable development, nevertheless focuses on keeping trade and environment policy-making on separate tracks.

Normative Framework

The main text of NAFTA does not differ significantly from the rules embodied in GATT 1994.[15] The main provisions follow the same 'rules of reason' as the GATT framework. Non-tariff trade restrictions are prohibited (art. 301(1)) and domestic measures must conform with the general principles of non-discrimination, that is, national-treatment obligations (art. 309(1)) and most-favoured-nation requirements. Similarly, NAFTA essentially reproduces GATT's article XX on environmental, health, and security exceptions (art. 2101).

While the environmental exception has yet to be tested significantly through NAFTA's dispute-resolution panels, the same legal limitations that have been found at the GATT level should also apply to the North American context. Consequently, the 'least trade-restrictive' and the 'primarily aimed at' tests would place the same high burden of proof on countries seeking to justify environmental policies having trade-restrictive effects.

In addressing the problem of environmental (and other) standards in the context of freer trade, the NAFTA parties opted for a loose call for harmonization. The chapters on technical barriers to trade (TBT) and on sanitary and phytosanitary (SPS) measures both declare that member states shall pursue, as much as possible, 'equivalence' or 'compatibility' of their standards. The agreements also encourage member states to use standards that have been adopted by an international standard-setting body (e.g., the ISO) as a guide to setting their own standards and specify that these international standards are deemed to be NAFTA-compatible.[16]

While calling for harmonization of both SPS and TBT standards, NAFTA also explicitly permits member states to set standards that are more stringent than international standards. And, at the request of American negotiators, the TBT agreement contains the additional statement that each party may 'establish the level of protection it considers appropriate.'[17]

However, in order to adopt standards more stringent than international norms, member states must meet a number of criteria. The more stringent domestic standard must be non-discriminatory, necessary to achieve the stated objective, and should not constitute a disguised restriction on trade. Moreover, SPS standards must also be based on a risk assessment and justified by 'scientific principles.' They must also be abandoned when a scientific basis can no longer be proved.[18] In essence, the TBT and SPS conditions for more stringent norms under NAFTA seem to match and extend the validity tests developed more generally for article XX of the GATT. While they are allowed, such norms will have to meet the 'least trade restrictive' and 'primarily aimed at' tests; and SPS measures will be more closely scrutinized for the scientific evidence at their basis.

Overall, these conditions seem to place significant constraints on member states choosing higher levels of environmental standards. The incorporation of GATT's validity criteria has led some analysts to conclude that 'harmonization of environmental standards to any level beyond international standards is not likely to occur.'[19] In any case, the combined emphasis on international standards and scientific evidence appears to work against the increase use of the precautionary principle as a means of dealing with environmental uncertainty in environmental policy.

In addition to these measures, which constitute the cornerstone of its normative structure, NAFTA also counts on a few additional distinctive articles that are meant to deal more favourably with potential trade and environment conflicts. First, its preamble declares the commitment of trading partners to pursue trade objectives in a way that is consistent with environmental protection and sustainable development. However, although it might help dispute-resolution panels interpret the main text, the preamble remains part of the context and its influence should not be overemphasized.

Second, article 1114 of the investment chapter also states that it is inappropriate to encourage domestic investment by waiving or derogating from environmental standards. But, in light of the expected difficulties of proving such a claim in the context of a panel investigation, this measure also appears mostly hortatory.[20] Moreover, some analysts have pointed out that, while the article appears to prohibit the attribution of *specific* waivers and derogations to attract *specific* investments, it seemingly permits lowering environmental standards more generally to improve 'national competitiveness' and make national jurisdiction more commercially attractive.[21] Nevertheless, if such action is alleged, member states must consult with the complaining party to address the issue. There are no obligations for the resolution of such disputes. The ban on performance requirements for foreign investments also exempts environmental measures, providing that the requirements are not found to be disguised protectionist measures and that they are not applied arbitrarily (art. 1106(6)).[22]

Finally, in a precedent-setting fashion, NAFTA recognizes and affirms the paramountcy of several MEAs over NAFTA obligations, including the Convention on the International Trade in Endangered Species (CITES), the Montreal Protocol on the Ozone Layer, and the Basel Convention on Waste Trade (art. 104). There is also the possibility for the North American Council to add new MEAs to the list. On this issue, by stating explicitly its relation to these MEAs, NAFTA is taking a step ahead of other trade regimes. The agreement nevertheless requests that the measure taken be the least trade-restrictive available to meet the MEAs' objectives. As a result, a recognized MEA trade measure could still be challenged under NAFTA as not being the least trade-restrictive measure available for achieving the MEA's stated objective.[23]

Organizational Framework

The organizational framework established by NAFTA constitutes one of its most innovative dimensions for a trade regime. In addition to traditional components, such as dispute-resolution panels, NAFTA and its side deal have created a series of trilateral bodies meant to address aspects of environmental policies in the context of continental market integration. The central component of this organizational structure is the North American Commission for Environmental Cooperation, tasked with furthering cooperative efforts to improve environmental conditions in North America and assisting the NAFTA trade institutions with environmental issues, but there are also a range of technical committees meant to address market access and integration issues from a perspective of sustainable development. This section reviews these three organizational components of the NAFTA regime.

While generally similar in approach to the WTO regime, the NAFTA dispute-resolution process does bear some distinctive features that have relevance to environmental issues. In contesting SPS and TBT measures that are allegedly incompatible with NAFTA provisions and principles, the burden of proof is with the complainant (art. 723 and art. 912(4)). This approach seemingly reverses the GATT's practice.[24] Given that dispute-resolution procedures give precedence to NAFTA over GATT, this distinction may prove environmentally favourable.[25]

The NAFTA dispute-resolution process also allows either one of the disputing parties (or the panels themselves) to convene a group of scientific experts to advise on the scientific issues involved in the case considered.[26] By allowing greater (third-party) scientific input in panel adjucation, NAFTA panels partly respond to some of the environmental criticism levelled against the GATT dispute-resolution process.[27] However, these changes must also be assessed in the broader context of NAFTA rules, including their more intense emphasis on the use of risk assessment in setting standards.

A structural limitation that the NAFTA dispute-resolution panels have emulated from GATT is the absence of meaningful public participation and inadequate transparency. As free-trade rules become increasingly important in shaping domestic regulatory regimes, the legitimacy of panel decisions affecting domestic policies can only be enhanced by granting citizens greater access to their proceedings. But under existing practices, the public cannot attend panel proceedings and the filing of amicus briefs is not permitted.[28]

An additional concern regarding dispute-resolution procedures, repeatedly voiced by Canadian environmentalists, is that NAFTA's investment chapter provides for the first time direct access to dispute procedures to private investors. Moving beyond the traditional intergovernmental approach of GATT, NAFTA allows investors who see their investment affected by an environmental measure to challenge directly the responsible state.[29] This unprecedented institutional feature is surprising in light of persistent objections by the same governments to granting direct access to panel proceedings to citizens on the rationale that governments democratically represent their nationals and that trade law should remain an intergovernmental affair. It clearly raises significant issues of equity and democratic control by granting corporations equal status with states and denying similar access to citizens and non-governmental organizations.

While only time will reveal the full significance of this new investment-protection procedure for environmental protection, its aggressive use by corporations to undermine environmental regulations on waste and fuel additives has already attracted much attention in Canada. Early cases, including the settlement by the Canadian government to compensate the U.S. Ethyl Corporation for banning MMT as a gasoline additive, have demonstrated that these investment procedures can be used aggressively by corporations against environmental regulations. Public worry about the issue led Canadian authorities to express some concern about them and the editorial pages of the *Globe and Mail* also advocated a re-examination of the issue. In a recent study, Howard Mann and Konrad von Moltke have also found the early application of the chapter 11 measures to be exceedingly favourable to corporations, which can count on unprecedentedly generous legal wording (e.g., on the criteria to qualify as an investor and on the concept of expropriation) as well as on an undemocratic, secretive dispute-resolution process to press their case for compensation.[30]

The North American Commission for Environmental Cooperation (NACEC) is the main trilateral organization created by the North American Agreement for Environmental Cooperation (NAAEC). Established in large part in order to calm public apprehension and win over part of the American environmental movement, the NAAEC represents a crucial aspect of the NAFTA regime. Nevertheless, the NAAEC remains a side deal: it supplements the main trade agreement without altering it and it brings in environmental considerations largely as an afterthought to the trade regime, as opposed to entering them on an equal footing with trade objectives. To illustrate this separate status, we note that one of the signatories could withdraw from the NAAEC without legally affecting its membership in NAFTA.[31] Formal links between the NAAEC institutions and the main text of NAFTA have been kept to a minimum.

In essence, the NACEC, although a valuable trilateral organization in itself, does not constitute a vehicle for the integration of trade and environmental objectives in the regulation of continental economic exchanges.[32] While NAFTA's main text exhorts members to harmonize standards upward, the Commission is not called upon to play any role in this regard. As an organization dedicated to continental environmental cooperation, its main purpose lies elsewhere. The emphasis of the side deal and the Commission is on the enforcement of national environmental laws by NAFTA's member states and on the promotion of continental environmental cooperation.

The bulk of the NACEC activities are dedicated to a program of research, capacity building, remediation, and conservation, supported by an annual budget of 2,910,000 $U.S. in 1998.[33] Its work program includes a wide range of projects and issues. The Commission aims at improving environmental conditions across the continent, recognizing that national environments are fundamentally integrated and that having fewer environmental problems is probably the best way to limit environmental trade barriers and conflicts in the future. But while greater continental cooperation is likely to be beneficial, in the context of the NAFTA debate, it could not have been sufficient to offset environmental concerns. In a further attempt at improving environmental assessment of the NAFTA deal, the NACEC was also presented as a potential 'counterweight to the North American Free Trade Commission in the dispute resolution procedure.'[34] The NACEC was to play this role by both assisting and informing the North American Free Trade Commission, and its related technical bodies, in dealing with environmental issues and in approaching their own mandates from a sustainable-development perspective. But the commision was also to operate a dispute-resolution process of its own, focusing on the adequate enforcement of domestic environmental laws in the member states.

Five years after its establishment, the NACEC's contribution to 'greening' the NAFTA, and its related trade bodies, has been poor. John Kirton and Rafael Fernandez de Castro, in an assessment conducted for the Commission itself, have found that there was 'a striking absence of contact and cooperation between the two institutional communities,' despite the many calls for such collaboration in the NAFTA text. Most notably, at the ministerial level, despite calls for a joint meeting between the Free Trade Commission and the NACEC, none has taken place. Cooperation between the secretariats of the two institutions remains 'virtually nonexistent.' Moreover, many economic bodies with environmental responsibilities, or with responsibilities relevant for the environment, have not involved stakeholders beyond industry in their work. With the limited exception of the production of an *Emergency Response Guidebook* for dangerous substances by the Land Transportation Standards subcommittee, the trilateral bodies created under NAFTA have seemingly neglected or disregarded the explicit, or implied, environmental dimension of their mandates.[35] This approach reflects an attitude that appears to be supported by the member states' emphasis on the commercial purposes of NAFTA.[36]

This clear shortcoming in fostering a balanced consideration of trade and environmental policy objectives is unlikely to be rectified by the operation of the NACEC's own dispute-resolution process. As mentioned above, the clear focus of the NACEC process is on the enforcement of domestic environmental laws. The Commission offers the possibility to member states, and to citizens and non-governmental organizations across North America, to file a complaint against a national government for 'a persistent pattern of failure to enforce' their environmental laws (art. 14). If the complaint is judged to be receivable by the NACEC, the council of ministers decides whether the preparation of a factual record is warranted. When such action is initiated, the

NACEC prepares a factual record after investigating the matter. If, on the basis of this record, the ministerial council fails to find an acceptable resolution, a majority in the council can decide to create a panel to consider the case.[37] If the alleged non-enforcement is confirmed, the council has another opportunity to find a resolution and to agree on an action plan to correct the situation. If this also proves impossible, the panel can then impose a fine on the guilty country for a maximum of the amount represented by 0.007 per cent of the value of total trade between the two countries concerned. If the member state fined refuses to pay, the other parties can finally withdraw trade benefits in an amount equivalent to the fine.[38]

In addition to the significant length of the process and the fact that much of it is permeable to political obstruction,[39] we should note that ultimately any fines imposed on guilty states are essentially to be paid to themselves through the NACEC. The funds received as a result of fines are to be spent by the commission in the country found guilty of the offence, in a manner consistent with its own laws.[40] This unusual system for sanctions suggests that penalties for non-enforcement were meant to have primarily symbolic value. As a result, not only does the possibility of fines and trade sanctions appear remote, but the fines themselves are unlikely to constitute a serious incentive to modify behaviour.

In addition to these difficulties, focusing on the enforcement of national standards is also likely to create perverse incentives for the three NAFTA partners. Despite the exhortation to strive for higher environmental standards contained in the main agreement, the creation of a supranational agency overseeing the enforcement of these standards constitutes an incentive for minimalist standards: by setting lower environmental targets and reducing statutory requirements for enforcement agencies, governments minimize the likelihood of facing complaints under the side deal.[41]

Given the poor state of enforcement of environmental measures, an alternative scenario is that governments will be reluctant to pressure trade partners to enforce their domestic laws unless they are themselves confident of their immunity to similar challenges. In such a case, member states may not make great use of the available mechanisms and would be reluctant to support actions put forward by non-governmental organizations. If trade partners use the process aggressively, however, pressure may build to lower standards or to alter the enforcement norm at the heart of the dispute mechanism. As Abbott points out, 'a legal standard which is virtually assured of continuing violation by each of the parties seems more likely to create political pressure for amendment of the standard than to cure the underlying violations.'[42]

Five years after the entry into force of NAFTA and NAAEC, the NACEC experience suggests that its specific dispute-resolution process has been of limited value. In the first four years of the NAAEC, fifteen complaints in total were filed with the Commission. While eight remain in process, seven cases have been concluded. In all these cases, only one led to a factual record being established.[43] In sum, to this point, none of the cases completed the dispute-resolution process and, consequently, none resulted in the imposition of fines. Overall, this record would appear to conform to early predictions that the structure of the dispute process would render its work slow and would not make it conducive to effectively challenge the enforcement behaviour of national governments. Despite what appears to be a modest record, the Commission has nevertheless already suffered harsh criticism by national governments unhappy to see it pass judgment on, or investigate, their activities.

Environmental problems should be dealt with through national policies and, when involving a supranational dimension, through global or regional environmental agreements. What trade agreements and institutions must do is clarify the interface between trade rules and domestic or international environmental laws. Although providing an interesting venue for ENGOs to seek better enforcement of domestic policies or to set the continental environmental policy agenda as well as encouraging further cooperation among countries, the NACEC actually does little to deal with the heart of the trade and environment issue.

The cooperative approach espoused by the NACEC is laudable and must be commended, but the fact remains that greater continental economic integration, if it is to avoid being detrimental to the social and environmental standards of the member countries, will require more-established and clearer rules about the appropriate ways to balance environmental and trade objectives. These rules do not need to give blanket exemptions for environmental measures; but they should place environmental objectives on an equal footing with economic objectives.

Despite the overall recognition of the primacy of some MEAs, the North American governance regime maintains the paramountcy of trade objectives over environmental protection. As we will see in the next section, the NAFTA framework in total does not go as far as the EC in allowing for the balanced consideration of environmental and trade objectives in the context of market integration.

The European Community

The European Community offers an approach to economic integration that is markedly and distinctively different from the one proposed by the multilateral trade regime or by NAFTA. The much greater degree of political integration and institutional development that characterize the EC are likely to hinder the transferability (to other trade regimes) of lessons learned by examining its experience. Nevertheless, an analysis of its approach for dealing with environmental policies in the context of deepening market integration may still reveal significant insights about the underlying process of arbitrating the potentially conflicting objectives of trade and environment policies.

Normative Framework

Since the 1957 Treaty of Rome, the principal objective of European governance has been the creation of a single economic market where internal trade barriers are abolished, and individuals and firms are 'free to work, invest, produce, buy and sell anywhere in the member states.'[44] However, despite this primary focus on creating a common market, dealing with environmental problems has long been an important issue in the European Community's internal process of integration.

While the protection of the environment did not figure among the explicit objectives in its founding text in 1957, the EC did not escape the emergence of growing environmental awareness that characterized the 1960s, and, in the aftermath of the 1972 Stockholm Conference, it adopted its first formal program of action on the environment.[45] With no explicit legal basis for environmental directives in force, however, environmental measures were either justified as necessary for the establishment of a common market (art. 100)[46] or as falling within the scope of the EC's 'residual authority' to take action for the achievement of Community objectives (art. 235).[47] While in both cases an explicit link with the creation and the operation of the common market was necessary to support the adopted directives, the Community's environmental policies were more far-reaching than this requirement may lead one to believe, including provisions on clearly subnational issues, such as the quality of drinking and bathing water, which appear to have little relation to the common market.[48]

Despite this implicit, and arguably tenuous, legal basis for environmental legislation, the EC adopted 118 environmental laws[49] between 1972 and 1986, clearly establishing the protection of the environment as an integral component of building a European common market.[50] Since community directives are binding on member states, national legislatures must either adapt existing domestic environmental legislation (or regulations) to meet community objectives or they must introduce new legislation where none previously existed.[51] In essence, the adoption of community laws constitutes a vehicle for a strategy of harmonization of differing national standards. Since the early days, the trend toward widening the scope and intensity of community intervention in the area of environmental protection has endured and today the *acquis communautaire* in the area of environmental policy comprises over 500 legislative items.[52]

In 1987, the Treaty of Rome was amended by the Single European Act (SEA). Among the changes brought about by the SEA, some amendments were included in order to address more explicitly the environmental implications of trade liberalization and the development of the common market. Under the SEA, the EC was given clear legal authority to formulate binding community-wide environmental policies[53] and some normative principles were entrenched to guide the arbitration between economic and environmental imperatives.

In particular, by amending article 100, the SEA provided a mandate of upward harmonization in the areas of health, safety, and environment, where community policies must take as a base 'a high level of protection' (art. 100a(3)). The SEA also introduced an alternative, and more explicit, basis for community environmental law through the adoption of article 130. This article now offers a legal basis for environmental policies without requiring a demonstration that the measures are tied to the workings of the common market. Moreover, while measures adopted on the basis of article 100a are limited to taking the form of directives, measures taken on the basis of article 130 can take the form of more direct regulations.[54]

Maybe more significantly, before the SEA, the well-established interpretation of community law prohibited member states from adopting more stringent standards in areas where harmonized standards existed.[55] To the insistent demands of Denmark and Germany, the SEA departed from this norm by explicitly allowing member states to adopt more stringent standards than the Community.[56] This option is valid both for community directives taken on the basis of article 100a and for those taken on the basis of article 130s.

By overcoming its previous concern that allowing member states to adopt norms more stringent than community standards would unreasonably impede the free trade of goods, the EC demonstrated an increased level of deference to environmental objectives and a greater tolerance of diversity. However, such tolerance has its limits. The national government opting for more stringent standards than those adopted by the Community under article 100a must register its intention before the European Commission and obtain its approval in order to avoid the proliferation of disguised protectionist measures.[57] However, this condition does not hold for community laws adopted on the basis of article 130s; for these measures, derogation does not require any approval by the Commission. While still unduly limited for some observers,[58] this approach to accommodating higher environmental norms still offers a safeguard against a 'race to the bottom' dynamic and against excessive uniformity across varying natural and economic conditions.

It must also be noted that, even without explicit derogation from community standards, member states are still afforded a fair degree of flexibility. As mentioned above, the preferred legal instrument of the EC, the directive, establishes only binding objectives for member states. In translating these objectives into national policies, member states can tailor the form of their intervention to local preferences and needs.[59] Moreover, as Esty and Geradin point out, EC history illustrates a clear ability to provide flexible conditions of harmonization, offering flexible implementation schedules and alternative options in standards setting, and even adapting standards somewhat across localities to take into account local environmental conditions or the technical characteristics of local firms.[60]

In addition to these measures for derogation and flexibility in dealing with community harmonization, the normative framework of the EC also demonstrates a clear willingness to recognize the special importance of environmental protection in areas where community harmonization has not occurred. Much like GATT and NAFTA, the Treaty of Rome contains an explicit environmental, health, and safety exception to the norm of free trade. Article 36 allows a member state to impose restrictions on trade for the objective of protecting the natural environment.[61] However, again much like GATT's article XX, article 36 requires that the environmental restriction be applied without discrimination and be considered necessary to meet the stated environmental objective.[62]

However, in contrast to both GATT and NAFTA, European jurisprudence has come to give importance to the principle of 'proportionality' in arbitrating trade-offs between the unimpeded flow of goods across borders and the retention of regulatory measures required for pursuing environmental objectives. On this basis (among others), the ECJ has proved more willing to uphold obstacles to trade when these measures were judged to be required for protecting the environment than has been the case so far under the GATT regime and is likely to be the case under the NAFTA regime.[63] As a result, the Community's normative order better incorporates both objectives: the free trade of goods in order to improve economic conditions *and* the explicit possibility of limiting trade when it is required for the protection of the natural environment. The importance of such a recognition in the ECJ's interpretative practices has been demonstrated in several of its decisions.[64]

In a first judicial decision rendered in 1985 on the implementation of a directive on the management of waste oils,[65] the ECJ stipulated that '[t]he principle of freedom of trade is not to be viewed in absolute terms but is subject to certain limits justified by the objectives of the general interest pursued by the Community ... The Directive must be seen in the perspective of environmental protection, which is one of the Community's essential objectives.'[66]

In effect, the ECJ clearly established that free trade did not constitute an objective supplanting all others, but that the overall objectives of the Community – the general interest – were to be assessed in determining the balance among competing objectives.

In the 1988 *Danish Bottles* case, the ECJ ruled again that the environmental objectives of member states could justify creating obstacles to intra-community trade. In a landmark decision, it found in favour of Denmark's 1981 recycling law requiring that all beer and soda bottles, foreign and domestic, be recycled and include an obligatory deposit at the time of sale. While the Commission (on behalf of importers) argued that the Danish law discriminated against foreign firms whose home countries did not have recycling programs, the ECJ ruled that a law requiring that beverage packaging be returnable was necessary in order to reach a high level of returns and that the measure was therefore 'in suitable proportion' to that goal. This decision ultimately opened the door for other European states to adopt more stringent packaging standards.[67]

Notwithstanding the overall outcome in Denmark's favour, it should be noted that the ECJ also invalidated the section of the recycling law that imposed a single, centralized container-approval scheme. The ECJ judged that the effects of the proposed approval system were disproportionate to the expected gains, noting that Danish authorities could refuse approval to foreign producers even if they could assure them that the returned bottles would be used again.[68] The *Danish Bottles* case offers an interesting illustration of the application of the proportionality principle. It shows both that the ECJ has not sought to impose an excessive burden of proof on responding parties to prove the 'proportionality' of their environmental restrictions on trade and that it could invalidate those measures that appeared to be excessive in meeting the stated objective.

In addition to these norms regarding harmonization, national derogation, and environmental exceptions, the legal framework of the EC has also explicitly incorporated a number of fundamental principles meant to guide the elaboration of community environmental policies. The 1987 SEA explicitly identified the polluter-pays principle, the rectification of damages at source, and preventive action as the principles upon which environmental policies should be based. The 1993 Maastricht Treaty made 'sustainable and non-inflationary growth respecting the environment' one of the fundamental objectives of the EC and formally introduced the precautionary principle as a basis for community action on environmental problems. Finally, the Amsterdam Treaty will improve upon the Maastricht language by making 'balanced and sustainable development' (instead of the more limited 'growth') one of the EC's objectives and by affirming that environmental-protection requirements must be integrated into the development of Community policies in all sectors.[69]

While the statement of general principles can often be interpreted as purely hortatory, there are signs that the inscription of these principles in the foundational community legislation could prove to be more meaningful in the context of the EC. In particular, since the EC legal texts are not solely objects of interpretation by trade panels but are also the constituting documents of a set of policy-making bodies, they are more likely to find their way into concrete policies. Moreover, the Community case law suggests that these principles do hold legal significance for the ECJ.[70] The ECJ's decision in the 1992 *Wallonia Waste* case offers an important illustration.[71]

The *Wallonia Waste* case involved an executive decree by the local government of the Belgian region of Wallonia prohibiting the storage, tipping, or dumping of 'foreign' waste within the region's territory. The decree applied equally to waste imported from other countries and from other regions of Belgium. It also covered both 'ordinary' and hazardous waste material. Responding to the Commission's challenge of the Wallonian decree, the ECJ first determined that existing legislative items on hazardous waste constituted a set of Community harmonization measures. Given the supremacy of Community laws and the incompatibility of these with the Belgian decree, the ECJ found the decree non-applicable with respect to hazardous waste. But, surprisingly, the ECJ also found that the decree constituted a legitimate restriction on the trade of ordinary waste. Consequently, the Wallonian measures on ordinary waste material were upheld.

While reiterating the Community's preference for harmonization as the prime strategy for dealing with potential trade and environment conflicts, the *Wallonia Waste* case is notable for the extent to which it illustrates a willingness to impede free trade for environmental reasons. Despite the fact that the Wallonian decree is prima facie clearly discriminatory (prohibiting to foreign firms activities that are allowed for domestic ones), the ECJ found that the 'special nature' of waste warranted that it be judged non-discriminatory.[72] In its reasoning, the ECJ relied significantly on the principle that 'environmental damages should as a priority be rectified at source' inscribed at article 130r(2) of the Treaty of Rome by the SEA.[73] It noted that, given the limited capacity of local or regional environmental systems to eliminate waste, unfettered accumulation would represent a threat to the environment. As a result, limitations on international and interregional trade were found to be justified.[74] The ECJ's rationale, and its decision in this case, clearly demonstrate that the EC's normative framework has more successfully incorporated environmental principles and imperatives in the region's trade regime than has been the case in North America.

Organizational Framework

While the Treaty of Rome, its subsequent amendments, and the case law provide the normative framework for dealing with trade and environment conflicts, the EC also possesses organizational features that facilitate a more balanced arbitration between trade liberalization and environmental protection.

The ECJ's authority to enforce community-wide environmental policies resonated in the 1980 legal case between the European Commission and Italy wherein the Commission brought an enforcement action against Italy for failing to comply with an EC directive on the sulphur content of liquid fuels. The binding quality of the ECJ's decisions contrasts markedly with decisions rendered by NAFTA trade panels, where political trade-offs become more clearly important at the adoption and implementation stages. There is also an important contrast with the GATT process, which has been illustrated by the unilateralism and political wrangling showed by the United States in its response to the tuna-dolphin decisions.[75] While U.S. actions may have been favourable to the protection of the commons in this specific instance,[76] this case nevertheless demonstrates the weakness of such an approach for establishing a predictable, rules-based framework for dealing with trade and environment conflicts.

The European Court of Justice also has the advantage of being more accessible and transparent than the dispute-resolution panels used by the WTO or NAFTA. The ECJ offers standing to member states, citizens, business corporations, and the Commission. It can also consider technical and scientific advice in rendering its decisions. It benefits from more leeway in considering the issues at stake, including the environmental objectives of domestic laws and other competing Community objectives expressed by its support for specific multilateral environmental agreements. Since the ECJ is also considered more objective and accountable by the interested public, its decisions are also likely to hold greater legitimacy than those rendered by panels of trade experts.

Moreover, given the high base level of environmental protection prescribed by article 100 for Community-wide environmental policies, the European Commission seems well placed to counter the lowest-common-denominator approach to the harmonization of environmental standards between trading partners. Assistance funds controlled by the Commission are an organizational feature that has assisted significantly in pursuing this upward harmonization strategy. The EC also controls funds that are used to help poorer member countries upgrade their environmental-protection measures. Member states can draw from the Cohesion Fund, the European Regional Development Fund, the European Social Fund, the European Agriculture Guidance and Guarantee Fund, and the LIFE Fund to assist in developing more stringent national standards or to undertake environmental remedial actions.[77] These funds provide the EC with 'more authority and a wider range of instruments than many other international institutions have in dealing with member countries' environmental policies.'[78] They support the EC's efforts to integrate environmental concerns and trade liberalization by ensuring that member countries will not have to sacrifice environmental interests to remain competitive in the common market. In effect, the EC has in place the kind of compensation mechanism that will be required at the global level to solve the stalemate between developed and developing countries and that the Global Environmental Fund experience has proved so difficult to establish.

The EC's striving toward the upward harmonization of Community environmental standards is also aided by the presence of environmentally progressive countries within the Community. The integration of environmental requirements into relevant European policies is supported by several member countries that advocate enhanced international cooperation in the area of sustainable development and trade.[79] On environmental issues, countries like Germany, Norway, and the Netherlands possess considerable influence in shaping the direction of Community policy.[80]

Environmental policy, like other potential policies justified by their link to the establishment of the common market, benefited from the introduction of the qualified majority voting procedure for the adoption of measures by the council of ministers. By reducing the possibilities for veto, the new procedure arguably expanded the possibilities for the adoption of new environmental measures at the Community level. The new procedure also reduced the risk that less environmentally progressive states, previously benefiting from a veto, could bring Community laws to the lowest common denominator of all state preferences.[81]

Many scholars identify this change in voting procedures as a turning point in the development of Community environmental policy. Around the same time, Germany is reported to have undergone a significant 'conversion' in favour of more stringent Community environmental directives.[82] Partly responding to domestic pressures and concerned that German firms would be disadvantaged by more stringent domestic laws, Germany became a driving force behind a significant expansion in environmental measures at the Community level in the late 1980s.[83] More generally, Steinberg estimates that the EC has developed more progressive rules for dealing with trade and environment conflicts in large part because, within Community institutions, power is 'relatively concentrated in favour of green countries.'[84]

Since the late 1980s, the expanding role of the European Parliament in Community policy-making (partly through the introduction of the cooperation and co-decision procedures) has also brought a measure of democratic input and control into the development of Community environmental legislation. David Judge even argues that the SEA's environmental provisions were largely added as a result of the EP's persistent strategy to promote public awareness about the necessity for greater democratic control of the Community's transborder policies.[85] In any case, the European Parliament (and its Committee on the Environment) are clearly considered to be aggressive supporters of a more balanced approach between commercial, social, and environmental imperatives.[86] Its growing status within European policy-making institutions is likely to increase both accountability in the process of integration and grant more weight to the Environment Committee in the evolution of Community environmental policies.

However, this positive evaluation of the less rigid organizational framework for decision-making within the EC system should be qualified to some extent. The use of qualified majority voting, in tandem with the growing influence of the European Parliament under the co-decision and cooperative procedures, do not necessarily ensure upward harmonization and higher levels of environmental protection. There clearly have been cases where the new decision-making procedures have led to the adoption of much tougher standards than 'laggard states' would have preferred, such as vehicle emission standards.[87] But there were also cases where sufficient coalitions were formed within the council and parliament to keep in check the more progressive forces in the Commission and within parliament, resulting in the adoption of a lowest-common-denominator standard. Golub's analysis of the adoption process of the Packaging Waste Directive is instructive in this regard.[88] Nevertheless, the fact that the EC adopted more environmental laws between 1989 and 1991 than in the previous twenty years combined may suggest that the new decision rules did in fact have a positive effect. Moreover, there seems to be widespread agreement among European scholars that EC legislation has, overall, clearly exceeded the lowest common denominator of state preferences and has in fact driven upwards the environmental standards of the 'laggard states.'[89]

This cursory review of the experience of the EC in dealing with environmental policy in the context of the common market leads me to conclude that it embraces a markedly different approach to reconciling trade and environment imperatives. The EC shows a clear preference for harmonization as a way of pre-empting trade problems associated with potentially trade-restrictive (or trade-distorting) national environmental-policy measures. While harmonization constitutes a policy choice that can be questioned on theoretical grounds, it must be added that the EC has pursued this option in parallel with compensatory measures that may be interpreted as alleviating some of its negative consequences. The Community requires harmonization while allowing for significant flexibility in achieving it and explicitly permits the adoption of more-stringent standards in most cases. The EC's historical experience suggests that it has avoided the pitfalls of a race to the bottom through a mix of favourable decision rules, 'integration through law' on the basis of entrenched principles that recognize the appropriate importance of environmental protection and an activist court, and the adoption of significant financial-assistance programs to support laggard states in their efforts to improve their environmental performance.

4. Regional Models of Environmental Governance in the Context of Market Integration

The EC model, embodying a strategy of *flexible harmonization*, seems to offer a promising avenue for dealing with environmental policies in a context of market integration. Providing that one takes for granted that freer trade is a desired social objective and that a more sustainable form of development is achievable by allowing a more balanced consideration of environmental and economic imperatives, the European approach offers a middle ground between unchallenged free trade and unchecked environmental protectionism.

Harmonization, tempered with possibilities for upward harmonization and for the maintenance of obstacles to trade for environmental objectives, recognizes that different local conditions may call for different policies. But, by assuring a Community floor in setting standards, it also alleviates the possibility of a race to the bottom and implicitly recognizes that low standards can often simply reflect regulatory failure rather than the careful matching of local environmental and economic conditions.[90] This multilevel governance regime may be complex and can undoubtedly result in a patchwork of entangled measures at different levels of jurisdiction. But at a time when rethinking the spatial basis of politics (and policy) appears necessary, the EC may offer a promising start.

In contrast, NAFTA's emphasis on 'environmental state autonomy,' combined with an exhortation to move toward international standards and strict limits on keeping more-stringent norms, seems less inspired.

Under the cover of maximizing state autonomy, it could fail to effectively alleviate international competitive pressures for lowering domestic standards, and it still generally submits environmental policy to trade imperatives.

EC institutions also offer a more democratic institutional environment for making the kind of continuous arbitration that the reconciliation of trade and environmental imperatives will increasingly require. While the EC's 'democratic deficit' is real and significant, as a post-national arrangement it remains superior to other experiences, including NAFTA. Recognizing that making decisions about the appropriate relationship between trade rules and environmental protection is fundamentally a political exercise, and certainly not a purely technical or legal matter, the trade-panel and technical-standardization-bodies model prevalent at the WTO and NAFTA comes significantly short of providing an adequate forum for such decisions.

The experiences of both continents also reveal the importance of international financial transfers in limiting 'race to the bottom' dynamics in the context of market integration. While trilateral cooperation is officially the strength of the NAFTA/NAAEC model, in practice, the European Community has invested more systematically and more substantially in supporting the adjustment process of states with lower standards. Evidence is found not only in the smaller budget of the NACEC for assisting in environmental improvements but also in the relative failure of the North American Development Bank, set up in 1994 to assist in improving the environmental conditions of the U.S.-Mexican border area.[91]

The comparative analysis also shows that the same rules can lead to significantly distinctive interpretations. While article 36 of the Treaty of Rome and article 2101 of NAFTA (and GATT article XX) are similar, the EC jurisprudence has come to provide more room for environmental objectives in judging the validity of trade-restrictive environmental measures. The rules of reason developed in GATT (and thus to be applied in future GATT cases) and by the ECJ have distinctly different flavours. While GATT's panels have emphasized the trade-restrictiveness of the contested measures, the ECJ has more conscientiously weighted the environmental objectives pursued by the challenged legislation.

While these divergent developments could partly be explained by path-dependent trajectories, flowing from (precedent-setting) early case law, the institutional framework of the EC seems to offer a more complete interpretation. The legal and institutional structure of European integration has allowed the ECJ to draw more significantly from environmental law and policy principles in passing judgment in trade/environment cases. NAFTA panels remain truly trade bodies, strongly entrenched in the law of international trade and its jurisprudence. While time may prove GATT's ability to build an independent, more qualified jurisprudence in trade/environment cases, experiences to date are cause for scepticism. So, in contrast to Esty and Geradin,[92] I find that the EC has developed a set of rules and procedures that better take into account the legitimate environmental objectives of trade-discriminatory measures in assessing their validity and that it has clearly demonstrated a greater willingness to accommodate environmental concerns in furthering economic integration.

In sum, the EC and NAFTA represent clearly different responses to environmental-policy concerns in the face of growing market integration. While the European Community has chosen a more dedicated strategy of flexible harmonization, providing room for locally tailored norms and support for improving the stringency of national standards, the NAFTA regime has chosen to emphasize the enforcement of domestic standards and to place more severe obstacles to adopting standards that are more stringent than international norms. Following more closely GATT's traditional approach, NAFTA has also chosen to limit the integration of trade and environmental policies, keeping them on separate tracks and generally emphasizing the conformity of environmental measures to trade principles, which are considered predominant in its normative order.

5. Epilogue: Lessons for the North American Debate

Drawing lessons from our examination of the European experience is a tricky endeavour. The European Community represents an exceptional experience in post-national governance. Transposition of its approach to the North American context without taking due consideration of the world of differences dividing the continents would be sociologically inept and probably constitute a recipe for irrelevance.[93] Nevertheless, comparative policy studies may offer valuable insights for developing original strategies. In this last section, I tentatively offer some preliminary thoughts on the options offered to North American policy-makers wanting to move beyond the current state of affairs. They are meant to encourage debate.

Overall, the European experience suggests to me the following approach. In the context of greater economic and social integration, the cornerstones of a progressive strategy may be found in flexible forms of upward harmonization; more accessible, transparent, and accountable continental institutions; and a commitment to the sharing and redistribution of resources to improve our shared environment. In this perspective, and keeping in mind the more limited form of integration in North America, potential options revolve around three areas: modifying the NAFTA text to limit its trade bias; improving the access and openness of the dispute-resolution process; and augmenting trilateral funding mechanisms to encourage upward harmonization.

1. The EC's experience demonstrates that a more expansive reading of trade-law principles is possible, if one accepts that, in the pursuit of a better life, social development can mean restraining economic exchanges. While it remains to be seen whether NAFTA will develop a different jurisprudence, its current normative framework is not promising. A minimalist approach to reform could focus on amending its environmental exception in order to clearly inscribe the precautionary principle, rectification at source, and preventive action as principles to be considered by adjudication bodies in dealing with disputes. The TBT and SPS agreements should encourage harmonization on the basis of the more stringent standards existing among member states (instead of international standards) and, in assessing the validity of more stringent norms, should abandon the requirement for a risk-assessment test. There is also a clear need to reform chapter 11 language to restrict its adoption to obvious traditional cases of expropriation and to prevent its adoption by corporations to undermine environmental laws.

2. The NAFTA dispute-resolution process should be opened to the public and the filing of amicus briefs should be permitted. If the winds of radical change were blowing, making domestic courts the arbitrators of NAFTA disputes could also be considered. It would improve the access to dispute-resolution procedures, increasing their transparency and legitimacy. It would also provide a legal setting that would allow judges to draw more freely from other bodies of law, including international and domestic environmental law. To ensure greater consistency and predictability (through the development of a joint body of case law, for example), a North American court could be established as an appellate body for cases dealing with NAFTA law, including cases brought up under the non-enforcement provisions of the side deal. The NACEC would maintain its fact-finding and alternative dispute-

resolution functions but, in the event of an inconclusive result at the intergovernmental level, citizens could bring the case to court for adjudication. Executable court decisions would also limit the potential for unilateralism, or heavy political pressure by the big markets, to override the competent application of legal reasoning.

3. Finally, international financial assistance appears to be an important part of a good strategy to prevent a 'race to the bottom' dynamic. In this regard, NACEC's cooperative efforts are to be praised. But greater financial contributions may be the cost of a serious trilateral strategy to ensure that greater market integration is not achieved at the cost of lower environmental standards. While environmental subsidies work against the polluter-pays principle, they may still be better than leaving governments with the sole option of promising deregulation and lower standards as a means to attract investment. In any case, they could be necessary to win states' commitment to an upward harmonization strategy.

The preceding comparative analysis of the normative and organizational frameworks of NAFTA and the EC offers a necessary point of entry into the problems and dilemmas emerging for environmental governance in an era of market integration. But, as pointed out in the first section, this remains a partial examination of the overall problem. The chapter's focus on continental institutions leaves out important considerations regarding the environmental impact of trade-generated growth, the relationship between trade regimes and multilateral environmental regimes (especially their use of trade sanctions), and even the likely impact that the emerging trade regimes will have on the choice and effectiveness of domestic environmental-policy instruments (e.g., the impact of border-tax adjustment rules concerning the use of environmental taxation or the impact of trade rules concerning scientific-proof requirements on the evolution of domestic regulatory processes). While I have chosen to leave these issues outside the scope of this paper, their examination will be important for our understanding of the impact of international trade regimes on sustainable-development policies.

NOTES

The author thanks Christine Holke for her excellent research assistance and the

Social Science and Humanities Research Council for financial support. Members of the Environmental Change Trends Project and the people who participated in its April 1999 workshop at Green College, University of British Columbia, provided many valuable comments. Ted Parson, Margaret Hill-Campbell, Michael Howlett, and Jennifer Clapp are especially thanked for their detailed and useful comments on earlier versions of the article.

  1 B. Jessop, 'The Schumpeterian Workfare State,' *Studies in Political Economy* no. 40 (1993): 7–39.
  2 M. Hart, 'Globalization and Governance,' *Policy Options* 16, no. 5 (1995): 52–3.
  3 R. Falk, 'Regional Experiences and International Environmental Order,' in G. Handl, ed., *Yearbook of International Environmental Law 1992* (Oxford: Clarendon Press, 1993), 1–46.
  4 While politically salient, the first issue has little to do with the new instruments of governance represented by continental economic institutions and it reads more like a replay, in the realm of international economics, of the debate about the compatibility of economic growth and environmental protection. As such, while it raises questions about the desirability of freer trade and the appropriate strategy for economic growth in many countries, especially the least-developed ones, this aspect of the debate seems to be of lesser significance for the actual forms of post-national governance. Consequently, I chose not to touch on it in this paper. The second issue, dealing with the trade measures of MEAs, concerns more specifically the intersection between international environmental policy and international economic policy. Being more concerned with the intersection between international trade policy and domestic environmental policy-making, I chose to exclude this issue as well from the scope of the study.
  5 J. Bhagwati, 'Trade and the Environment: The False Conflict?' in D. Zaelke, P. Orbuch, and R. Housman, eds, *Trade and the Environment* (Washington: Island Press, 1993), 159–90.
  6 D. Mander and P. Perkins, 'Trade Disputes and Environmental "Regulatory Chill": The Case of Ontario's Environmental Levy,' *World Competition* 18, no. 2 (1994): 57–76; and E. Perkins, 'Trade Agreements and Environmental Policy: Ontario Examples,' unpublished paper presented at Swedish-Canadian Academic Foundation 3rd annual conference on 'Environmental Issues in Canada and Sweden: The Challenge of Sustainability,' York University, Toronto, May 1996.
  7 F.M. Abbott, 'The NAFTA Environmental Dispute Settlement System as Prototype for Regional Integration Arrangements,' in G. Handl, ed., *Yearbook of International Environmental Law 1995* (Oxford: Clarendon Press, 1996), 20–1.

8 J. Whalley, *The Trading System after the Uruguay Round* (Washington: Institute for International Economics, 1996), 10–11.
9 J. Clapp, 'Foreign Direct Investment in Hazardous Industries in Developing Countries: Rethinking the Debate,' *Environmental Politics* 7, no. 4 (1998): 92–113.
10 This point was suggested to me by Jennifer Clapp and Ted Parsons.
11 See Whalley, *The Trading System*. The main forum to advance the trade and environment debate within the WTO is the Committee on Trade and the Environment (CTE). Progress within this forum, which functions as a committee of the whole and within which national positions are widely divergent and polarized, promises to be slow, difficult, and minimal. The first report of the CTE, tabled at the December 1996 ministerial meeting in Singapore, did not report significant progress. The meeting's main result was to extend the CTE's mandate to study the issues for another two years. Its report mainly described the different positions taken by members on the varying points of contention. It reiterated the WTO policy of prohibiting countervailing measures for lax environmental standards and exhorted members not to lower their environmental standards in the hope of improving the competitiveness of their industries. It concluded that further study was needed to determine whether changes to the multilateral trade regime were required to accommodate MEAs. The committee also judged that the recent decision to declassify internal documents after a period of six months was sufficient to ensure greater transparency and stipulated that national governments were the appropriate forums for ENGO consultations. In effect, the only significant concrete measure proposed by the CTE was to establish a database on the trade-related environmental measures of member countries. Since then, the CTE has built its work program around two clusters of issues: market access and the linkages between MEAs and the GATT 1994. In essence, the focus on market access has led the CTE to emphasize the abolition of subsidies and the study of necessary disciplines on trade restrictions caused by ecolabelling programs as a win-win approach to liberalize trade and eliminate perverse environmental incentives. Overall, the CTE seemed much more concerned with investigating the economic implications of environmental policies than with considering the potential detrimental effects that trade agreements might have on environmental measures. The committee reiterated its belief that more trade would result in more economic growth, which would mean countries would be able to afford better environmental protection. It proposed to further study the positive environmental effects of freer trade.
12 Falk, 'Regional Experiences.'

13 The claim has been made by William Reilly, former head of the U.S. Environmental Protection Agency, among others. See D.C. Esty and D. Geradin, 'Market Access, Competitiveness, and Harmonization: Environmental Protection in Regional Trade Agreements,' *Harvard Environmental Law Review* 21 (1997): 265–336.

14 See, e.g., the paper by Stewart Hudson (National Wildlife Federation), 'The NAFTA-NACE Relationship,' in S. Richardson, ed., *The North American Free Trade Agreement and the North American Commission on the Environment*, 16.

15 As the negotiating periods overlapped, it is not surprising to find similarities. On the central issue of the sanitary and phytosanitary measures (SPS agreement), the NAFTA draft borrowed directly the 'Dunkel Text' negotiated at the GATT and, in the end, the NAFTA negotiators accepted the same rules and principles as the GATT regime. See R.H. Steinberg, 'Trade-Environment Negotiations in the EU, NAFTA, and WTO: Regional Trajectories of Rule Development,' *American Journal of International Law* 91 (1997): 245.

16 Esty and Geradin, 'Market Access,' 311.

17 Steinberg, 'Trade-Environment Negotiations,' 245–6.

18 R.J. King, 'Regional Trade and the Environment: European Lessons for North America,' *Journal of Environmental Law* 14 (1996): 232.

19 Ibid.

20 P.-M. Johnson and A. Beaulieu, *The Environment and NAFTA: Understanding and Implementing the New Continental Law* (Washington: Island Press, 1996), 43–7; C. Thomas and G.A. Tereposky, 'The NAFTA and the Side Agreement on Environmental Co-operation,' *Journal of World Trade* 27, no. 6 (1993): 5–34; Abbott, 'The NAFTA,' 9.

21 S. Charnovitz, 'The North American Free Trade Agreement: Green Law or Green Spin?,' *Law and Policy in International Business* 26 (1994): 1–77.

22 A. Baker Fox, 'Environment and Trade: The NAFTA Case,' *Political Science Quarterly* 110, no. 1 (1995): 58.

23 Johnson and Beaulieu, *The Environment*, 108.

24 GATT jurisprudence regarding the burden of proof is in fact more complex. The general rule is that the burden of proof rests upon the party, whether complaining or defending, that asserts the affirmative of the claim at issue. So, in a typical case, the complaining party would bear the burden to prove that the contested measure violates the free-trade principles of the GATT by constituting a prohibited non-tariff barrier. The defender would then typically bear the burden to prove that the contested discriminatory measure qualifies as a permissible environmental exception (and therefore meets the usual tests for doing so). For the statement of the general rule, see United

States, *Measure Affecting Imports of Woven Wool Shirts and Blouses from India*, WT/DS33/AB/R, 23 May 1997. See also Abbott, 'The NAFTA,' 5; and Baker Fox, 'Environment and Trade,' 58.

25 More precisely, only with regard to environmental disputes, NAFTA party defenders have the right to shift disputes from the WTO to NAFTA for their resolution. See Abbott, 'The NAFTA,' 24–5.

26 Ibid., 5–6.

27 International Institute for Sustainable Development, 'The World Trade Organization and Sustainable Development: An Independent Assessment' (Winnipeg: IISD, 1996), 41. The recent decision by the appellate body of the GATT in the *Shrimp Case* illustrates this point. The *Shrimp Case* decision clarified the matter of scientific input into panel adjudication. It showed some minimal openness to scientific expertise by encouraging the American government (the defender) to include scientific briefs it wanted considered in response to allegations by India, Malaysia, Pakistan, and Thailand as part of its second submission. As a result, expertise originally submitted by ENGOs as amicus briefs, and consequently rejected, nevertheless made it into the panel's considerations. However, the panel also clearly reiterated the GATT's practice of not accepting amicus briefs. We should also note that, since the adoption of GATT 1994, panels have acquired the ability to call on scientific expertise at will, but the panels are the sole authority to request scientific advice and to select the experts called upon to provide it. In the *Shrimp Case*, the panel also availed itself of this provision to deal with conflicting scientific conclusions submitted by the parties. For details of the *Shrimp Case* decision, see *American Shrimp Case*, WT/DS58/R, 1998.

28 Abbott, 'The NAFTA,' 10.

29 A.M. Rugman, J. Kirton, and J. Soloway, 'NAFTA, Environmental Regulations, and Canadian Competitiveness,' *Journal of World Trade* 31, no. 4 (1997): 139.

30 H. Mann and K. von Moltke, NAFTA's Chapter 11 and the Environment: Addressing the Impacts of the Investor-State Process on the Environment' (Winnipeg: International Institute for Sustainable Development, 1999).

31 Johnson and Beaulieu, *The Environment*, 127.

32 For example, as a separate institution, the NACEC is not even called upon to clarify the meaning of the hortatory language of article 1114 concerning the relationship between investment and environmental norms. See Johnson and Beaulieu, *The Environment*, 126–30.

33 This figure includes only the funds allocated to directly support' projects. Program funding (which includes publication costs, public meetings, council sessions, salaries associated with substantive programs, etc.) amounts to

8,694,000 $U.S. The total budget in 1998 was 10,472,000 $U.S. See North American Commission for Environmental Cooperation, 'Annual Workplan 1998' (Montreal, 1998), 86–7.

34 S. Hudson, 'The NAFTA-NACE Relationship,' 16.

35 J. Kirton and R. Fernandez de Castro, 'NAFTA's Institutions: The Environmental Potential and Performance of the NAFTA Free Trade Commission and Related Bodies' (Montreal: North American Commission for Environmental Cooperation, 1997), 17–19.

36 Ibid., 15–16.

37 We should note that, for such a panel to be convened, the issue considered must concern a sector or firms that produce goods that are traded among the NAFTA countries.

38 K. Raustiala, 'The Political Implications of the Enforcement Provisions of the NAFTA Environmental Side Agreement,' *Environmental Law* 25 (1995): 40–3. Canada negotiated a different system for dealing with its own refusal to pay. In such a case, the NACEC will have special standing in Canadian courts and will be able to register its report under Canadian law to obtain a legal order to force payment.

39 L. Juillet, J. Roy, and F. Scala, 'Sustainable Agriculture and Global Institutions: Emerging Institutions and Mixed Incentives,' *Society and Natural Resources* 10 (1997): 309–18.

40 Johnson and Beaulieu, *The Environment*, 215.

41 Raustiala, 'Political Implications,' 31–56. Empirical studies testing this hypothesis are lacking and, in any case, identifying the precise impact of the NAAEC's particular dispute-resolution structure among the variety of factors influencing standard setting will be a difficult task. In the last five years, downward trends in standards and deregulation appear evident in some jurisdictions but may have more to do with broader political shifts in ideology than with specific institutional factors. In contrast, in a glowing review of enforcement trends in Mexico since NAFTA took effect, R.H. Steinberg notes a significant increase in enforcement resources and activities. See 'Trade-Environment Negotiations,' 249–53.

42 Abbott, 'The NAFTA,' 15.

43 There were in addition three cases under article 13 of the NAAEC, which triggers a fact-finding procedure culminating in a report to be considered by the ministerial council. These procedures do not concern any failure to enforce by the concerned party and cannot lead to sanctions. The best-known case was an investigation of the death of 40,000 birds in the Silva reservoir in Mexico in 1995.

44 L. Henderson, 'Forging a Link: Two Approaches to Integrating Trade and

Environment,' *Alternatives* 20, no. 1 (1993): 30; T.L. Joseph, 'Preaching Heresy: Permitting Member States to Enforce Stricter Environmental Laws than the European Community,' *Yale Journal of International Law* 20, no. 2 (1995): 228.

45 A. Jordan, 'The Construction of a Multilevel Environmental Governance System,' *Environment and Planning C: Government and Policy* 17 (1999): 3. This original program, adopted in 1973, was also partly triggered by the adoption of Dutch and German pollution legislation that was perceived as being potentially trade distorting. See A. Sbragia, 'Environmental Policy: The "Push-Pull" of Policy-Making,' in H. Wallace and W. Wallace, eds, *Policy-Making in the European Union*, 3rd ed. (Oxford: Oxford University Press, 1996), 243.

46 Article 100 allowed the EC to take measures to 'approximate' different national legislation that could affect directly the workings of the common market. It should be noted that, while the term 'approximate' suggests the pre-existence of national regulations, historical experience has clearly demonstrated that article 100 supports EC intervention in areas where none exist.

47 Article 235 allowed the EC to take measures 'necessary to attain the objectives of the Community' for which the Treaty of Rome did not provide the necessary powers. Again, a clear link (even if tenuous) must be established with the operation of the common market.

48 A. Weale, 'European Environmental Policy by Stealth: The Dysfunctionality of Functionalism,' *Environment and Planning C: Government and Policy* 17 (1999): 37.

49 The number goes up to 195 if environmental amendments to existing laws are included.

50 A.R. Zito, 'Task Expansion: A Theoretical Overview,' *Environment and Planning C: Government and Policy* 17 (1999): 19.

51 For a clear statement that community law is supreme over national legislation, see *Pubblico Ministero v. Ratti*, C-148/78, ECR [1979], 1629–44. It should be noted as well that some community laws also have direct effect in member states and will be applied by national courts even in the absence of national legislation. See Steinberg, 'Trade-Environment Negotiations,' 258. Since the Maastricht Treaty, the European Court of Justice (ECJ) can also impose fines on member states that fail to implement a directive (art. 171) and, through case law, the possibility of finding a member state liable for damages incurred by individuals as a result of its failure to implement a directive. On this latter case, see *Francovich v. Italian Republic*, C-6/90, C-8/90, ECR [1991], I-5357.

52 Jordan, 'Construction,' 12.

53 As the wide-ranging nature of community environmental law and its significant implications for national states became apparent, some debates about the binding nature of environmental directives emerged. In response to a legal challenge in 1980 by the Italian government arguing that environmental directives (regarding the sulphur content of liquid fuels) were simply non-binding international conventions, the European Court of Justice, in its first ruling in an environmental case, affirmed their binding character and upheld the use of article 100 as a basis for community environmental law. See C.F. Runge, *Freer Trade, Protected Environment: Balancing Trade Liberalization and Environmental Interests* (New York: Council on Foreign Relations Press, 1994); and Jordan, 'Construction,' 8.

54 While equally binding, directives require national legislatures to adopt domestic laws implementing the objectives that they enunciate. National legislatures must meet the directives' objectives but are free to determine the methods used to achieve them. As such, directives are less-direct forms of intervention than are regulations. While having the benefit of leaving more room to national jurisdictions for tailoring the form of interventions to their specific needs, directives are also blamed by some for contributing to the 'implementation deficit' of community policies. See A. Jordan, 'The Implementation of EU Environmental Policy: A Policy Problem without a Political Solution?' *Environment and Planning C: Government and Policy* 17 (1999): 83.

55 Joseph, 'Preaching Heresy,' 230.

56 Steinberg, 'Trade-Environment Negotiations,' 255. The amendments are articles 100a(4) and 130t.

57 The modalities for applying this measure remain ambiguous. To the author's knowledge, only one decision rendered by the ECJ provided some guidance on the matter. In a decision on a 1989 German law effectively banning PCP in products, the ECJ did establish that the Commission's approval should not be automatic and must be properly justified by a substantive analysis. After seeing its first approval overturned by the ECJ, the Commission published a second approval of the German law, based on a more detailed analysis. Since this second decision has not been challenged by other member states, the more stringent German law is now enforced. While useful, this clarification still leaves many issues unresolved. For example, some legal scholars argue that the more stringent measures justified by article 130s would not apply to new legislation. It also remains unclear whether the tests of 'proportionality,' 'necessity,' and 'non-discrimination' (discussed in the following pages) should apply in judging

the validity of the more stringent standards. For the German case, see *France v. Commission*, C-41/93, ECR [1994], 1829–46. For an exposition of the different legal arguments, see Joseph, 'Preaching Heresy,' 227–71.

58 Joseph, 'Preaching Heresy,' 227–71.

59 Jordan, 'Implementation,' 78.

60 Esty and Geradin, 'Market Access,' 304–8.

61 In fact, the text of article 36 does not explicitly include environmental protection as grounds for an exception. In its 1979 *Cassis de Dijon* decision, the ECJ found that the categories listed in article 36 were not to be considered as exhaustive and that other 'essential objectives' of the Community could be covered by the exception. Then, in the 1985 *Association de défense des brûleurs d'huiles usagées*, the ECJ stipulated that environmental protection was such an objective. *Cassis de Dijon*, C-120/78, ECR [1985]; and *Procureur de la République v. Association de défense des brûleurs d'huiles usagées*, C-240/83, ECR [1985].

62 King, 'Regional Trade,' 214; and Joseph, 'Preaching Heresy,' 236.

63 Steinberg, 'Trade-Environment Negotiations,' 254.

64 C. London, 'Droit communautaire de l'environnement,' *Revue trimestrielle de droit européen* 30, no. 2 (1994): 291–325.

65 It is worth noting that this first judgment precedes the adoption of the SEA in 1986.

66 *Procureur de la République v. Association de défense des brûleurs d'huiles usagées*, C-240/83, ECR [1985], 549. Also quoted in Jordan, 'Construction,' 9.

67 L. Hempel, *Environmental Governance: The Global Challenge* (Washington: Island Press, 1996), 192.

68 Joseph, 'Preaching Heresy,' 244.

69 Jordan, 'Construction,' 11–12. Article 3 would read: '[E]nvironmental protection requirements must be integrated into the development and implementation of Community policies and activities [...] in particular with a view to promoting sustainable development.'

70 For example, the ECJ has previously relied on text found in the preamble of the Treaty of Rome to guide its adjudication. See the *Van Gen en Loos* case, ECR [1963], 12. In all likelihood, principles included in the more substantive parts of the treaties would have at least as much significance.

71 *Commission v. Belgium*, C-2/90, ECR [1992], 4431.

72 The ECJ did not find that it needed to examine whether the decree was proportional to the objectives sought.

73 It also referred to the 'proximity principle' in the 1989 Basle Convention on the Control of Transboundary Movements of Hazardous Waste and Their Disposal.

74 It is interesting to note that this outcome stands in sharp contrast with the struggle of the Ontario government and neighbouring American states who have tried for years to establish their right to ban waste trade in order to preserve landfill capacities and support the principle of local management of locally generated wastes. Perkins, 12–14.

75 D. Black, 'International Trade v. Environmental Protection: The Case of the U.S. Embargo on Mexican Tuna,' *Law and Policy in International Business* 24 (1992): 123–56.

76 B. Kingsbury, 'The Tuna-Dolphin Controversy, the World Trade Organization, and the Liberal Project to Reconceptualize International Law,' in G. Handl, ed., *Yearbook of International Environmental Law 1994* (Oxford: Clarendon Press, 1995), 17–20; T.J. Schoenbaum, 'International Trade and Protection of the Environment: The Continuing Search for Reconciliation,' *American Journal of International Law* 91 (1997): 268–313.

77 Jordan, 'Construction,' 12; Steinberg, 'Trade-Environment Negotiations,' 257. The European Parliament calculates that 2.3 billion ECU was spent for environmental protection in 1994, the bulk of it channelled through these structural funds – an amount forty times greater than in 1988. See Joseph, 'Preaching Heresy,' 242.

78 Runge, *Freer Trade*, 36.

79 OECD Trade Directorate, 'Joint Session of Trade and Environment Experts: Draft 1995 Report to Ministers' (Paris: OECD, April 1995), 15.

80 Sbragia, 'Environmental Policy,' 238–41.

81 The EC's two main standard-setting bodies, the European Committee for Standardization and the European Committee for Electrotechnical Standardization, also share the weighted voting procedure. See King, 'Regional Trade,' 231.

82 Jordan, 'Construction,' 10.

83 Sbragia, 'Environmental Policy,' 239–41. It should be noted that this outburst in environmental policy in the late 1980s was not confined to Europe and can be associated with broader changes in public opinion. For an examination of Canada, see L. Juillet, 'Les politiques environnementales canadiennes,' in M. Tremblay, ed., *Les politiques publiques canadiennes* (Ste-Foy: Les Presses de l'Université Laval, 1998), 161–204.

84 Steinberg, 'Trade-Environment Negotiations,' 254.

85 D. Judge, '"Predestined to Save the Earth": The Environment Committee of the European Parliament,' *Environmental Politics* 1, no. 4 (1992): 186–212.

86 J. Golub, 'State Power and Institutional Influence in European Integration: Lessons from the Packaging Waste Directive,' *Journal of Common Market Studies* 34, no. 3 (1996): 320.

87 Sbragia, 'Environmental Policy,' 249.
88 Golub, 'State Power,' 313–39.
89 Sbragia, 'Environmental Policy,' 235–56; Jordan, 'Construction,' 10; and King, 'Regional Trade,' 235.
90 Esty and Geradin, 'Market Access,' 304.
91 Steinberg, 'Trade-Environment Negotiations,' 252–3.
92 'Market Access,' 318.
93 R. Rose, *Lesson-Drawing in Public Policy* (Chatham, NJ: Chatham House Publishers, 1993).

5. Aboriginal Peoples in Canada: Their Role in Shaping Environmental Trends in the Twenty-first Century

Patricia Doyle-Bedwell and Fay G. Cohen

On 1 April 1999, Nunavut, which means 'our home' in Inuktituk, became the third territory in Canada. The new flag features an image of an *inuksuk*, the type of stone assemblage used by Inuit to guide people on the land and to mark sacred and other special places. The North Star, *Niqirtsituk*, guides navigation and remains unchanged, like the leadership of the community elders.[1] Nunavut, carved out of the Northwest Territories, covers an area one-fifth the size of Canada.[2] It is a unique political unit in the world today. Aboriginal[3] people hold a numerical majority in the population of 50,000. With the Nunavut Land Claims Agreement, the Inuit will have a clear and unequivocal role in shaping the future of their homeland.[4]

Nunavut reflects a broader trend. Today, Aboriginal peoples in Canada number approximately one million persons speaking over fifty different languages.[5] Despite government policies aimed at eradicating traditional practices and disrupting communities, Aboriginal peoples have resisted oppression[6] and survived by forcefully articulating their rights and responsibilities in national and international arenas.[7] They see their rights flowing from their traditional occupation of the land from time immemorial, and from historical processes and agreements between the colonizers and Aboriginal peoples.

In 1982, the Canadian constitution[8] recognized existing Aboriginal and treaty rights. Court decisions such as *Calder*, *Sparrow*, and *Delgamuukw*[9] and modern land-claims agreements[10] have further delineated the Aboriginal peoples' role in the resource and environmental policy arena.

Many Aboriginal people still depend on traditional resource-based pursuits for their livelihood.[11] Aboriginal environmental stewardship principles guide and inform relationships to land, sea, and resources.[12] Traditional ecological knowledge,[13] based on centuries of experience within a specific territory, informs the appropriate use of animals, plants, and resources. However, conditions of extreme poverty in Aboriginal communities create a catalyst for participation in the contemporary market economy. Third-party interests in land and resources compete with traditional economic activities. Today, Aboriginal peoples face the challenge of balancing environmental stewardship with requirements for economic security.

In this paper, we provide an overview of legal developments supporting the inclusion of Aboriginal participation in environmental policy. We then describe Aboriginal stewardship principles, with emphasis on Mi'kmaq culture and environment and two case examples: (1) the traditional Nuxalk food fishery[14] and (2) the provisions for a wildlife management board in the Nunavut land-claims agreement.

As part of legal developments since 1975, Canadian Aboriginal peoples have negotiated agreements to share governance of natural resources.[15] The term co-management frequently is used to describe systems of shared authority between local communities – in this case Aboriginal communities – and state-level agencies. The durability of these institutional arrangements implementing Aboriginal values and environmental stewardship has been well documented by ecologists, anthropologists, historians, and political scientists, in terms of both general theory and case studies, but is beyond the scope of this paper.[16]

In the conclusion, we argue that the Canadian legal framework provides Aboriginal peoples with an essential role in the access to and management of natural resources. Recent Supreme Court decisions require governments to include Aboriginal peoples' interests and values in the development of environmental policy and its practical implementation. Further, the inclusion of Aboriginal environmental stewardship in governance regimes has the potential to make major contributions to the protection of lands and resources in the future.

1. Aboriginal Peoples and Canadian Law

Canadian jurisprudence and legislation on Aboriginal issues fall into three distinct phases. First, in the pre-Confederation period, British law established parameters of the common law applicable to Aboriginal peoples. During this period the British Crown and the Mi'kmaq people created Peace and Friendship treaties. The second phase, from Confederation to the repatriation of the constitution in 1982, the federal government signed eleven numbered treaties with First Nations in the west and north and assumed jurisdiction for Aboriginal peoples through section 91(24) of the Constitution Act, 1867.[17] Further, in 1876 the federal government passed the Indian Act,[18] which, among other provisions, created band councils on reserves and determined membership in the band. Courts during this period created the concept of Aboriginal title, whereby Aboriginal people had rights to the land based on historical use and occupancy.[19]

After 1982, existing Aboriginal and treaty rights received constitutional protection under section 35 of the Constitution Act of 1982.[20] The Supreme Court of Canada has considered the meaning of Aboriginal and treaty rights, the concept of Aboriginal title, and the nature of the special trust relationship between the government and Aboriginal peoples known as the fiduciary responsibility. These four fundamental areas create a space for discourse and the inclusion of Aboriginal perspectives on environment and policy-making. We discuss here key aspects of the legal framework and consider the recent Supreme Court of Canada interpretation of Mi'kmaq Peace and Friendship treaties in *R. v. Marshall*.[21]

Aboriginal Rights

Section 35(1) of the Constitution Act, 1982, recognizes and affirms existing Aboriginal and treaty rights. The Supreme Court has reaffirmed the *sui generis* nature of Aboriginal title, and the historic powers of the Crown constitute the source of the fiduciary obligation, which guides the interpretation of s. 35.[22] In defining an existing Aboriginal right, the Court found the government has the responsibility to act in a fiduciary capacity with respect to Aboriginal people. Later, in *R. v. Van der Peet*, the court stressed the importance of reflecting an Aboriginal perspective on the meaning of the rights themselves.[23]

R. v. Sparrow concerned Musqueam fishing in the Fraser River. Dickson C.J. held that '"existing Aboriginal rights" must be interpreted flexibly to permit their evolution over time.'[24] The Court confirmed the necessity of interpreting Aboriginal rights in their contemporary context and employed a liberal, purposive analysis of section 35(1). The Court also found that Musqueam Aboriginal rights still existed since the fisheries regulations at issue did not meet the test of showing clear and plain intention to extinguish them. Thus, the Aboriginal right to fish for social and ceremonial purposes survived the imposition of Crown sovereignty. The Court held that for a right to be continuing and within the protection of section 35(1), the right must be existing and unextinguished. Section 35 does not revive extinguished Aboriginal or treaty rights. [25]

Since the entrenchment of Aboriginal and treaty rights in the constitution, the question of extinguishment has taken on significant importance. Matthew Mukash, Chief of the Whampmagoostui, further states that 'extinguishment is part of the centuries old scheme to take and consolidate control over our lands by the government.'[26] Once an existing Aboriginal right receives the protection of section 35(1), however, only a constitutional amendment, with the consent of Aboriginal peoples, may extinguish that right.

Moreover, courts assume that Parliament has ultimate jurisdiction over Canada's First Nations and may extinguish Aboriginal rights, if done appropriately.[27] Macklem asserts: 'The principles laid down in *Sparrow* maintain a relationship of legal dependence between native peoples and the Canadian state ... Applying a reasonableness standard to the determination of whether a particular law infringes Aboriginal rights inevitably leads the judiciary into an assessment of the reasons for the legislative initiative. The contents of s. 35(1) rights becomes dependent in part on the legislative purpose and effect of laws which affect the interests that the right is designed to protect.'[28] *Sparrow* made it clear, according to Macklem, that state regulation of common-law Aboriginal rights is now subjected to constitutional review.[29] Consultation and consent of Aboriginal peoples, within the process as set out in *Sparrow*, are required to meet the standard of the fiduciary relationship.

In *R. v. Van der Peet*,[30] the Court further defined an Aboriginal right. The correct analysis of Aboriginal rights claims required consideration of several factors. The Court examined the nature of the action taken pursuant to an Aboriginal right, the government action said to infringe the Aboriginal right, and the practice, custom, or tradition relied upon to establish the Aboriginal right.[31] Any activity claimed to be an Aboriginal right must be part of a practice, custom, or tradition that, prior to European contact, was an integral part of the distinctive Aboriginal society of the Aboriginal people in question.[32] The definition of Aboriginal rights depends on the particular group; what may be an Aboriginal right for one may not be for another. This could be more difficult to show if there has been a long period of contact, as in the Mi'kmaq situation.

In summary, existing Aboriginal rights include all rights not extinguished before 1982. The Crown has the burden of proof to show the right had been extinguished by the clear-and-plain-extinguishment test.[33] Government policy cannot extinguish an Aboriginal right without clear and plain intention. Government regulation cannot delineate the Aboriginal right. Regulations do not extinguish the Aboriginal right, but can regulate the exercise of that right.[34] History and the normal social customs of the particular First Nation must determine the scope of an Aboriginal right.

The fiduciary relationship guides the parameters of the relationship between First Nations and the Crown. In the next section, we examine, in general terms, the nature of the fiduciary relationship.

Fiduciary Relationship

The fiduciary relationship has its origins in the original relationship between First Nations and the Crown. The Royal Proclamation of 1763 provided for the protection of Aboriginal lands by establishing that Indian tribes could not sell their lands to third parties, but must sell first to the Crown. 'The Crown assumed a general obligation to protect Aboriginal peoples and their lands and generally look out for their best interests – what the judges have described as a fiduciary or trust-obligation. In return, Native peoples were required to maintained [sic] allegiance to the Crown, to abide by her laws and to keep the peace.'[35]

The Supreme Court first established the nature of the fiduciary duty owed to Aboriginal peoples in *R. v. Guerin*.[36] Chief Justice Dickson ruled in *Guerin*: 'The fiduciary obligation which is owed to the Indians by the Crown is *sui generis*.'[37] The relationship has its origins in Aboriginal title: 'The conclusion that the Crown is a fiduciary depends upon the further proposition that the Indian interest in the land is inalienable except upon surrender to the Crown.'[38] This relationship also flows from the Royal Proclamation of 1763.

The Supreme Court further developed the fiduciary obligation in *R. v. Sparrow*.[39] *Sparrow* stated that the honour of the Crown is at stake in dealings with Aboriginal people. The relationship is trustlike, not adversarial.[40] The Supreme Court also stated that the fiduciary relationship guides interpretation under section 35(1).[41]

In *Delgamuukw*,[42] the Court further articulated principles ensuring that the federal government adheres to the fiduciary standard. The test for infringement of Aboriginal title depends upon the fiduciary duty to ensure that the legislative objectives are sufficiently pressing to justify the infringement and, further, that the federal government engages in meaningful consultation with Aboriginal peoples.

Aboriginal Title

Aboriginal title will have a central role in the development of environmental policy with respect to land on which the Crown has not cleared Aboriginal title. Before *Delgamuukw*, Aboriginal title was used 'in litigation as a bar to mining, exploration and production of oil and gas, construction of multi-million dollar oil and gas pipelines and hydro-electric dams and diversions, and forestry cutting regimes.'[43] We argue that Aboriginal title, because it receives constitutional protection under section 35, further entrenches the protection of the land and opens the door to further litigation. In other words, *Delgamuuwkw* created further protections of lands subjected to Aboriginal title from widespread development.[44]

In *Delgamuukw v. British Columbia*, the Court examined four issues: the proof of Aboriginal title, the relationship of Aboriginal title to section 35(1) of the Constitution Act of 1982, the issue of who can extinguish Aboriginal title, and the justification for infringement of Aboriginal title. Unlike the trial court, Lamer C.J. ruled that weight and credence should to be given to the Gitskan's oral history provided by elders as testimony in the case. The Court also created a nexus between the fiduciary duty owed to Aboriginal peoples by the federal government and Aboriginal title.

Aboriginal title is a right to land itself.[45] As defined by the Court, Aboriginal title 'encompasses the right to exclusive use and occupation of the land held pursuant to that title for a variety of purposes, which need not be aspects of those Aboriginal practices, customs and traditions which are integral to distinctive Aboriginal cultures; and ... those protected uses must not be irreconcilable with the nature of the group's attachment to that land.'[46]

The Supreme Court also held that land subject to Aboriginal title could not be used in a manner inconsistent with the nature of the claimant's attachment to the land.[47] If a group holds land pursuant to Aboriginal title, and claims a special attachment to that land because of its cultural and ceremonial significance, Aboriginal peoples may not use that land in such a way as to destroy the relationship.[48] The Court also held that lands subject to Aboriginal title could not be alienated except to the Crown.[49]

Further, the Supreme Court developed a test to determine proof of Aboriginal title. The test involved examining occupancy of the land before the assertion of British sovereignty, establishing continuity between present and pre-sovereignty, and demonstrating substantial maintenance of the connection between the people and the land.[50] Further, at the time of assertion of British sovereignty, occupation must have been exclusive.[51]

In *Delgamuukw*, the Court also stated that Aboriginal title was protected in its fullest form by s. 35(1) of the Constitution Act of 1982.[52] Since *Calder*[53] preceded the constitution and recognized Aboriginal title, the constitution must also afford that protection to Aboriginal title. Only the federal government, not the provinces, may extinguish Aboriginal title.[54] Infringement of unextinguished Aboriginal title rests upon the clear justification tests set down in *Sparrow*. The range of legislative objectives that justify infringement include 'the development of agriculture, forestry, mining and hydroelectric power, the general economic development of the interior of British Columbia, protection of the environment or endangered species, the building of infrastructure and the settlement of foreign populations to support these aims ... [These] are the kinds of objectives that are consistent with this purpose and in principle, can justify the infringement of Aboriginal title.'[55] The Court stated that infringement of Aboriginal title could lead to compensation: The economic role of Aboriginal title leads itself to the question of compensation and is relevant to the question of justification of infringement of Aboriginal title.[56] The Court states that development issues may justify the infringement of Aboriginal title if the Crown satisfies its fiduciary duty to Aboriginal peoples by involving them in decisions taken with respect to their lands.[57]

The court emphasized the duty of consultation that must occur when Aboriginal title may be infringed. The fiduciary duty also plays a significant role in determining whether or not an activity can be justified in order to infringe upon Aboriginal title.

The manner in which the fiduciary duty operates with respect to the second stage of the justification test – both with respect to the standard of scrutiny and the particular form that the fiduciary duty will take – will be a function of the nature of Aboriginal title. Three aspects of Aboriginal title are relevant here. First, Aboriginal title encompasses the right to exclusive use and occupation of the land; second, Aboriginal title encompasses the right to choose to what uses land can be put, subject to the ultimate limit that those uses cannot destroy the ability of the land to sustain future generations of Aboriginal peoples; and third, that lands held pursuant to Aboriginal title have an inescapable economic component.[58]

The Court also held that 'consultation must be in good faith ... and some cases may require the full consent of an Aboriginal nation, particularly when provinces enact hunting and fishing regulations in relation to Aboriginal lands.'[59] Thus, the Court emphasizes that First Nations who have Aboriginal title must be consulted by the government if an activity threatens their land and the Aboriginal connection to it. Moreover, First Nations may be entitled to compensation for infringement of Aboriginal title. If provinces attempt to impose regulations in relation to Aboriginal land, as noted, full consent of the Aboriginal band is required. *Marshall* provides a ready backdrop to establish when the Province must consult with Mi'kmaq people with respect to fishing regulation in their traditional territory, as Aboriginal title has not yet been cleared on Mi'kmaq lands.

Delgamuukw presents some difficulties. Here the Court relies on prior use and occupancy, but still does not elevate Aboriginal title to full ownership. Land subject to Aboriginal title must not be used in such a way as to disconnect the relationship that Aboriginal people have with the land in question. This goes beyond reserve land, and applies to traditional territory. Furthermore, despite the need of the government to consult with Aboriginal peoples to meet the fiduciary duty, the Court does not outline the process required to do so; it states that 'the nature and scope of the consultation will vary with the circumstances.'[60]

In next section, we examine treaties and attempt to reconcile the *Delgamuukw* decision with *Marshall*.

Treaties

The treaties signed by Aboriginal people fall into three distinct categories: Peace and Friendship treaties such as the Treaty of 1752 between the British and the Mi'kmaq Nation; the land-cession or numbered treaties to gain title to Aboriginal lands following Confederation; and contemporary land-claims agreements such as the James Bay Agreement and the recent Nisga'a Agreement, which include provisions for land, governance, and funds in exchange for the extinguishment of Aboriginal title over the traditional territory. Recently, the Supreme Court of Canada has decided that several treaty rights cases affirmed the validity of the rights, explicated rules for interpreting them, and created the necessity for developing policy to implement the rights.

Judicial interpretations of the pre-Confederation Mi'kmaq treaties of 1752 and of 1760–1 assert the rights of Mi'kmaq people to hunt, fish, and take commodities for trade in their traditional territories. In *Simon*,[61] the Supreme Court found that the Treaty of 1752 continued to be in force and effect. Dickson C.J. stated, 'Given the serious and far reaching consequences of a finding that a treaty right has been extinguished, it seems appropriate to demand strict proof of the fact of extinguishment in each case where the issue arises.'[62]

In *R. v. Badger*,[63] the Court affirmed these principles and established the test for infringement of treaty rights from *Sparrow*. The Supreme Court stated:

> First, it must be remembered that a treaty represents an exchange of solemn promises between the Crown and the various Indian Nations. It is an agreement whose nature is sacred. Second, the honour of the Crown is always at stake in its dealing with Aboriginal Peoples. Interpretations of treaties and statutory provisions, which have an impact upon treaty or Aboriginal rights, must be approached in a manner, which maintains the integrity of the Crown. It is always assumed that the Crown intends to fulfil its promises. No appearance of sharp dealing will be sanctioned. Third, any ambiguities or doubtful expressions must be resolved in favour of the Indians. A corollary to this principle is that any limitations which restrict the rights of Indians must be narrowly construed. Fourth, the onus of proving a treaty or Aboriginal rights has been extinguished lies upon the Crown. There must be 'strict proof of the fact of extinguishment' and evidence of a clear and plain intention on the part of the Government to extinguish treaty rights.[64]

The Court held that treaty interpretation must take into account the Aboriginal understanding of the treaty at the time of the signing.[65] Oral promises made by representatives of the Crown also have great significance.[66]

The infringement of a treaty right must also meet a justification test. First, the Court asks, is there a valid legislative objective? If yes, then the analysis examines the honour of the Crown, as it must be a priority.[67]

In *R. v. Marshall*,[68] released in September 1999, Donald Marshall Jr was charged with three offences under the federal fisheries regulations: selling eels without a licence, fishing without a licence, and fishing during the closed season with illegal nets. He admitted to all three offences and stated that he had caught and sold 463 pounds of eels. His defence relied on the 1760–1 treaty right to catch and sell fish. Reversing the lower-court ruling, the Supreme Court upheld the Mi'kmaq treaties of 1760–1 and affirmed Mi'kmaq treaty rights to hunt, fish, and sell the commodities. In effect, the Court protected Mi'kmaq rights to a commercial fishery.

The essential issues in this case concern the interpretation of the treaty in question, the right to fish for a moderate livelihood, and the right to regulate the commercial use of natural resources. The majority decision held that the interpretation of the treaty should uphold the honour of the Crown. Further, the ruling stated that Mi'kmaq people had not lost their right to trade and sell their goods because of the demise of 'truckhouses' (those trading places specified in the treaty). The Court used extrinsic evidence such as oral negotiations leading up to the treaty to determine that it supported a right to trade. Binnie J. states: '[w]here a Treaty was concluded verbally, and afterwards written up by representatives of the Crown, it would be unconscionable for the Crown to ignore the oral terms while relying on the written terms.'[69] The Court continued: 'The bottom line is the Courts' obligation is to "choose from among the various possible interpretations of the *common* intention [at the time the treaty was made] the one which best reconciles" the Mi'kmaq interests and those of the British Crown' (*Sioui*, per Lamer J. at p. 1069; emphasis added).[70]

The court also placed limits on the right to access natural resources for commercial activity by holding that the treaty right did not give Mi'kmaq people a wholesale right to exploit natural resources for commercial gain. Binnie J. stated: 'The recorded note of February 11, 1760 was that "there might be a truckhouse established for the furnishing them with *necessaries*" [emphasis added]. What is contemplated therefore is not a right to trade generally for economic gain but rather a right to trade for necessaries. The treaty right is a regulated right and can be contained by regulation within its proper limit.'[71]

The court interpreted 'moderate livelihood' to mean basics such as '"food, clothing, housing, supplemented by a few amenities," but not the accumulation of wealth.'[72] As a result, the Mi'kmaq treaty right to trade could be regulated within these limits and would not need to be justified by the *Badger* justification standard.

Since the Supreme Court released this decision, controversy has erupted over the interpretation of the treaty, particularly with respect to the lobster fishery. Mi'kmaq people have suffered violence and threats by non-native fishers. *Marshall* illustrates quite clearly the lack of policy development in terms of Aboriginal access to the fishery or any other natural resource. This policy vacuum created a situation, immediately following the release of the decision, where some non-native fishers advocated using violence to protect their share of the lobster fishery. Many meetings during the winter of 1999–2000 between the Atlantic chiefs, the Department of Fisheries and Oceans, non-native fishers, and the Minister of Fisheries failed to develop a framework of conservation and limits acceptable to all parties. Despite the fact that Mi'kmaq fishers make up a very small percentage of the lobster fishery, non-native fishers continue to assert that the Mi'kmaq people will decimate the resource. The situation remains uncertain and volatile.

Marshall presents several difficulties. First, the court did not clearly define 'moderate livelihood.' Although the court did say that food, housing, and other basic needs would constitute a moderate livelihood, one could argue that the standard to be applied should be sufficient to lift Mi'kmaq people out of poverty. The Court supports limits placed on the right to trade based on the moderate livelihood standard. However, some Mi'kmaq people have seen the judicial support of the right to trade as one of their first chances to earn a living. Current conditions on the reserve prevented the Mi'kmaq people from taking full advantage of access to the lobster fishery without boats, traps, and other necessities required for fishing. The concept of 'moderate livelihood' remains open to several interpretations.

Who can exercise rights under the Mi'kmaq treaties remains uncertain. At this point, the Mi'kmaq chiefs have stated clearly that only status Indians may fish commercially under the treaty. However, the Native Council of Nova Scotia has fought for inclusion in the fishery because the division between status and non-status Indians did not exist at the time of the treaty, but arose from the Indian Act. Further negotiations with non-status people will likely occur. The Native

Council, the representative agency for non-status Indians, may engage in litigation to establish their right to the fishery.

The lack of federal planning for the possibility of a decision in favour of Donald Marshall has created an adversarial and volatile situation in this region. The federal government must deal with these issues while balancing the rights of the resource users in the region in order to ensure a positive response to the new allocations required by the Marshall case. The transition from judicial recognition of treaty rights to their practical implementation remains a major challenge.

In November 1999, the Supreme Court clarified the initial decision in *R. v. Marshall*.[73] In an unprecedented move, the West Nova Fisherman's Coalition asked for a rehearing of the appeal and a stay of the judgment with respect to the impact of the decision on the lobster fishery.

At trial and on appeal, the Crown did not argue the issue of regulatory justification of an infringement of treaty rights. As the Court stated, 'The issue of justification was not before the Court and no judgement was made about whether or not such restrictions could have been justified in relation to the eel fishery had the Crown led evidence and argument to support their applicability.'[74] Infringement of the treaty right by catch limits that produce a moderate livelihood can be established by regulation and enforced without violating the treaty right.[75] The eel fishery is not endangered and is not a commercial enterprise in the Maritimes. The treaty right is in itself a limited right.[76]

The Court also stated that 'the primary regulatory objective is the conservation of the resource. This responsibility is placed squarely on the Minister and not on the Aboriginal or non-Aboriginal users of the resource.'[77]

The Court held that the federal government must consult with Aboriginal peoples about limitations on Aboriginal and treaty rights.[78] Limitations could include economic and regional fairness.[79] The Court stated that economic and regional fairness could justify a limitation on a treaty right, while stating that the treaty right is itself limited to 'necessaries.'

In current negotiations, limits placed on the fishery involve very low dollar amounts, which do not provide basic 'necessaries.' In the Marshall rehearing, the Court stated that 'regulatory limits take the Mi'kmaq catch below the quantities reasonably expected to produce a moderate livelihood, or other limitations that are not inherent in the limited nature of the treaty right itself, have to be justified according to the Badger test.'[80] Most importantly, the courts mandated that effective consultation must occur. Negotiations remain ongoing.

Non-Native resource users fear the decimation of the fishery. Mi'kmaq people reply that they will exercise conservation and stewardship with respect to the fishery and management of the land. We now turn to a discussion of Aboriginal and Mi'kmaq environmental stewardship.

2. Aboriginal Stewardship, Mi'kmaq Culture, and Environment

In the previous section, we briefly outlined how key elements of Canadian law – Aboriginal rights, the fiduciary responsibility, Aboriginal title, and treaty rights – have provided the constitutional and jurisprudential cornerstones for the participation of Aboriginal peoples in accessing natural resources. Moreover, Aboriginal people must play essential roles in resource and environmental decision-making, subject to certain conditions and regulations. The transition from recognition of the Aboriginal role to its implementation is critical. An understanding of Aboriginal environmental stewardship beliefs and practices is essential to inform policy-making based on this legal foundation, because Aboriginal societies provide the substantive basis within which participation will occur. We identify several philosophical streams that create the concepts of environmental stewardship that are common to many Aboriginal societies in Canada.[81]

In any writing about Aboriginal environmental stewardship and practice, Aboriginal voices must be included in a respectful manner. To understand the connection to the land and the environment from a Mi'kmaq perspective means understanding the role of personal experience in the development of environmental ethics and recognizing the validity of oral tradition. Battiste shows that 'indigenous knowledge exists and is a legitimate research issue. Many parts of the existing Eurocentric academy have not fully accepted this principle, arguing that there is no such thing as an Indigenous perspective.'[82] Henderson states: 'Aboriginal perspectives are just now being heard in Canada in a climate that is not mired in racial discrimination and hostility to our very presence.'[83]

Aboriginal people define 'experts' as those elders with wisdom and vision from lived experience. Aboriginal cultures depend heavily on the 'I' and one's personal experience. In this paper, we depend on the first author's personal experiences, as well as Mi'kmaq oral tradition, which has been passed down from generation to generation.

We also utilize ethnographies that offer detailed information based on extensive fieldwork, such as those of Wallis and Wallis, Cruikshank, and Feit.[84] Collections of case studies describing Aboriginal resource management in relation to state systems include Cohen and Hansen and Berkes and Folke.[85] As Borrows states: 'Indigenous ideas regarding the environment comprise a field of knowledge with its own disciplinary integrity. Through both observation and contemplation, Indigenous peoples devised empirically testable methods for checking the impact of certain practices. This methodology also has its limitations. Indigenous insights regarding the environment, while valuable, are partial and must be pooled with information from other disciplines to answer the pressing questions we face.'[86]

By utilizing a variety of sources and case studies, we hope to avoid the possibility of idealizing Aboriginal relationships to the environment, an issue that has been the subject of many recent commentaries.[87] Mythologizing Aboriginal virtues or vices defeats the purpose of developing environmental governance regimes that respect Aboriginal societies and their legal rights within the contemporary context. White provides a useful approach by emphasizing that reciprocal relationships exist between culture and nature and that, further, the connection between spiritual belief, individual action, and social institutions underpins cultural perspectives of sustainability.[88] As Anderson states, 'The world's traditional societies have come to some kind of terms with their environments, or they would not have lasted long enough to become "traditional." Most of them encode in their moral teachings practical wisdom about the environment and the individual's duty to treat it with respect. These injunctions are lived; they enter daily practice.'[89]

Berkes and Folke also emphasize the importance of a people-oriented approach when they analyse non-Western resource management regimes. Using the concept of 'cultural capital,' they describe a society's 'means and adaptations to deal with its natural environment.'[90] They also provide concrete examples of how such systems work by describing how different cultures use traditional knowledge in responding to feedbacks from the ecological system.[91]

The Royal Commission on Aboriginal Peoples states, 'Elders tell us that currently fashionable terms such as 'environmentally friendly' and 'sustainable development' are ancient concepts inherent in Aboriginal societies.'[92] Aboriginal people see the world holistically, making it difficult to differentiate between the two concepts of stewardship and sustainability within the Aboriginal cultural and linguistic paradigm.

The Aboriginal concept of equality rests upon the inherent sacredness of all creation. Since all creation is sacred, all creation is equal. Aboriginal peoples infuse this connecting principle of love and sacredness into all things and animals and people. 'Nature is sacred because it reveals the Great Mystery.'[93] The whole earth is sacred because it is the source of life. Mother Earth, as tribal elders refer to the earth, continuously renews herself. Creation is an ongoing process. Aboriginal peoples see nature as constantly in flux and motion.[94] That does not mean, however, that all parts of creation are the same. Therefore, Aboriginal people accepted differences among members of the community, animals, and plants. Aboriginal cultures believe in the interconnectedness and sacredness of animals, humans, and land. Traditional spiritual practices, developed to acknowledge the sacredness of the land, reflect respect for the spiritual power of nature within a specific geographic context.

Respect for the earth provides the spiritual basis for the parameters of conduct and government. Land, including its plants, animals, and humans are interdependent. Aboriginal perspectives construct responsibilities to land as holistic, based on oral traditions and lived experience. Aboriginal peoples see the earth as 'our Mother,' a vision that illustrates a close personal and spiritual connection to the land. The power of nature informs all relationships. According to Barsh, 'Like Euro-Asian monotheism, Native Americans attribute creation to a first principle, often identified as Grandfather or Grandmother, Maker, or Great Mystery. Unlike Euro-Asian monotheism, this Creator is not a personal god supervising the human affairs, but an ultimate, pure and aloof power identified with love.'[95]

The responsibility of one generation to other generations is very important in Aboriginal culture. For example, the seven-generation concept of the Haudenosaunee is based on family structure. The seven generations are the ones that an individual person can know: great-grandparent, grandparent, parent, self, child, grandchild, and great-grandchild.[96] However, other Aboriginal societies speak of the seven generations as those that flow only into the future.[97] 'Some Elders say that the only people who truly own the land are the generations yet unborn. Once born, you no longer own the land. Instead, it becomes your responsibility to take care of the land for its rightful owners: the coming generations.'[98]

In addition to caring for other humans, Aboriginal societies in Canada also have clear and personal responsibilities for the non-human animals on which they rely. As documented in numerous accounts,[99] many believe animals live in societies of their own, and that they sacrifice themselves so that humans can live. Moose, deer, salmon, and other animals of their locality gave themselves to humans. In return, humans had to show proper respect to all the animals. Respectful behaviours included performing sacred rituals, not taking more than was offered or needed, letting land rest for regeneration, and other practices. Aboriginal peoples use the circle to epitomize the connectedness and equality of all people, plants, and animals. The Royal Commission on Aboriginal Peoples states:

> Traditional knowledge of the ways of the land was rooted in an understanding of the holistic, interrelated nature of the earth's ecosystems, of the Circle of Life ... Their philosophy is that all things are connected, that you cannot isolate one part of water, for instance, sport fishing. They don't see it that way. When they talk about water, they talk about everything that is connected to water. It starts with the smallest living thing right on up to the largest. They talk about water as being a big chain in a big circle, and we are part of that circle. We have to look after everything that is within that circle. If we destroy anything within that circle, we destroy ourselves.[100]

The use and protection of the land and all within it reflects this interconnectedness. Noonan states: 'Territoriality is essential to Indian [sic] spirituality. It dictates that certain ceremonies occur at particular locations within the landscape such as previously dedicated sacred burial grounds. While all of nature is considered sacred, there are certain designated points on the landscape where renewal and communication with spiritual forces can be achieved.'[101]

No one escapes from natural law, which provides the doctrinal underpinnings of Aboriginal perspectives of equality, interdependence, and responsibility to the land. Aboriginal leader and statesman Oren Lyons defines natural law as follows:

> The one thing you want to understand about nature and its law is that there is no place for mercy, no compromising. It is absolute. If you go out without clothes when you go hunting, you will freeze to death. The natural law prevails, no matter what any international tribunal may decide. The natural law, in its most basic form, is simply that if you do not eat, you will die. If you don't drink water, you will die. There is no way you

can violate this law and get away with it. We are all bound by this law. It is basic, it is simple and it is eternal.'[102]

Despite commonalties in basic principles of environmental steward-ship among Aboriginal groups, it is also important to recognize that various Aboriginal peoples relate to their surroundings and define environmental stewardship on the basis of their own particular tradi-tions. It is difficult to discuss universal practices that rely on broad environmental stewardship principles, because actions based on these principles depend significantly on the territory of the specific First Nations people. In the next section, we explore Mi'kmaq perspectives on environment.

The Mi'kmaq Perspective on Environment

Mi'kmaq culture involves a different way of thinking about and relat-ing to the world. Five main themes emerge with respect to environ-mental management: identity, stewardship, language, sharing, and the maintenance of harmony through ceremonies, which leads to sustainable use of the resources. The Mi'kmaq[103] people continue to define their relationship to the environment through the concept of *Netukulimk*, the Mi'kmaq term for 'resource management and harvest-ing which does not jeopardize the integrity, diversity or productivity of our environment.[104]

In this section, we examine the Mi'kmaq relationship to the land and how this relationship determines tribal identity. Mi'kmaq people have lived in Mi'kma'ki for more than 12,000 years.[105] They governed them-selves through the Grand Council, also known as the Sante Mawiomi, and had government systems, institutions, laws, and a property sys-tem that sustained and nourished all members of the community. 'Mi'kma'ki' describes what the allied people, Wabinaki, called their national territory.[106]

Mi'kmaq tribal consciousness depends upon a process of respecting the land in order to establish spirituality, sacredness, sustainability, and resource-sharing. In Mi'kmaq culture, people respect the earth as sacred. Relationships to the land link Mi'kmaq culture, history, clan, and identity. The Mi'kmaq do not separate land and identity. The Mi'kmaq world includes both the invisible and visible realms.[107] Mi'kmaq oral tradition tells us that lived personal experience to land develops wisdom and status in Mi'kmaq society. Further, spiritual experience comes from our relationship to the land. Ceremonies take care of the land and all those on it. Humans will reciprocate when we die and return our bodies to the earth, where we will become part of our mother again.

The Mi'kmaq world view relies upon the concept of an orientation around space as opposed to a material consciousness. For example, Mi'kmaq people value land in terms of the land itself, not according to how the land is developed. The space itself has value, history, and a connection to identity.

The orientation towards space as opposed to a material consciousness reflects a view that is grounded in the practical and geographical. As Henderson states, 'Generally, Algonquin People and their linguistic worldview do not have a defined concept of territory or land. Instead, they had a concept of *space*. Their vision of the concept is different realms enfolded into a sacred space. Their earth is a series of ecological spaces, each filled with natural resources, sights, sounds and memories. The relationship between the earth and their ancestors informs their spirituality and religion.'[108] The Mi'kmaq concept of 'space' provided for Mi'kmaq identity, a sharing of resources, and a record of their history.[109] Mi'kmaq language reflects a relationship to the land. It is verb-oriented, which means that the focus is on action.[110] Mi'kmaq people believe that the world is in constant flux and motion.[111] Henderson identifies this series of spaces that orders Aboriginal language as Langscape.[112] The Langscape speaks of the history of the Mi'kmaq people in the territory of Mi'kma'ki. Recognition of the sacredness of the land and of the connection of Mi'kmaq people to the land and to their community and family dictated resource use and sharing.

The word *Nestomou*[113] 'describes the Mi'kmaq experiences on a part of the earth ... [It] describes everything for which they have experiences.'[114] The land itself held those memories, as Henderson describes: 'Every tree, every shore, every mist in the dark woods, every clearing was holy in their memory and experience, recalling not only their lives but the lives of their ancestors since the world began. Hence the entire langscape is a symbolic, historical and educational record, testifying to the unique experience and identity of the people.[115] The land determined identity and a sense of belonging, not only to the land but also to the nation. History, oral tradition, and language flowed from the experiences of Mi'kmaq people with the land. For example, Chapel Island remains important to Mi'kmaq people due to the shared experience and history of that space, both for the first author and for the nation. The island belongs to the entire nation. Its history is embedded in the ground in the form of circles where our ancestors danced. Elders point this connection out as we walk past the circles. Being Mi'kmaq means understanding the significance of the island. As Henderson states: 'Belonging, then, is directly tied both linguistically and experientially to a space ... as well as to shared knowledge of a series of common space ... [I]t is viewed as a special responsibility.'[116]

The Sante Mawiomi, the Grand Council, was and is the trustee of the Mi'kmaq sacred order and territory for the future generations. Members have the duty to regulate the natural resources of Mi'kmaki among the people and through trading customs. This is a responsibility of managing the space to ensure discipline in the consumption of resources, not an expression of ownership.[117] 'The Grand Council is the governing body of the nation and is led by several officers, including a kji'saqmaw (grand chief), a putus (treaty holder and counselor), and a kji'keptan (grand captain, advisor on political affairs). The Sante Mawiomi determined where families might hunt, fish, and set up their wumitki (camp).'[118]

The Mi'kmaq see space and land as sacred, subject to natural law. In other words, natural law meant that if a person does not take care of the land's resources, that person or the community will die. 'This basic law held for every living thing on earth. If the people were to deplete the animal or plant resources of their immediate environment, pain and suffering could be expected. This understanding gave rise to a relationship that is intimately connected to the sustainability of the earth and its resources.'[119] Mi'kmaq people recognize the interdependence of all things: 'Given the Mi'kmaq view that all things in the world have their own spirit, and all things must work in harmony with each other, Mi'kmaq show respect for the spirit by extending certain rituals to our interactions with nature. We extend a certain amount of recognition of the spirit of the tree, animal, plants and elements we disturb for our own use ... We do not apologise for our needs but accept the interdependence of all things.'[120]

For the Mi'kmaq, risk avoidance recognizes the interdependence of all beings and operates through the non-accumulation of material resources. Sharing and mobility discourage the accumulation of resources not considered essential. Risk avoidance also involves travelling throughout the people's region to prevent excessive consumption of resources in any one place and to utilize seasonal resources. Travel contributes to a sustainable way of life and cemented the relationship of Mi'kmaq people to their territory as well as increasing biodiversity and trade opportunities.[121] Since accumulation and hoarding represent imbalance and harm, Mi'kmaq people consider greed reprehensible. The sharing of space and all of its resources with the clan and family creates the basis of meaning for all Aboriginal life.[122]

Hunters perform rituals to honour the spirits of the hunted animals. Mi'kmaq people believe that animals such as deer and moose give themselves to humans for their survival. In return, the people must show proper respect for the animals. 'If anyone caught any meat, like deer, it was shared with everyone.'[123] Netukulimk refers to the hunters' and fishers' responsibility to be mindful of the Creator, the land, and the human community:[124] 'For this reason, fishing peoples have maintained a high degree of discipline over harvesting and coastal development. A wide variety of methods were traditionally used to keep harvesting within sustainable levels, including the assignment of fishing sites to individuals (who served more as managers than as owners), and restrictions on the times and places each species could be harvested. Relying on experience accumulated for generations, community leaders and fishing-site owners were able to adjust harvest levels to observed changes in abundance.'[125] Ceremonies ensured respect for the hunted animals and reminded the hunter to be mindful of both the Creator and the human community: 'These renewal rituals and ceremonies brought the people and the land into balance thereby achieving basic subsistance and material well being. These rituals and ceremonies created a harmony, which emphasized stability and the minimization of risk for the harvesting of resources rather than the growth or accumulation of wealth.'[126] Henderson states that 'managing a space and sharing is viewed as an integral part of the ethical development of the Mi'kmaq.'[127] The notion of space here reflects Aboriginal ecological consciousness: their language appropriates a space and attaches responsibility to it. 'Their notion of self does not end with their flesh, but instead, continues with the reach of the senses into the land, thus they can talk of the land as their flesh.'[128] The land is not simply natural wilderness, but a creation that must be cared for in a proper and respectful way.

The ultimate ownership of the land, if it could exist, rests with unborn children, seven generations into the future, in the invisible realm. As Henderson states: 'The relationship between the Mi'kmaq and the land embodies the essence of the intimate sacred order. As humans, they have and retain an obligation to protect the order and a right to share its uses, but only the future, unborn children in the invisible sacred realm of the next seven generations had any ultimate ownership of the land.'[129] Aboriginal efforts to protect places considered sacred continue today. If economic development endangers Aboriginal identity and disconnects Aboriginal people from their land, their very existence becomes threatened.

Examining stewardship from a Mi'kmaq perspective involves the inclusion of experience and diversity. Stewardship, as practised by Mi'kmaq people, offers a positive step towards the protection of the environment. Alex Denny, the Grand Captain of the Grand Council, provides guidance here: 'We are convinced that our assets are not being conserved, and not being put to the best use. We consider this an emergency, and can not delay action any longer. The *living resources of the Maritime Region – our Mi'kmakik – are simply disappearing while we speak*' (emphasis added).[130]

Seeing resources as living entities illustrates the connection of Mi'kmaq people to the land. Natural law demands that, in order to survive, we take as little as possible and refocus energy towards conservation, not simply economics. Denny states: 'They [the Europeans] use up resources as fast as they can get away with it, usually just a little too fast. They all chase what will get them the most money, and after it's gone, they look for something else. Why is anyone surprised that the ocean and forests are dying?'[131] Mi'kmaq concepts of stewardship and respect for experience and the sacredness of the land can only encourage responsible development for the long term. In the next section, we examine two examples of the complexities of integrating traditional Aboriginal perspectives into new institutions emerging from recent legal and policy developments.

The Nuxalk Food Fishery

Judicial affirmation of Aboriginal and treaty rights has led federal, provincial, and First Nations governments to enter into new institutional arrangements for harvesting, enhancing, and protecting resources. Winbourne describes the relationship between traditional fishing practices and emerging government policy in her study of the Nuxhalk food fishery.[132]

The Nuxalk of northern British Columbia have maintained their traditional salmon food fisheries for centuries.[133] Despite increasing pressures from disturbances to their territory, particularly through logging, the Nuxalk people continue to rely heavily on the salmon food fishery for cultural, social, and economic purposes. They use the 'salmon economy' to provide a livelihood. It also reinforces social ties within the community and, through traditional trade, provides links between communities.[134]

Nuxalk stewardship practices include selective fishing methods and close monitoring of fish stocks and habitat. Twenty years ago, the Nuxalk elders banned motorized vessels on the river so that the spawning fish and their eggs would not be disturbed. Traditional fish weirs (which permit close monitoring of harvested fish and the live release of weaker stocks) are now being reintroduced in some areas. Winbourne also reports on a three-day-per-week closure on the food fishery to ensure adequate escapement, and restrictions on dumping waste and pollutants in the river. The Nuxalk protect the fish and their environment by ceremonial and social means as well. They feel obligated to care both for the salmon and the river.[135]

The nature of the community at Bella Coola contributes to the likelihood that stewardship norms will be respected. As Winbourne states: 'Notions of greed, social stigma and shaming continue to play a role in Nuxalk salmon stewardship. In this small, tight-knit community, everyone knows what everyone else is doing; fishing and processing activities are highly visible.'[136] The designation of certain individuals as 'River Guardians' (*Ixwanaisa*) who hold special responsibilities to enforce protection of the river is a longstanding, traditional practice that has recently been reinstated:

> In 1994, during a feast at which the opening of the Nuxalk-run fish plant was celebrated, nine fishermen were appointed as River Guardians; their names were publicly acknowledged at that time ... The bestowal of the name and the profession *Ixwanaisa* at this point had important political, social and ecological implications: the appointment of the Nuxalk Guardians sent a message that there would be a watchful eye on illegal fish sale activity, at the same time as letting state management representatives know that the Nuxalk were upholding their responsibilities for caring for the fish. More recently, during a potlatch in August 1997, the *staltimx* (head chief) of the traditional village site of the present town of Bella Coola (*Q'omq'ots*) gave this name to a tribal biologist to acknowledge his role in protecting salmon populations.'[137]

The Nuxalk of Bella Coola have become involved in the Aboriginal

Fisheries Strategy (AFS) initiated by the Department of Fisheries and Oceans following the *Sparrow* decision. DFO developed the AFS in 1992 as a seven-year program and negotiated co-management agreements with Aboriginal communities across Canada for co-management of food fisheries and, in some cases, for pilot-project commercial fisheries.[138] The AFS has included components such as allocation quotas and increasing Native management control. It has also featured increased Aboriginal involvement in developing monitoring, and reporting on fisheries plans, habitat restoration and enhancement, and training.[139]

Winbourne reports that the application of the AFS has involved considerable conflict involving Nuxalk fishers, members of neighbouring communities, DFO representatives, and non-Aboriginal user groups.[140] Community members are particularly concerned about the federal government's attempts to impose a new communal licence on their food fishery. This process would involve an allocation quota and the requirement to share harvest data, an undertaking that requires a firmer basis of trust than currently exists.

The Aboriginal cultural approach to the fishery differs from the quantitative emphasis held by federal managers, so that applying numerical models and quotas is seen as inappropriate.[141] Some Nuxalk community members have expressed concern that the AFS does not respect their traditional trading practices. The Nuxalk see such practices as being an integral part of their Aboriginal rights.[142]

The Nuxalk case illustrates key aspects of environmental-stewardship practices in one Aboriginal community. It highlights some areas of potential conflict between communities and DFO programs such as the AFS. As such, it underscores the need for federal policy-makers to understand and to take into account the values and practices of Aboriginal communities, and to give greater weight to consultation in developing co-management programs in the future.

The Nunavut Wildlife Management Board

Nunavut officially became a territory in April 1999 after more than twenty years of negotiations. Following the *Calder* ruling that recognized the existence of Aboriginal title, the federal government began to negotiate comprehensive land claims with Aboriginal peoples in areas where no previous treaties had been made.[143] These included the 1975 *James Bay and Northern Quebec Agreement (JBNQA)* and the 1984 *Inuvialuit Agreement*.[144] The Nunavut Land Claims Agreement follows the pattern of establishing regimes of co-management, or shared decision-making regimes, that emerged earlier in the Canadian North.[145]

Wildlife is central in the agreement, as would be expected in a region where Aboriginal subsistence harvesting activities continued relatively undisturbed until after the Second World War, and where a significant proportion of the population still depends upon 'country food.'[146] The following key objectives of the agreement are stated in its preamble:

- to provide for certainty and clarity of rights to ownership and use of lands and resources and of rights for Inuit to participate in decision-making concerning the use, management and conservation of land, water and resources, including the offshore,
- to provide Inuit with wildlife harvesting rights and rights to participate in decision-making concerning wildlife harvesting,
- to provide Inuit with financial compensation and means of participating in economic opportunities, and
- to encourage self-reliance and the cultural and social well-being of Inuit.[147]

The Nunavut Act establishes the Nunavut Wildlife Management Board as one of several co-management boards to serve as advisers to the Nunavut government. Others include the Nunavut Planning Commission (NPC), for land-use planning (including pollution control), and the Nunavut Impact Review Board, to assess the environmental and economic impacts of new developments.[148] Inuit organizations and governments have equal numbers of representatives on each of these agencies.

The implementation of the new institutional arrangements in Nunavut is now under way. The Nunavut Wildlife Management Board, whose members will receive compensation (section 12), will work with the territorial government, and with the Hunters and Trappers Organizations and Regional Wildlife Organizations, thus linking the board with resource users in widespread communities. The board will also deal with matters such as conservation areas and national parks. It has been reported that national parks managers have already recognized that consumptive human use of wildlife is not incompatible with ecological integrity in northern parks and that the question is not 'if but how parks and Aboriginal groups are going to work together.[149]

It is too early to evaluate the operation of the Nunavut Wildlife Management Board, but it will be closely monitored in the coming years.

However, Inuit managers express hope for the future. As Brian Aglukark states, 'The creation of these co-management bodies through the implementation of the Nunavut Land Claims Agreement puts the future well-being of our land and wildlife in the hands of the Inuit. With our history of survival, strength, unity and our love of the environment, Inuit can be assured that, like that morning years ago when I walked out of the tent and saw not only the geese flying over, but also saw the sheer beauty of the land, future generations will know this same experience.'[150]

3. Discussion and Conclusion

Our analysis of Canadian Aboriginal law illustrates the complexity of Aboriginal land rights, treaties, and Aboriginal rights. Policy-makers must understand these issues if they hope to include Aboriginal peoples in shaping environmental trends. Moreover, Aboriginal title, Aboriginal rights, and treaty rights receive protection under the highest legal order, section 35(1) of the constitution. The Constitution Act of 1982 opened the door and the Supreme Court decisions began to pave the way for Aboriginal participation in deliberations on resource management, development, and policy.

Both federal and provincial governments have the fiduciary obligation to support Aboriginal inclusion at the policy table. However, the division of powers under the Constitution Act, 1867[151] impedes the realization of full inclusion of Aboriginal peoples. Professor Borrows agrees, stating: 'Participation in environmental planning is hindered by the *Indian Act* because it limits the steps indigenous peoples could take to more directly address environmental challenges. Compressing First Nations from the other side are the deep waters of provincial authority. Indigenous peoples are often submerged and invisible in their own land because the province does not make provisions for their interests.'[152] The federal government must recognize that Aboriginal peoples have secured their rights within the constitution. Even if the Supreme Court, on the basis of different factual situations, reverses some gains made in Aboriginal law, Aboriginal people will remain fundamental players in the environmental sphere. The current conflict over the *Marshall* decision illustrates the difficulties faced by Mi'kmaq people and the federal government when the government fails to acknowledge the extent of its fiduciary obligation to include Aboriginal people in resource management decisions.

Some essential questions remain unanswered at this point. The boundaries of the fiduciary relationship and of the exact duty owed to Aboriginal peoples remain unclear. The courts have not elaborated upon the exact limits on this relationship. The political nature of Aboriginal and treaty rights has caused some commentators to question the litigation process because of the complexity of the issues presented to the court and the length of time and money needed for the courts to decide on any particular issue. For example, the *Delgamuukw* case had been before the courts for over twelve years. After hearing the case, the Supreme Court sent it back for a new trial. Due to such difficulties, policy-making and negotiation become necessary, and are sometimes preferred to litigation. Relevant jurisprudence does dictate a particular path to take with respect to these issues and offers some guidance towards implementation.

As Bruce Doern states, 'Aboriginal groups bring a particular intensity and range of environmental values to the table, in part, because their centuries-long traditions and beliefs stress a unity and compatibility that Western cultures have tended to neglect.'[153] Western culture must begin to respect Aboriginal values and principles when creating and implementing environmental policies.

Other relevant issues that remain include the following:

- *Delgamuukw* implies that Aboriginal title and consultation should not be limited to the reserves. What impact does this aspect have in the Mi'kmaq context, since the Mi'kmaq did not sign treaties that ceded land? Will Mi'kmaq people be included in the development of environmental policy for reserves only, or throughout their traditional territory, which encompasses five provinces?
- As noted earlier, translating traditional Aboriginal understanding of the environment and applying it in a modern context presents linguistic and cultural challenges, as alluded to by John Burrows and Janet Winbourne. Sallenave states that the use of traditional ecological knowledge [TEK] in northern environmental impact agreements 'requires an understanding of how Aboriginal peoples perceive and use the environment. TEK cannot be used outside of its political and social context.'[154]
- On the matter of Aboriginal identity, with whom will the federal and provincial governments consult on environmental policy-making? For example, the Indian Act divides the Mi'kmaq people. Status, non-status, on-reserve, and off-reserve Mi'kmaq people have vari-

ous political representations. The Native Council of Nova Scotia (NCNS) represents non-status Mi'kmaq people. Off-reserve Mi'kmaq people fall into the cracks, as both the band and the NCNS claim to represent their interests. The NCNS does not participate in the current self-government discussions, but advocates for their inclusion in the Aboriginal fishery.

Developing policy that honours the existing legal framework and the federal obligation remains paramount. Implementing Aboriginal and treaty rights to resources will also affect the non-Aboriginal users of these resources. Thus, the Mi'kmaq people and both levels of government need to deal fairly with the competing and conflicting demands concerning access. Moreover, both levels of government must take seriously the fiduciary obligation to include Aboriginal peoples by seeking a deeper understanding of Aboriginal viewpoints and community life.

Canadian policy-makers have included traditional ecological knowledge in both environmental-impact assessment[155] and land claims settlements.[156] However, much more needs to be done in this area. International forums have increasingly recognized Aboriginal rights and the wisdom to be gained from traditional ecological knowledge. For example, the Rio Summit Agenda 21 recommended the need to include Aboriginal and other indigenous traditions with respect to the sustainability of the environment.

However, we acknowledge the danger in entrusting the saving of the planet to Aboriginal peoples. A superficial examination of Aboriginal land relations can only lead to raising Aboriginal persons and cultures to a superordinate status, to their detriment. Huffman argues that such a view can only hurt Native Americans, who continue to live in poverty on reservations.[157] And Professor John Borrows further suggests: 'The fact that Indigenous Peoples may contribute to the creation of better communities should not be taken to mean that all of our environmental problems will be solved if we heed their knowledge. There are many intricacies these peoples have not faced because of the scale of our current troubles ... [W]hat was successful in one time and place, as a response to a particular historical, environmental, and social circumstances, may not always be translated appropriately to other settings.'[158]

Despite these challenges and the lack of clear guidance from the courts, Aboriginal peoples in Canada have made progress with respect to exercising their legal rights and responsibilities. Nunavut, the Nuxalk fishery, and the current struggles over implementation of the

Marshall decision show the tenacity of Aboriginal peoples in establishing their role in resource management. The complexity of conditions in the twenty-first century means that Aboriginal peoples must seek a balance between traditional perspectives and present political conditions in their participation in managing resources such as forestry and fisheries, as well as in discussions on sustainable development.[159] This is a dynamic and ongoing process.

But it remains to be seen if both levels of government possess the political will to include Aboriginal peoples in a more fundamental way in a constructive environmental-policy process. To permit them to exercise the rights and responsibilities to which history, treaties, and law entitle them demands nothing less.

NOTES

1 www.nunavut.com/nunavut99/english/name.html *under* gg.ca/heraldry/nun/sym-desc-e.html.
2 Nunavut Handbook, http://www.nunavut.com/basicfacts/english/basicfacts_1territ ory.html#17.
3 With respect to names – First Peoples, First Nations, American Indians, Native peoples, indigenous peoples, and Aboriginal peoples – debate exists about the definition, appropriateness, and inclusiveness of these names in various contexts. The use of Aboriginal in this paper parallels the usage in the Constitution Act, 1982, sect, 35. 'Indigenous' predominates in international discourse, particularly at the United Nations. We use the word 'peoples' rather than 'people' depending on the context, which differs under international law with respect to individual and collective rights. For general information about Aboriginal peoples in Canada see T.R. Berger, *A Long and Terrible Shadow: White Values, Native Rights in the Americas* (Vancouver: Douglas and McIntyre, 1991); and B. Richardson, *People of Terra Nullius: Betrayal and Rebirth in Aboriginal Canada* (Toronto: Douglas and McIntyre, 1993).
4 Nunavut Land Claims Agreement Act, chap. N-28.6, N-28.7 (1993, c. 28), Statutes of Canada.
5 *Report of the Royal Commission on Aboriginal Peoples*, vol. 1 (Ottawa: Supply and Services Canada, 1996), 15.
6 Recent examples include the Oka Crisis of 1990. See G.R. Alfred, *Heeding the Voices of Our Ancestors: Kahnawake Mohawk Politics and the Rise of Native Nationalism* (Toronto: Oxford University Press, 1995); and G. York and

L. Pindera, *People of the Pines: The Warriors and the Legacy of Oka* (Toronto: Little, Brown, 1991). For information on the protest at Voisey's Bay, see M. Lowe, *Premature Bonanza: Standoff at Voisey's Bay* (Toronto: Between the Lines, 1998).

7 For further information on indigenous peoples on the international stage, see D.E. Saunders, 'The Indian Lobby and the Canadian Constitution, 1978–82,' in N. Dyck, ed., *Indigenous Peoples and the Nation State: Fourth World Politics in Canada, Australia and Norway* (St John's: Memorial University Institute of Social and Economic Research, 1985), 151; O. Mercredi, 'Address to the United Nations,' in A. Ewen, ed., *Voice of Indigenous Peoples* (Santa Fe: Clear Light Publishers, 1994), 64; F.G. Cohen, A. Luttermann, and A. Bergen, 'Comparative Perspectives on Indigenous Rights to Marine Resources in Canada and Australia,' in L.K Kriwokin et al., eds, *Oceans Law and Policy in the Post-UNCED Era: Australian and Canadian Perspectives* (London: Kluwer, 1996), 389; and J. Zinsser, *A New Partnership: Indigenous Peoples and the United Nations System* (Paris: UNESCO, 1994). For a historical account on Aboriginal delegations from Canada to Europe, see C. Feest, ed., *Indians and Europe: An Interdisciplinary Collection of Essays* (Aachen: Alano, 1989).

8 Constitution Act 1982, being Schedule B to the Canada Act 1982 (U.K.).

9 *Calder v. Attorney-General of British Columbia*, [1973] S.C.R. 313; *R. v. Sparrow*, (1990) 3 C.N.L.R. 98, [1990] 1 S.C.R. 1075, 56 C.C.C. (3d) 263, 46 B.C.L.R (2d) 1, [1990] 4 W.W. R. 410, 70 D.L.R. (4th) 385, 11 N.R. 241, cited to C.N.L.R.; *Delgamuukw v. British Columbia*, [1997] 3 S.C.R 1010.

10 See, e.g., Canada, Dept. of Indian and Northern Affairs, *Federal Policy for the Settlement of Native Claims* (Ottawa: DIAND, 1993); and ibid., *The Western Arctic Claim, The Inuvialuit Final Agreement* (Ottawa: DIAND, 1984).

11 J. Huffman, 'An Exploratory Essay on Native Americans and Environmentalism,' *University of Colorado Review* 63 (1992): 901–17.

12 R. Kapashit and M. Klippenstein, 'Aboriginal Group Rights and Environmental Protection,' *McGill Law Journal* 36, no. 3 (1991): 925.

13 T. Greaves, ed., *Intellectual Property Rights for Indigenous Peoples: A Source Book* (Oklahoma City: Society for Applied Anthropology, 1994); P. Sillitoe, 'The Development of Indigenous Knowledge: A New Applied Anthropology,' *Current Anthropology* 39 (1994): 223; J. Cruikshank, *The Social Life of Stories: Narrative and Knowledge in the Yukon Territory* (Lincoln: University of Nebraska Press, 1998); M. Johnson, ed., *Lore: Capturing Traditional Ecological Knowledge* (Hay River, NWT, and Ottawa: Dene Cultural Institute and International Development Research Centre, 1992); R. Simonelli, 'Sustainable Science: A Look at Science through Historic Eyes and through the Eyes of

Indigenous Peoples,' *Bulletin of the Science and Technology Society* 24 (1994): 1; V. Deloria, Jr, *Red Earth, White Lies: Native Americans and the Myth of Scientific Fact* (New York: Scribner 1995).

14 J.L. Winbourne, 'Taking Care of Salmon: Significance, Sharing, and Stewardship in a Nuxhalk Food Fishery,' Master of Environmental Studies thesis, Dalhousie University, Halifax, 1998; J.L. Winbourne, 'Meeting Needs: A Consideration of the Aboriginal Fisheries Strategy and the Future of First Nations Food Fisheries,' in *Abstracts: Crossing Boundaries*, 297–8, 7th conference of International Association for the Study of Common Property, Vancouver, June 1998.

15 Gouvernement du Québec, *The James Bay and Northern Quebec Agreement* (Quebec: Éditeur Officiel du Québec, 1975).

16 F. Berkes, ed., *Common Property Resources: Ecology and Community Based Sustainable Development* (London: Belhaven 1989); E. Pinkerton, 'Local Fisheries Co-Management: A Review of International Experiences and Their Implications for Salmon Management in British Columbia,' *Canadian Journal of Fisheries and Aquatic Sciences* 51 (1994): 2363; E. Pinkerton, ed., *Co-operative Management of Local Fisheries: New Directions for Improved Management and Community Development* (Vancouver: University of British Columbia Press, 1989); F. Berkes, P. George, and R.J. Preston, 'Co-Management: The Evolution in Theory and Practice of the Joint Administration of Living Resources,' *Alternatives* 18 (1991). For information on U.S. inter-tribal commissions, natural resource management plans, and links to other relevant sites, see Columbia River Inter-Tribal Fish Commission (www.critfc.org/index.html), Great Lakes Indian Fish and Wildlife Commission (www.glifwc.org), and Northwest Indian Fisheries Commission (www.nwifc.wa.gov).

17 Constitution Act, 1867 (U.K.), 30 & 31 Vict., c. 3, s. 91 (24), which assigns jurisdiction to the federal government with respect to Indians and lands reserved for Indians.

18 An Act to Amend and Consolidate laws respecting Indians, S.C. 1876, c. 18. Indian Act, 1876, S.C. 1876; currently cited as The Indian Act.

19 *St. Catherine's Milling and Lumber Co. v. the Queen* (1888), 14 A.C. 56 (P.C.); *Calder v. British Columbia* (A.G.), [1973] S.C.R. 313.

20 *R. v. Sparrow*, 160.

21 *R. v. Marshall* [1999] 3 S.C.R. 456. Appeal from a judgment of the Nova Scotia Court of Appeal (1997), 159 N.S.R. (2d) 186, 468 A.P. R. 186, 146 D.L.R. (4th) 257, [1997] 3 C.N.L.R. 209, [1997] N.S.J. no. 131 (QL), affirming [1996] N.S.J. no. 246 (QL).

22 *Sparrow*, 180.

23 R. v. Van der Peet [1996] 2 S.C.R. 507.

24 Sparrow, 171.

25 Ibid., 169–70.

26 W. Nichols, 'Masters of Conquest,' The Nation 1 (February 1994): 10. See also J. Henderson, 'Aboriginal Rights in Western Legal Tradition,' in M. Boldt and J.A. Long, eds, The Quest for Justice: Aboriginal People and Aboriginal Rights (Toronto: University of Toronto Press 1985).

27 For further discussion of the Sparrow case and its implications for self-government, see P. Macklem, 'First Nations Self-Government and the Borders of the Canadian Legal Imagination,' McGill Law Journal 36, 383 (1991): 382–456, 450.

28 Ibid., 449–50.

29 Ibid., 447.

30 Van der Peet [1996] 2 S.C.R. 507, at p. 553.

31 Ibid., 552.

32 Ibid., 553.

33 Sparrow, 175.

34 Ibid., 176.

35 B. Slattery, 'Understanding Aboriginal Rights,' Canadian Bar Review 66 (1987): 736.

36 R. v. Guerin, [1984] 2 S.C.R. 335, 13 D.L.R. (4th) 321, [1985] 1 C.N.L.R 120 [hereinafter Guerin cited to C.N.L.R.]

37 Ibid., 139.

38 Ibid., 131.

39 R. v. Sparrow, (1990) 1 S.C.R 1075, 70 D.L.R. (4th) 427 (1990) 3 C.N.L.R. 160 [hereinafter Sparrow cited to C.N.L.R].

40 Ibid., 180, 183, 184.

41 Ibid., 180.

42 See n. 9 above. S. Persky, Delgamuukw: The Supreme Court of Canada's Decision on Aboriginal Title (Vancouver: Greystone Books, 1998).

43 R. Bartlett, Resource Development and Aboriginal Land Rights (Calgary: Canadian Institute of Resources Law, 1991), 1.

44 In 1970, in Calder v. A.G. British Columbia, the Supreme Court ruled that once Aboriginal title is found to exist, it continues until the contrary is proved. Calder affirms and recognizes that Aboriginal title exists based on the prior historical occupancy of the land in question. Aboriginal peoples enjoyed rights that arose from that occupancy.

45 Ibid., 99.

46 Persky, Delgamuukw, 88.

47 Ibid., 93.

48 Ibid.
49 Ibid.
50 Ibid., 104, 105.
51 Ibid., 105
52 Ibid., 95.
53 *Calder v. Attorney General of British Columbia*, [1973] S.C.R. 313, where the court held that Aboriginal title exists, is held collectively, and is inalienable except to the Crown.
54 Persky, *Delgamuukw*, 116.
55 Ibid., 112.
56 Ibid., 113.
57 Ibid., 113.
58 Ibid., 112.
59 Ibid., 113.
60 Ibid.
61 *Simon v. The Queen*, [1985] 2 S.C.R. 387.
62 Ibid., 405–6.
63 *R. v. Badger* [1996] 1 S.C.R. 771, [1996] 2 C.N.L.R. 77. The facts of the case involve three people hunting per Treaty 8, which protected hunting rights. All accused were status Indians. Cited to C.N.L.R.
64 Ibid., 92.
65 Ibid., 96.
66 Ibid., 97.
67 In *Badger*, the Crown did not present evidence with respect to justification, so the court did not proceed with the analysis. The important point here is that the court asserted that the same test must be applied to an infringement of a treaty right.
68 See n. 21.
69 *Marshall*, 472.
70 Ibid., 474.
71 Ibid., 501–2.
72 Ibid., 502.
73 [1999] 3 S.C.R 533.
74 Ibid., 544.
75 Ibid., 543.
76 Ibid., 559.
77 Ibid., 561.
78 Ibid., 564.
79 Ibid., 562.
80 Ibid., 561.

81 See V. Deloria, Jr, *God Is Red* (New York: Grossett and Dunlap, 1973); B. Deloria, V. Deloria Jr, K. Foehner, and S. Scinta, eds, *Spirit and Reason: The Vine Deloria Jr. Reader* (Golden, CO: Fulcum Publishing, 1999); A. Hultkantz, *Belief and Worship in Native North America* (Syracuse, NY: Syracuse University Press, 1981).

82 M. Battiste, ed., *Reclaiming Indigenous Voice and Vision* (Vancouver: UBC Press, 2000), xix–xx.

83 J. Henderson, 'Empowering Treaty Federalism,' *Saskatchewan Law Review* 58 (1994): 245.

84 W.D. Wallis and R.S. Wallis, *The Micmac Indians of Eastern Canada* (Minneapolis: University of Minnesota Press, 1955); J. Cruikshank, in collaboration with A. Sidney, K. Smith, and A. Ned, *Lives Lived Like a Story: Life Stories of Three Yukon Native Elders* (Lincoln: University of Nebraska Press, 1990); H. Feit, 'Waswanipi Realities and Adaptation: Resource Management and Cognitive Structure,' Ph.D. thesis, McGill University, 1973. For additional works by Feit and by Berkes on the Cree, see bibliography at pp. 83–91 in F.G. Cohen and A.J. Hanson, *Community-based Resource Management in Canada: An Inventory of Research and Projects* (Ottawa: Canadian Commission for UNESCO, 1989); and F. Berkes and C. Folke, eds, *Linking Social and Ecological Systems: Management Practices and Social Mechanisms for Building Resilience* (Cambridge: Cambridge University Press, 1998).

85 Cohen and Hansen, *Community-based Resource Management*, 25; Berkes and Folke, *Linking Social and Ecological Systems*. For two perspectives, see W.R. Swagerty, ed., *Scholars and the Indian Experience: Critical Reviews of Recent Writing in the Social Sciences* (Bloomington: University of Indiana Press, 1984) and T. Asad, *Anthropology and the Colonial Encounter* (London: Ithaca Press, 1975).

86 J. Borrows, 'Living between Water and Rocks – First Nations, Environmental Planning and Democracy,' *University of Toronto Law Journal* 47 (1997): 418.

87 For a discussion on the highly politicized question of Aboriginal people and conservation, see A. Agrawal, *Community in Conservation: Beyond Enchantment and Disenchantment, Discussion Paper* (Gainesville: CDF, 1997); and A.M. Stearman, 'Revisiting the Myth of the Ecologically Noble Savage in Amazonia: Implications for Indigenous Land Rights,' *Culture and Agriculture* 49 (1994): 2. For an example of the debate about whether or not Aboriginal people were 'conservationists,' and its implications, see C. Martin, *Keepers of the Game* (Berkeley: University of California Press, 1978); and its critique, S. Krech II, ed., *Indians, Animals and the Fur Trade: A Critique of Keepers of the Game* (Athens: University of Georgia Press, 1981). As Peter

Usher points out in 'Some Implications of the Sparrow Judgement for Resource Conservation and Management' (*Alternatives* 18 [1991]: 20), conservation is an extremely complex and often controversial issue. He queries, 'Conservation of what, for whom, and to what ends, and by what means? How do we decide on appropriate conservation objectives, how do we know the chosen methods are the best ones, and how do we know when and if the objectives are being achieved?' These questions point to the importance of careful consideration of the biological, economic, political, and socio-cultural aspects of conservation in order to address what is legally permissable regulation of conservation under recent Canadian Supreme Court decisions.

88 R. White, 'Native Americans and the Environment,' in W.R. Swagerty, ed., *Scholars and the Indian Experience* (Bloomington: Indiana University Press, 1984), 179–204.

89 E. Anderson, *Ecologies of the Heart: Emotion, Belief and the Environment* (New York: Oxford, 1996), 174. Also see F. Berkes, *Sacred Ecology* (Philadelphia: Taylor and Francis, 1998).

90 Berkes and Folke, eds, *Linking*, 13.

91 Ibid.

92 *Report of the Royal Commission on Aboriginal Peoples (RCAP)*, *Perspectives and Realities* (Ottawa: Minister of Supply and Services, 1996), vol. 4, chap. 3: 139.

93 A. Hultkrantz, *Belief and Worship*, 127.

94 J. Henderson, 'Ayukpachi: Empowering Aboriginal Thought,' in M. Battiste, ed., *Reclaiming Indigenous Voice and Vision* (Vancouver: UBC Press, 2000), 258.

95 R. Barsh, 'The Illusion of Religious Freedom for Indigenous Americans,' *Oregon Law Review* 65 (1986): 364–5.

96 H. Lickers, personal communication.

97 L. Clarkson, Y. Morrissette, and G. Regallet, *Our Responsibility to the Seventh Generation: Indigenous Peoples and Sustainable Development* (Winnipeg: International Institute for Sustainable Development, 1992).

98 *RCAP*, vol. 4, chap. 3: 139.

99 E. Anderson, *Ecologies*; H. Feit, 'Waswanipi'; J. Cruikshank, *Life Lived*; J. Winbourne, 'Taking Care.'

100 *RCAP*, vol. 4, chap. 3: 139.

101 P. Noonan, 'Mining Desecration and the Protection of Indian Sacred Sites: A Lesson in First Amendment Hurdling,' *University of Pittsburgh Law Review* 50 (Summer 1989): 1131–4.

102 O. Lyons, 'Spirituality, Equality and Natural Law,' in M. Boldt, J.A. Long,

and L. Little Bear, eds, *The Quest for Justice: Aboriginal People and Aboriginal Rights* (1985), 12.

103 According to research undertaken by Bernie and Virick C. Francis, the word Mi'kmaq means 'the people'; see http://mrc.uccb.ns.ca/miscellany.html#1, and n. 106 below.

104 S. Berneshawi, 'Resource Management and the Mi'kmaq Nation,' *Canadian Journal of Native Studies* 17, no. 1 (1997): 118. Also see Mi'kmaq Grand Council, Union of Nova Scotia Indians, and Native Council of Nova Scotia, in cooperation with Department of Fisheries and Oceans, *Mi'kmaq Fisheries: Netukulimk – Towards a Better Understanding* (Truro, NS: Native Council of Nova Scotia, 1993).

105 Mi'kmaq tribal societies of Eastern Canada, Newfoundland, Prince Edward Island, Quebec, New Brunswick, and the state of Maine have inhabited these regions for over 10,000 years (J. Henderson, 'First Nations Legal Inheritances,' paper prepared for University of Manitoba Legal History Project; used with permission, 1991). The territory may have covered as much as 121,760 square kilometres.

106 J. Henderson, 'Mikmaw Tenure in Atlantic Canada,' *Dalhousie Law Journal* 18, no. 2 (Fall 1995): 239. The Mi'kmaq are the 'People of the Dawn,' as they are the most eastern peoples of the Wabnaki Confederacy, a loose coalition that included the Maliseets, the Passamaquoddys, the Penobscots, and the Eastern and Western Abenakis of present-day Maine, New Hampshire, and Vermont. At its peak, this confederacy influenced tribal life from the Gaspé Peninsula to northern New England. See http://mrc.uccb.ns.ca/mikmaq.html.

107 Ibid., 228.

108 Ibid., 218.

109 For example, the first author, speaking from her experience, remembers being told by her elders about the sacredness of Chapel Island, a place for Mi'kmaq gatherings for the past thousand years. The place itself reflects the history of the Mik'maq people. Elders tell us stories about ancestors whose spirits inhabit the island. Dancing circles still exist from 300 years ago.

110 *RCAP*, vol. 4, 123–4.

111 Henderson, 'Mi'kmaw Tenure,' 228.

112 Ibid., 220.

113 Ibid., 226.

114 Ibid., 226.

115 Ibid., 230.

116 Ibid., 219.

117　Ibid., 232.
118　http://mrc.uccb.ns.ca/mikmaq.html; E. Johnson, 'Mi'kmaq Tribal Consciousness in the Twentieth Century,' in S. Inglis and J. Manette, eds, *Paqtatek* (Halifax: Garamound Press, 1990).
119　Clarkson, Morrissette, and Regallet, *Our Responsibility,* 4.
120　M. Marshall, 'Values, Customs and Traditions of the Mi'kmaq Nation,' in L. Choyce and R. Joe, eds, *The Mi'kmaq Anthology* (Lawrencetown Beach, NS: Potterfield Press, 1997), 53.
121　Henderson, 'Mi'kmaw Tenure,' 219.
122　Ibid., 232.
123　Oral History Five with Daniel J. Stevens, http://mrc.uccb.ns.ca/oralhis. html#4.
124　Henderson, 'Mi'kmaw Tenure,' 233.
125　http://mrc.uccb.ns.ca/mdc/fishing.htm.
126　Henderson, 'Mi'kmaw Tenure,' 232.
127　Ibid., 233.
128　Ibid., 221.
129　Ibid., 232.
130　Text of speech given by Alex Denny, Grand Captain of the Mi'kmaq Grand Council, on Treaty Day, 1 October 1994.
131　Ibid.
132　'Taking Care of Salmon'; see also Winbourne, 'Meeting Needs' (see n. 14). It should be noted that the Nuxalk community was politically divided on the Aboriginal Fisheries Strategy and other issues. Winbourne worked primarily with the hereditary chiefs of the House of Smayusta at Bella Coola.
133　T.F. McIlwraith (1948), *The Bella Coola Indians,* 2 vols. (Toronto: University of Toronto Press, 1992). N.J. Turner and J.T. Jones, 'Occupying the Land: Traditional Patterns of Land and Resource Ownership among First Peoples of British Columbia,' presented at 'Constituting the Commons,' 8th annual conference of the International Association for the Study of Common Property, June 2000; www.indiana.edu/~isascp2000.htm.
134　Winbourne, 'Meeting Needs,' 298.
135　Winbourne, 'Taking Care,' 106–8.
136　Ibid., 107.
137　Ibid., 111.
138　Canada, Dept. of Fisheries and Oceans, Industry Services and Native Fisheries, 'Federal Aboriginal Fisheries Strategy,' unpublished outline 1995; Cohen et al., 'Comparative Perspectives,' 392–4.
139　Cohen et al., 'Comparative Perspectives,' 393.
140　Winbourne, 'Meeting Needs,' 298.

141 Ibid.

142 Ibid.

143 For policy directly prior to this period, see S. Weaver, *Making Canadian Indian Policy: The Hidden Agenda 1968–1970* (Toronto: University of Toronto Press, 1981). For further information on land claims policies, see G. Dacks, ed., *Devolution and Constitutional Development in the Canadian North* (Ottawa: Carleton University Press, 1990); Indian and Northern Affairs Canada, *Comprehensive Land Claims Policy* (Ottawa: INAC, 1987); and INAC, *Federal Policy for the Settlement of Native Claims* (Ottawa, 1993).

144 P. Usher, 'Contemporary Aboriginal Land, Resource and Environmental Regimes: Origins, Problems and Prospects,' report prepared for Royal Commission on Aboriginal Peoples, 1996. Available also on CD-ROM: For Seven Generations, 'The Information Legacy of the Royal Commission on Aboriginal Peoples' (Ottawa: Libraxus, 1997); this CD-ROM contains extensive studies commissioned by RCAP.

145 P. Clancy, 'Political Devolution and Wildlife Management,' in Dacks, ed., *Devolution*, 87.

146 Usher, *Contemporary Aboriginal Land*, 18–19.

147 Nunavut Lands Claims Agreement Act, preamble.

148 G. Dacks, *Nunavut: Aboriginal Self-Determination through Public Government*. Prepared for Royal Commission on Aboriginal Peoples, 1996.

149 J.P. Morgan and J.D. Henry, 'Hunting Grounds: Making Co-operative Wildlife Management Work,' *Alternatives* 22 (1996): 26.

150 B. Aglukark, 'Inuit and the Land as One,' on Nunavut website found at http://www.nunavut.com/nunavut99/english/inuit_land.html.

151 Constitution Act, 1867 (U.K.), 30 & 31 Vict., c. 3, s. 91 (24) states that federal government has jurisdiction with respect to 'Indians and lands reserved for Indians.'

152 Borrows, 'Living between Water and Rocks,' 420–1.

153 G.B. Doern, *Green Diplomacy: How Environmental Policy Decisions Are Made* (Toronto: C.D. Howe Institute, 1993), 12.

154 http://www.carc.org/pubs/v22no1/know.htm.

155 D.J. Nakashima, *Application of Native Knowledge in EIA: Inuit, Eiders and Hudson Bay Oil* (Ottawa: Canadian Environmental Assessment Research Council, 1999). See also T. Berger, *Northern Frontier, Northern Homeland: The Report of the Mackenzie Valley Pipeline Inquiry* (Toronto: J. Lorimer, 1977) for a pioneering approach to including Aboriginal voices in EIA in Canada.

156 M.G. Reed, *Environmental Assessment and Aboriginal Claims: Implementation of the Inuvialuit Final Agreement* (Ottawa: Canadian Environmental Assessment Research Council, 1990).

157 J. Huffman, 'An Exploratory Essay on Native Americans and Environmentalism,' *University of Colorado Law Review* 63 (1992): 901.
158 Borrows, 'Living between Water and Rocks,' 424.
159 C. Notze, *Aboriginal Peoples and Natural Resources in Canada* (North York, ON: Captus Press, 1994); C. Burda, R. Collier, and B. Evans, 'The Gitxsan Model: An Alternative to the Destruction of Forests, Salmon and the Gitxsan Land' (Victoria, BC: Eco-Research Chair of Environmental Law and Policy, University of Victoria, 1999); Aboriginal Fisheries Commission of British Columbia, 'Framework: Co-Management,' www.afcbc.org; Atlantic Policy Congress of First Nations Chiefs Secretariat, 'Atlantic First Nation Sustainable Development Consultation Report' (1997), www.apcfnc.ca.

6. Voluntarism and Environmental Governance

Kathryn Harrison

In recent years, governments throughout the world have expressed increasing dissatisfaction with 'command and control' environmental regulation, which is widely criticized as economically inefficient, adversarial, and administratively cumbersome. However, despite decades of advice from academic policy analysts, few governments have embraced market-based forms of regulation, such as marketable permits and discharge fees, as the leading alternative to traditional regulation. Rather, in recent years governments of industrialized countries have increasingly experimented with a variety of less coercive policy instruments predicated on cooperation between the state and business. 'Cooperation' and 'partnership' are thus gradually replacing 'command and control' in the environmental policy lexicon. For example, the European Union's Fifth Action Plan states: 'Whereas previous environmental measures tended to be prescriptive in character with an emphasis on the "though shalt not" approach, the new strategy leans more towards a "let's work together" approach. This reflects the growing realization in industry and in the business world that not only is industry a significant part of the (environmental) problem but it must also be part of the solution. The new approach implies, in particular, a reinforcement of the dialogue with industry and the encouragement, in appropriate circumstances, of voluntary agreements and other forms of self-regulation.'[1]

Some recent environmental policy reforms merely represent more flexible forms of regulation, such as negotiated compliance agreements, and less demanding regulatory requirements, including discharge reporting requirements, which mandate disclosure of information about environmental discharges but not actual reductions of those discharges. However, in other cases the state has embraced voluntary alternatives to regulation. Some take the form of hortatory public policies, including government-sponsored eco-labelling programs, 'challenge' programs such as Canada's Accelerated Reduction/ Elimination of Toxics (ARET) program, and negotiated voluntary agreements between government and business, perhaps best exemplified by the Dutch 'covenants.' In other cases governments have deferred to non-governmental voluntary initiatives, such as the chemical industry's self-regulatory Responsible Care program and third-party environmental management systems, such as ISO 14001, as an alternative or complement to public policy.

The growing reliance on less-coercive regulatory and voluntary programs reflects a trend toward greater reliance on civil society to achieve collective goals,[2] even with respect to the management of externalities and common-pool resources. The state's embrace of voluntary programs in such cases is striking in its rejection of the inevitability of a 'tragedy of the commons' in the absence of resource management by government.[3] Rather than looking to the state, voluntary programs rely instead to varying degrees on the willingness of non-governmental actors, including industry associations, environmental groups, and individual consumers to resist the temptation to exploit common-pool resources.

After situating this recent trend within a typology of environmental policy instruments, this chapter addresses two critical and related questions. First, how can we explain the trend away from coercive regulation in the 1990s? And, second, what do we know about the effectiveness of these new policy instruments? The chapter concludes with reflections on the broader implications of the shifting boundary between the state and civil society in the field of environmental protection.

A Typology of Environmental Policy Instruments

Among the plethora of competing typologies of policy instruments available in the literature, one of the most straightforward is that offered by Doern and Phidd, who argue that governments choose among five broad classes of policy tools: public enterprise, expenditure, regulation, exhortation, and inaction.[4] The majority of environmental policy reforms in recent years fall into the three categories of regulation, exhortation, and government inaction. Assuming equally ambitious policy objectives, these three can be placed along a continuum of state coerciveness from regulation to exhortation to government inaction, albeit with considerable variation within each category.[5]

These categories are, of course, not always as simple as they seem given the multidimensional nature of policy instruments. For instance, a question that arises within the context of this chapter is whether a voluntary program that is not mandated by regulation, but is driven primarily by the threat of regulation, should be considered a form of exhortation or of regulation. While a typology based on formal expressions of public policy (e.g., whether or not there is an actual law in place prohibiting or requiring certain actions) would situate such a program within the category of exhortation, Vedung emphasizes the 'dimension of state power' being exercised (coercion, financial inducements, or persuasion) and would thus consider the program to be inherently regulatory.[6] Consideration of both government's intentions and the motives of target populations is central to understanding the efficacy of any policy instrument, and will be a theme revisited throughout this chapter.[7]

For the purposes of this chapter, however, Doern and Phidd's typology, based on formal manifestations of policy, will be adopted for two reasons. First, different target populations may have different motives in responding to the same policy instrument. Thus, following Vedung's approach, the same voluntary program would have to be classified as regulatory with respect to some firms and persuasive with respect to others. While that is important to bear in mind in examining how different firms respond to the program, it does not offer a helpful shorthand for distinguishing between different programs. Second, the options available to government – and often to private actors as well – in response to non-compliance differ depending on the formal expression of policy. The application of sanctions such as fines and jail terms is available in response to regulation but not persuasion. Even if a voluntary program is driven by the threat of regulation, if that threat fails to motivate the desired actions, the state still must adopt actual regulations, in effect shifting to an alternative policy instrument. While the discussion here will thus adhere roughly to Doern and Phidd's categories based on the formal expressions of public policy, it should be recognized that there is considerable variation within each category along other dimensions, including government intent and target population motives.

Regulation

Regulation can be defined as formal rules of behaviour backed by sanctions legitimately available to the state. It thus represents a broad category of policies, from criminal laws to parking restrictions, with various forms of economic and social regulation in between. Of particular relevance to environmental policy is an important distinction between the traditional regulatory approach, often referred to as 'command and control,' where a group of actors or facilities is subjected to uniform process or performance standards, and more flexible, market-based forms of regulation, such as those predicated on discharge or user fees and marketable permits, which grant greater flexibility to the regulated interests. These market-based approaches offer the potential to achieve societal objectives with greater flexibility for those regulated and, correspondingly, lower cost than traditional regulation. However, they remain inherently regulatory in that they mandate behavioural change by polluters under threat of legal sanctions – whether by requiring that firms pay discharge fees, or by requiring discharge permits and allocating fewer of them than would exist in an unregulated market.

Although examples of market-based regulatory approaches do exist, most of the policy reforms adopted in recent years are in fact adaptations to more traditional regulation. For instance, there is renewed interest in cooperative approaches to enforcement, particularly via negotiated compliance agreements, as an alternative to legalistic enforcement.[8] As discussed by Dorcey and McDaniels in this volume, there has also been experimentation with a variety of models for input by both regulated interests and other stakeholders at the regulation-development stage. Finally, there have been reforms to reduce the coerciveness of regulatory mandates. Examples include planning requirements, which demand development, but not necessarily implementation, of pollution-prevention plans, and discharge reporting requirements, such as those underlying the U.S. Toxic Release Inventory and the Canadian National Pollutant Release Inventory, which mandate dissemination of information about toxic discharges but not necessarily the reduction of those discharges. Although this paper will focus primarily on voluntary approaches that fall within the categories of exhortation and government inaction, it is noteworthy that most of the regulatory reforms noted above also follow the trend toward reduced coercion, whether by relaxing regulators' expectations or increasing regulated interests' discretion with respect to compliance.

Exhortation

Although exhortation has been described as a category of policy instruments 'largely overlooked by the scholarly community,'[9] it has not been overlooked by the state in recent years. Hortatory approaches differ from regulation in that no formal statutory or regulatory requirements are applied. However, such approaches can vary significantly in degree of coerciveness, from those that rely exclusively on moral or intellectual appeals by the state to those driven by explicit threats of regulation. In the discussion that follows, I focus on three categories of state-sponsored voluntary programs: voluntary agreements, voluntary challenges, and eco-labels.[10]

Closest to regulation along a spectrum of coercion lie 'voluntary agreements' between business and government. Examples include agreement between the federal and Ontario governments and Dofasco[11] and the Dutch covenants discussed below. Voluntary agreements are characterized by strong expectations on the part of government that the parties to the agreements (typically industry) will comply, and such agreements are thus often accompanied by an explicit threat of traditional or market-based regulation should the voluntary approach fail. Voluntary agreements or codes are typically negotiated by government and the private sector, either an individual firm or an entire sector. Although most voluntary agreements take the form of non-binding 'gentlemen's agreements,' some have been entrenched in legally binding contracts. Such contracts can still be considered voluntary, however, in the sense that the parties must consent to assume negotiated obligations, in contrast to laws and regulations, which apply equally to all regardless of their consent.

In contrast to voluntary agreements, governmental efforts to persuade target groups to change their behaviour via 'voluntary challenges' typically involve less arm-twisting in the form of explicit threats of regulation or other punitive measures. Examples include the U.S. Environmental Protection Agency's 33/50 program and, in Canada, the ARET Challenge, the Canadian National Packaging Protocol, and the Voluntary Challenge and Registry for greenhouse gases. The central difference between voluntary agreements and voluntary challenges is that the latter represent an open-ended challenge that the audience is not committed to accept. In contrast, parties to voluntary agreements offer a commitment, if only an informal one, to live up to the terms of the agreement. Thus, EPA's 33/50 program called on any and all firms releasing seventeen specified toxic substances to reduce their discharges of those substances. Given the diversity of the target population typically affected, challenges tend to be less detailed, and there is accordingly less need to negotiate the details with the industries in question.[12] In practice, the requirements of participation in challenge programs tend to be very flexible. For instance, in both the 33/50 and ARET programs, participants were expected to *commit to make some* reductions of the listed substances, but they were not required in practice to meet any particular performance standard. Again, following from the number and diversity of target firms, announcements of voluntary challenge programs tend to emphasize who participates, rather than who does not. The appeal of participation in voluntary challenge programs thus may lie less in avoiding a threat of regulation than in seizing an opportunity for positive publicity.

Closely related to voluntary challenge programs, eco-labelling attempts to harness market forces by helping environmentally aware consumers identify products that are less harmful to the environment. They do so by licensing manufacturers of preferred products to display a certification symbol indicating their products' reduced burden on the environment. The primary inducement is thus recognition of a firm's environmental performance via certification of a product or process.[13] As with voluntary challenge programs, all firms within the relevant product or service sector are welcome to participate. However, in contrast to voluntary challenges, certification criteria for particular products tend to be quite specific and firms are required to comply with those criteria in order to maintain their certification. Since West Germany launched the first environmental labelling program, the 'Blue Angel,' in 1978, eco-labelling initiatives have emerged in more than two dozen other jurisdictions, including Canada, the European Union, and Scandinavia.

Government Inaction

The final category of policy instrument is for the state to choose not to intervene at all in private markets and civil society. However, the absence of government action need not imply that no one else is acting. Indeed, there has been a great deal of activity with respect to voluntary non-governmental initiatives in recent years. In many respects, non-governmental programs parallel the state-based voluntary programs described above, but with someone other than government doing the coercing or encouraging. Thus, the chemical industry's Responsible Care program can be viewed as a non-governmental version of the voluntary agreements discussed above. Similarly, non-governmental eco-labelling and product-certification programs, including those operated by Green Seal in the United States and the Forest Stewardship Council internationally, closely parallel governmental eco-labelling. The participants in non-governmental voluntary programs vary, from individual firms to sectoral trade associations, to non-partisan third parties such as the International Organization for Standardization, to environmental groups, with various permutations in between, including industry-environmentalist collaborations (e.g., McDonalds and the U.S. Environmental Defense Fund).[14]

The absence of governmental involvement does not mean that non-governmental programs are without coercion. The primary motive for self-regulation may still be the threat of government regulation. Moreover, participants in voluntary programs may be subject to rules, compliance audits, and sanctions, similar in at least some respects to those associated with regulation. For instance, the Canadian Chemical Producers Association requires that all its members participate in their Responsible Care program, audits their compliance, and has ejected one member for persistent non-compliance. This element of coercion by non-governmental actors has lead some to downplay the distinction between governmental and non-governmental programs.[15] However, a critical difference between state coercion and coercion by non-state actors lies in the fact that only the state has legitimate authority to coerce (subject of course to constitutional limitations). Thus, although firms have strong incentives to respond to consumer demand, one would not speak of firms being 'coerced' by their customers, since they choose which customers to cater to and how. Similarly, although the Canadian Chemical Producers' Association makes participation in its Responsible Care program a condition of membership, there is no requirement for a chemical company to belong to the CCPA, and some (particularly smaller firms) choose not to. However, when a government indicates that it expects all firms within a sector to comply with a voluntary code, that is likely to carry much greater weight given the punitive recourses to non-compliance, including the authority to levy fines and revoke business licences, uniquely available to the state.

Combined Policy Instruments

A typology of voluntary instruments would not be complete without noting the potential for combinations of different policy instruments.[16] At present, there is particular interest in combinations of regulation and voluntary programs.[17] One can conceive of regulatory and voluntary programs interacting in different ways, with different implications for environmental effectiveness.[18] Voluntary programs could support regulatory programs, for instance by encouraging adoption of environmental management systems that enhance internal operational controls. Indeed, it is noteworthy that one Canadian government department, Transport Canada, has sought certification to ISO 14001, a non-government standard for environmental management systems, in order to promote and confirm compliance with its own laws. In turn, regulations could shore up voluntary programs, by setting minimum performance standards to discourage free-riding, by promoting compliance through entrenchment of voluntary commitments in regulatory permits, or by facilitating the monitoring of progress under the voluntary program through regulatory discharge-reporting requirements.

On the other hand, regulation and voluntary programs may not always be complementary. For instance, it is conceivable that a voluntary program could undermine the effectiveness of regulation if a court excuses non-compliance on the grounds that adherence to a voluntary code constitutes 'due diligence.' Or, firms may decline to pursue certification of some of their facilities or products, lest that raise due-diligence expectations for other facilities of same company. Finally, to the extent that the threat of regulation of unknown stringency motivates participation in a voluntary program, the promulgation of a 'back-up' regulation could undermine some firms' inclinations to take more aggressive actions by clarifying just how far the government is willing to go.

Explaining Instrument Choice

The shift in recent years away from coercive regulation raises two related questions: how can we explain this trend, and what are the implications of these novel approaches for our ability to achieve policy objectives, especially protection of the environment? This section considers the first of those questions.

'Good Policy Motives'

Since a voluntary program will only be agreed to if all parties to the agreement perceive benefits to participation, it is pertinent to consider the theoretical benefits of voluntary approaches relative to regulation from the perspectives of both government and business. From *government*'s perspective, one oft-cited advantage of voluntary approaches is that they take advantage of business expertise with respect to what can be accomplished and how, and thus can incorporate better solutions to environmental problems. Indeed, a key rationale behind the Dutch 'environmental covenants' was the government's belief that it simply did not have the expertise to specify via regulation what industry should do to achieve long-term national environmental objectives. For the same reason, Georg has argued that voluntary agreements are particularly well suited to pollution prevention, which can only succeed by relying on industry's knowledge of what goes on inside its facilities.[19] It is noteworthy, however, that the same arguments can be made for negotiated performance-based regulation and market-based approaches as for a voluntary, non-regulatory approach.

Various arguments also have been made about the 'soft effects' of voluntary approaches.[20] For instance, many authors have stressed that voluntary agreements improve relations between business and government, and thus inculcate norms of shared responsibility in business.[21] In effect, this takes the arguments made by proponents of cooperative regulation one step further, to the complete withdrawal of regulation. Voluntary approaches may also be less costly than regulation from government's perspective because industry bears a greater share of the costs of monitoring and standards development.

From *business*'s perspective, one can suggest three reasons why a firm motivated by profits would voluntarily reduce its environmental impacts. First, there may be immediate financial benefits from reducing energy use or preventing losses of valuable reactants. A firm would have incentives to realize such benefits whether or not consumers or government demand improved environmental performance. However, information dissemination and technology transfer by the state may help firms recognize and take advantage of the full market potential of waste reductions and energy-efficiency improvements.[22]

Second, firms may be able to enhance competitiveness by responding to consumer demand, whether at home or abroad, for environmentally preferred products or a 'greener' corporate reputation.[23] Again, these incentives would exist regardless of public policy. However, government recognition of industry's voluntary efforts may enhance the credibility of a firm's own environmental claims with consumers.

The third type of business incentive for voluntary actions lies not in the marketplace, but with the state.[24] A firm may opt for additional voluntary measures above and beyond those promoted by market forces in order to forestall or avoid regulation, since in practice voluntary actions typically offer greater flexibility with respect to timing and control options. It is noteworthy that in this case the challenge for government is not merely to enhance existing market incentives, but to create incentives in the first place in the form of a credible threat of regulation. Therein lies the paradox of a voluntary approach: coercive government is often a necessary prerequisite for cooperation.[25]

Critics of voluntary approaches view this last mechanism with scepticism, however. Many have argued that government limits itself unnecessarily by pursuing only those measures to which industry consents. As Ayres and Braithwaite note, 'The very conditions that foster the evolution of cooperation are also the conditions that promote the evolution of capture and indeed corruption.'[26] Similarly, Rennings, Brockmann, and Bergmann have argued that 'once the government commits itself to a corporatist style of environmental policy, the other negotiating partner is granted a potential to delay and water down goals that should not be underestimated.'[27] While the state may well reduce its monitoring and enforcement costs when industry consents to change its behaviour voluntarily, the price of that consent may be relaxed expectations in terms of environmental performance. To return to the question of industry motives discussed above, a critical question when voluntary action is driven by the threat of regulation is thus whether the appeal of voluntarism from business's perspective lies merely in greater flexibility in terms of techniques and timing to achieve the same degree of control anticipated in regulations, or rather in relaxed performance expectations relative to regulation.

Heterogeneity within a sector can complicate matters further. While a subset of firms may well have incentives to voluntarily change their behaviour in response to demands by 'green consumers,' firms catering to 'brown consumers,' who are concerned primarily with price, will seek only to minimize their costs, including environmental control costs. While a voluntary program offering the reward of government recognition may encourage firms in the former category, it would not be expected to wield much influence over those in the latter category.

The voluntary nature of participation in business networks also raises the spectre of free-ridership, which occurs when firms either decline to participate in a voluntary program or participate but fail to adhere to their voluntary commitments. The temptation to free-ride can be great if a firm can gain the benefits of participation, be it the withdrawal of proposed regulations or an improved public image, simply by virtue of being in a participating sector, regardless of whether or not it changes its own behaviour. Free-riders are not only problematic because some fraction of firms fail to take desired actions to protect the environment, but because their failure to do so may undermine the commitment of those firms initially inclined to participate. Concerns about free-ridership have prompted some proponents of voluntary approaches to emphasize that voluntary agreements or codes are more likely to be effective if there is a relatively small number of partners or a stable, well-organized trade association, and if compliance costs are manageable (i.e., expectations are not too high) and evenly distributed across the sector.[28]

Critics of voluntary programs have also raised a number of concerns about democratic participation and accountability. Environmentalists argue that the purported ease with which voluntary agreements can be negotiated and implemented owes much to their operation beyond the procedural safeguards of administrative law, which reduces opportunities for participation and access to information by third parties.[29] Concerns have also been raised that there are insufficient opportunities for involvement by democratically elected legislatures when the executive relies on informal agreements and contracts rather than statutory authority to achieve its environmental objectives.[30]

Political Analysis of Instrument Choice

Implicit in the forgoing discussion is an assumption that policy-makers are motivated by 'good policy motives,' that is, they embrace voluntary approaches because they believe they will be effective in advancing collective policy objectives such as environmental protection and economic efficiency. However, even if one were to accept such an idealized image of policy-makers, in light of the competing arguments presented above it is not readily apparent that voluntary approaches represent the obvious 'good policy' choice. An alternative, political analysis of instrument choice accepts both that political actors may have motives other than the public interest and that even well-intentioned actors must make choices in the face of political, economic, and institutional constraints. As Baggott has observed, the popularity of cooperative approaches may reflect their political appeal rather than their administrative effectiveness.[31]

The potential for divergence between 'good policy' and 'good politics' lies in the obstacles to collective action that arise when a large number of people are jointly affected by changes in environmental quality.[32] While each member of the public benefits from improvements in the quality of the shared environment, in the absence of reassurances that others will act the same way, individuals may be reluctant to take action to protect shared resources, or even to take the time to inform themselves about threats to those resources. Although a healthy environment is in everyone's interest, it does not necessarily follow that individuals will take unilateral actions to protect the environment, for instance via green consumerism, nor that they will be well informed about actions being taken by either government or the private sector.

In this regard, it is relevant that public attention to the environment has been cyclical in recent decades, with peaks in 1969 and 1989.[33] Although in 1989 'the environment' was the most common response to the survey question, 'What is the most important problem facing Canada today,' by the mid-1990s, it was cited by only 1 or 2 per cent of respondents. The first and second peaks in the salience of environmental issues saw a flurry of new legislation in both North America and Europe, as politicians scrambled to deliver strong environmental programs in response to unprecedented public demand for action. The late 1980s and early 1990s also saw the emergence of a deluge of self-proclaimed 'green' products, as firms scrambled to respond to consumers' environmental interest. However, after public attention to environmental issues declined in both the early 1970s and the early 1990s, governments faced the challenge of delivering on their promises and implementing their ambitious new statutes in a very different political environment than that which gave rise to them. The green marketing movement had lost much of its momentum[34] and the business community that stood to bear the brunt of governments' promises was unwavering in its opposition to burdensome regulatory programs. In contrast, the public, though still supportive of environmental policies when prompted, was no longer paying attention.

This shift in the balance of support for and opposition to regulation is consistent with a shift from coercive regulation during periods of peak public attention to the environment to more cooperative voluntary programs when public attention wanes. Backed by overwhelming public demand during periods of heightened salience, politicians are quick to claim credit by depicting industry as the culprit to be controlled with strong regulations. But when public attention subsides, the state is more inclined to extend a cooperative hand in 'partnership.' Ironically, the result may be that governments are most inclined to pursue regulation when it is least needed – that is, when the attentive public is most likely to exert independent pressure on firms via green consumerism – and to embrace voluntary approaches when they are least likely to be effective in light of reduced market pressures.

As public attention to the environment has declined, it has been replaced, not coincidentally, by increased public attention to economic issues. Domestic insecurity about jobs is exacerbated by globalization and increasingly free trade. Indeed, it is concern about unemployment and economic competitiveness that have to a large degree replaced the environment in public-opinion polls and the governmental agenda. The re-emergence of economic concern not only accounts for the declining salience of environmental issues, but also strengthens the hand of industry in opposing environmental regulation. Governments may be increasingly reluctant to impose the costs of regulatory compliance on, and thus jeopardize the competitiveness of, domestic producers competing in international markets.

The trend toward less coercive policy instruments has also been supported by a significant shift in environmental policy discourse with the emergence of the 'sustainable development' paradigm in the late 1980s.[35] In asserting that continued economic development (typically taken to mean economic growth) and environmental conservation can coexist, the sustainable development paradigm has conveniently been read by many to mean that we can have it all. If business can profit from environmental protection, there is no need for coercive regulation; gentle encouragement and the dissemination of pollution-prevention information should suffice. The sustainable development paradigm has thus prompted politicians to focus on 'win-win' scenarios, clearly preferable to the traditional 'win-lose' politics of regulation. The problem is that this train of thought tends to overlook the many enterprises that are still profiting very nicely from environmentally unsustainable economic activities, and that have little immediate incentive to change their behaviour voluntarily.

Finally, the recent efforts by OECD countries to address their deficits by reducing expenditures have led in many cases to significant budget cuts to environment departments. This could enhance governments' interest in voluntary programs if bureaucrats and politicians perceive them to be capable of delivering the same environmental benefits as regulation, but at reduced administrative cost. However, less optimistic environment departments may also embrace voluntarism out of desperation, simply because they no longer have the resources to regulate.

The preceding discussion suggests two models of decision-making at opposite ends of a spectrum of human motivation, from public spiritedness to self-interest. According to the first model, state decision-makers are motivated by 'good policy motives' to protect the environment at least cost. This explanation bodes well for the efficacy of voluntary approaches, since well–intentioned government actors would not embrace voluntary approaches in the first place, nor continue to support them in the long run, if they do not prove to be effective. Moreover, their efforts would ideally be reinforced by an electorate that is well informed on environmental issues, and willing to play its part. On the other hand, the political explanation for instrument choice assumes that politicians seeking re-election will cater disproportionately to the interests of business, since the public that stands to benefit from environmental protection will tend to be rationally (in the Olsonian sense) uninformed and apathetic. Self-interested consumers would be expected to place few environmental demands on business.[36] This alternative, rational-choice model offers less sanguine predictions concerning the effectiveness of voluntary environmental policy instruments, implying that they are, in effect, adopted *because* they are less likely to be effective.

Policy Evaluation

The suggestion that cooperative approaches may be adopted for reasons that have little to do with environmental or other policy objectives (other than re-election) provides all the more reason to evaluate carefully the effectiveness of these new approaches to environmental protection. Given the variety of voluntary approaches that have been introduced in many countries in the last decade, the discussion that follows can at best provide a cursory overview of the burgeoning literature on voluntary approaches, supplemented by illustrative case studies.

A critical question in evaluating voluntary programs concerns the appropriate baseline against which to measure performance. While coercive regulatory programs tend to be measured against a yardstick of complete compliance and optimal economic efficiency, there is a tendency for proponents of voluntary programs to hail any accomplishments above the current baseline as a success. This standard may be quite appropriate if the voluntary program is the only realistic alternative to the status quo. However, to the extent that voluntary and regulatory programs are being considered substitutes, the relevant question is how they compare to each other in practice.[37]

One can, in fact, consider several different levels of analysis of environmental effectiveness.[38] The first, and simplest to achieve, is a measure of environmental or behavioural change relative to a reference year. A second, and more rigorous standard, is to ask to what degree the observed changes are in fact attributable to the program in question, acknowledging that actors' behaviour might have changed anyway in response to other factors, including market forces and other government policies. This standard necessitates development of a 'business-as-usual' baseline that would have prevailed in the absence of the voluntary program. Finally, the third and most difficult standard of analysis is to compare the chosen policy to alternative policies, a counterfactual–laden task that is even more challenging than establishing the 'business-as-usual' baseline and, as a result, seldom undertaken.

This section follows the typology of instruments introduced at the outset of the paper in considering in turn three categories of government-sponsored voluntary programs – voluntary agreements, voluntary challenges, and eco-labels – as well as non-governmental voluntary codes.

Voluntary Agreements

Voluntary agreements have grown dramatically in popularity in Europe since the mid-1980s.[39] An inventory of environmental agreements conducted by the European Commission in 1996 found 305 such agreements among the member countries, with roughly two-thirds equally divided between the Netherlands and Germany.[40]

The Dutch 'covenants' are arguably the best-known example of voluntary agreements. Reliance on negotiated covenants increased in the Netherlands after the first National Environmental Policy Plan in 1989 called for a more cooperative approach to environmental protection. The government typically negotiates with trade associations to identify measures to achieve objectives set by the national plan. Individual firms then sign on to the sectoral covenants via letters of declaration. To date, far-reaching agreements have been negotiated with eighteen sectors responsible for most industrial pollution in the Netherlands, though there are dozens of other covenants concerning energy efficiency and other environmental issues.[41]

Evaluation of the Dutch approach is complicated by considerable variation among covenants within the Netherlands.[42] To some degree, this variation reflects evolution of the approach. The early covenants in particular were criticized for exclusion of third parties and the elected legislature, unclear objectives, and inattention to monitoring. A 1995 study of 154 covenants, including 85 in the environmental field, by the Dutch auditor general concluded that a majority lacked sufficient safeguards to ensure effective implementation.[43] In two-thirds of the substantive covenants examined, the parties agreed only to 'strive to achieve' their obligations, not to actually achieve them, while deadlines were unclear in half the cases studied. Similarly, a study of voluntary agreements throughout Europe by the European Commission found that environmental groups participated in negotiation of only 20 per cent and labour in 7 per cent of agreements reviewed, that just two-thirds contained requirements for monitoring, that just over half contained any provisions concerning verification by public authorities, and only one in seven provided for public reporting of results.[44]

In response, more recent covenants place greater emphasis on clarity of commitments, monitoring requirements, and legal formality.[45] However, bipartite negotiation is still the norm and concerns remain about public access to the details of agreements and reports on performance.[46] Despite the considerable variation among covenants, two unique features of the Netherlands' approach warrant emphasis, particularly since they distinguish this approach from that used in other countries, including Canada, and thus may limit the applicability of lessons learned from the Dutch covenants to other voluntary programs that do not share those characteristics.

First, it is significant that negotiations take place within the context of national performance objectives. The government sets non-negotiable goals – percentage reductions in discharges, energy use, and so on – and then negotiates the means to achieve those goals with the target groups. The issue is thus 'how,' not 'what.' Glachant offers a compelling formal analysis of the importance of this distinction.[47] When collective performance objectives are previously established, government and industry have compatible objectives for negotiations: to find the most cost-effective means to achieve those goals (although, as Glachant notes, this might be achieved more efficiently through a system of marketable permits than via negotiation). However, when the goals themselves are negotiable, strategic behaviour and 'capture' by industry are serious threats.

A second distinctive feature, at least of more recent covenants, is that they are legally binding. Recent covenants tend to take the form of legally binding private contracts, with commitments in many cases also being incorporated in statute-based permits.[48] It is noteworthy, however, that the effort to recognize negotiated commitments in formal permits seems to have been motivated not only to strengthen enforcement of covenants, but also to protect bilaterally negotiated agreements from legal challenges by third parties, including environmental groups.[49]

The Dutch Ministry of the Environment believes that '[l]ong range covenants (5–10 years) which permit some flexibility over the nature and timing of implementation actions are proving more efficient and effective than direct regulation in many cases.'[50] A 1997 review of progress by the Netherlands government concluded that good progress was being made with respect to most national objectives for the year 2000, with the notable exceptions of emissions of nitrogen oxides and carbon dioxide.[51] It is, however, difficult to assess to what extent that progress is attributable to the covenants approach, as opposed to other concurrent policy reforms, including extension of the regulatory permit system to cover virtually all pollution sources, introduction of environmental taxes, and significantly enhanced regulatory enforcement.[52]

Negotiated voluntary agreements are also popular in Germany. However, many authors have been quite critical of their effectiveness in that country. Rennings and colleagues conclude that voluntary agreements concerning climate change and CFCs yielded only 'no-regrets' measures that firms would have had incentives to take in the absence of the agreements.[53] The European Environmental Agency was sceptical of the benefits of the cross-sectoral declaration on climate change, concluding that it 'runs the risk of achieving little more than an increase in the dissemination of information by the industry associations.'[54] Storey concluded that the agreement was actually *less* ambitious than the business-as-usual scenario.[55] Rennings and colleagues also noted that an agreement involving fifteen industrial sectors concerning end-of-life used automobiles was comparable to a regulatory proposal that had launched negotiations four years earlier, thus offering no additional environmental benefits to compensate for the delay.[56] A study of that agreement conducted for the European Commission stressed that a variety of exceptions negotiated by the industry are likely to limit its effectiveness and ultimately demand renegotiation.[57]

Interest in voluntary agreements in North America has lagged behind that in Western Europe by several years.[58] In Canada, pollution prevention 'memoranda of understanding' (MOUs) have been signed in recent years by the federal government with various industry sectoral organizations, including the Canadian Chemical Producers' Association, the Motor Vehicle Manufacturers Association, and the Ontario Fabricare Association.[59] In several respects, the Canadian MOUs appear vulnerable to the same critiques as many European voluntary agreements: they are not legally binding, few have measurable objectives, and most have been negotiated between only the relevant industry and federal and provincial governments.[60] In a manner reminiscent of the first generation of Dutch covenants, a draft MOU between the federal government and the Canadian Chemical Producers' Association commits members only to 'work to achieve' targets for benzene reductions, rather than to actually achieve them.

Voluntary Challenges

The two most prominent and promising voluntary challenge programs to date arguably are the U.S. EPA's 33/50 program and Canada's ARET program. In 1991, the U.S. EPA challenged the business community to voluntarily reduce its releases and transfers of seventeen high-priority chemicals by 33 per cent by the end of 1992, and 50 per cent by the end of 1995, dubbing the program '33/50.' Consistent with the voluntary challenges discussed above, requirements for participation were very flexible. A firm needed only to write to the EPA pledging some degree of reduction of its discharges of any of the 33/50 chemicals. In turn, the EPA would provide a certificate of appreciation and recognize 33/50 participants in its annual report on the Toxic Release Inventory (TRI).

Even though only 16 per cent of firms contacted by the EPA agreed to participate,[61] the goal of a 33 per cent reduction relative to the reference year was achieved one year early, by the end of 1991, and the 50 per cent reduction goal was also achieved early, by the end of 1994. That has prompted many, including the EPA, to cite the 33/50 program as an example of the potential of voluntary approaches. However, when one considers whether reductions were achieved relative to a 'business as usual' baseline, the benefits of the 33/50 program are not as clear. The first concern is that one-quarter of the reported reductions in total discharges and transfers were made by firms that chose not to participate in the program. A second problem lies in the fact that when the program was launched in 1991, the EPA chose 1988 as the reference year, since it was the most recent year for which discharge data were available. As a result, one-third or more of the reported 51 per cent reductions occurred before the program's inception.[62]

There is, however, circumstantial evidence that 33/50 encouraged firms to make reductions over and above what they would have made otherwise. Firms participating in the program reduced their discharges of the 33/50 chemicals by more than 49 per cent from 1990 to 1994, as compared to 30 per cent for non-participating firms.[63] This 19 per cent difference in reductions by participating firms constitutes only an 11 per cent reduction relative to the total releases and transfers of 33/50 chemicals in the 1990 reference year, considerably less than the 50 per cent typically claimed by the EPA. Even then, questions remain. Firms already inclined to make reductions of 33/50 chemicals, whether in response to negative publicity associated with mandatory reporting of discharges to the Toxic Release Inventory (TRI), market forces, or other regulatory requirements, simply may have been the ones to sign on for credit. This likelihood is supported by Arora and Cason's finding that the larger a firm's releases and transfers the more likely it was to participate in 33/50, since these are the firms that would be expected to respond most aggressively to the release of TRI data in the absence of the 33/50 program.[64] Thus, the fact that 33/50 participants made greater reductions than non-participants does not necessarily indicate that those reductions were prompted by the 33/50 program. It is also problematic that none of the analyses of the 33/50 program conducted to date has controlled for the effects of concurrent regulations.[65] In summary, it is not possible to conclude with any confidence what benefits the 33/50 program had, though it appears to have prompted discharge reductions of specified chemicals by less than 11 per cent.

The Canadian ARET (Accelerated Reduction/Elimin. tion of Toxics) Challenge, launched in 1994, is similar in many respects to the 33/50 program, though more ambitious. Industry is challenged to reduce discharges of 30 chemicals considered to be toxic, persistent, and bioaccumulative by 90 per cent by the year 2000, and of 87 others by 50 per cent by the same year. As is characteristic of a voluntary challenge program, there is no threat of penalties for failure to achieve those goals. Indeed, as in 33/50, firms that choose to participate are not required to commit to the full 90 and 50 per cent reductions. In contrast to 33/50, however, the ARET challenge emerged from extensive negotiations with stakeholders. It is noteworthy, though, that agreement on the voluntary challenge was reached by only industry and government, after Aboriginal, labour, and environmental group participants withdrew from the negotiations in protest over what they perceived as excessive reliance on voluntarism and insufficient emphasis on source reduction.[66]

Preliminary assessments of the impact of ARET based on the first three years of participant reports are promising. By the end of 1997, action plans had been received from 303 industrial and government facilities.[67] Discharges of ARET substances had already been reduced by 64 per cent relative to base-year levels. Reduction levels of the class of substances targeted for 50 per cent reductions had been surpassed four years ahead of schedule, with further reductions promised.

As with 33/50, however, the degree to which these reductions are attributable to the ARET program is unclear. The base-year problem is exacerbated in the ARET case, since each participating facility can pick its own base year anytime after 1987. This allows firms to claim credit toward the ARET program for discharge reductions they made as much as six years before the program's inception, and to strategically choose a year with particularly high discharges to maximize apparent reductions.[68] In fact, ARET program figures indicate that roughly half of the 64 per cent reductions claimed by the end of 1997 had been achieved before the program was launched.[69]

As with 33/50, there are questions about whether the reductions attributed to ARET are in fact voluntary, and if so, whether they are attributable to the program. No analysis has been done of the extent of regulatory overlap at the federal or provincial levels, though anecdotal evidence provides cause for concern that some fraction of the reported voluntary reductions are attributable to mandatory measures.[70] As with 33/50 and TRI, voluntary reductions may have been driven less by the positive publicity associated with the ARET challenge than by the negative publicity associated with public reporting of discharges of half of the ARET chemicals covered by Canada's National Pollutant Release Inventory (NPRI). Finally, the absence of any provisions for third-party verification of firms' own claims of discharge reductions is troubling, particularly for the half of ARET chemicals not covered by the regulatory NPRI program.[71]

Free-ridership is less problematic than in the 33/50 program. The ARET secretariat has claimed a participation rate of 70 per cent across eight sectors.[72] However, other measures reported by the program suggest a higher degree of free-riding. Although 162 firms and government organizations are participating in ARET, approximately 190 others that report discharges of ARET substances to the NPRI inventory have chosen not to participate.[73] Preliminary efforts to elicit further participation via letters to CEOs have not been encouraging.[74] In summary, although there clearly have been promising reductions of industrial discharges of some toxic substances in Canada in recent years, it is not clear to what degree that is attributable to ARET.

Eco-labelling

As with other voluntary programs, it is difficult to assess the impact of eco-labelling programs, which seek to reduce environmental impacts by encouraging consumers to shift their purchases to less environmentally harmful products within the same product category. Rigourous measurement of the environmental benefits of eco-labels would require data on the environmental burden posed by different products throughout their life cycle, as well as analysis of the impact of an eco-label on the market share of labelled and unlabelled products, controlling for other factors, such as manufacturers' own marketing strategies, that might also cause concurrent changes in consumption patterns.[75] A recent study by the OECD concluded that such an analysis is impracticable since data concerning the market impact of eco-labelling is difficult to obtain and, when it does exist, typically confidential to participating firms.[76]

The OECD found mixed anecdotal evidence of the efficacy of eco-labelling. On the one hand, some producers appear to be investing considerable sums to qualify for and obtain certification to display some eco-labels, suggesting that they perceive a potential market value. Weyerhauser's efforts to obtain certification for its products by the non-governmental Forest Stewardship Council provide a case in point.[77] In other cases, producers have invested considerable time and effort to oppose eco-labels that they fear could negatively affect their market share, again suggesting that they perceive the labels as having the potential to affect consumer demand. The OECD found the strongest evidence of eco-labelling impacts in a few product categories, such as paper and detergents, that have been emphasized by environmental group campaigns, and that have attained symbolic importance for environmentally-motivated consumers.[78] Greater impacts were also observed in Scandinavian countries, which exhibit a higher degree of green consumerism.

On the other hand, it is commonplace for eco-labelling programs to attract the vast majority of their licensees in three or four product categories, while a significant fraction of product guidelines attract no licensees at all.[79] Given the limited interest by both producers and consumers in the majority of eco-label product categories, the OECD study concluded overall that 'eco-labelled products have not had a significant impact on the market.'[80] A similar conclusion was drawn by a review of the Canadian Environmental Choice Program, and in a broader review of international programs by Salzman.[81]

In the absence of proprietary marketing data, I have examined the underlying premises of eco-labelling through case studies of the eco-labelling of paper products by government-sponsored agencies in Canada, the Nordic countries, and the European Union.[82] Each of three premises examined was violated to varying degrees in each jurisdiction. The first assumption tested is that certification criteria can be set at an optimal level to distinguish between products based on their impacts across the product life cycle.[83] A significant problem for eco-labelling bodies, though, is that environmentally laggard firms seek to water down certification standards in order to resist a loss of market share. In practice, to the extent that eco-labels have the potential to cause regional dislocations, politicians (and, in international programs, national governments) tend to intervene to protect their constituents, thus yielding weaker standards. Standards that are weaker than optimal not only fail to capture the full potential for environmental benefits, but may actually increase environmental impacts if consumers lulled by an eco-label fail to distinguish between products produced by genuine environmental leaders and by less progressive firms.

The second fundamental premise of eco-labelling programs is that manufacturers and retailers will apply for certification if their products are eligible. Evidence of boycotts of eco-labels by trade associations, in which even those qualified for certification decline to apply, suggests that this assumption often does not always hold.[84] Finally, eco-labelling assumes that consumers are in fact motivated by an altruistic willingness to assume their share of the costs to conserve and protect public goods.[85] However, consumer demand for 'green' products generally has declined in North America and Europe (though discrete instances of consumer pressure concerning particular products continue to surface), and in some cases consumers even seem to be less willing to buy such products than comparably priced alternatives because they perceive a decline in quality.[86]

Non-Governmental Codes

As noted above, non-governmental voluntary programs take a variety of forms, from actions by individual citizens or firms to national sectoral codes, to international cross-sectoral codes.[87] Based on a review of eighty-eight industry-sponsored voluntary initiatives world-wide, Börkey and Lévêsque conclude that industry initiatives typically 'make no provisions for monitoring, reporting or sanctions.'[88]

Among non-governmental voluntary programs, an important distinction can be drawn between those that establish actual environmental performance objectives and 'environmental management systems' (EMSs), which leave the setting of goals to individual participants and focus instead on processes to ensure those goals will be achieved. The latter appear to be the norm among industry-sponsored programs, although ENGO-sponsored product-certification schemes represent an important exception. The extent to which some in the business community have advocated process-oriented voluntary environmental management systems as an alternative (as opposed to a complement) to government regulation is ironic in light of those same industries' criticism of command-and-control regulation for focusing on means rather than ends.[89]

The chemical industry's Responsible Care program has been described as 'not only the single most advanced and sophisticated scheme of self-regulation in the environmental area, but one of the most developed and far-reaching schemes of self-regulation to be found anywhere in the western world.'[90] Responsible Care was conceived by the Canadian Chemical Producers Association (CCPA) in 1979, when it adopted a statement of principles with respect to the environment. The program has grown considerably in scope and sophistication since then, and now includes a statement of policy, guiding principles, six codes of practice collectively comprising more than 150 discrete elements, a compliance verification process, a national advisory panel, and a referral centre for chemical information.[91] Since 1991, participation in the Responsible Care program has been a condition of membership in the CCPA.

In the wake of the Bhopal tragedy in 1984, the Canadian Responsible Care approach was promoted internationally by the International Council of Chemical Associations. Responsible Care programs can now be found in forty-three countries,[92] accounting for more than 86 per cent of world chemical production.[93] The program has received numerous international awards, including recognition by the United Nations Environment Programme. Its success has also prompted other national trade associations to follow the example of the chemical industry in pursuing self-regulation via sectoral codes of practice.[94]

Several strengths of the program are immediately evident. The

Canadian version of Responsible Care demands that members commit to continuous improvement of their environmental performance, with a minimum baseline of compliance with all applicable laws in both letter and spirit. Firms are required to publicly report their discharges, and in so doing, CCPA members report on more substances than required by the NPRI regulations. Public involvement is promoted through a national advisory panel and local committees at the facility level, though the latter are encouraged rather than required.[95] In 1993 a compliance verification program was adopted, which requires that each facility periodically fund an audit by an external team comprising two industry and two non-industry representatives, one of which must be from the local community.[96]

In terms of results, the CCPA reports a 50 per cent reduction in total discharges from 1992 to 1996, including a 79 per cent reduction of carcinogens. Although program supporters tend to attribute this reduction entirely to Responsible Care,[97] no effort has been made to assess to what degree improvements are attributable to the government-sponsored ARET challenge or to concurrent regulations, including NPRI reporting requirements and the phase-out of CFCs.

Responsible Care is not without its critics. The nature of Responsible Care programs varies significantly among participating countries. Many have adopted only the cursory statement of principles, without the detailed codes of practice.[98] There is no requirement to make compliance audits public in the United States;[99] indeed the U.S. Chemical Manufacturers Association (CMA) leaves it to individual member companies to define what constitutes 'full implementation' for their own circumstances.[100] The code development and implementation process is generally less open in Europe than in North America.[101] And the Canadian trade association's external verification process appears to be the exception to the rule,[102] with participating companies in other countries effectively 'grading their own exam papers.'[103]

Even in Canada, arguably the strongest example of Responsible Care, membership in the CCPA, and thus participation in Responsible Care, is no guarantee of regulatory compliance. Firms have three years from the date they join the CCPA to achieve compliance with the elements of the Responsible Care program, and in any case, expulsion from the CCPA is by no means automatic when non-compliance with any element of Responsible Care (including regulatory compliance) is detected. Indeed, one of the largest penalties for regulatory non-compliance in Canadian history was levied against a then-member of both the CCPA and Responsible Care.[104] Moreover, the sanction of expulsion is a limited threat depending on the perceived benefits of membership in the trade association. Gunningham and Grabosky report that an association representing smaller chemical companies simply withdrew from the Australian chemical-industry group implementing Responsible Care when they perceived the requirements to be too onerous.[105]

Most importantly, at its core Responsible Care remains an environmental management system, which focuses on the means to achieve environmental objectives, rather than the objectives themselves. Whether or not it is effective as such, it can not be viewed as a substitute for goal-oriented public policy. For instance, the manufacturing code of practice commits participants to 'be aware of all effluents and emissions to the environment, monitor those for which it is necessary, and implement plans for their control when necessary' (sec. 2.5), to 'identify and evaluate on a regular basis potential safety, health and environmental hazards and associated risks, and work to minimize these risks' (sec. 2.1), and to 'provide information to employees, other people on site and interested people in the community about the materials handled, processes and equipment, related hazards and associated risks and the procedures for their control, and respond to community and public concerns' (sec. 2.4). It is striking that no specifics are provided about which substances should be monitored, what to report to the community, when control is 'necessary,' or how far firms should go in 'responding to community concerns.' The management focus of Responsible Care also sheds light on the significance of external compliance audits, in that the audit team focuses exclusively on a facility's compliance with the elements of the environmental management system, not on the facility's environmental performance per se, including its compliance with applicable laws.

Parallels in this regard between Responsible Care and the International Organization for Standardization's ISO 14001 environmental management system are worth noting. As with Responsible Care, third-party certification of compliance with ISO 14001 focuses on elements of the company's *management* system, including training programs, performance monitoring systems, management accountability, and record-keeping. Like Responsible Care, ISO 14001 leaves the choice of environmental performance objectives up to the firm, with the exception of a requirement that firms 'commit to comply' with legal requirements, though not that they must actually comply in practice.[106]

It is noteworthy that eight of the first nine ISO-certified firms in Mexico were in non-compliance with Mexican environmental laws.[107] It is also noteworthy that, in contrast to both public laws and the Responsible Care codes, the ISO 14001 standard is not even available to the public free of charge.

The factors that prompted the CCPA to create Responsible Care appear to be a combination of the three forces discussed above: opportunities to capture direct savings, opportunities to respond to (or, more accurately, avoid being penalized by) consumer pressure, and a desire to avoid regulation. The last is particularly noteworthy in light of the contrast noted above between goal-oriented regulation and Responsible Care as a management system. All accounts of the origins of Responsible Care, including the CCPA's own, emphasize a decline in the reputation of the chemical industry in the late 1970s and early 1980s. Particularly relevant was the fact that surveys sponsored by the industry found that members of the public did not distinguish between the reputation of individual firms and that of the chemical industry as a whole. Industry leaders concluded that they would stand together or fall together. A series of high-profile disasters within the chemical industry played a central role in both the decline in public confidence and the industry's response.[108] For instance, a chemical-plant accident in Seveso in Italy in 1979 prompted the CCPA's original statement of principles. Thereafter, the prominence of Love Canal (at Niagara Falls, New York) in the early 1980s provided the impetus for the first dozen members of CCPA to finally agree to sign the statement of principles in 1983. The subsequent Bhopal tragedy in 1984 was the catalyst for the spread of Responsible Care world-wide.[109]

While declining credibility of the industry with the public clearly played a central role, it is not readily apparent whether the CCPA members' concern was the immediate costs of declining customer confidence or the indirect costs should widespread public concern provoke government regulation. A recent account by the CCPA of the program's origins suggests that both were viewed as problematic.[110] Moffet and Bregha also conclude that the 'threat of regulation served as a major incentive for the development of Responsible Care.'[111] In particular, the authors argue that the Canadian government's efforts to revise its Environmental Contaminants Act in the mid-1980s prompted the CPPA to adopt its six codes of practice, based on principles developed by the federal government's own stakeholder advisory body.

Fifteen years later, the CCPA reports that its members have experienced direct financial benefits from Responsible Care through lower energy use, reduced losses of raw materials, lower insurance rates, better lending rates from financial institutions, and reduced legal liability, as well as indirect benefits in the form of less burdensome regulatory requirements.[112] For instance, the association boasts that the Responsible Care reporting scheme heavily influenced NPRI, thus saving 'CCPA member companies well over a million dollars in needless data collection costs compared with the alternative templates such as the [U.S.] TRI.'[113] Similarly, an author from the European chemical industry emphasizes German state governments' willingness to enter into 'voluntary agreements ... about deregulation' as a measure of success of the Responsible Care program.[114]

Effectiveness of Voluntary Programs: Summary

No claim can be made that the case studies summarized here are representative of the broad range of voluntary programs that have been initiated in recent years, though the emphasis on 'success stories' might be expected if anything to overstate the effectiveness of voluntary programs. Some patterns are evident in the forgoing discussion, however. First, reports of the environmental benefits of voluntary programs relative to reference years almost certainly exaggerate program effectiveness, since some fraction of improvements typically would be attributable to market incentives in the absence of the voluntary program and/or concurrent regulatory requirements. It is important to acknowledge that it is extremely difficult to control for overlapping effects in any program evaluation; certainly researchers evaluating the effectiveness of regulatory programs have demonstrated no greater inclination than those evaluating voluntary programs to rise to that challenge. However, overstatements concerning the ARET and 33/50 programs are less easily forgiven, since proponents have claimed reductions undertaken before the programs' inception or by non-participants, for which adjustments can quite easily be made.

Second, although policy evaluation is never straightforward, it is especially challenging with respect to voluntary programs for several reasons. Since participation is voluntary, claims of benefits beyond 'business as usual' can be viewed with less confidence since firms may be selectively signing on only to do what they would have done anyway. In addition, the measurement of rates of compliance and environmental benefits can be more difficult since voluntary agreements are seldom backed by legal mechanisms to compel disclosure. Finally, the potential for strategic behaviour presents a special problem for voluntary programs. To the extent that participation in voluntary programs is motivated by a desire to avoid regulations, firms have incentives to exaggerate the economic and environmental benefits of voluntary programs.

The one clear area of consensus among studies of voluntary approaches is that there has been too little attention to evaluation of either the economic or environmental benefits of voluntary programs.[115] In part, this reflects the novelty of voluntary approaches; it is simply too early to assess their effectiveness in many cases. However, it also reflects a pathology of unclear targets and inattention to the kinds of monitoring, verification, and public reporting needed to support program evaluation. While there is provision for independent compliance audits for at least some non-governmental codes, they typically confirm only that environmental management systems are in place to achieve firms' own environmental objectives, and not that those objectives (whatever they may be) are being achieved.

Returning to the theoretical arguments offered above, with respect to whether government co-optation by business has resulted in weaker standards in voluntary agreements, Rennings and colleagues conclude, based on their analysis of German agreements: 'For the government side the price for an agreement often consists in reducing the announced level of environmental protection ... [A]s the case studies in connection with this study bear out, a "decrease in the stringency of regulations" is always observable.'[116] The fact that voluntary agreements often lack clear targets, reporting requirements, and deadlines[117] lends support to this conclusion. Similarly, the fact that fewer than 40 of 587 action plans submitted to the Voluntary Challenge and Registry for climate change contained targets for greenhouse-gas emissions[118] and the extreme flexibility of the ARET program with respect to baselines are also indicative of compromises by government, since it is difficult to conceive of regulatory programs with such unclear requirements.

A critical issue underlying the effectiveness of voluntary approaches is the question of what motivates business to participate in the first place. Storey has argued that non-binding approaches are more likely to be effective (though it's questionable how much value they add) when the actions being promoted are already in firms' economic self-interest.[119] However, a strong threat of regulation and binding agreements is critical if that is not the case. There is reason to believe that the latter scenario is more common. A survey by the European Commission found that the potential to forgo or postpone regulation was cited as the most important benefit of voluntary environmental agreements by roughly two-thirds of industry respondents.[120] In Canada, KPMG reported that 95 per cent of firms cited compliance with regulations as one of the top five factors motivating their environmental improvements.[121] In contrast, factors such as cost savings, customer requirements, and public pressure were all cited by less than half of respondents, which suggests that government coercion, rather than market forces, remains the most important factor driving firms to improve their environmental performance.

In such cases, it is essential that government maintain a credible threat of regulation.[122] Ironically, however, the very fact of a government embracing voluntary approaches may undermine their effectiveness. As Rennings and colleagues note, 'A binding commitment giving priority to cooperative solutions can deprive the instrument of voluntary agreements of the basis for effective environmental policy improvements.'[123] Thus, Chang and colleagues attribute the failure of Ontario's voluntary agreement to promote municipal recycling programs through industry subsidies to relaxation of the threat of regulation after the election of a government openly committed to deregulation.[124]

The implication of the foregoing is that the rush by the state to embrace voluntary approaches to environmental protection is premature. When one probes beyond proponents' rhetoric, it becomes clear just how little is known about the benefits and costs of these programs. What evidence does exist is sometimes of questionable validity. Governments' premature enthusiasm for voluntary programs risks not only forgoing a potentially more effective choice of policy instrument, but also undermining the effectiveness of the voluntary program itself, by reducing the credibility of the threat of regulation often needed to motivate voluntary compliance. The answer to well-justified critiques of traditional command-and-control regulation is not to rush headlong to any one untested alternative, but to experiment with a variety of instruments, including improved regulation, tradeable permits, discharge fees, and voluntary programs, with a careful eye to program evaluation in each case. At a minimum, this evaluation demands that those designing voluntary programs include clearer targets, more effective mechanisms for public reporting, and independent verification of actual environmental performance (as opposed to verification of the presence of internal management systems).

Conclusion: Voluntarism and Governance

Earlier in the paper, a tension was noted between competing explanations for instrument choice that are predicated on public-spiritedness and narrow self-interest. The former assumes that government and, to a lesser degree, consumers are motivated by a desire to protect the shared environment, even if that involves personal costs (political or monetary). The latter assumes that politicians primarily motivated by a desire for re-election will respond preferentially to profit-driven industries that resist the costs of environmental protection, since the public at large will be vulnerable to obstacles to collective action. Reality, of course, undoubtedly lies between these two idealized extremes.

The critical task is to determine where one lies along this continuum in each case. On the one hand, the very existence of environmental groups, environmental laws, and green consumerism flies in the face of a rational-choice analysis. On the other hand, as Andrews cautions, voluntary approaches, 'while enjoying a resurgence in the 1990s, in fact represent the dominant approach throughout history. Self-regulation was the norm prior to the 1970s, and its failure was the reason we started regulating in the first place.'[125] Society's track record of managing common-pool resources on a large scale in the absence of government intervention has not been a stellar one. 'This history ... places a special burden on advocates of voluntary approaches to demonstrate how their proposals will in fact achieve equal or better results than government regulation.'[126]

A culture of encouragement, recognition, and reward is growing alongside, and to some degree replacing, that of shame and punishment associated with traditional regulation. This trend represents an important shift in environmental governance, with potentially significant implications not only for environmental protection, but also for democratic participation and accountability. As the role of civil society in environmental management is growing, the role of the state in environmental protection is changing in significant ways. Increasingly, the state can be seen pursuing its objectives much like a private actor. Thus, in negotiations leading to the voluntary ARET program, the Canadian federal government opted to play a role as merely another 'stakeholder.' Moreover, many voluntary agreements negotiated by European governments and industry have taken the form of contracts under civil law, with the state pursuing its objectives through private contractual agreements rather than public laws. Interestingly, at the same time non-governmental organizations are increasingly assuming governance functions traditionally conducted by the state, such as standard setting, compliance monitoring, and application of sanctions to their members.[127]

Encouragement for civil society to play a growing role in addressing the challenge of sustainability is laudable. The challenges we face are immense, and demand integration of questions of environmental sustainability into everyday decisions by both consumers and business. However, it is noteworthy that for most of the voluntary programs discussed in this chapter the state has been selective in inviting only the business community to participate in cooperative decision-making, a situation reminiscent of the closed business-government bargaining that characterized Canadian environmental policy in the 1970s.[128] Although voluntary programs may well improve the relationship between business and government,[129] that cooperation has often been achieved at the expense of openness and opportunities for more widespread participation.[130] Yet as Gunningham and Grabosky have argued, when the state opts to 'govern at a distance' via voluntary initiatives, it is all the more important that environmentalists and other third parties be in a position to step in as 'surrogate regulators' to defend the interests of a sympathetic but often distracted public.[131]

The growing popularity of voluntary programs also threatens, in some cases, the fundamental function of the state in setting public-policy objectives in the first place, even if the means to achieve them are left to industry. As it now stands, as business is being given increasing flexibility, even to set its own objectives and grade its own performance in the case of many environmental management systems, the role of both government and other non-governmental actors is being curtailed by the move to voluntarism. Given that the business community is the last place many would look for altruism, that trend represents a significant leap of faith.

NOTES

This chapter builds on work previously published by the author in 'Talking with the Donkey: Cooperative Approaches to Environmental Protection,' *Journal of Industrial Ecology* 2 (1999): 51–72.

1 European Commission, Communication from the Commission to the Council and the European Parliament on Environmental Agreements, COM(96) 561 (Brussels: European Commission, 1996).

2 I interpret the term 'civil society' to include business associations.
3 G. Hardin, 'The Tragedy of the Commons,' *Science*, 162 (1968): 1143–8; F. Lévêque, 'Externalities, Collective Goods and the Requirements of a State's Intervention in Pollution Abatement,' Fondazione Eni Enrico Mattei, Working paper 20.97, February 1997.
4 G.B. Doern and R.W. Phidd, *Canadian Public Policy: Ideas, Structure, Process*, 2nd ed. (Scarborough, ON: Nelson Canada, 1992).
5 Ibid.
6 Vedung identifies three categories of instruments – coercion, expenditure, and persuasion – which roughly correspond to Doern and Phidd's regulation, expenditure, and exhortation. E. Vedung, 'Policy Instruments: Typologies and Theories,' in M.-L. Bemelmans-Videc, R.C. Rist, and E. Vedung, eds, *Carrots, Sticks and Sermons: Policy Instruments and Their Evaluation* (New Brunswick, NJ: Transaction, 1998).
7 Vedung's emphasis on the dimension of state power could be further unpacked, to distinguish between the state's intentions (i.e., which dimension of power it intends to use) and target populations' perceptions (i.e., which dimension of power, if any, actually influences their behaviour in practice).
8 It is noteworthy, however, that studies of the effectiveness of cooperative vs. adversarial enforcement strategies are conflicting, with some scholars concluding that strict enforcement produces higher levels of compliance and others asserting that 'going by the book' is counterproductive and that flexible, cooperative enforcement is more effective. Commission for Environmental Cooperation, *Voluntary Measures to Ensure Environmental Compliance* (Montreal: CEC, 1998); J.T. Scholz, 'Cooperative Regulatory Enforcement and the Politics of Administrative Effectiveness,' *American Political Science Review* 85 (1991): 115–36; R.J. Burby and R.G. Paterson, 'Improving Compliance with State Environmental Regulations,' *Journal of Policy Analysis and Management* 12, no. 4 (1993): 753–72; K. Harrison, 'Is Cooperation the Answer? Canadian Environmental Enforcement in Comparative Context,' *Journal of Policy Analysis and Management* 14 (1995): 221–44.
9 Vedung, 'Policy Instruments,' 30.
10 As noted above, any simple taxonomy of hortatory programs is bound to be less than fully satisfying, since programs can vary along several dimensions. At least four dimensions are relevant here: government involvement or not; strength of the sponsor's expectations concerning compliance; motivations for compliance from the perspective of target populations (i.e., threat of regulation or promise of positive publicity); and unilateral vs negotiated origins. The OECD relies on the last of these as an organizing

principle, distinguishing between unilateral (non-governmental) programs, negotiated agreements, and public voluntary programs, which roughly correspond to my categories of government inaction (though unilateral industry programs would only constitute a subset of that category), voluntary agreements, and voluntary challenges. OECD, *Voluntary Approaches for Environmental Policy: An Assessment* (Paris: OECD, 1999).

11 L. Lukasik, 'The Dofasco Deal,' in R. Gibson, ed., *Voluntary Initiatives: The New Politics of Corporate Greening* (Peterborough, ON: Broadview, 1999).

12 The ARET challenge was negotiated by a multi-sectoral task force, while 33/50 was a unilateral initiative of the U.S. EPA. However, consistent with other voluntary challenges, the parties to the ARET negotiations then issued a broad challenge to all sectors, which even the parties to the negotiations were not bound to accept.

13 However, it is noteworthy that, as the Hickling report observes, the primary reason cited by firms that sought certification under the Canadian government's Environmental Choice Program guideline for paints, one of the program's few successful guidelines, was the desire to fend off a perceived threat of product regulation, rather than to impress consumers. Hickling Corporation, 'Evaluation of the Environmental Choice Program: Final Report,' prepared for Environment Canada, 29 November 1993.

14 The EDF-McDonalds collaboration is reviewed in C.L. Hartman and E.R. Stafford, 'Green Alliances: Building New Business with Environmental Groups,' *Long Range Planning* 30 (1997): 184–96.

15 See, e.g., J. Nash and J. Ehrenfeld, 'Codes of Environmental Management Practice: Assessing Their Potential as a Tool for Change,' *Annual Review of Energy and Environment* 22 (1997): 487–535.

16 N. Gunningham and P. Grabosky, *Smart Regulation: Designing Environmental Policy* (New York: Oxford, 1998).

17 Combinations with instruments other than regulation are also conceivable. For instance, public education programs promoting green consumerism would support environmental labelling programs, as would 'green procurement' policies.

18 K. Webb, 'Voluntary Initiatives and the Law,' in R. Gibson, ed., *Voluntary Initiatives: The New Politics of Corporate Greening* (Peterborough, ON: Broadview, 1999).

19 Susse Georg, 'Regulating the Environment: Changing from Constraint to Gentle Coercion,' *Business Strategy and the Environment* 3, no. 2 (1994): 11–20.

20 European Environment Agency, *Environmental Agreements: Environmental Effectiveness* (Copenhagen: EEA, 1997).

21 European Commission, Communication; Nash and Ehrenfeld, 'Codes.'

22 M. Storey, 'Demand-Side Efficiency: Voluntary Agreements with Industry,' Annex I Expert Group on the UN FCCC, supported by the OECD and IEA, December 1996.

23 R. Kerr, A. Cosbey, and R. Yachnin, *Beyond Regulation: Exporters and Voluntary Environmental Measures* (Winnipeg: IISD, 1998).

24 Pressures (and thus financial inducements) from shareholders, insurers, and lenders are also often cited as explanations for adoption of voluntary measures by business. However, each of these influences would follow from one or more of the reasons discussed above (i.e., cost savings, consumer pressure, and threat of regulation).

25 M. Glachant, 'The Setting of Voluntary Agreements between Industry and Government: Bargaining and Efficiency,' *Business Strategy and the Environment* 3, no. 2 (1994): 47; R.B. Gibson, 'Conclusion,' in R. Gibson, ed., *Voluntary Initiatives: The New Politics of Corporate Greening* (Peterborough, ON: Broadview, 1999), 244.

26 I. Ayres and J. Braithwaite, *Responsive Regulation: Transcending the Deregulation Debate* (New York: Oxford University Press, 1992), 55.

27 K. Rennings, L. Brockmann, and H. Bergmann, 'Voluntary Agreements in Environmental Protection: Experiences in Germany and Future Perspectives,' *Business Strategy and the Environment* 6 (1997): 253.

28 European Environment Agency, *Environmental Agreements*; Canada, Treasury Board Secretariat, Office of Consumer Affairs and Regulatory Affairs Division, *Voluntary Codes: A Guide for Their Development and Use* (Ottawa: Government of Canada, 1998).

29 Friends of the Earth, *A Superficial Attraction: The Voluntary Approach and Sustainable Development* (London: Friends of the Earth Trust, 1997).

30 K. Bastmeijer, 'The Covenant as an Instrument of Environmental Policy: A Case Study from the Netherlands,' in OECD, *Cooperative Approaches to Regulation* (Paris: OECD Public Management Occasional Papers no. 18, 1997); R. Baggott, 'By Voluntary Agreement: The Politics of Instrument Selection,' *Public Administration* 64 (1986): 51–67.

31 Baggott, 'By Voluntary Agreement,' 59.

32 M. Olson, *The Logic of Collective Action* (Cambridge, MA: Harvard University Press, 1965); Hardin, 'Tragedy.'

33 K. Harrison, *Passing the Buck: Federalism and Canadian Environmental Policy* (Vancouver: UBC Press, 1996).

34 J. Lawrence, 'Green Marketing Jobs Wilt at Big Companies,' *Advertising Age* 27 (1993): 54. A decline in green consumerism was also evident in surveys: the Yankelovich Monitor reported that Canadians' willingness to pay a 10%

premium for environmentally preferred products fell from 70% in 1990 to 55% in 1996 (data courtesy of Creative Research International).

35 G. Hoberg and K. Harrison, 'It's Not Easy Being Green: The Politics of Canada's Green Plan,' *Canadian Public Policy* 20 (1994): 119–37.

36 A distinction can be drawn, however, between the environmental attributes of a product, such as energy efficiency or contamination with pesticides, which are in a consumer's immediate self-interest to consider, and other, public-good attributes, such as the degree of air and water pollution released during manufacturing, which demand public-spirited behaviour from consumers.

37 Indeed, even when a voluntary program is considered a complement to a baseline regulation, it is still a substitute for more stringent regulation.

38 European Environment Agency, *Environmental Agreements*.

39 Ibid.

40 European Commission Directorate General III.01 – Industry, *Study on Voluntary Agreements Concluded between Industry and Public Authorities in the Field of the Environment. Final Report* (Brussels: European Commission, January 1997).

41 The Netherlands, Ministry of Housing, Spatial Planning and the Environment, *Towards a Sustainable Netherlands* (The Hague, 1997); D. Beardsley, T. Davies, and R. Hersh, 'Improving Environmental Management,' *Environment* 39, no. 7 (1997): 6–9, 28–35.

42 Bastmeijer, 'The Covenant.'

43 Algemene Rekenkamer, 'Convenanten van het Rijk met bedrijven en instellingen,' Tweede Kamer, vergaderjaar 1995–1996, 24 480, nos. 1–2, November 1995.

44 European Commission, *Study*.

45 Bastmeijer, 'The covenant'; H. Van Zijst, 'A Change in the Culture,' *Environmental Forum* May/June 1993: 12–17.

46 J.W. Biekart, 'Environmental Covenants between Government and Industry: A Dutch NGO's Experience,' *Review of European Community and International Environmental Law* 4, no. 2 (1995): 141–9; Van Zijst, 'Change in the culture.'

47 Glachant, 'Setting of voluntary agreements.'

48 Bastmeijer, 'The covenant'; Organisation for Economic Co-operation and Development, *Extended Producer Responsibility: Case Study on the Dutch Packaging Covenant* (Paris: OECD, 1997).

49 Van Zijst, 'Change in the culture,' 16; Biekart, 'Environmental covenants,' 144–5.

50 Ministry of Housing, *Towards a Sustainable Netherlands* 18.

51 Ibid.
52 The number of enforcement staff and prosecutions both rose by roughly one-third from 1991 to 1992 alone. Ibid.
53 Rennings, Brockmann, and Bergmann, 'Voluntary Agreements.'
54 European Environmental Agency, *Environmental Agreements*. A similar analysis is also offered by E. Jochem and W. Eichhammer, 'Voluntary Agreements as an Instrument to Substitute Regulating and Economic Instruments. Lessons from the German Voluntary Agreements on CO_2 Reduction,' in C. Carraro and F. Lévêsque, eds, *Voluntary Approaches in Environmental Policy* (Boston: Kluwer Academic Publishers, 1999).
55 Storey, 'Demand-Side Efficiency,' 28.
56 Rennings, Brockmann, and Bergmann, 'Voluntary Agreements.'
57 European Commission, *Study*, annex 5, 26–7.
58 On voluntary agreements in the U.S., see J. Mazurek, 'The Use of Unilateral Agreements in the United States: An Initial Survey,' ENV/EPOC/ GEEI(98)27/FINAL (Paris: OECD, 1998).
59 Commission for Environmental Cooperation, *Voluntary Measures*; K. Clark, *The Use of Voluntary Pollution Prevention Agreements in Canada: An Analysis and Commentary* (Toronto: Canadian Institute for Environmental Law and Policy, 1995).
60 Commission for Environmental Cooperation, *Voluntary Measures*. However, one pollution prevention agreement concerning mercury use in hospitals was co-signed by an environmental group, Pollution Probe.
61 J.C. (Terry) Davies and J. Mazurek, *Industry Incentives for Environmental Improvement: Evaluation of US Federal Initiatives* (Washington: Global Environmental Initiative, 1996).
62 K. Harrison, 'Talking with the Donkey: Cooperative Approaches to Environmental Protection,' *Journal of Industrial Ecology* 2 (1998): 51–72.
63 Ibid.
64 S. Arora and T.N. Cason. 'Why Do Firms Volunteer to Exceed Environmental Regulations? Understanding Participation in EPA's 33/50 Program,' *Land Economics* 72, no. 4 (1996): 413–32.
65 Arora and Cason note that two of the 33/50 chemicals were being phased out by regulations concerning ozone-depleting substances. The 1990 Clean Air Act Amendments also mandated further regulation of discharges of volatile organic compounds (in order to achieve ground-level ozone objectives) and hazardous air pollutants, both of which could be expected to cover all seventeen 33/50 chemicals. Ibid.
66 W. Leiss and Associates, 'Lessons Learned from ARET: A Qualitative Survey of Perceptions of Stakeholders, Final Report,' Working Paper Series

96–4, Environmental Policy Unit, School of Policy Studies, Queen's University, June 1996; D.L. Van Nijnatten, 'The Day the NGOS Walked Out,' *Alternatives* 24, no. 2 (1998): 10–15

67 ARET, *Environmental Leaders 3: Voluntary Action on Toxic Substances* (Ottawa: ARET, 1999).

68 G. Gallon, 'Accuracy Is Optional in Reporting Voluntary Success,' *Alternatives* 24 (1998): 12.

69 ARET reports total discharges of 37.6 tonnes in participants' various base years, 25.8 tonnes in 1993, and 13.5 tonnes in 1997. Thus, at least 11.8 of the 24.1 tonnes of reductions were achieved before the launch of the program in early 1994. ARET, *Environmental Leaders 3.*

70 Gallon notes that the 90% reduction in sulfur dioxide emissions claimed by INCO's Sudbury smelter under the ARET program were in fact legally mandated. Gallon, 'Accuracy Optional.'

71 Leiss and Associates, 'Lessons Learned.'

72 ARET, *Environmental Leaders 2: Update* (Ottawa: Ottawa, 1998).

73 This lower figure presumably understates the total number of non-participants, since about half of ARET chemicals are not reported to NPRI. Ibid.

74 In July 1997, the ARET program sent letters to the CEOs or presidents of 20 of the largest emitting firms among the 190 non-participants identified. However, as of 1999, only two had agreed to join the program, though five others had committed to do so. ARET, *Environmental Leaders 3.*

75 One would also need to investigate the impact of the eco-label on total consumption to rule out the possibility that the presence of an eco-label could invite a net increase in 'guilt-free' product purchases, which might outweigh the environmental benefits of a shift to less harmful products.

76 Organisation for Economic Co-operation and Development, *Eco-Labelling: Actual Effects of Selected Programmes*, ECDE/GD(97)105 (Paris: OECD, 1997), 5.

77 However, it is unlikely that all, or even most, of the environmental improvements that may be achieved by Weyerhauser can be attributed to the ecolabel itself, since a company that chooses to pursue certification presumably has strong incentives to cater to consumer demand for more sustainable environmental practices even in the absence of certification.

78 OECD, *Eco-Labelling.*

79 Organisation for Economic Co-operation and Development, *Environmental Labelling in OECD Countries* (Paris: OECD, 1991).

80 OECD, *Eco-Labelling* 67.

81 Hickling Corp., *Evaluation*; J. Salzman, 'Informing the Green Consumer:

The Debate over the Use and Abuse of Environmental Labels,' *Journal of Industrial Ecology* 1 (1997): 11–21.

82 K. Harrison, 'Racing to the Top or Bottom? Industry Resistance to Ecolabelling of Paper Products in Three Jurisdictions,' *Environmental Politics* 8 (1999): 110–36.

83 Standard setting for eco-labels is normally an optimization exercise, in which the potential environmental benefits of stringent certification criteria must be balanced against a reduction in consumer demand associated with a price increase to achieve those environmental benefits.

84 See also H.U. De Haes, 'Slow Progress in Ecolabelling: Technical or Institutional Impediments,' *Journal of Industrial Ecology* 1 (1997): 4–6.

85 OECD, *Environmental Labelling* 11.

86 Scott Canada sells a brand of toilet paper in Eastern Canada that is made from 100% recycled fibre. However, the company has declined to label the product accordingly because it believes that consumers will be less willing to purchase it. Harrison, 'Racing to the Top or Bottom?'; United Nations Environment Programme, *Voluntary Industry Codes of Conduct for the Environment* Technical Report no. 40 (Paris: UNEP Industry and Environment, 1998).

87 UNEP, *Voluntary Industry Codes of Conduct*.

88 P. Börkey and F. Lévêsque, *Voluntary Approaches for Environmental Protection in the European Union* (Paris: OECD, 1998).

89 Davies and Mazurek, *Industry Incentives*.

90 Gunningham and Grabosky, *Smart Regulation,* 160.

91 Codes of practice have been developed for community awareness and emergency response, research and development, manufacturing, transportation, distribution, and hazardous-waste management.

92 Industry Canada, *The Power of Partnerships: Industry and Government Working Together for Economic Growth and a Cleaner Environment* (Ottawa: Industry Canada, 1998).

93 F. Druckrey, 'How to Make Business Ethics Operational: Responsible Care – An Example of Successful Self-Regulation?' *Journal of Business Ethics* 17 (1998): 979–85.

94 For examples, see Kerr, Cosbey, and Yachnin, *Beyond Regulation*.

95 Moreover, Nash and Ehrenfeld report that local advisory committees 'only rarely' include ENGO representatives. 'Codes,' 502.

96 Curiously, CCPA's web page refers to a '*three-member* compliance verification team consist[ing] of two chemical industry representatives and one non-industry representative,' with *participation of* 'one local community representative selected via the company's community dialogue process' (emphasis added.)

97 Industry Canada, *The Power of Partnerships*.

98 By way of support, Druckrey offers only that 'more than half' of participating national associations are collecting performance data. 'How to
Make Business Ethics Operational.'
99 Nash and Ehrenfeld, 'Codes.'
100 J. Mazurek, 'The Use of Unilateral Agreements in the United States: The
Responsible Care Initiative,' ENV/EPOC/GEEI(98)25/FINAL (Paris:
OECD, 1998).
101 R. Tapper, 'Voluntary Agreements for Environmental Performance
Improvement: Perspectives on the Chemical Industry's Responsible Care
Program,' Business Strategy and the Environment 6 (1997): 287–92.
102 Ibid.
103 Gunningham and Grabosky, Smart Regulation, 167.
104 J. Moffet and F. Bregha, 'The Canadian Chemical Producers' Association's
Responsible Care Program,' in K. Webb and D. Cohen, eds, Voluntary
Codes: Private Governance, the Public Interest and Innovation (Ottawa: Carlton
University, forthcoming).
105 Gunningham and Grabosky, Smart Regulation, 166.
106 Commission for Environmental Cooperation, Voluntary Measures, 70.
107 Ibid.
108 Moffet and Bregha, 'Responsible Care.'
109 Nash and Ehrenfeld, 'Codes.'
110 The CCPA noted: 'Leading thinkers in the Canadian chemical industry
[believed] that the survival of the industry was very much in jeopardy.
Public outrage over the health and ecological impacts of incidents and
chronic problems associated with the life cycle of chemicals was growing
and coalescing into calls for restrictive regulation and curtailment of the
development of the industry and its products. This also translated into
insurance and financing problems, community nervousness, higher inci-
dent response costs, diversion of management time to crisis control and
erosion of employee, customer and shareholder confidence in the industry.' Canadian Chemical Producers Association, 'Does Responsible Care
Pay? ... A Primer on the Unexpected Benefits of the Initiative.'
www.ccpa.ca.
111 Moffet and Bregha, 'Responsible Care.'
112 CCPA, 'Does Responsible Care Pay?'
113 The CCPA also points to expedited permitting in Quebec, and the federal
government's willingness to 'prune the chlorine tree rather than cutting it
down.' Ibid.
114 Druckrey, 'How to Make Business Ethics Operational.'
115 Storey, 'Demand-Side Efficiency'; Davies and Mazurek, Industry Incentives;
United States National Research Council, Fostering Industry-Initiated Envi-

ronmental Protection Efforts (Washington: National Academy Press, 1997); D. Beardsley, *Incentives for Environmental Improvement: An Assessment of Selected Innovative Programs in the States and Europe* (Washington: Global Environmental Management Initiative, 1996); European Environment Agency, *Environmental Agreements*; OECD, *Voluntary Approaches*.

116 Rennings, Brockmann, and Bergmann, 'Voluntary Agreements,' 247.

117 European Environment Agency, *Environmental Agreements*.

118 R. Hornung, 'The VCR Is Broken,' in R. Gibson, ed., *Voluntary Initiatives: The New Politics of Corporate Greening* (Peterborough, ON: Broadview, 1999).

119 Storey, 'Demand Side Efficiency.'

120 European Commission, *Study*.

121 KPMG, *Canadian Environmental Management Survey* (Toronto: KPMG, 1994).

122 Glachant, 'Setting Voluntary Agreements'; K. Segerson and T.J. Miceli, 'Voluntary Approaches to Environmental Protection: The Role of Legislative Threats,' in C. Carraro and F. Lévêsque, eds, *Voluntary Approaches in Environmental Policy* (Boston: Kluwer Academic Publishers, 1999).

123 Rennings, Brockmann, and Bergmann, 'Voluntary Agreements,' 253.

124 E. Chang, D. MacDonald, and J. Wolfson, 'Who Killed CIPSI?' *Alternatives* 24, no. 2 (1998): 21–5.

125 R.N.L. Andrews, 'Environmental Regulation and Business "Self-Regulation,"' *Policy Sciences* 31 (1998): 179.

126 Ibid.

127 I am indebted to Bruce Doern for this observation.

128 A. Thompson, *Canadian Environmental Regulation* (Vancouver: Westwater Research Centre, UBC, 1980); G. Hoberg, 'Environmental Policy: Alternative Styles,' in M. Atkinson, ed., *Governing Canada: Institutions and Public Policy* (Toronto: Harcourt Brace Jovanovich, 1993).

129 Beardsley, *Incentives for Environmental Improvement*; European Environment Agency, *Environmental Agreements*; Commission for Environmental Cooperation, *Voluntary Measures*.

130 Addressing this concern may not be a simple matter of adding chairs around the bargaining table, since participants in at least some programs stress that agreement was facilitated by the exclusion of environmental groups (Beardsley, *Incentives for Environmental Improvement*, 13; European Commission, *Study*, annex 5, 31). Agreement was also achieved in the ARET case only after labour, environmentalists, and First Nations withdrew.

131 Gunningham and Grabosky, *Smart Regulation*. On this point, see also Ayres and Braithwaite, *Responsive Regulation*.

7. Great Expectations, Mixed Results: Trends in Citizen Involvement in Canadian Environmental Governance

Anthony H.J. Dorcey and Timothy McDaniels

The trend toward greater citizen involvement (CI) is beyond doubt one of the most influential and yet least well-defined aspects of environmental decision-making in Canada and other countries. How a nation involves its citizens in defining, structuring, and analysing key environmental questions can have a major influence on what is decided. The emergence of this trend is demonstrated by the proliferation of diverse CI efforts in environmental governance processes around the world. Its growing importance is underscored by recent recommendations for greater CI in environmental policy and sustainability choices, such as those by Canada's National Round Table on the Environment and the Economy,[1] two prestigious advisory panels in the United States,[2] and the World Bank.[3]

At the same time, recommendations for greater CI are not without controversy. For example, responses to the U.S. advisory panels' recommendations for greater CI in managing environmental risks have ranged from wholehearted endorsement to deep scepticism. Such a range in responses is understandable. On the one hand, it is clear that policy for environmental and health risk management involves public resources and public values, so it is easy to argue that judgments by the public should be used to help guide such decisions. On the other hand, all concerned parties would agree that risk-management decisions are enormously complex, replete with technical uncertainties and perplexing value trade-offs. Making and implementing wise policy choices is difficult, even for those who have specialized in risk-management efforts for decades. How then could members of the interested lay public hope to understand and play a meaningful role in making such complex, high-stakes choices? Given the experience with adversarial politics and the high costs associated with CI processes, when if at all should the public be involved? How can CI best be structured and conducted to meaningfully integrate deliberation and analysis as a basis for public policy? While questions like these have been the subject of fundamental debate and controversy for thousands of years, the biophysical, technological, socio-economic, and political–institutional context of the late twentieth century is novel.

Both the significance and diversity of CI make it difficult to treat comprehensively as a single trend, or to address completely the range of issues it raises. Further, the topic is characterized by widely differing ideological, disciplinary, and academic/practitioner perspectives, distributed among diverse literatures, and confounded by limited and often inconclusive and contradictory empirical research. We have therefore chosen to view the topic in terms of several selected trends that represent slices of a huge and complex field, focusing on Canadian experiences in the context of the North American literature.[4]

The organization of this chapter reflects our desire to consider CI in terms of several different sub-trends. Each section is approached in varying ways appropriate to the particular sub-trend being examined while cumulatively and selectively building an overall perspective on CI trends. The first section defines CI in environmental governance and introduces a set of important concepts and typologies for examining trends within CI. It draws on North American literature and reveals the scope for immense differences in views on the trends that are discussed in following sections.

Section 2 highlights trends in the evolution of CI activities in Canada, focusing particularly on British Columbia, over the last three decades. This regional perspective illustrates how CI has evolved, waxed, and waned in its role amidst the changing politics of one part of the country where there has been a high degree of experimentation. It concludes that there have been two major bursts of innovation in CI associated with the periods of heightened environmental concerns in the early 1970s and again in the early 1990s. Further, there is an underlying longer-term trend toward not only greater utilization of CI but potentially more fundamental transformation of the environmental governance system.

Section 3 examines in more detail the trends in CI approaches and techniques employed in British Columbia and Canada during the second burst of innovation. It focuses on two key aspects: the growing use of negotiation-based techniques, including negotiation, facilitation, and mediation, and the proliferation of approaches to CI in environmental governance utilizing these techniques, such as co-management and partnerships. Highlighted is the emergence of a remarkably interdisciplinary literature with shared themes that is moving the discussion and practice of CI toward a potential transformation of environmental governance.

Section 4 considers this transformative potential more specifically and critically. Two extremes of current practice on a continuum running from maximal to minimal stakeholder control of CI activities are assessed and potential middle-ground approaches are explored. At one extreme are approaches to CI that place control over the process design and management entirely in the hands of the stakeholders, while at the other extreme control is entirely in the hands of those experts designing and managing the process. We propose middle-ground approaches, drawing on the literatures relating to structured, progressive, contingent, and adaptive decision-making, giving particular attention to the key design and management functions of the sponsors and conductors of the CI process.

Section 5 briefly reviews four recent evaluations of CI in order to illustrate the theoretical and empirical strengths and weaknesses of different types of assessments. Attention is focused on the critical need for clarity about the goals of CI and on the challenges of specifying them and measuring their achievement in practice.

The concluding section suggests a strategy for more effectively learning while implementing the middle-ground approaches we have explored. It indicates our views on future trends and research issues that will become increasingly important for CI.

1. Defining CI and Its Objectives

Citizen involvement (CI) has been defined in many different ways. For the purposes of this chapter we have defined it broadly as processes for the involvement of citizens in advising and making decisions on matters under government authority that augment or supplant decision-making through established channels of representative government.

A potential source of confusion in analysing CI trends is that different processes or writers may use the words 'public' or 'civic' or 'community' or 'stakeholder' instead of 'citizen,' and 'participation' or 'engagement' or 'consultation' in place of 'involvement.' Sometimes these terms are used synonymously, other times there are significant differences in meaning. For example, in certain instances 'stakeholder involvement' is differentiated from 'citizen involvement,' by limiting the former to only those who have a specific interest in the issue as opposed to being generally interested as citizens (e.g., the effected landowners versus all voters in the jurisdiction). In other situations, the term 'stakeholder' may be used to identify the non-governmental interests and imply that the participants represent discrete constituencies. On yet other occasions, 'participation' is distinguished from 'involvement' or 'engagement' as being somehow more passive (e.g., citizens being merely informed versus actively contributing to or making decisions). Commonly, 'consultation' is differentiated from 'involvement' as being a purely advisory process, as opposed to providing for direct decision-making. In this chapter we use each of these terms as they are relevant to the particular CI process or literature being discussed, and wherever it is important we explicitly recognize specific differences in the intent of the users.

Governance is the larger context for considering CI and is broadly conceived to be the interrelated set of processes within which individuals in varied roles make decisions about the environment. Potentially these include roles as varied as voter in elections and referenda, elected representative, political activist, buyer and seller in markets, volunteer producer, petitioner in the courts, or participant in government or business processes. *Environmental governance* is that subset of processes relating to decision-making with respect to the biophysical environment. As will be seen, one of the notable current trends is that CI in environmental decision-making has increasingly been viewed in the larger governance-system context, under the rubric of sustainability, with its ecological, socio-economic, and institutional dimensions.

In a manner reflecting the differing theoretical and practical perspectives, many varied taxonomies of CI have been employed to organize investigation of this vast and complex field. Three common types derive from focusing on (1) democratic theory, (2) power relationships, and (3) tools. For example, Beierle describes how differing views on the nature of democracy can lead to different views on the role of CI in democratic process:

A *managerial* perspective entrusts elected representatives and their appointed administrators with identifying and pursuing the common good.[5] While knowledge of public preferences is vital to a managerial approach, the direct involvement of the public in decision-making is seen as a threat to the common good because it opens the door to self-interested strategic behavior. A *pluralist* perspective views government, not as a manager of the public will, but as an arbitrator among various organized interest groups. In pluralism, there is no objective 'common good' but a relative common good arising out of the free deliberation and negotiation among organized interest groups.[6] The *popular* perspective calls for the direct participation of citizens, rather than their representatives, in making policy. Popular democratic theory stresses the importance of direct representation in instilling democratic values in citizens and strengthening the body politic.[7]

The power perspective is well illustrated in the seminal paper by Sherry Arnstein that provides a taxonomy for CI based on the decision-making role of the participants within the process. At the bottom rung of her public-involvement ladder, the interested public is only *informed of* policy issues; at the top rung, the interested public *makes* the decision (see figure 7.1).[8] Drawing on her experiences in the United States as Chief Advisor on Citizen Participation for HUD's Model Cities Administration during the second half of the sixties, Arnstein was concerned that the 'heated controversy over "citizen participation," "citizen control," and "maximum feasible involvement of the poor," has been waged largely in terms of exacerbated rhetoric and misleading euphemism.'[9] For her, 'citizen participation is a categorical term for citizen power. It is the redistribution of power that enables the have-not citizens, presently excluded from the political and economic processes, to be deliberately included in the future. It is the strategy by which the have-nots join in determining how information is shared, goals and policies are set, tax resources are allocated, programs are operated, and benefits like contracts and patronage are parceled out. In short, it is the means by which they can induce significant social reform which enables them to share in the benefits of the affluent society.'[10] For Arnstein, citizen participation is citizen empowerment and the ladder is her typology for differentiating non-participation and tokenism from meaningful citizen power. Thirty years later, controversy about the terminology of citizen participation and its real intent continues and Arnstein's ladder and adaptations of it are still widely used to indicate the extent to which citizens are empowered to decide.[11]

The tools perspective is commonly found in the numerous manuals on citizen involvement. In these, the focus is on the approaches and techniques that can be used for conducting CI and on where and how

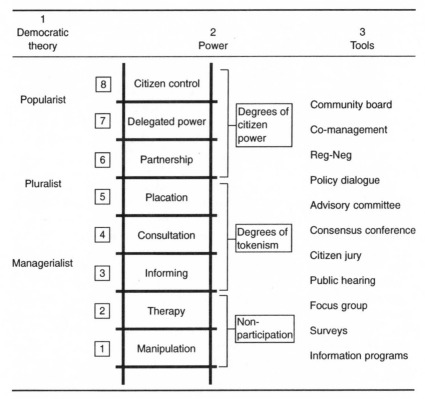

Figure 7.1 Three perspectives for structuring Citizen Involvement

they might be used in the process. In figure 7.1 we list some of the key approaches and techniques that are usually discussed in such typologies. The list is ever growing and the development of variants results in different names. For example, another common typology would include arbitration, mediation, facilitation, and negotiation.

We have arrayed the three perspectives beside each other in figure 7.1 in order to show their potential interrelationships. While there may appear to be some broad correlations, mapping across the perspectives should be done with care, as multiple combinations are possible. One complicating factor is that a CI program may well employ a wide variety of tools either at the same time or at different stages in the program. For example, a popularist approach might start with an information program and surveys before going on to add consensus processes (i.e., the combination and sequence of tools used is critical to understanding use of CI).

A second complication is the differences between use in principle and in practice. For example, it should not be assumed that the managerialist perspective will only be associated with the lower rungs of Arnstein's ladder and with the use of tools such as information programs. A CI program may well be using tools higher up the array, such as negotiation, in a consultation process while the intent of the sponsors remains nonetheless managerial (i.e., the true intent of the sponsor is crucial to understanding use of CI).

Differing normative perspectives, complications associated with varying typologies, and practical difficulties in undertaking empirical assessments present major challenges to the evaluation of CI programs and approaches. Any evaluation needs to be explicit about the viewpoint being taken and the specific objectives that provide the bases for its evaluation. Four viewpoints from which evaluation could be conducted are the sponsor of the CI program, the citizens or groups directly involved, the larger society, and external analysts.[12] Not only will goals and objectives likely vary between these four groupings, they will also probably vary among the constituent members of each (e.g., while the environmental NGOs want a popularist approach, the developers prefer a managerialist approach).

Goals and objectives for CI could focus on either the process or desired outcomes. Process goals relate to who is involved, when, and how, whereas outcome goals relate to the desired consequences. Process-oriented goals are well exemplified by the ten Guiding Principles of Consensus Processes developed by the Round Tables of Canada through a consensus process (table 7.1). In contrast, Beierle has proposed a set of six outcome-oriented social goals by focusing on the problems that CI is intended to fix:

1 Educating and informing the public.
2 Incorporating public values into decision-making.
3 Improving the substantive quality of decisions.
4 Increasing trust in institutions.
5 Reducing conflict.
6 Achieving cost-effectiveness.[13]

As can readily be seen, process and outcome goals are often expressed

TABLE 7.1
Guiding Principles of Consensus Processes

1. **Purpose driven:** People need a reason to participate in the process.
2. **Inclusive not exclusive:** All parties with a significant interest in the issue should be involved in the consensus process.
3. **Voluntary participation:** The parties who are affected or interested participate voluntarily.
4. **Self design:** The parties design the consensus process.
5. **Flexibility:** Flexibility should be designed into the process.
6. **Equal opportunity:** All parties must have equal access to relevant information and the opportunity to participate effectively throughout the process.
7. **Respect for diverse interests:** Acceptance of the diverse values, interests, and knowledge of the parties involved in the consensus process is essential.
8. **Accountability:** The parties are accountable both to their constituencies, and to the process that they have agreed to establish.
9. **Time limits:** Realistic deadlines are necessary throughout the process.
10. **Implementation:** Commitment to implementation and effective monitoring are essential parts of any agreement.

Source: National Round Table on the Environment and the Economy (1993)

in similar ways even though their concerns are different. Implicitly, process goals are frequently seen as means for achieving ends; for example, making the process inclusive not exclusive (principle 2 in table 7.1) contributes to reducing conflict. Comprehensive though the Round Tables' and Beierle's goals may be, some other goals could also be identified from various viewpoints (e.g., while some of the goals might be related to empowerment, it is not readily obvious how, if at all, this is to be considered).

Beyond the complexities in specifying the goals and objectives to be used in an evaluation of CI are immense practical difficulties in undertaking empirical assessments of the extent to which they are achieved. It is difficult to design and implement appropriate methods and instruments for assessing CI for a particular decision. Also the immense differences among the governance contexts within which decisions are made create major challenges in undertaking assessments of the use of CI. Not surprisingly, Beierle concludes that 'the state of evaluation still resembles one researcher's 1983 description: "the participation concept is complex and value laden; there are no widely held criteria for judging success and failure; there are no agreed-upon evaluation methods; and there are few reliable measurement tools."'[14] Given the infant state of the assessment art and its relatively infrequent and uneven application, there are severe limitations on our ability to assess evaluative comments and conclusions about CI in discussing trends. As will be seen, we have elected to base our evaluative comments in part on the range of claims in the literature and in part on our own experience, while pointing out where research is needed. In the concluding sections we suggest strategies for proceeding in light of the critical need for better evaluative information.

2. Two Bursts of Innovation: Great Expectations, Mixed Results[15]

It was not until the mid-1960s that citizen involvement in Canadian environmental governance began to involve the approaches and techniques that have become so common today.[16] The next two subsections highlight some of the key events and trends in the context for and use of CI since the mid-1960s. It identifies two bursts of innovation, focusing particularly on British Columbia while relating these to developments elsewhere in Canada.

Mid-Sixties to Late Eighties: Should Citizens Be Involved in Environmental Decisions?

During the 1960s concerns about environmental problems increased greatly and environmental issues rose on the public agenda in unprecedented ways.[17] The publication in 1962 of *Silent Spring*, in which Rachel Carson raised an alarm about threats to the environment and human health from the increasing use of pesticides and other synthetic chemicals, is often cited as one of the key catalysts. Widespread concerns arose about water, land, and air pollution and habitat destruction. Canadian attention was focused on these issues by the 1966 national symposium on *Pollution and Our Environment* organized by the newly formed Canadian Council of Resource Ministers. The response was a remarkable period of innovations in environmental policies and associated citizen-involvement processes, often following similar developments in the United States.[18]

Three major foci for these initiatives in Canada were planning for urban development, river-basin management, and assessments for project developments. The planning process for Greater Vancouver's Livable Region Strategy, beginning in the early seventies, was a pathbreaking example of the new approaches to citizen involvement in urban planning that began to develop across the country.[19] Environmental concerns were central to the growth-management issues that were emerging. In Greater Vancouver these revolved around proposals for major new developments such as freeways, subways, and expansion of the airport. A growing alienation of citizens from their governments, the increasing complexity of government, and the rapidity of technological and social change were among the reasons given at the time for the unprecedented creation of nine citizen policy committees that took a central role in the development of the Livable Region Strategy.

In 1967 the federal government offered to fund a comprehensive river-basin planning experiment with provinces in each region of Canada.[20] Initially, intergovernmental cost-shared agreements were negotiated for the Okanagan, Qu'Appelle, and Saint John basins. Through the first half of the 1970s major basin planning studies were undertaken across Canada and introduced the newly emerging techniques of multiple-purpose, multiple-means, and multiple-objective analyses. At the same time, the federal and provincial governments introduced project-review processes designed to assess the environmental and social impacts of developments that had previously been neglected in cost-benefit analyses. The assessments focused particularly on megaprojects such as the W.A.C. Bennett Dam and its impact on the Peace-Athabasca Delta, exploration drilling in the Beaufort Sea, and the James Bay hydro project.

In response to growing demands for greater public involvement, these planning and project-review initiatives experimented with a wide diversity of communication and participation techniques. For example, the river-basin planning studies included the use of information brochures, media releases, citizen surveys, public hearings, workshops, task forces, and advisory committees.[21] They also explored strategies for involving the public in different ways from the beginning to the end of the studies. At the time, an independent reviewer of the Greater Vancouver citizen policy committees concluded that they were a 'highly innovative and astonishingly successful experiment in the area of citizen involvement.'[22] In reviewing the basin planning experience, Sewell pointed out that while the techniques had been used in various Canadian governance contexts before, they had not been utilized as intensively as in the water and related environmental-resources planning. Using Arnstein's ladder the reviewer concluded: 'While it is probably true that Non-Participation occurs in water resources planning, there is usually some Degree of Tokenism, and increasingly a move towards Citizen Power.'[23] However, he cautioned that the programs 'must not be a facade, giving the impression that the public's views are being sought and taken into account but in reality not considered at all. Nor must information programs be titled participation or involvement programs.'[24]

Through the mid-seventies a series of major public inquiries relating to the development of mega-energy projects set new precedents for CI: the Mackenzie Valley Pipeline Inquiry under Berger (1977), the Alaska Highway Pipeline Inquiry under Lysyk (1977), and the Kitimat Pipeline Marine Terminal Inquiry under Thompson (1977). While each of these introduced innovations into the traditional public-hearing process, Berger's inquiry is renowned worldwide for its unprecedented commitment and approaches to community involvement. To quote one review at the time: 'The Mackenzie Valley Pipeline Inquiry must now rank as one of the most successful public participation events in Canadian history. By almost any criteria it achieved results far beyond the expectations of those who took part. It has produced massive documentation on the environment, economy and society of the Mackenzie and Western Arctic; everyone who wished a say had one; and the commissioner has become the unlikeliest folk hero of the seventies and his report a best-seller that struck a mortal blow to the largest engineering project ever proposed. To question the success of the inquiry seems foolish, if not sacrilegious, for its results have been generally satisfying to the vast majority of citizen participants.'[25]

Not all innovations during the 1970s were viewed with such enthusiasm; opinions differed among the interested parties. In the second half of the decade increasing disenchantment with the results of planning and impact assessment led to questioning of the innovations.[26] The river-basin studies were seen by some as unproductive in resolving issues and too time-consuming and costly. The experiments with public involvement were criticized for delaying the process, overemphasizing the interests of the active publics, and usurping the role of elected officials. There were commonly delays of up to two years in responding to recommendations, which frustrated the heightened expectations that had been created by public involvement and sometimes meant that the recommendations were overtaken by events. There was equal, if not greater, dissatisfaction with impact-assessment processes. Project proponents increasingly questioned their costs and benefits,[27] environmental interests were critical of their effectiveness,[28] and technical analysts savagely critiqued their data, methods, and conclusions.[29] At a time when the Canadian economy was weak, negative perceptions seemed to overwhelm the positive and for the ensuing decade there was relatively much less attention to environmental policy and CI in environmental governance. Yet, major precedents had been set and there was no longer widespread questioning of the role for CI, as there had been when the innovations began.

The Nineties: Sustainable Development and Multi-stakeholder Processes

In the second half of the 1980s environmental issues resurfaced as major public concerns in Canada. With the release of the Brundtland Report in 1987 these concerns gained momentum in the new context of the concept of sustainable development.[30] The National Task Force on the Environment and the Economy established by the federal government to make recommendations on Canada's response to the new imperatives for sustainable development was an example of a new generation of citizen-involvement approaches based on multi-stakeholder and consensus processes. The diverse mix of senior governmental and non-governmental members of the task force was highly impressed by the potential usefulness of such approaches for building understanding about their different perspectives on the environmental, economic, and social dimensions of sustainable development. They therefore recommended that similar multi-stakeholder round tables be established by each of the provinces and mandated to draft sustainable-development strategies. Through the early 1990s the federal and provincial governments established various forms of round tables and a multitude of others were created by governments and non-governmental groups from the local to the national levels as mechanisms for reaching agreement on sustainable-development strategies.[31]

Although the specifics varied greatly across the country, events in British Columbia, where great enthusiasm emerged for experimenting with new multi-stakeholder approaches, illustrate some of the key trends. The BC Round Table on the Environment and the Economy was established by the provincial government in 1990. It had thirty-one governmental and non-governmental members and, in comparison to other provinces, was distinctive in including no cabinet ministers and a mandate emphasizing the development of conflict-resolution and consensus processes.[32] Its use of multi-stakeholder mechanisms and consensus in drafting recommendations on sustainable-development strategies, along with two early reports on the potential for using them in all aspects of sustainability governance, elevated interest in using the new approaches.[33]

The two-volume report defined consensus processes as encompassing 'techniques that go by a variety of names – negotiation, dispute resolution, mediation, facilitation and getting-to-yes ... [A]ll have a common basis in collaboration and seeking agreement.'[34] The reports assessed twenty cases where consensus processes had already been tried in the province and proposed guidelines for their improved and more extensive use. Recommendations for using multi-stakeholder processes for negotiating agreements on environmental regulations (so-called 'reg-neg') and for incorporating consensus processes into environmental permitting and licensing were developed using consensus processes that involved key governmental and non-governmental stakeholders. In the ensuing two years the National Round Table led a dialogue among all the Canadian round tables that built on the BC consensus proposals and resulted in the widely cited guidelines *Building Consensus for a Sustainable Future: Guiding Principles* (see table 7.1).[35]

Within British Columbia multi-stakeholder consensus processes began to be extensively utilized and were given additional impetus by the establishment of the BC Commission on Resources and Environment (CORE), which was designed to address growing conflicts over land use, particularly in relation to forestry. While the Round Table had popularized the focus on 'consensus processes,' CORE introduced 'shared decision-making processes.' Shared decision-making was defined as 'an approach to public participation in decision-making (especially land use planning) in which, on a certain set of issues for a defined period of time, those with authority to make a decision and those affected by that decision are empowered jointly to seek an outcome that accommodates, rather than compromises, the interests of all concerned.'[36] After four tumultuous years of testing this new approach in practice and a higher degree of stakeholder involvement than had ever been attempted before, the commission drew together the results of its work in bold and far-reaching proposals for an overarching Sustainability Act, including major innovations in public-participation processes and dispute-resolution systems[37] that were seen to be essential to the successful pursuit of sustainability. Recommendations on citizen involvement included: (1) enshrining general rights of participation in law; (2) adopting a public-participation policy covering all agencies of government and including procedures for reviewing compliance and performance; and, (3) arguably the most far-reaching of all, creating community resource boards 'as a vehicle for supporting direct, democratic and intensive public participation in land use and resource and environmental management.'[38] The recommendations on a provincial dispute-resolution system were designed to complement the preventive measures expected from improved stakeholder-participation processes by strengthening adjudicative procedures and including explicit provisions for review, appeal, notification, standing, use of mediation, and publication of reasons for decisions.[39]

By 1992, a bewildering array of initiatives involving multi-stakeholder and consensus processes were under way in British Columbia. These included processes being conducted by the Round Table and CORE, as well as province-wide 'policy dialogues' on new water, energy, and environmental legislation. In addition, agencies were beginning to incorporate multi-stakeholder and consensus processes into their ongoing planning and management programs, most notably the BC Ministry of Forests in land and resource-management Planning efforts. At the same time, initiatives associated with the federal government's $1.4 billion Green Plan (a multi-sectoral initiative to implement new environmental-protection and sustainable-development programs) were starting similar multi-stakeholder processes as part of a strategy of building partnerships.[40] In British Columbia, there were major Green Plan initiatives relating to forestry, agriculture, fisheries, and environment. These included a special focus on the Fraser Basin, specifically a $100 million program for pollution control, habitat restoration, and improved fish and wildlife management. Not only did communities have to cope with this tsunami of federal and provincial initiatives, they also became preoccupied with their own, some of which were launched by local and regional governments, others by non-governmental groups in the communities.[41] These local processes were strongly encouraged and supported by guidebooks from the national and provincial round tables and aided by funding from the federal Green Plan.

By 1993 stakeholders across the province were struggling to cope with all the processes claiming their time and attention. Even though some steps were taken to coordinate the initiatives, such as through the use of the newly established Fraser Basin Management Board, they were often seen as being more part of the problem than a potential solution.[42] Recognizing the seriousness of the emerging problems, the BC Round Table produced a report recommending ways to use the array of citizen-involvement approaches more strategically and efficiently, arguing that multi-stakeholder consensus processes should be reserved for selected purposes.[43] It proved impossible to halt a major backlash. High-profile conflicts and controversies surrounding CORE's round tables (dramatized by upwards of 15,000 stakeholders marching on the provincial legislature to protest its forest land-use proposals for Vancouver Island and the commissioner being hung in effigy in the Cariboo) contributed to a perception that things were getting worse rather than better. In the context of a deteriorating economy and anticipating an upcoming election, the provincial government closed down or restricted many of the initiatives. The Round Table and Energy Commission were quickly terminated in 1994 and CORE was eventually closed down completely in 1996. Of the major initiatives only the Fraser Basin Management Board (FBMB) (now the Fraser Basin Council) and the Land and Resource Management Planning (LRMP) have continued to the time of writing. However, recent assessments of experience with each of these have raised doubts about their abilities to put into practice the innovative principles they espoused, given uncertain government commitments and the huge challenges of implementation.[44] Many of the local and watershed round tables are also still operating, although some have faded away with the declines in government funding and burnout among their stakeholders.

Even though this sketch of events in British Columbia omits other key initiatives relating to citizen involvement in environmental governance (e.g., processes relating to First Nations treaty negotiations and water-use plans), it does illustrate the rise and fall of a second burst of innovations that in varying ways has been experienced in Canada during the nineties. A variety of other innovations across the country further advanced the opportunities and techniques for citizen involvement. These included the introduction of freedom-of-information legislation, court decisions (e.g., recognizing aboriginal fishing rights), establishment of ombudsman offices (including a federal Sustainable Development Commissioner), the provision of mediation options (e.g., in federal project-review processes), and the development of the Internet. Also notable was the expansion of CI into environmental governance processes relating to international and global issues and agreements (e.g., NAFTA)

As in British Columbia, enthusiasm across Canada for the new citizen-involvement initiatives waned in the mid-nineties as governments at all levels became doubtful about their worth and as concerns about economic issues came to dominate their agendas. One stark illustration of the turnaround in views was the Canadian Institute of Planners 1998 award for an article that severely critiqued Vancouver's innovative approaches to citizen involvement in CityPlan, innovations that the Institute had recognized in another award only three years before.[45] Drastic budget cuts by the federal and provincial governments have had major impacts on environmental departments and environmental policies have been made less stringent (e.g., in Ontario the department's budget has been cut by more than 40 per cent and staff have been instructed to not enforce some regulations). Local governments have struggled to cope as environmental responsibilities have been shifted to them through federal and provincial government downsizing. At the same time, governments at all levels are commercializing or privatizing activities related to the environment.[46] Increasingly, governments are also looking to non-profit societies and volunteers to take on greater responsibilities for environmental management. Finally, in response to earlier successes with more-activist strategies (e.g., at Clayoquot Sound) and a growing concern that participation in governmental multi-stakeholder processes has co-opted them, some ENGOs are considering a return to more adversarial and direct action.

Thus, in the late nineties, citizen involvement in environmental governance in Canada appears once again to have gone through a period of great innovation followed by second thoughts. Now it seems to be moving towards another major change in its evolution; just how quickly and in what ways cannot be predicted with any certainty.

Cycles Trending Upwards and Outwards

Two broad trends are evident from this brief sketch of experience with CI. First, the use of CI in environmental governance in Canada has clearly been increasing and diversifying over the last three decades, despite falling away from the two peaks of interest. Second, while environment has been a primary focus for expanding CI, other areas of governance, such as community development and social policy, have also been significant, particularly over the last decade, when environmental issues have been considered in the more comprehensive context of sustainable development. Overall, there has been a broad trend towards more participatory forms of governance in Canada, which is potentially leading towards transformation of the governance system, as explored more fully in following sections.

Even though it is not easy to separate out the influence of the swings in governmental enthusiasm for environmental policies per se, the longer-term trend in CI in environmental governance appears to be upwards as well as outwards into the wider context of ecological, social, and economic sustainability. Clearly, the second burst of innovation began from a higher base of general acceptance and understanding and quickly moved beyond previously established approaches and techniques, and into broader areas of application. What are some of the key changes and trends that have emerged over the last three decades?

- While debate in the initial decade often dwelt on whether there was a role for CI, it progressively shifted to questions of how and how much.
- At its peak, CI in the 1990s was generally more widespread, diverse, and time-demanding than in the 1970s (e.g., BC in the early 1990s).
- As planning and environmental-impact assessment (EIA) processes were advanced and refined, opportunities for CI in them were diversified (e.g., from scoping through to monitoring implementation in EIA processes).
- Involvement expanded from the focus on planning and impact assessment into the processes for developing the context-setting policy, legislation, and regulations (e.g., drafting CEPA legislation in the mid-eighties was an early federal example) and for subsequent implementation of environmental management (e.g., community-based watershed round tables).
- The topics addressed became more comprehensive and integrated as pollution and habitat issues were placed in the wider context of environmental, economic, and social sustainability (e.g., sustainable communities).
- Originally, CI generally entailed government and, occasionally, business initiating processes, increasingly non-governmental groups are now initiators and some processes might even exclude government, at least initially (e.g., some community-based watershed round tables).
- The shift to multi-stakeholder processes, involving participants from diverse agencies and all levels of government, has often resulted in these processes becoming means for 'intragovernment involvement,' in that they involve a variety of agencies from various levels of government, as much as 'citizen involvement' (e.g., CORE's round tables).
- While the earlier involvement processes tended to focus on relatively discrete and short-term events, over time there has been

increasing use of ongoing mechanisms and partnerships (e.g., boards and co-management mechanisms).

- In the second period innovations gave particular emphasis to approaches and techniques that would avoid adversarial interactions and facilitate cooperation (e.g., the more recent emphasis on consensus-based multi-stakeholder processes).
- While relatively little progress has been made in enshrining rights to participation in law in Canada (in contrast to the U.S.), there has been increasing expression of policy commitments by governments and business to their inclusion in environmental governance (e.g., the Land Use Charter adopted in principle by the BC cabinet in 1993).
- Non-governmental stakeholders have become increasingly organized and skilled in participating in environmental governance processes (e.g., the environmental networks found from the local to international level).
- Non-governmental stakeholders have become increasingly sophisticated in their lobbying of governments and business and use of the media, courts, and markets to extend and strengthen their participation in environmental governance beyond the citizen-involvement processes established by governments (e.g., the multi-faceted strategies employed to influence forestry decisions in BC).

Overall, the tools, approaches, and strategies that have come to be used today have generally moved CI processes significantly further up Arnstein's Ladder than they were at the end of the first burst of innovation, although they are still only occasionally reaching the upper levels of 'delegated power' and 'citizen control.' There has been a general shift, at least in principle, by governments from Beierle's *managerialist* perspective to a greater emphasis on the *pluralist* perspective, and citizens have increasingly become interested in the *popular* perspective. Such a shift could imply that a potential transformation in environmental governance is under way, but only time and research will tell whether the change is significant. Next we briefly review the literature on recent innovations in CI, in order to better understand this potential.

3. Negotiation-based CI Innovations in Sustainability Governance

This section briefly examines in more detail the negotiation-based approaches to citizen involvement in sustainability governance because they are central to the CI approaches that emerged in the second burst of innovation. These approaches have received growing attention, both in practice and in an increasingly interdisciplinary literature, as governments ànd business search for ways to reduce costs and citizens seek empowerment. For the most part, these negotiation-based innovations have their origins in the United States and so we widen our consideration to the North American literature, while continuing to emphasize applications in Canada, in this and the remaining sections of the chapter.

Negotiation, Facilitation, Mediation, and Consensus

By the second half of the 1980s, negotiation-based approaches to citizen involvement were beginning to be used in Canadian environmental governance.[47] Various forms of negotiation along with facilitation and mediation were employed. Sometimes, they were proactive elements designed into the stakeholder-involvement processes of planning and management initiatives. Other times, they were a response to the emergence of conflict.[48] Often they were loosely referred to as 'environmental mediation' or ADR (Alternative Dispute Resolution).[49] In other instances, they were collectively referred to as 'consensual approaches.'[50]

Negotiation-based approaches originated in the United States, during the 1960s and 1970s, where there was growing exploration of the potential for applying in new contexts the facilitation and dispute-resolution approaches and techniques originally developed in the labour, peace, and international-relations fields.[51] Environmental conflicts were one of the major new areas of attention; others included community disputes, divorce settlements, and business disputes.

A key motivation for much of this development in the United States was the search for alternatives to court action that would provide less-costly, quicker, and more-predictable ways to resolve disputes. Often assisted by foundation funding, practitioners and academics developed, tested, and promoted new theory and techniques. CI approaches were strongly influenced by the resulting spate of publications, including *Getting to Yes: Negotiating Agreement without Giving In, The Art and Science of Negotiation, The Mediation Process, Breaking the Impasse: Consensual Approaches to Resolving Public Disputes,* and *Managing Public Disputes.*[52] These books were widely used by those experimenting with negotiations, facilitation and mediation, and other forms of third-party assistance in negotiated approaches to CI consensus-building.

Facilitation as a form of third-party assistance has distinctive origins in the 1960s protest movements in the United States against racial discrimination, poverty, and the Vietnam War.[53] Subsequently, it has become widely used not only in diverse economic, social, and environmental protest movements, but increasingly in the 1980s and 1990s in all kinds of governmental and business meetings.[54] Reflecting the term's origins and current practices, Kaner and colleagues define a facilitator as 'an individual who enables groups and organizations to work more effectively; to collaborate and achieve synergy. She or he is a "content neutral" party who, by not taking sides or expressing or advocating a point of view during the meeting, can advocate for fair, open and inclusive procedures to accomplish the group's work. A facilitator can also be a learning or dialogue guide to assist a group in thinking deeply about its assumptions, beliefs and values and about its systemic processes and context.'[55] Facilitators thus assist with the logistics and conduct of meetings, focusing on the process and on communications, as well as on details such as room arrangement, agendas, and recording. They are knowledgeable about group dynamics and are skilled in techniques for encouraging active listening, brainstorming new ideas, and identifying opportunities for consensus.

While mediators often may use similar techniques to those of facilitators, their entry into a citizen-involvement process is much more likely to be in response to a conflict than a proactive attempt to reach agreement. Moore defines mediation as 'an extension or elaboration of the negotiation process that involves the intervention of an acceptable third-party who has limited or no authoritative decision-making power. This person assists the principal parties in voluntarily reaching a mutually acceptable settlement of the issues in dispute ... [Mediation] is usually initiated when the parties no longer believe that they can handle the conflict on their own and when the only means of resolution appears to involve impartial third-party assistance.'[56] It is generally distinguished from facilitation in that the third party is more actively involved in assisting and persuading parties to reach formal agreements including the use of private caucuses with the individual parties and carrying messages between them. There is, however, enormous variety among mediators, the principles they espouse, and the practices they employ.[57] For example, Susskind believes that effective mediation requires the mediator to have and use substantive knowledge of the issues, but other mediators would put much less emphasis on this aspect and some would argue that substantive involvement jeopardizes trust in their role. In addition, as one might expect given the relative newness of the field and particularly its application to newer issues such as environment and sustainability, highly regarded mediators are found to not necessarily practise the principles they espouse.[58]

Although negotiation-based approaches started more slowly in Canada than in the United States, a growing variety were found by Dorcey and Riek to be in use by the mid-1980s in Canadian environmental governance.[59] While the vast majority of these were unassisted negotiations, a growing number involved some type of third-party assistants who, depending on the nature and extent of their assistance, were variously labelled 'conciliators,' 'convenors,' 'facilitators,' 'fact-finders,' 'problem-solvers,' and 'mediators.' From a review of thirty-two published case studies, Dorcey and Riek reached a number of conclusions, including the following:

- The use of negotiation-based approaches was slower to develop in Canada than in the United States, in large part because of the lack of foundation funding for the development of theory, techniques, and practice.
- A major reason for developing negotiation-based approaches in Canada was to avoid the delays, uncertainty, and costs associated with governmental administrative processes, in contrast to the U.S. focus on alternatives to the courts.
- Negotiation-based approaches were being employed in settling environmental disputes involving water and energy-resource developments, as well as air, land, and water pollution, at all levels in the hierarchy of governance and in all provinces.
- While largely concentrated on specific projects, negotiation-based approaches were being used in five different contexts of environmental governance: project evaluation (17), multiple-use phanning (4), policy analysis (3), domestic rights (4), and international rights (4).
- Half the cases involved some form of mediation, often referred to as 'environmental mediation,' and were concentrated on the project (12) and policy levels (3).
- Although thirteen cases involved only governments, eighteen also involved various mixes of non-governmental parties, including citizens, interest groups, industry, and native Indians, and one did not involve government at all.

• At the project level, most negotiations (14 of 17) were designed to produce agreements to be implemented by the parties, thus putting them highest on the Arnstein ladder; the policy-level negotiations were largely (2 of 3) consultative in that agreements were only advisory to government, and thus were lower on the ladder.

No comparable overview has been undertaken subsequently, but it is clear that use of negotiation-based approaches has expanded enormously in Canada over the last decade, as highlighted in section 2. While continuing to draw on the U.S. development of theory and principles, Canada has arguably been ahead in experimenting with their practical application in the context of sustainability governance. Negotiation, facilitation, and mediation have come to be seen as approaches in their own right, as well as techniques that can be employed within the breadth of approaches to citizen involvement in environmental and sustainability governance that span Arnstein's ladder (e.g., facilitation of information programs, negotiation of agreements within consultation initiatives, and mediation in the implementation of co-management agreements through committees and boards).

Growing experience with these approaches and techniques throughout North America over the last decade has resulted in a major increase in awareness of their potential among stakeholders. Many have become practised in their use. Growth in demand for facilitators and mediators has resulted in the United States in a proliferation of public- and private-sector training programs. Universities have developed degree programs from the bachelor's to the doctoral level as well as research centres. Accompanying this upswing has been the emergence of professional organizations to both advance new principles and practices and address issues of competency and ethical conduct. Particularly notable in the last few years have been the heightened efforts to develop collaborative efforts between the sub-fields. For example, two of the most important and relevant organizations in North America, the Society of Professionals in Dispute Resolution (SPIDR) and the Association of Public Participation Professionals (AP3), have been holding joint sessions at their annual meetings, with the environment being a particular focus of discussions. Out of all this experience has come a deeper appreciation of the state-of-the-art and best practices for negotiation-based approaches.[60] In retrospect, the last decade has been a period of remarkable growth in development, use, and convergence on negotiation-based approaches that are transforming citizen involvement in environmental and sustainability governance.

Co-Management, Civic Engagement, and Transformation of Governance

While some CI innovations have been focused on the use of negotiation-based techniques per se, others have focused on new approaches to governance that employ them as central tools. Here we briefly examine two key examples: 'co-management' and 'civic engagement.' We also discuss the increasingly diverse and interdisciplinary literature on the transformation of CI in environmental and sustainability governance, of which these are major examples.

Over the last two decades increasing attention has been given to 'co-management,' which is also variously referred to as 'co-operative management,' 'joint management,' or 'collaborative management.' After reviewing the many different ways in which these terms have come to be used, the National Round Table on the Environment and the Economy adopted the following definition: '[C]o-management is a system that enables a sharing of decision-making power, responsibility, and risk between governments and stakeholders, including but not limited to resource users, environmental interests, experts and wealth generators.'[61] In a manner that reflects the growing interest in ways to devolve responsibilities from government and involve stakeholders more directly and fully in environmental and sustainability governance, co-management reaches upwards towards the top rungs of Arnstein's ladder and embodies Beierle's popularist perspective.

Interest in co-management has grown out of the search for more effective, efficient, and equitable ways to manage natural resources such as fish, water, forests, and agricultural lands.[62] Theoretical and empirical studies have focused particularly on self-governing associations of local users and their relations with the state. Special attention has been given to the practices of indigenous peoples and their use of traditional knowledge in making decisions. While state or private ownership regimes provide two extreme options, common property ownership and co-management provide an array of joint alternatives for involving the state and citizens. Co-management advocates argue that these options can offer efficiency benefits while avoiding the costs of damage to community and democratic values that so often accompany management under state or private ownership.

After reviewing experience in Canada and abroad, the National Round Table has recommended that co-management should be a central element of sustainability strategies.[63] Their report demonstrates a convergence of their own and others evolving ideas on CI in sustainability governance. Co-management is described as just one of the types of 'partnerships' that have been seen as central to sustainability initiatives. It is also viewed as a way to implement 'community-based management' utilizing 'multi-stakeholder processes' and 'consensus principles.' While the report focused on ocean governance, many of its proposals could be extrapolated to other applications such as watersheds and forests, and an extensive appendix reviews the growing numbers of examples that can be found.

A second major focus on CI in environmental and sustainability governance has been the diverse literature addressing the role of ENGOs and, more generally, 'civil society.' Pross describes the phenomenal proliferation of interest groups including environmental groups over the last thirty years in Canada. Reflecting Beierle's pluralist perspective, he concludes that interest groups are necessary in an era of highly diffused power because the political system depends on them to articulate, implement, and monitor the general will. 'Pressure groups contribute vitally to the life of policy communities. They perform functions that other institutions cannot perform. They are necessary. At the same time, they create a major problem in democratic representation, threatening to substitute sectoral representation for the geographically based representation upon which our legislative system depends ... Pressure groups must therefore be contained and other institutions strengthened.'[64]

Analysing the increasing involvement of environmental, interest groups in ways that go beyond the traditional role of government-initiated public participation programs, Gardner distinguishes three roles in relation to government: advocacy, supplemental, and transformative. Advocacy 'encompasses the broad range of activities undertaken by ENGOs to strengthen and expand the accountability of government and industry without restructuring economic or governance systems.'[65] 'The supplemental role refers to the work undertaken by ENGOs to supplement government functions for environmental conservation.'[66] 'The transformative role encompasses ENGO activities that strive to transform government and society.'[67] Gardner discusses how a particular ENGO might employ a mix of these roles and associated strategies, how these can evolve over time, and the widely differing views among moderates and radicals about their respective merits and efficacy. She concludes that 'most observers of the current state of the environmental movement, whether reformist or radicals, agree that the naively apolitical days of earlier phases are past, and that ENGOs are increasingly obliged to enter the political forum.'[68]

ENGOs are just one part of civil society, whose restored and enhanced engagement in governance, to counterbalance and work with government and business, is seen by an increasing number of writers as crucial to sustainable development. In *Beyond Prince and Merchant: Citizen Participation and the Rise of Civil Society*, Burbidge reviews the varied concepts of civil society and the impetus to a groundswell of interest in its revitalization around the world: 'In many countries, the driving force is the struggle to attain or preserve basic human rights or the demand of disenfranchised minorities to participate fully in the society ... In other countries, the call to empower civil society seems to spring more from a deep cynicism about the role of government, a growing concern about a runaway global economy and the encroaching power of market forces, and the belief that voluntary associations which have been part of the bedrock of society are in decline.'[69] Participation in voluntary associations, embodying norms of trust, reciprocity, tolerance, and inclusion, and activating networks of public communication, are believed to build and maintain the social capital upon which the vitality of the governance system and sustainable development are dependent. In his most recent book, Barber clarifies the ideals of 'civil society' and differentiates among the often misleading uses of the term, in particular distinguishing the nostalgists, who want to recreate old-fashioned (and discriminatory) small communities, from the free-marketeers, who associate the term with unfettered commercial activity.[70] The phenomenal growth of civic engagement through the creation of and participation in associations and networks relating to sustainability issues from the local to the global level is seen as one of the most hopeful signs that the daunting challenges posed by looming environmental, social, and economic crises might be met.[71]

The trends in co-management and civic engagement are broadly consistent with themes evident in the rich breadth of theoretical and applied literature relating to CI. For example, the trends reflect the interest among democratic theorists in moving from the predominantly 'thin' or representative forms of democracy towards the 'strong' or direct forms.[72] Associated with this has been increasing interest among a growing number of political theorists over the last decade in forms of 'deliberative democracy' or 'decision making by discussion among free and equal citizens.'[73] An increasingly strong influence has been Habermas's work, notably his *Theory of Communicative Action*.[74] Drawing on his ideas and their observations of how planners interact with citizens in practice, planning theorists have begun to articulate a new paradigm of planning ('communicative action') that sees approaches, such as multi-stakeholder processes, and techniques, such as negotiation and consensus-based decision-making, as the central components of a progressive practice that addresses the many inequitable faces of power.[75] Theorists and practitioners have challenged conventional ideas with proposals for 'transformative approaches' to negotiation, facilitation, and mediation.[76] 'Environmental justice' has been a specific focus,[77] as has 'health and environmental risk,'[78] and the term 'civic science' has been coined to describe the use of such approaches and techniques in addressing the complexities and uncertainties that are inherent in ecosystem management.[79]

Thirty years later, Arnstein's concerns about disempowerment are still much alive, yet there are potentially mitigating trends in CI evident in the theoretical and applied literatures focusing on negotiation-based approaches and sustainability governance. However, the retreat in Canada in the second half of the 1990s from the vigorous innovations of the decade's first half raises major questions about political commitment to these innovations, as well as their effectiveness in practice. In the next section, we draw on our own experience to address this latter question before returning to the question of political commitment in the conclusions.

4. Consensus-based Approaches: Experience and Reform

This section considers four important approaches to citizen involvement, which we term 'consensus-based approaches,' 'structured decision processes,' 'progressive approaches,' and 'contingent approaches.' It begins by outlining two extremes of CI practice in Canada and the United States. Then it briefly considers consensus-based approaches, in terms of the judgmental and political issues they raise. This discussion is followed by an alternative perspective that we term a 'structured decision process' approach to CI. We outline a set of principles that, based on limited experience, appear innovative and relevant for how CI should be conducted. We then briefly review how one might build on this approach by incorporating 'progressive approaches' to the intrinsic political and ethical issues and 'contingent approaches' to the choice of when to use CI and how. In this section we draw on both the North American literature and our own experience in consensus-based processes from the local to the global level.

Two Extremes of Current CI Practice

One could characterize much of CI practice in North America by considering two extremes on a continuum of 'stakeholder control' of CI activities, which in turn is related to control over the decision-making process. One extreme involves group processes, relying on consensus among participants as the decision rule, which can be reasonably viewed as a subset of the wider set of negotiation-based processes for CI. One form of this approach, which has wide endorsement, argues that the decision process a particular group should adopt should be designed by the group itself. For example, consider the set of principles developed by the Canada National Round Table on the Environment and the Economy intended to encourage improved decision-making to achieve a sustainable future for Canada (table 7.1).[80] The principles call explicitly for 'self-design' involving 'all parties with a significant interest' as the prescription for improved decision-making.

The other camp, the polar opposite from such consensus processes, allows CI only in the form of specific, formally structured value judgments. For example, members of the public may only provide judgments about specific non-market-value trade-offs cast in terms of willingness-to-pay in dollar terms.[81] Other aspects of the decision process (such as the range of objectives considered, the nature of the alternatives proposed, and the characterization of the impacts of alternatives) may be influenced by the values of focus groups or media reviews, but are presented in a distilled form based on judgments made by the analyst or project proponent. This extreme approach is standard practice for social benefit/cost analysis based on welfare economics.

In reviewing the writing and practice on CI, readers would find an increasing preponderance of attention and effort devoted towards the 'consensus' end of this continuum. For example, the *Understanding Risk* report of the U.S. National Research Council implicitly seems to have adopted consensus as the archetype for CI in its latter chapters.[82] The other extreme of CI has its proponents among economists or policy analysts who are interested in CI only as a means to obtain value judgments that will allow them to impute quantitative values (often in dollars) for non-market goods. Some critics would say that formally structured value judgments do not constitute a meaningful form of CI.

They are concerned with the lack of input by citizens regarding problem definition or the nature of the decision process, not to mention the cognitive and ethical difficulties.[83]

Later in this section, we consider a relatively new generic approach to CI that adopts a middle course between these two extremes. It employs a group process, with substantial responsibility placed on group participants to provide judgments, to assimilate information, and to provide views on the acceptability of alternatives. Yet it also adopts a clear structure for the decision process, requiring both formal and informal benefit/cost comparisons. The general outlines of this structure are established with the assistance of the facilitators, and although participants have the ability to fine-tune, the scope of their role falls well short of a licence to continually redesign the process. Before discussing this approach, we turn our attention to considering consensus-based approaches as often practised.

Conceptual Aspects of Consensus as a CI Norm

The conceptual appeal of consensus among diverse stakeholders as the basis for complex environmental and sustainability policy choices is easy to understand. The possibility of all participants seeing their interests reflected in the outcome gives hope for overcoming polarization and turning 'win-lose' into 'win-win' decisions, through creativity and negotiation. All would likely agree that consensus among all affected parties is an egalitarian (though not necessarily democratic) ideal for multi-party decisions. In this ideal, established interests share their power with others concerned with the decision, in order to devise approaches that are more widely acceptable, and protective of minority interests. There is also evidence that the process of conducting consensus-based activities can sometimes lead to new problem formulations, additional information about alternatives, and greater insight about the views of others, even if consensus does not result.[84] These are all laudable goals and desirable outcomes for CI.

Yet, how is consensus, in self-designed processes, likely to work in practice? What are the possible barriers that may arise in pursuing this egalitarian ideal?

Individual and Group Behavioural Decision Research

Consensus-based decision-making, particularly in processes designed by the participants, places heavy reliance on the cognitive abilities of individuals to make wise choices that require compromise about technically complex, emotionally charged issues. How well could we expect the average person to do in such circumstances?

Behavioural decision research with individuals has developed over the last three decades as a major theme in social psychology. These research findings show consistently that, in experiments and real-life situations, 'humans are quite bad at making complex, unaided decisions.'[85] Individuals naturally respond to complex tasks by using their judgmental instincts to find an easy or adequate way through the problem at hand. They respond to probabilistic information or questions involving uncertainties with predictable biases that often ignore or misprocess important information.[86] They seem to have little instinctive ability to clarify objectives, create a wide variety of alternatives, or structure decision tasks.[87] When asked to consider value trade-offs   or select among alternatives, they may employ a number of heuristic reasoning processes that are susceptible to a variety of contextual or task-related influences.[88] In short, there are many reasons to expect that, left to their own devices, individuals (either lay or expert) will often not make informed, thoughtful choices about complex issues involving uncertainties and value trade-offs.

Behavioural research regarding group decision processes is equally discouraging about the unaided ability to make wise choices about complex tasks. In general, groups can (at best) do about as well as the more deliberative or well–informed members would on their own in addressing complex judgment tasks. Groups can have improved performance over individuals because more perspectives may be put forward for consideration, and because the chances of having natural systematic thinkers involved is higher. On the other hand, the performance of unaided groups is susceptible to the tendency to establish entrenched positions, a tendency that makes discussion of compromise difficult. Groups also are subject to adopting a common perspective and ignoring contrary information, a tendency termed 'group think.'[89] As a result, a single forceful or cantankerous member can have a dramatic effect on a group's activities.

These findings should not be taken as a blanket condemnation of CI on the grounds of cognitive shortcomings. They relate to *unaided* efforts at judgment tasks, not to situations in which individuals or groups are aided within structured decision processes. Thus, these findings (intentionally) ignore the crucial role played by those who help the participants structure, understand, and grapple with the required decision tasks. Rather, the findings focus attention on the issue of what facilitators do in guiding CI activities, and on the tasks and decision processes that are placed before participants.

Legitimacy of Stakeholder Consensus as Governance

Consensus-based CI could be viewed as a new form of governance. In it, established government institutions, such as regulatory agencies, invite affected parties to craft a negotiated settlement to a complex question. The prospect of overcoming disagreement, designing an implementable solution, and taking pressure off elected officials account for its conceptual appeal. How legitimate are such processes as a new form of governance?

One important criterion for legitimacy is representativeness. Within standard governance in Canada, we elect representatives to make policy on our behalf. In consensus processes, we have the ideal of representation of all affected parties; they involve a shift from a *managerial* to a *populist* perspective on democratic governance. Yet, those who are most directly affected by a decision, and who will reap concentrated benefits or bear concentrated costs, have a strong incentive to organize a power base and participate in consensus processes in order to affect the outcome. The broader public, which may bear the largest share of the benefits or costs, but for which these impacts are more diffuse (i.e., lower per capita), has far less incentive to participate.[90] Hence, the interests of important but more diffusely affected parties, ranging from the public at large to future generations, are not directly represented in consensus-based governance unless facilitators take special steps to ensure the sponsors and other participants address this concern.

A second criterion is the nature and legitimacy of rules. It is an open question whether power can ever be legitimately delegated to ad hoc governance processes, within which there is no mechanism for broad social accountability or established rules of procedure. In their traditional governance structures, Canadians have constitutional, institutional, and procedural norms that are sanctioned by legitimate agencies. Some critics are hard pressed to see the merits of new governance structures, particularly when the sponsors of these processes (referring to the organizations that convene them rather than the facilitators that conduct them) do not clearly delineate the specific mandate of the process. Overcoming this problem requires that lines of account-ability and responsibility for final decisions be made clear by sponsors and facilitators.

In its reports on the implementation of consensus processes the BC Round Table on the Environment and the Economy specifically addressed concerns about compromising government authority, making four points.[91] First, the collaborative approach should not seek to limit an official's discretion, rather the process should be seen as a means for confirming the will of the constituents and building a solid foundation on which to make decisions. Second, the primary role of government in the process should be to represent the broad public interest and to ensure that statutory requirements and public policies are observed. Third, the ultimate decision-maker (e.g., director or minister) should not participate directly in the process; other staff members should be responsible for representing the government perspective and public policy. Finally, any agreement reached as a result of the consensus process should be advisory in nature. Within this framework cabinet authority can be respected and civil-service secrecy maintained.

A third criterion for legitimacy of governance for science-based issues such as environmental regulation is how technical information is used as a basis for decisions. One can find examples of consensus processes in which technical information has been used in responsible ways, and examples of the opposite situation.[92] Yet, this comment is equally relevant for standard governance institutions, in that the difficulties posed for elected officials by scientific uncertainty are widely recognized. Dealing with technically complex issues involving uncertainty appears to be an ongoing difficulty for elected and non-elected governance processes, one that leads some writers to argue that facilitators need to be substantively knowledgeable about the issues to be resolved.[93]

It is worth noting that all three of these concerns over legitimacy can arise in any CI process. They can be particularly problematic in situations where the sponsors and facilitators of the process are not sensitive to their critical importance, and where legitimacy may be questioned because of the nature of the issue under consideration. In the early days of experimenting with consensus-based processes, when all parties are relatively inexperienced with the implications of these approaches, such problems have commonly arisen.

Status Quo Bias

The best alternative to a negotiated agreement, as seen from the viewpoints of the various parties, is widely recognized as a huge influence on the final outcome of a negotiation process.[94] The alternative to a negotiated agreement in a consensus process is often the status quo. In such situations, interests favoured by the status quo have a strong incentive to only accept alternatives that are substantially similar to the status quo. Consensus processes (or any form of negotiation) can in such situations be said to have a *status quo bias*. Hoberg has discussed this issue, with examples involving consensus processes in Canada.[95] Other writers, including people from the environmental movement, have made similar points that question the role of consensus because of its status quo bias. McCloskey, former head of the Sierra Club in the United States, has questioned the role of stakeholder processes in locally based land-use decisions in the United States, in which the status quo favours resource-extraction activities.[96] Thus, key stakeholders who are only interested in changes that differ significantly from the status quo may choose not to participate in the consensus process and pursue other opportunities such as the courts, lobbying, or civil disobedience. A critical role of the facilitator therefore is to ensure that the sponsors and the participants clearly understand the scope of opportunities for agreement under the mandate in the specific situation.

Structured Decision Processes in Consensus-based CI

Given the potential cognitive difficulties, uncertain legitimacy, and status quo bias of consensus in self-designed processes, it is not surprising that attention has been directed towards approaches that can overcome these obstacles. Below we discuss what we refer to as a 'structured decision process' as one of three possible approaches for strengthening consensus-based CI processes. We use the term 'decision process' because the intent is to aid the interactions and decisions about recommendations among the CI participants. In addition, the CI results are intended to aid actual decisions by the sponsors and other legitimate decision-makers. Some observers might say that much of what is outlined below simply consists of good practice that is already evident in many consensus processes. In our experience, it is only too seldom the case.

Orientation

We focus on CI as largely a process of decision-making with groups, particularly when addressing important, controversial environmental issues. The crucial features of this approach are how the process is structured, and what it is deciding.

The views of two eminent decision scientists help clarify what is needed to assist individuals and groups to responsibly address complex environmental risk-management questions within CI efforts. March draws attention to the need for help with identifying and defining goals by observing that 'human beings have unstable, inconsistent, incompletely evolved and imprecise goals at least in part because human abilities limit preference orderliness.'[97] Simon emphasizes the need for an effective decision structure and workable tasks: '... [h]uman rational behavior is shaped by a scissors whose two blades are the structure of task environments and the computational capabilities of the actor.'[98] The implication is that efforts to assist citizen-involvement processes in making defensible choices should stress methods for clarifying fundamental individual or social objectives and for structuring the decision tasks so they are meaningful, and within the capabilities of those involved. At the same time, the goals and tasks must be useful for making responsible choices in the given decision context.

The decision to be addressed in a CI group-decision process will differ from one situation to the next, but can be addressed in general terms. In our view, a major stumbling block in consensus-based CI processes is the expectation that the group should be empowered to 'make the decision,' when sponsors and facilitators fail to address explicitly the mandate and its limits. Except on those still relatively infrequent occasions when mandates provide for the group to make decisions (e.g., co-management boards), it is essential that stakeholders understand their task as one of making recommendations.

Such recommendations could address the issues outlined below, among others:

• The nature of the decision to be made. These recommendations could address all the elements of a responsible, well-informed decision process, including problem formulation, the relevant objectives that should guide the decision process, a wide range of attractive alternatives, an understanding of the impacts of the various alternatives, including the range of views among technical experts, and the key trade-offs that arise in choosing among the alternatives.

• The alternatives the various stakeholders within a CI process could support. These recommendations would characterize the range of societal views and coalitions of support about the choice among the alternatives.

One view about how processes could be conducted to provide these recommendations is discussed next.

Concepts for Group Decision Processes

Four concepts are particularly important for group decision processes for complex environmental risk-management choices. All involve the pragmatic application of formal decision analytic concepts.

Value-focused thinking. Keeney describes 'value-focused thinking' in simplest terms as 'deciding what is important and how to achieve it.'[99] Value-focused thinking emphasizes the pre-eminent role of values in all decision-making. It involves value-structuring approaches drawn from multi-attribute utility theory. It uses these judgments to create more attractive alternatives that stand a better chance of wide support, determine the information needed to characterize impacts of alternatives, and, formally or informally, evaluate alternatives.

Adaptive management. Holling, Walters, and others developed 'adaptive management' as a means of coping with profound uncertainties in managing complex natural-resource systems involving predator-prey relationships such as fisheries.[100] Since then, this concept has been applied to a wide range of resource-management issues as well as strategy design and other management contexts.[101] In simple terms, adaptive management could be characterized as follows: when faced with profound uncertainties, take a purposeful step forward, monitor the consequences, learn from the results, and avoid costly failures. It sees decision-making as an iterative process, rather than a one-time exercise, and emphasizes the role of learning from successive management choices. While adaptive management could be applied in a formal experimental design, it is also helpful as an informal impetus to seek opportunities for learning over time in any iterative decision context.[102]

A structured decision process. The basic steps of decision analysis, which are essentially the steps of any structured planning or decision framework, provide a responsible, informative, and complete structure for a decision process.[103] For the purposes of designing CI with groups of stakeholders, these steps can be cast in terms of a series of questions:

1 What ends (objectives) are important to achieve in selecting a management alternative for the question at hand?
2 What alternatives can be constructed to achieve these objectives?
3 What information is needed to characterize the impacts of these alternatives, in terms of measures for the stated objectives?
4 What trade-offs arise in selecting among the alternatives?
5 What alternatives can the participants support?

An 'informative' decision rule. The preceding question raises the issue of the appropriate decision rule for group CI processes that consider environmental risk-management policy issues. Perhaps the most common is a consensus rule, in which every participant effectively has a veto over the decisions of the group (and often over every step of the process). A different, perhaps more informative decision rule is to ask participants what alternative(s) each can support. By 'informative' we mean a decision rule that fosters learning about the process, the alternatives, and the values of participants (which should be important for CI). Greater insight occurs throughout the process because less time is spent dealing with objections that might occur with a veto-based consensus rule, and as a result every step is more straightforward.

An informative decision rule is akin to approval voting as opposed to unanimous agreement.[104] However, the group does not make its ultimate recommendations based on majority or plurality voting, because typically the number of participants and of groups they represent are not required to be representative of the citizenry as a whole, as in a legislative body. Instead, the decision rule is simply to report to the elected or appointed decision-makers which alternatives the various stakeholders can support. This approach is in keeping with the role of decision analytic approaches with multiple stakeholders, where utility functions for various groups could be used to inform the decision-maker about the preferences of constituents.[105]

The approach can also be greatly enhanced by the facilitator having participants focus on reaching consensus among alternative 'packages,' as opposed to each individual component of the decision, and using graduated scales of consensus instead of just all-or-nothing decisions.[106] For example, a group might agree to the following graduated scale reaching from 'I like it' to 'I veto this proposal': endorsement; agreement with reservation; abstain; stand aside; formal disagreement but willing to go with majority; formal disagreement with request to be absolved of responsibility for implementation; block. Working with packages and scales of consensus increases the likelihood of the group being able to reach an agreement that can be recommended.

Progressive Approaches in Consensus-based CI

A second and potentially complementary way in which decision-making may be aided focuses on the issues relating to information and power. Ignoring the political and ethical dimensions of CI will undermine the assistance that might be provided by structured decision-making. Drawing on the work of Habermas, Forester contrasted five different perspectives on information as a source of power: the technician, the incrementalist, the liberal-advocate, the structuralist, and the progressive.[107] It is the last, integrating the views of the first four, that is of particular interest as a possible second approach for strengthening CI in consensus-based processes. While Forester was focusing on planners, his ideas for progressive practice can be applied to any sponsor of CI.

> [T]he progressive approaches information as a source of power because it can enable the participation of citizens and avoid the legitimizing functions of which the structuralist warns. The planner's information can also call attention to the structural, organizational, and political barriers that needlessly distort the information that citizens rely on to act. The progressive perspective thus combines the insights of the liberal and structuralist views and goes one step further. It recognizes that political-economic power may function systematically to misinform affected publics, by misrepresenting risk or costs and benefits, for instance. The progressive view anticipates such regular, structurally rooted, misinformation and organizes information to counteract this 'noise.'[108]

Forester argues that misinformation can effect action by shaping citizen's comprehension, trust, consent, and beliefs.[109] The role of the progressive practitioner is therefore to anticipate and counteract this possibility. Such a role does not require

> any new progressive social technology or political gimmickry. Planners already have a vast repertoire of practical responses with which they can

counteract mis-information: commonplace acts of checking, double-checking, testing, consulting experts, seeking third-party counsel, clarifying issues, exposing assumptions, reviewing and citing the record, appealing to precedent, invoking traditional values (democratic participation, for example), spreading questions about unexplored possibilities, spotlighting jargon and revealing meaning, negotiating for clearly specified outcomes and values, working through informal networks to get information, bargaining for information, holding others to public commitment, and so on.[110]

Forester and other communicative planning theorists[111] who have built on his ideas have seen the facilitator in CI as having a crucial role in determining how progressive processes will be. To the extent that facilitators are committed to a progressive ethics of practice, they can aid the decision-making process in anticipating and counteracting both the systematic and ad hoc sources of distortion and inequity. If sponsors and participants are not committed to comparable standards of progressive practice, the task of the facilitator is more challenging but not impossible. Progressive practice thus has the potential to extend and complement the trend towards structured decision-making by explicitly recognizing and addressing the political and ethical issues that suffuse CI.

Contingent Approaches to Consensus-based CI

A third and again potentially complementary way in which decision-making may be aided is by selecting and designing CI approaches and techniques so that they best fit the context and goals of the sponsor. Relatively little explicit attention had been given to addressing these critical choices until recently, when Thomas proposed his 'Effective Decision Model of Public Involvement.'[112] His model is an attempt to balance the 'pure enthusiasm of the proponents of public involvement' and 'the scepticism of the critics' by taking a contingent perspective on the choice of CI approaches and techniques. Thomas argues that

[t]he desirability of public involvement depends primarily on the relative need for quality versus the need for acceptability in an eventual decision. Some public issues embody greater needs for quality, that is, for consistency with professional standards, legislative mandates, budgetary constraints and the like. Other issues carry greater needs for acceptability, for

public acceptance of or compliance with any decision. Where the needs for quality are greater, there is less need to involve the public. Where, on the other hand, the needs for acceptability are greater, the need to involve the public and to share decision-making authority will be greater. Where both needs are substantial, there will be competing needs for public involvement and for constraints on the involvement.[113]

The model is based on research by Vroom and Yetton and Vroom and Jago, who addressed the question of when and how managers should involve subordinates in making decisions.[114] Thomas argues that, while the model requires adaptations to recognize the special nature of public-sector and public-involvement issues (e.g., greater difficulty in defining the relevant public), private-sector decisions involve questions of quality and acceptability comparable to decisions regarding CI. The model's predictive power was tested by Thomas through re-analysis of forty governmental decisions made with varying degrees of public involvement. Consistency with the model's recommendations proved the best predictor of the effectiveness of those decisions.

Using the term 'manager' for the sponsor of the CI, Thomas differentiates five basic choices:

- *Autonomous managerial decision.* The manager solves the problem or makes the decision alone without public involvement.
- *Modified autonomous managerial decision.* The manager seeks information from segments of the public, but decides alone in a manner that may or may not reflect group influence.
- *Segmented public consultation.* The manager shares the problem separately with segments of the public, getting ideas and suggestions, then makes a decision that reflects group influence.
- *Unitary public consultation.* The manager shares the problem with the public as a single assembled group, getting ideas and suggestions, then makes a decision that reflects group influence. (This approach requires only that all members of the public have the opportunity to be involved, such as in well-publicized public hearings, not that everyone participate.)
- *Public decision.* The manager shares the problem with the assembled public, and together the manager and the public attempt to reach agreement on a solution.[115]

To make an appropriate choice among the five approaches, Thomas argues that the manager must ask a series of seven questions about the characteristics of the context and the goals of the process:

- What are the quality requirements that must be incorporated in any decision?
- Do I have sufficient information to make a high-quality decision?
- Is the problem structured such that alternative solutions are not open to redefinition?
- Is public acceptance of the decision critical to effective implementation? If so, is that acceptance reasonably certain if the manager decides alone?
- Who is the relevant public? And, does that public consist of an organized public, more than one organized group, or some combination of the three?
- Does the relevant public share the agency's goals to be obtained in solving the problem?
- Is there likely to be conflict within the public on the preferred solution?

The decision tree in figure 7.2 demonstrates the CI choices that the sponsor should make depending on the answers to the seven questions. Depending on the answers to the first four questions, the sponsor may decide to make a managerial decision or go on to consider involving stakeholders in a consultation or public decision. Depending on the specifics, the consultation or public decision would selectively utilize potential approaches and techniques. For example, the model indicates that sponsors should use a unitary consultation first for any situation that features (a) a need for information, (b) a lack of clear problem structure, (c) a need for acceptance that requires involvement, and (d) public disagreement with the sponsor's goals. 'The latitude for public influence is so great in a situation in which information is needed and the problem is unstructured that a unitary consultation is recommended despite the public's disagreement with the [sponsoring] agency's goals. Using a unitary consultation, a manager can decide in a manner that reflects both public input and agency priorities.'[116] Such consultation could be assisted by the use of progressive facilitators and structured decision-making approaches in negotiation and consensus-based approaches as described in previous sections.

Those who generally believe that there is a need for more CI in environmental governance are often uncomfortable with Thomas's model because of its potential recommendations for no or limited CI. It is not

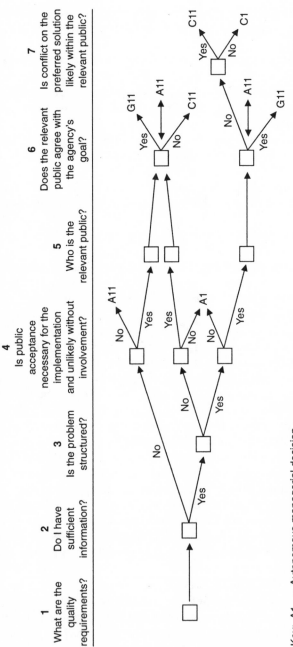

1
What are the quality requirements?

2
Do I have sufficient information?

3
Is the problem structured?

4
Is public acceptance necessary for the implementation and unlikely without involvement?

5
Who is the relevant public?

6
Does the relevant public agree with the agency's goal?

7
Is conflict on the preferred solution likely within the relevant public?

Key: A1   = Autonomous managerial decision
A11 = Modified autonomous managerial decision
C1   = Segmented public consultation
C11 = Unitary public consultation
G11 = Public decision

Source: Thomas, *Public Participation in Public Decisions* (1995).

Figure 7.2 The effective-decision model of public involvement

easy for them to accept that from the sponsor's perspective there are situations where the costs exceed the benefits of any or more extensive CI. On the other hand, they should be reassured by Thomas's conclusion from his re-analysis that in 91 per cent of the cases examined the model indicated the need for public involvement in which influence is shared with the public.[117]

5. Evaluation of CI

As indicated at the beginning of this chapter, evaluation of CI is very difficult and is an infant art that has only infrequently been applied and then usually with partial or limited results. This is illustrated in various ways by four recent assessment attempts, each of which represents different types of approaches to CI evaluation with associated combinations of theoretical and empirical strengths and weaknesses. Renn, Webler, and Weidmann made an ambitious attempt to evaluate approaches to CI based on the underlying principles of 'critical theory,' particularly the work of Jürgen Habermas.[118] Starting with primary goals of 'fairness' and 'competence,' they developed a set of evaluative questions that were applied by contributing authors to eight different 'models' of CI, each of which involves elements of negotiation-based approaches (citizen advisory committees; citizen panels or planning cells; citizen juries; citizen initiatives; negotiated rule-making; mediation; compensation and benefit-sharing for facility siting; and Dutch study groups). The major overall conclusion was that no single 'model' of CI, as defined in the study, is clearly preferable over another in terms of their broadly defined objectives of fairness and competence. Rather, their assessments emphasize the importance of practice-oriented issues (how any of these approaches is implemented) and the need to consider approaches in light of the characteristics of the problem at hand. However, while the strength of this work lies in its attempt to be explicit about the normative and theoretical framework and specific goals and objectives upon which the evaluation is based, the editors are refreshingly candid about the unforeseen difficulties that were encountered when proponents and reviewers of each of the models applied the evaluative questions and found it exceedingly difficult to resolve differences among their subjective judgments.

More recently, Chess and Purcell attempted to synthesize the findings of existing evaluation studies of CI involving public meetings, workshops, and community advisory committees. While the authors recognized the need for objectives, they did not present their own explicit objectives to serve as the basis for the analysis. In their view, 'developing a definition [of success] is problematic because of the limited theory and the diversity of perspectives about the goals of public participation.'[119] Instead, they relied on the various implicit or explicit objectives adopted by the authors of the reviewed studies. They did distinguish between process and outcome criteria and concluded that 'the forms of participation do not determine process or outcome success,' and that 'participants' satisfaction with participatory processes is clearly not associated with satisfaction with an outcome.'[120] In response to the difficulties they encountered in synthesizing results, they argued that criteria for evaluating CI efforts need greater attention, and should be drawn from stakeholders and agencies involved in the effort, as well as from universal criteria based on theory. Finally, they observed that actions of agencies can have a major influence on outcome and process success, and that there is some supportive evidence for what they referred to as 'practitioner rules of thumb' regarding 'what works' in process design.

A third type of approach is illustrated by Yosie and Herbst's study involving interviews with several key informants knowledgeable about the practice of CI in the United States, as well as in-depth assessments of the structure and outcomes of several CI case studies.[121] Their overall goal was to identify 'lessons learned, key issues and future challenges.' It is notable that this evaluation did not proceed by developing an explicit set of objectives for CI, nor does it explicitly acknowledge the range of CI approaches and techniques that could be employed in various circumstances. Although their key findings are broad generalizations, they reiterate those found in various assessments:

- The increased use of stakeholder-involvement processes over the past decade in the U.S. represents a societal interest in more interactive forms of decision-making. Rather than being a transitory phenomenon, this development reflects a culmination of a series of developments that have begun to yield significant changes in the methods of making environmental decisions.
- Environmental-stakeholder processes are frequently not well managed because a number of convenors, facilitators, and participants are not aware of, or have not made effective use of, knowledge and practices developed over time.
- There is a significant need to achieve a better match between the

choice of a stakeholder process and the problem it is attempting to solve.

• The decision whether or not to utilize a stakeholder process should be guided by an evaluation of key issues.

• Stakeholder processes challenge the ability of the scientific community to participate effectively in a growing number of environmental decisions. New approaches to delivering and communicating scientific information are needed to better inform stakeholder deliberations.

• While increasingly participating in stakeholder processes, environmental and business groups have growing concerns about their use.

• The future use of stakeholder processes will be significantly influenced by the ability to successfully manage five major challenges: (1) achieving quality management of stakeholder processes; (2) measuring stakeholder processes and results; (3) engaging the scientific community in stakeholder processes; (4) integrating stakeholder deliberations with existing decision-making processes; and (5) determining whether improved stakeholder processes yield improved decisions.

Finally, a recent study evaluating public participation in Land and Resource Management Planning (LRMP) in British Columbia illustrates a fourth type of approach, one that is focused on a specific CI program and in a Canadian context.[122] It began with an extensive literature review to identify criteria appropriate to evaluating the eighteen consensus-seeking, multi-stakeholder planning processes initiated at the sub-regional scale under LRMP. Two sets of criteria were defined. The first set included ten criteria focused on the evaluation of the planning process and relating to support for the process, representation, resources, and process design. Their detailing reflected commonly recommended best-practice principles and procedures emerging in the recent literature on negotiation-based CI approaches, such as the round tables (table 7.1) and others referenced in section 3. The second set innovatively focused on CI outcomes for 'community capacity' defined as 'the ability of residents in the planning area to maintain and build meaningful involvement in the ongoing planning and management of public lands.'[123] Four criteria relating to information, resources and skills, structures, and attitudes were defined respectively for participants, organizations, and government agencies involved in the CI process. These drew more specifically on the literature relating to negotiation-based decision-making, community development, community health planning, community psychology, organizational development, and planning and political theory.

Data was collected by telephone surveys of participants in thirteen of the LRMPs, using questions based on the criteria. Results were summarized in terms of perceived strengths, weaknesses, challenges, lessons, and advice. Using these results, questions were designed for more detailed studies of three cases, one of which focused on capacity-building outcomes. The interviews generated an exceptionally rich qualitative assessment of the participants' evaluations, with detailed insights into performance according to the wide array of indicators. A notable strength of this approach to evaluation is the extent to which it reveals whether the principles and procedures of CI established at the outset of a program were actually followed and achieved in practice as perceived by participants. This study once again indicates the immense difficulties encountered in putting what are thought to be 'best practices' of CI into practice. The reasons are numerous, include both intentional and unintentional actions by the participants, and relate to not only the CI processes themselves but also the specific issues being addressed and the particulars of the governance and political context within which they take place. The notable weakness of this approach follows from its strength in that generalizations about the merits of CI approaches are difficult to make. As evident in this study, conclusions and recommendations tend to focus predictably on what needs to be done to faithfully implement the 'best practices' espoused at the outset rather than on questioning whether they are the 'best practices' and how they can be made 'better.'

Despite the weaknesses in evaluation of CI as it has been practised to date, there is much that is known about what constitute 'best practices' in the use of the tools and their appropriateness to particular environmental issues, and how choices about these are influenced by the different normative perspectives on the governance system that are desired. Susskind and colleagues 1150-page *Consensus Building Handbook* provides a comprehensive overview of the state of the art, demonstrating the breadth of agreement about 'best practices' while highlighting where significant differences in views persist.[124] This understanding can be utilized in adopting an adaptive strategy to accelerate the development of knowledge about 'best practices' for CI by building on insights into the strengths and remedying the weaknesses in evaluation methods.

6. Future Trends in CI Policies and Research

Three decades of experience with CI in Canada and elsewhere have yielded one incontrovertible conclusion: It is not easy to achieve. Some would say CI is the worst part of environmental governance. Yet, most would agree that environmental governance without CI is not an alternative that will be considered seriously in the future. In our view, the general trend towards increasing and diversifying CI in environmental governance, in particular the use of negotiation-based approaches, will continue. Further, despite the weaknesses in the evaluation literature, we believe there is much to learn from the experience over the last three decades that can guide improved CI policy and research. In this concluding section we highlight key components of a trend towards a contingent and adaptive strategy for CI policy. This means a strategy that applies the emerging understanding of CI approaches that are appropriate to specific goals and contexts. It also means adopting best practices in employing techniques, while incorporating explicit procedures for learning, assessment, and experimentation. We present these as trends that we perceive emerging in Canada today and carrying us into the first decade of the new millenium.

Trends in the Environmental-Governance Context for CI

Overall, the shift from managerialist towards more pluralist and popularist philosophies and forms of governance will continue. The longer-term trend towards the downsizing of governments and devolving of responsibilities to local governments will also continue, and this will be accompanied by increasing reliance on business and civil society in governance. These are continuing and more fundamental trends in governance that are to a substantial extent independent of the cycles of concern for specific issues such as environmental protection and sustainability. Before too long, in response to the rebuilding concerns about threats to the environment, there will be a third burst of enthusiasm for environmental initiatives and associated innovations in CI. Once again, the innovations in CI will take off from a base of ongoing practice that is considerably more extensive, intensive, and diverse than it was at the beginning of the previous wave. In all likelihood this third burst of innovation will take the principles and practices of CI into new territories for negotiation-based approaches before the wave once again breaks under the twin pressures of increasing questioning of overly ambitious experiments and the resurfacing of greater priorities than environmental issues. The extent and durability of innovation in the next wave depends importantly on other emerging trends that are discussed below.

Trends towards Contingent Approaches

If the first burst of innovation was largely about gaining acceptance for using CI at all and the second burst was focused on diversifying and extending its utilization, in particular through negotiation-based methods, then the third burst will be about contingent approaches. There has been growing recognition of the critical need to select and customize CI approaches and techniques to the particular situations to which they are being applied. Increasing understanding of the costs and benefits of different approaches and techniques of CI is making it possible to judge better when CI is merited and, if it is, which combination of approaches and techniques are most appropriate to each part of the process. Progress in the next wave of innovations will be hugely dependent on the extent to which contingent approaches are implemented based on this growing understanding.

Trends in Best Practices

Despite the enormous challenges inherent in assessing experience with CI approaches and techniques, there is clearly a trend towards a substantial and growing core of agreement about many of the key considerations in selecting, designing, and implementing what is needed in a particular situation. It is significant that much of what practitioners have developed over the years through long and extensive experience as rules of thumb is now being found to be consistent with a growing body of literature based on more explicit theorizing and experimentation. In particular, there is a good understanding of the key questions that should be addressed by sponsors of CI and the critical role that they need to play in the process. Likewise, the pivotal importance of the facilitators' role and the principles and practices that they should employ are increasingly well understood. Among the newly emerging ideas on best practices there is some convergence around the middle-ground potentials of progressive and structured decision-making within negotiation-based processes. The productivity of the innovations in the next wave will depend greatly on the sponsors' and facilitators' skills in bringing to bear the established and newly emerging best practices.

Trends towards Adaptive Strategies

While much can be learned from past experiences, there remain enormous uncertainties surrounding CI approaches and techniques, which are driving a nascent trend towards more learning-oriented and adaptive strategies. Recognizing the relatively untried nature of many newer approaches, such as those utilizing consensus, CI programs are increasingly incorporating assessment procedures to learn from experience. These procedures are employed to adapt lessons learned into future programs. Ongoing assessments are also built into the CI process so that changes can be made in real time. Accompanying this emphasis is increasing attention to observing what 'successful' practitioners do. It can be anticipated that research and assessment will be extended to include the revolutionary opportunities for CI approaches and techniques that are being created by the development of information technologies and the World Wide Web.[125] Clearly, progress and the longevity of the next wave of CI innovations will be affected critically by the ability to test the emerging new hypotheses and apply the results in further innovations incorporating further rounds of experimentation. Fundamental to success will be the utilization of evaluation frameworks that give explicit consideration to (1) the hierarchy of CI goals and objectives, ranging from the ideology adopted to the tools employed, and how these vary among the differing viewpoints of sponsors, participants, and society; (2) the specifics of the environmental and sustainability issues to be addressed; and (3) the structure and politics of the governance context within which CI takes place.

Reasonable Expectations, Better Results

Whether the trends we have suggested materialize depend on a multitude of factors, and a wide variety of scenarios are possible. However, from the first two waves of innovation we are confident in suggesting two major lessons. First, the genesis and path of the next wave will be powerfully influenced by the unpredictable vagaries of public opinion, politics, and environmental events. Based on experience to date, we would do well to have more reasonable expectations of CI the next time. Second, substantial progress in the art and science of CI will continue to be made as sponsors, facilitators, and participants become more skilled and practised in applying and advancing best practices. Better results can reasonably be expected.

NOTES

This paper was funded as part of the SSHRC/PRC Environment Trends Project. Most valuable comments on an earlier draft were provided by Elizabeth Dowdeswell, Edward Parson, and participants in the workshop at Green College, University of British Columbia, 23–4 April 1999.

1 See National Round Table on the Environment and the Economy, *Building Consensus for a Sustainable Future: Guiding Principles* (Ottawa: National Round Table, 1993); National Round Table, *Building Consensus for a Sustainable Future: Putting Principles into Practice* (Ottawa: National Round Table, 1996); National Round Table, *Sustainable Strategies for Oceans: A Co-Management Guide* (Ottawa: National Round Table, 1998).

2 See United States National Research Council, Committee on Risk Characterization, *Understanding Risk: Informing Decisions in a Democratic Society* (Washington: National Academy Press, 1996); Presidential/Congressional Commission on Risk Assessment and Risk Management, *Framework for Environmental Health Risk Management*, Final report, vol. 1 (Washington: 1997).

3 See World Bank, *The World Bank Participation Sourcebook* (Washington: World Bank, 1996).

4 The authors have had experience with CI in environmental governance, both as practitioners and academics, from the local to the global level since the early 1970s. However, they have not previously worked together and approach the field from different traditions: McDaniels emphasizing the use of the analytical techniques of decision theory and Dorcey focusing on the design of institutional arrangements and processes. These differing traditions and our varied experiences, particularly in British Columbia, have had a strong influence on how we have chosen to examine CI trends in this chapter. Indeed, the confluence of these two traditions in recent times is one of the significant trends we highlight.

5 See F.N. Laird, 'Participatory Analysis, Democracy and Technological Decision Making,' *Science, Technology and Human Values* 18, no. 3 (1993): 343.

6 See B.A. Williams and A.R. Matheny, *Democracy, Dialogue and Environmental Disputes: The Contested Language of Social Regulation* (New Haven: Yale University Press, 1995).

7 See T. Beierle, 'Public Participation in Environmental Decisions: An Evalua-

tive Framework Using Social Goals,' Discussion paper 99–06 (Washington: Resources for the Future Inc, 1998), 2.

8 See S. Arnstein, 'A Ladder of Citizen Participation,' *Journal of the American Institute of Planners* 35 (1969): 216–24.

9 Ibid., 216

10 Ibid.

11 See F. Berkes, 'Co-management: Bridging the Two Solitudes,' *Northern Perspectives* 22, no. 2–3 (1994): 18–20; E.M. Rocha, 'A Ladder of Empowerment,' *Journal of Planning Education and Research* 17 (1997): 31–44.

12 See O. Renn, T. Webler, and P. Wiedemann, *Fairness and Competence in Citizen Participation* (Dordrecht: Kluwer Academic Press, 1995).

13 See T. Beierle, *Public Participation*, 3.

14 Ibid., 2. See also J.B. Rosener, 'User Oriented Evaluation: A New Way to View Citizen Participation,' in G.A. Daneke et al., eds, *Public Involvement and Social Impact Assessment* (Boulder, CO: Westview Press, 1983), 45.

15 The literature on CI in Canadian environmental governance is widely scattered, partial, and uneven in its description and analysis. The brief overview in this section is very preliminary and is not the result of comprehensive or detailed studies. It leaves many questions that need to be addressed in future research analysing experiences with CI in Canadian environmental governance over the last three eventful decades.

16 In pointing to the diverse earlier roots of CI in Canada, commentators have variously emphasized the significance of extending the franchise in the twentieth century (Tester, 1992); the role of education and community-development organizations, tenant and taxpayers associations, and co-operative unions since the 1930s depression (Draper, 1978); the influence of the British tradition of public involvement in town-planning decisions, which was already evident in Canada by the 1920s, and the U.S. politics of protest in the 1960s (Lucas, 1978).

17 See A.H.J. Dorcey, 'Research for Water Resources Management: The Rise and Fall of Great Expectations,' in M.C. Healey and R.R. Wallace, eds, *Canadian Aquatic Resources* (Canadian Bulletin of Fisheries and Aquatic Sciences 215 (Ottawa: Fisheries and Oceans Canada, 1987).

18 See, e.g., the National Environmental Policy Act, 1969.

19 See H. Lash, 'Planning in a Human Way: Personal Reflections on the Regional Planning Experience in Greater Vancouver' (Ottawa: Ministry of State for Urban Affairs, 1976).

20 See Dorcey, 'Research.'

21 See W.R.D. Sewell, 'Public Involvement,' in *Monograph on Comprehensive River Basin Planning* (Ottawa: Environment Canada, 1975), 75.

22 See D. Smith, *Monitoring Report on the Public Participation Program of the GVRD* (Vancouver: Greater Vancouver Regional District and Ministry of State for Urban Affairs, October 1974), quoted in H. Lash, *Planning in a Human Way*, 31.
23 See Sewell, 'Public Involvement,' 75.
24 See ibid., 108.
25 See G. Beakhust, 'The Berger Inquiry,' in B. Sadler, ed., *Involvement and the Environment*, vol. 2 (Edmonton: Environment Council of Alberta, 1979), 312.
26 See B. Brule et al., *An Evaluation of the River Basin Planning and Implementation Programs* (Ottawa: Environment Canada, 1981).
27 See Economic Council of Canada, *Reforming Regulation* (Ottawa: Supply and Services Canada, 1981).
28 See W.E. Rees, 'Environmental Assessment and Planning Process in Canada,' in S.D. Clarke, *Environmental Assessment in Australia and Canada* (Vancouver: Westwater Research Centre, UBC, 1981).
29 See D.M. Rosenberg et al., 'Recent Trends in Environmental Impact Assessment,' *Canadian Journal of Fisheries and Aquatic Sciences* 38 (1981): 591–624.
30 See A.H.J. Dorcey, 'Perspectives on Sustainable Development in Water Management: Towards Agreement in the Fraser River Basin' (Vancouver: Westwater Research Centre, 1991).
31 See M. Howlett, 'The Round Table Experience: Representation and Legitimacy in Canadian Environmental Policy-making,' *Queen's Quarterly* 97, no. 4 (1990): 580–601; Projet de Société, *Planning for a Sustainable Future: Canadian Choices for Transitions to Sustainability* (Ottawa: National Round Table on Environment and Economy, 1995).
32 See Howlett, 'The Round Table Experience.'
33 See British Columbia, Round Table on the Environment and the Economy, *Reaching Agreement: Implementing Consensus Processes in British Columbia*, vol. 2 (Victoria: BC Round Table, 1991).
34 Ibid., 2
35 See National Round Table, *Building Consensus*.
36 See Commission on Resources and Environment, *Strategic Land Use Planning Source Book* (Victoria: CORE, 1996), 167.
37 See Commission on Resources and Environment, *A Sustainability Act for British Columbia – Provincial Land Use Strategy*, vol. 1 (Victoria: CORE, 1994).
38 See Commission on Resources and Environment, *Public Participation – Provincial Land Use Strategy*, vol. 3. (Victoria: CORE, 1994), 11.
39 See Commission on Resources and Environment, *Dispute Resolution – Provincial Land Use Strategy*, vol. 4 (Victoria: CORE, 1994).

40 See G. Hoberg and K. Harrison, 'It's Not Easy Being Green: The Politics of Canada's Green Plan,' *Canadian Public Policy* 20 (1994): 119–37.

41 See BC Round Table on the Environment and the Economy, Commission on Resources and Environment, Fraser Basin Management Program, and National Round Table on the Environment and the Economy, *Local Round Tables: Realizing Their Full Potential* (Vancouver: Fraser Basin Management Board, 1994).

42 See A.H.J. Dorcey, 'Collaborating towards Sustainability Together: The Fraser Basin Management Board and Program,' in Dan Shrubsole and Bruce Mitchell, eds, *Practising Sustainable Water Management: Canadian and International Experiences* (Cambridge, ON: Canadian Water Resources Association, 1997).

43 See A.H.J. Dorcey, L. Doney, and H. Rueggeberg, *Public Involvement in Government Decision-Making: Choosing the Right Model* (Victoria: BC Round Table on the Environment and the Economy, 1994).

44 See Dorcey, 'Collaborating towards Sustainability'; D. Duffy et al., *Improving the Shared Decision-Making Model: An Evaluation of Public Participation in Land and Resource Management Planning (LRMP) in British Columbia*, vols 1 and 2 (Vancouver: Dept. of Geography and School of Resource and Environmental Management, Simon Fraser University, 1998).

45 See A. McAfee, 'When Theory Meets Practice – Citizen Participation in Planning,' *Plan Canada* 37, no. 3 (1997): 18–22; M. Seelig and J. Seelig, 'City-Plan: Participation or Abdication?' *Plan Canada* 37, no. 3 (1997): 18–22.

46 See M. Charih and A. Daniels, *New Public Management and Public Administration in Canada* (Toronto: Institute of Public Administration in Canada, 1997).

47 See A.H.J. Dorcey and C.L. Riek, 'Negotiation-based Approaches to the Settlement of Environmental Disputes in Canada,' in *The Place of Negotiation in Environmental Assessment* (Ottawa: Canadian Environmental Assessment Research Council, 1987).

48 See B. Gray, *Collaborating: Finding Common Ground for Multiparty Problems* (San Francisco: Jossey-Bass, 1989).

49 See D.J. Amy, *The Politics of Environmental Mediation* (New York: Columbia University Press, 1987).

50 See L. Susskind and J. Cruikshank, *Breaking the Impasse: Consensual Approaches to Resolving Disputes* (New York: Basic Books, 1987).

51 See S. Kaner et al., *Facilitator's Guide to Participatory Decision-Making* (Gabriola Island, BC: New Society Publishers, 1996); and C.W. Moore, *The Mediation Process: Practical Strategies for Resolving Conflicts*, 2nd ed. (San Francisco: Jossey-Bass, 1996).

52 See R. Fisher and W. Ury, *Getting to Yes: Reaching Agreement without Giving In* (Boston: Houghton Mifflin, 1981); H. Raiffa, *The Art and Science of Negotiation* (Cambridge, MA: Harvard University Press, 1982); Moore, *The Mediation Process*; Susskind and Cruikshank, *Breaking the Impasse*; and S.L. Carpenter and W.J.D. Kennedy, *Managing Public Disputes: A Practical Guide to Handling Conflict and Reaching Agreement* (San Francisco: Jossey-Bass, 1988).

53 See V. Coover et al., *Resource Manual for a Living Revolution: A Handbook of Skills and Tools for Social Change Activists* (Philadelphia: New Society Publishers, 1977).

54 See Kaner et al., *Facilitator's Guide* 1996; and R.M. Schwartz, *The Skilled Facilitator: Practical Wisdom for Developing Effective Groups* (San Francisco: Jossey-Bass, 1994).

55 Ibid., xi.

56 See Moore, *The Mediation Process*, 8.

57 See D.M. Kolb, *When Talk Works: Profiles of Mediators* (San Francisco: Jossey-Bass, 1994).

58 Ibid. The distinction between a facilitator and mediator is highly important, for while mediators are skilled at facilitation, facilitators are not trained in mediation. Yet often in practice facilitators find themselves being drawn into situations where mediation is required. At a time when the practice of mediation is striving to become a credible profession, there are major concerns that facilitators who are not competent mediators could bring mediation into disrepute. It is important to keep this distinction in mind, even though we do not discuss its implications further in the remainder of the paper.

59 See Dorcey and Riek, 'Negotiation-based Approaches.'

60 See L. Susskind, S. McKearnan, and J. Thomas-Larmer, *The Consensus Building Handbook: A Comprehensive Guide to Reaching Agreement* (Thousand Oaks, CA: Sage, 1999).

61 See National Round Table, *Building Consensus* (1998), 14.

62 See E. Ostrom, *Governing the Commons: The Evolution of Institutions for Collective Action* (New York: Cambridge University Press, 1990); D.W. Bromley, *Making the Commons Work: Theory, Practice and Policy* (San Francisco: Institute for Contemporary Studies Press, 1992).

63 See National Round Table, *Building Consensus* (1998).

64 See P.A. Pross, *Group Politics and Public Policy*, 2nd ed. (Toronto: Oxford University Press, 1992), 18.

65 See J.E. Gardner, 'Environmental Non-Government Organisations and the Management of the Aquatic Environment for Sustainable Development,' in

A.H.J. Dorcey, ed., *Perspectives on Sustainable Development in Water Management: Towards Agreement in the Fraser River Basin* (Vancouver: Westwater Research Centre, 1991), 326.

66 Ibid., 329.

67 Ibid., 331.

68 Ibid., 335.

69 See J. Burbidge, *Beyond Prince and Merchant: Citizen Participation and the Rise of Civil Society* (New York: Pact Publications, 1997), 8–9.

70 See B. Barber, *Strong Democracy: Participatory Politics for a New Age* (Berkeley: University of California Press, 1984).

71 See T. O'Riordan and H. Voisey, 'The Political Economy of the Sustainability Transition,' in O'Riordan and Voisey, eds, *The Transition to Sustainability: The Politics of Agenda 21 in Europe* (London: Earthscan, 1998). Contrary to this optimistic view, Putnam ('Bowling Alone,' 1995) has argued that there has been a decline in civic engagement that is reflected in falling electoral and civic-group participation in the United States.

72 See Barber, *Strong Democracy.*

73 See J. Elster, *Deliberative Democracy* (Cambridge: Cambridge University Press, 1998), 1.

74 See J. Habermas, *The Theory of Communicative Action*, trans. T. McCarthy (Boston: Beacon Press, 1984).

75 See J.E. Innes, 'Planning Theory's Emerging Paradigm: Communication Action and Interactive Practice,' *Journal of Planning Education and Research* 14, no. 3 (1995): 183–9.

76 For example, R.A.B. Bush and J.P. Folger, *The Promise of Mediation: Responding to Conflict through Empowerment and Recognition* (San Francisco: Jossey-Bass, 1994); and F.E. Dukes, *Resolving Public Conflict: Transforming Community and Governance* (Manchester: Manchester University Press, 1996).

77 See R.O. Washington and D. Strong, 'A Model for Teaching Environmental Justice in a Planning Curriculum,' *Journal of Planning Education and Research* 16 (1997): 280–90.

78 For example, W. Leiss and C. Chociolko, *Risk and Responsibility* (Montreal: McGill-Queen's University Press, 1994).

79 See K.N. Lee, *Compass and Gyroscope: Integrating Science and Politics for the Environment* (Washington: Island Press, 1993).

80 See National Round Table, *Building Consensus* (1993).

81 See R. Mitchell and R. Carson, *Using Surveys to Value Public Goods: The Contingent Valuation Method* (Washington: Resources for the Future, 1989).

82 See National Research Council, *Understanding Risk.*

83 See S. Kelman, 'Cost-Benefit Analysis: An Ethical Critique,' *Regulation* 5,

no. 1 (1981): 33–40; R. Gregory, S. Lichtenstein, and P. Slovic, 'Valuing Environmental Resources: A Constructive Approach,' *Journal of Risk and Uncertainty* 7 (1993): 177–97.

84 See National Research Council, *Understanding Risk.*

85 See P. Slovic, B. Fischhoff, and S. Lichtenstein, 'Behavioural Decision Theory,' *Annual Review of Psychology* 28 (1977): 1–39.

86 See D. Kahneman, P. Slovic and A. Tversky, *Judgment under Uncertainty: Heuristics and Biases* (New York: Cambridge University Press, 1982).

87 See J. March, 'Bounded Rationality, Ambiguity, and the Engineering of Choice,' *Bell Journal of Economics* 8, no. 4 (1978): 587–608; R. Keeney, *Value-Focused Thinking: A Path to Creative Decisionmaking* (Cambridge, MA: Harvard University Press, 1992); and H. Simon, 'Invariants of Human Behaviour,' *Annual Review of Psychology* 41 (1990): 1–19.

88 See J. Payne, J. Bettman, and E. Johnson, 'Behavioural Decision Research: A Constructive Processing Perspective,' *Annual Review of Psychology* 43 (1992): 87–132.

89 See I. Janis and L. Mann, *Decision Making: 'A Psychological Analysis of Conflict, Choice, and Commitment* (New York: Free Press, 1977).

90 See M. Olson, *The Logic of Collective Action: Public Goods and the Theory of Groups* (Cambridge, MA: Harvard University Press, 1965).

91 BC Round Table, *Reaching Agreement*, vol. 2.

92 See National Research Council, *Understanding Risk.*

93 See Susskind and Cruikshank, *Breaking the Impasse.*

94 See Fisher and Ury, *Getting to Yes.*

95 G. Hoberg, 'Environmental Policy: Alternative Styles,' in M.M. Atkinson, ed., *Governing Canada: Institutions and Public Policy* (Toronto: Harcourt, Brace, Jovanovich, 1993).

96 See M. McCloskey, 'The Limits of Collaboration,' *Harper's Magazine,* November 1996: 34–6.

97 See March, 'Bounded Rationality,' 598.

98 See Simon, 'Invariants of Human Behaviour,' 7.

99 See R. Keeney, *Value-focused Thinking: A Path to Creative Decisionmaking* (Cambridge, MA: Harvard University Press, 1992), 4.

100 See C.S. Holling, *Adaptive Environmental Assessment and Management* (New York: John Wiley and Sons, 1978); C. Walters, *Adaptive Management of Renewable Resources* (New York, Wiley: 1986).

101 See T. McDaniels, M. Healey, and R. Paisley, 'Cooperative Fisheries Management Involving First Nations in British Columbia: An Adaptive

Approach to Strategy Design,' *Canadian Journal of Fisheries and Aquatic Science* 51, no. 9 (1994): 2115–25.

102 See Walters, *Adaptive Management*.

103 See Keeney, *Value-focused Thinking*; and D. von Winterfeldt and W. Edwards, *Decision Analysis and Behavioral Research* (Cambridge: Cambridge University Press, 1986).

104 See S. Brams and P. Fishburn, *Approval Voting* (Boston: Birkhauser, 1983).

105 See von Winterfeldt and Edwards, *Decision Analysis*.

106 See Kaner et al., *Facilitator's Guide*.

107 See J. Forester, *Planning in the Face of Power* (Berkeley: University of California Press, 1989).

108 Ibid., 69.

109 Ibid., 36.

110 Ibid., 40.

111 E.g., Innes, 'Planning Theory's Emerging Paradigm'; J.E. Innes and D.E. Booher, 'Consensus Building as Role Playing and Bricolage: Towards a Theory of Collaborative Planning,' *Journal of the American Planning Association* 65, no. 1 (1999): 9–26.

112 See J.C. Thomas, *Public Participation in Public Decisions: New Skills and Strategies for Public Managers* (San Francisco: Jossey-Bass, 1995).

113 Ibid., 36.

114 See V.H. Vroom and P. Yetton, *Leadership and Decision Making* (Pittsburgh: University of Pittsburgh Press, 1973); V.H. Vroom and A.G. Jago, *The New Leadership: Managing Participation in Organizations* (Englewood Cliffs, NJ: Prentice-Hall, 1988).

115 See Thomas, *Public Participation*, 39–40.

116 Ibid., 80.

117 Ibid., 75.

118 See Renn, Webler, and Wiedemann, *Fairness and Competence in Public Participation*; Habermas, *Theory of Communicative Action*.

119 See C. Chess and K. Purcell, 'Public Participation and the Environment: Do We Know What Works?' *Environmental Science and Technology* 33, no. 16 (1998).

120 Ibid.

121 T.F. Yosie and T.D. Herbst, *Using Stakeholder Processes in Environmental Decisionmaking: An Evaluation of Lessons Learned, Key Issues, and Future Challenges* (Washington: Ruder Finn and ICF Inc., 1998).

122 See Duffy et al., *Improving the Shared Decision-Making Model*.

123 Ibid., 10.

124 See Susskind et al., *The Consensus Building Handbook*.
125 D.A. Schon, B. Sanyal, and W.J. Mitchell, *High Technology and Low-Income Communities: Prospects for the Positive Use of Advanced Information Technology* (Chicago: University of Chicago Press, 1999); D. Barney, *Prometheus Wired: The Hope for Democracy in the Age of Network Technology* (Chicago: University of Chicago Press, 2000).

8. Complex Network Management and the Governance of the Environment: Prospects for Policy Change and Policy Stability over the Long Term

Michael Howlett

1. Introduction: Modern Governance and Policy Change[1]

Contemporary governance takes place within a very different context than that of past decades. Government capacity in terms of human and organizational resources has increased, but its autonomy or ability to effect change independently has been eroded. This is due, at the international level, to the growth of powerful international and transnational actors and systems of exchange.[2] At the domestic level, however, modern governments have also been affected by the restructuring of societies into complex networks of interorganizational actors.[3] As a result of both movements, states have undergone a kind of 'hollowing' out, as various functions and activities traditionally undertaken by governments now involve a variety of significant non-governmental actors. This is true of services previously provided directly by government employees – from highway maintenance to psychiatric care – which have been contracted out to non-governmental organizations; the replacement or augmentation of legal and regulatory enforcement – in areas such as energy conservation and drinking and driving – by information-based quasi-private public relations campaigns; a general shift in regulatory activities from 'enforcement' to 'compliance' regimes; and a shift in the use of financial instruments away from subsidies towards the increased use of tax expenditures.[4] Intentionally or not, these changes have all had the effect of further deepening the network structure and complex character of contemporary life by fostering the creation and interaction of non-governmental and governmental organizations.[5]

These processes and paradoxes pose challenges to public administration at the turn of the century. The result, in practice, has been for many governments to develop a renewed interest in types of policy instruments that can deal with the complexities of modern societies. That is, governments in many countries have turned away from the use of a relatively limited number of traditional, more or less command-and-control-oriented, 'substantive' policy tools – such as public enterprises, regulatory agencies, subsidies, and 'moral suasion' – that attempt to influence directly the allocation of goods and services in society. Instead, modern governance more and more entails the use of a different set of tools, 'procedural' instruments such as government-NGO partnerships, public advisory commissions, interest-group funding, and information dissemination, which act in a less direct fashion to guide or steer social actors in the direction government wishes.[6]

As such, modern governance is becoming less and less a matter of direct service delivery and more and more one of indirect network management,[7] in which governments attempt to influence network actors, or restructure networks themselves, in order to manage change and achieve their ends.[8] Thus, contemporary governance, in contradistinction to government in past epochs, is very often indirect, subtle, and largely invisible. However, it requires a great deal of pre-planning and much foresight to steer the immense ship of state indirectly in what are largely uncharted waters.

This chapter examines how changes in a specific sector, the environment, are likely to affect policy outcomes in a single jurisdiction, Canada. It develops a model of policy change and assesses the manner in and extent to which such change can be led by governments, rather than simply reacted to. As such, it provides the foundation for a discussion of how Canadian governments can best position themselves to steer policy in the environmental sector in the near future.

2. Understanding Policy Change

Assessing the likely impact of developments in any particular sector on government policy-making requires an understanding of the general processes through which policies change. Moreover, it requires, at the outset, a clear understanding of exactly what the dependent variable, 'policy change,' entails.

At the present time, several competing definitions of policy change can be found in the literature of the policy sciences. Peter Hall, for example, has developed one notion of policy change as involving an alteration in either the means or ends of policy-making. In his work, Hall identified three types or 'orders' of change: *first-order* change, in which only the settings of policy instruments vary; *second-order* change, in which the types of instruments used to effect policy change; and *third-order* change, in which the goals of policy are altered.[9] Examples of first-order changes would include increasing the safety requirements that automobile manufacturers must follow or altering the level of allowed emissions from a factory. In these examples, second-order changes might involve such actions as adding or substituting financial incentives for regulation in the traffic-safety field or changing the type of instrument used in pollution control, such as changing from an administered emission standard to the imposition of a tax on emissions. Third-order changes would involve a shift in policy goals, such as moving away from a focus on private vehicles to one on public transit in the traffic-safety area or, in the pollution case, shifting from a focus upon *ex post* end-of-pipe regulation to a focus upon *ex ante* preventative production-process design.

Although this formulation has some advantages in terms of simplicity and clarity, there are some difficulties associated with its focus on changes in policy outputs as an exclusive measure of policy change. That is, as Hernes has pointed out in the context of a general discussion of sociological change processes, change can involve not only changes in outputs but also changes in inputs and in processes.[10] A focus on instrument change, in particular, is problematic in the case of public policy-making. This is because (1) the same types of instruments can be used for different ends, meaning a change in instrument will sometimes be evidence of a change in goals and other times not, (2) it is sometimes very difficult to disentangle goals and means in the way that is required for the analysis to proceed, and (3) even a change in the setting of an instrument can sometimes reflect a major shift in policy goals, as occurs, for instance, when income tax rates are increased in a progressive or punitive direction.[11]

Case studies of instances of policy change have in fact revealed a variety of different types of change and a number of distinct processes through which change has occurred. These same studies have also uncovered a number of processes and factors that inhibit policy change. Taking these together, it is possible to identify the key elements of policy change, the basic types of change, and the relationships that exist between basic processes and types of change.[12]

Policy Change and Policy Stability: Different Processes and Different Outcomes

Until fairly recently, it was often thought that policy change occurred largely as a result of events and occurrences that took place outside of stable policy-making systems or sets of relatively stable actors, instruments, institutions, and ideas related to specific policy-issue areas.[13] That is, it is possible to identify in almost any policy area a policy system consisting of the current collectively accepted definition of an issue, the current state of relevant policies (laws, regulations, fiscal instruments, and government programs and relationships) on the issue, and the people and institutions, both inside and outside government, actively engaged in and debating the policies' maintenance and modification.

The notion that such systems change only due to exogenous events or 'shocks' arose from the assumption that policy systems or subsystems were a form of stable or self-adjusting 'homeostatic' system.[14] Given an initial set of characteristics and composition, it was argued, policy systems would adjust to any internal changes and could only be thrown out of equilibrium by external events that introduced new dynamic elements into the system.[15] In addition, it was often argued that a policy system had a set capacity for action that, once reached, would prevent or restrict any internal changes from occurring – the 'overload' thesis.[16] This notion of the exogenous nature of policy change focused attention on the various types of external crises that could provoke a government response or policy change.

Although aspects of these models remain useful,[17] more recent conceptions of policy systems are more chaotic, abandoning notions of dynamic equilibria in favour of adaptive concepts in which systems can affect their environments and therefore alter the nature of their own constraints.[18] In the policy sciences, this shift has manifested itself in the acknowledgment that crises are not the only external source of policy change, and that factors internal or endogenous to policy-making systems and subsystems can also independently, or in conjunction with external factors, lead to policy change.[19]

This recognition has led to more-systematic efforts to measure, chronicle, and account for policy change. These efforts have moved well beyond the original 'external–internal' distinction and have identified both a number of distinct processes that influence the type and speed of change, and a number of distinct types of change determined by the scope and tempo of change. In particular, four major processes that underlie policy change and four major processes that enhance policy stability have been identified. Listed in order of their appearance in the literature, the processes that facilitate policy change are *systemic perturbations, venue change, policy-learning,* and *subsystem spillovers.* In contrast, the processes that enhance policy stability are *non-decisions, hard issues, path dependency,* and *closed networks.* Each of these processes is briefly described below.

Policy Change: Four Processes

The formal term *systemic perturbations* describes the oldest known form of policy change–enhancing process – that originating in external crises which upset established policy routines.[20] These can include idiosyncratic phenomena such as wars or disasters, or repeating events such as critical elections and leadership rotations. The well-known American student of policy processes, Paul Sabatier, for example, has argued that 'changes in the core aspects of a policy are usually the results of perturbations in non-cognitive factors external to the subsystem such as macro-economic conditions or the rise of a new systemic governing coalition.'[21] The principle mechanism by which change occurs is via the introduction of new actors into policy processes, often in the form of enhanced public attention being paid to a policy issue as a result of a perceived crisis situation.

Venue change refers to a second process of facilitating policy change, one related not so much to changes in external conditions as to changes in the strategies that policy actors follow in order to pursue their interests.[22] In their work on policy formation in the United States, for example, Baumgartner and Jones noted several strategies employed by actors currently excluded from policy systems or subsystems to gain access to policy deliberations and affect policy outcomes.[23] This usually involved members of policy communities attempting to 'break into' more restricted networks of central policy actors, but also can involve a jockeying for advantage among network actors.[24] Venue-shifting strategies usually involve the redefinition of a policy issue in order to facilitate the alteration of the location in which policy formulation occurs. These include notable instances such as when environmental groups attempt to redefine an issue like waste disposal from a technical issue to a public-health or property-rights one susceptible to lawsuits and recourse to the courts.[25] Not all policy issues are susceptible, or as susceptible, to re-framing or image manipulation, and not all political systems contain any, or as many, alternative policy venues. However, Baumgartner and Jones argue that actors outside of formal policy processes, especially, will attempt to alter existing policy images in the hope that an alternative venue can be located successfully in which their issues and concerns will be accorded a favourable reception.

Policy-learning refers to the third change-enhancing process described by policy scholars. It concerns the manner in which, as Hugh Heclo has noted, a relatively enduring alteration in policy results from policy-makers and participants learning from their own and others' experience with similar policies.[26] What is learned is often the experiences of other jurisdictions, but can also involve reflection on experiences originating within the confines of the subsystems' existing boundaries.[27] This behaviour can result in a variety of feedback-like policy-learning processes.[28] These include instances ranging from those in which policy actors in one country investigate and report on activities in another to situations in which administrators attempt to emulate 'best practices' in service delivery. While some types of learning are limited to reflections on existing practices, others are much more far-reaching and can affect a wide range of policy elements.[29] All involve the development and diffusion of new ideas into existing policy processes.

Finally, *subsystem spillovers* refers to the most recently described change process, one that occurs in situations in which activities in otherwise distinct subsystems transcend old policy boundaries and affect the structure or behaviour of other subsystems.[30] Instances such as those that have occurred as Internet-based computing collided with existing telecommunications regimes, or when long-established natural-resource policy actors find it necessary to deal with aboriginal land-claims issues, are examples of this phenomenon. Although this particular process of policy change has just begun to be examined, it would appear that spillovers can occur on specific issues without any permanent change in subsystem membership – subsystem intersection – or they can be more long-term in nature – subsystem convergence.[31] This general process, like systemic perturbations, affects policy processes largely through the introduction of new actors into otherwise stable subsystems. Unlike the case of systemic perturbations, however, here the new actors tend to be policy specialists and interested parties, rather than simply members of the aroused public.

Policy Stability: Four Processes

The question of policy stability and resistance to change has also been addressed in the policy literature over the course of the past thirty years. This literature, built up from numerous case studies, has highlighted the manner in which ideological and institutional factors insulate policy issues from the change processes outlined above.

Policy-making is about both making, and failing to make, decisions on policy issues. *Non-decisions* was a term used in the 1960s to describe situations in which policy debates remained mired in the status quo because alternatives were simply not considered or debated.[32] Examples of such instances range from the failure to deal with issues important to the urban poor to similar inaction on a wide range of women's issues. Non-decision-making has been the subject of many inquiries and studies, beginning with the community-power debates in political science in the early 1960s and 1970s[33] and extending into contemporary discourse analysis which reflects upon the manner in which ideologies operate to filter and colour the types of options put forward in the policy-making process.[34] All of these studies point to the significance of policy 'frames,' or relatively stable sets of overarching policy ideas that serve to filter out alternative visions of public policy.[35]

Hard issues is a term coined more recently to describe the oft-noted phenomenon in which the nature of a particular policy issue can insulate it from external change processes.[36] As students of the public-policy process in the 1970s (such as Cobb, Ross, and Ross) had noted, issues follow different routes onto government agendas, with a significant difference in policy processes being related to whether an issue involves significant elite or public mobilization.[37] More recently, May and Pollock, Lilie, and Vittes have argued that certain issues either fail to ignite popular interest or, if they do, fail to deliver a popular consensus on what kinds of change are required.[38] They argue that some issues like toxic regulation or utility rate-setting are 'hard' in that they generate policy discourses that are technical, legalistic, means-oriented, or, simply, unfamiliar to most members of the public. Such issues are more likely to involve smaller sets of specialized policy actors than issues such as traffic safety or health, which are more likely to generate public attention and discussion. Hard issues, therefore, are more likely to involve only a limited number of specialized policy actors and serve as a barrier to the entry of new actors into existing subsystems.[39]

Path dependence is another recent term for an older observation, one that refers to the manner in which current policy decisions are influenced by the institutional and behavioural legacies of past ones.[40] Policy legacies affect current policy-making due to factors such as sunk costs or institutional routines and procedures that can force decision-making in particular directions – by either eliminating or distorting the range of options available to governments.[41] Hence, for example, a decision to alter an existing nuclear energy program in which billions may already have been invested is much more difficult to make than if the program had not yet been started. As Weir, March and Olsen, and others have argued, stability is expected to occur when an issue is routinized or institutionalized.[42]

Closed networks refer to a more recently identified source of policy stability, which is based simply on the ability of existing key policy actors to prevent new members from entering into policy debates and discourses. This can occur, for example, when governments refuse to place prominent environmentalists on environmental advisory boards or regulatory tribunals, when funding is not provided for intervenors at environmental assessments, when the creation of such boards and procedures is resisted, or due to the behaviour of interest groups in pursuing specialized issue niches.[43] Rhodes, Schaap and van Twist, and many others have argued that actors in all subsystems tend to construct 'policy monopolies' in which the interpretation and general approach to a subject is more or less fixed.[44] Only when this monopoly is broken and new members emerge into these subsystems would a policy be expected to change in any significant sense of the term.

Key Variables and Measures of Policy Change

This brief outline of the major processes of policy change and stability found in the policy literature highlights the commonalities found in the central variables affected by and involved in these policy dynamics. At first glance, the central variables are the nature of the actors, institutions, issues, and ideas found in a policy sector. However, as Table 8.1 suggests, the eight processes identified above in fact share only two common variables. That is, these processes underline the significance of the entrance of (1) new actors, be they the public or policy 'elites,' and (2) new ideas, whether specific new knowledge or more-

TABLE 8.1
Key variables involved in policy change and stability processes

Change variable	Change process	Stability process	Variation causing (stability)/change
Actors	Subsystem spillovers	Closed networks	(Lack of) Entrance of new actors into subsystem
	Systemic perturbations	Hard issues	(Lack of) Mobilization of public around issue
Ideas	Policy-learning	Non-decisions	(Lack of) Entrance of new ideas into subsystem
	Venue/Image change	Path dependency	
			(Lack of) Change in institutional discourses

general image frames, as the major factors affecting both policy change and policy stability.

Actors, of course, come in different types and occupy different locations in the policy-making process. Generally speaking, they can usefully be thought of as existing in the general public or *policy universe*; in the set of attentive actors within the policy universe who have some knowledge of affairs in the policy area in question, or the *policy community*; or in the set of those actors who have some interest in a particular area that lead them to interact routinely with other interested actors in more restricted *policy networks*.[45] 'New' actors in this context can refer either to the movement of actors from the policy universe into a policy community or network, or the movement of actors from a policy community to a network.

Ideas, similarly, come in different shapes and sizes. They exist at both the cognitive and normative levels and can play a significant role in affecting either the foreground propositions or background assumptions of policy debate.[46] Each type of idea – programmatic principles and discursive frames, in the case of the foregrounded ideas of policy experts and the public, or paradigmatic idea-sets and attitudinal values, in the case of background assumptions of either group – can have significant policy implications. New ideas of any of these types can result in policy change, although the extent of change will vary directly with the generality of the types of ideas involved. That is, a shift in public sentiments and attitudes, for example, can be expected to have a broad, but diffuse, impact on policy content. By contrast, the introduction of a new programmatic idea by a policy elite would be expected to have a much more specific and concentrated impact.

3. A Vector Theory of Policy Change: A Taxonomy and Analytical Model

Specifying the basic variables involved in policy change and stability begs the question of how these two processes are related to each other. Here it is not unreasonable to suggest that the nature and type of policy change that occurs in a specific sector is linked to the manner in which policy processes enhancing stability or encouraging change are linked together.[47] That is, a policy process promoting change can be impeded by another process encouraging stability, resulting in only a gradual change from the status quo. Or a situation can exist where two or more change processes can be under way, without any countervailing stability process, hence promoting more rapid or fundamental change. By contrast, in the opposite situation, a change process can be limited or negated by the existence of multiple stability processes.[48]

In this regard, it should be noted that several of the change and stability processes are closely linked to each other. For example, extensive path dependency implies that a fairly costly effort is required to alter the status quo. This is likely to come about rapidly only if a systemic crisis occurs that undermines the status quo to such an extent that it is cheaper to alter policy than retain it. Similarly, a process such as a policy spillover can serve to undermine a closed network. Estimating exactly what the typical relationship is between policy outcomes and the forces of change and stability, however, requires further elaboration of the nature of patterns of policy change and how they are linked to the two basic change variables – ideas and actors – described above.

Typical Patterns of Policy Change

It is important to note that many observers have remarked upon the fact that most policies made by governments are, for the most part and most of the time, in some way a continuation of past policies and practices. Even what are often portrayed as 'new' policy initiatives are often simply variations on existing practices.[49] In normal circumstances a policy problem or issue will be dealt with by reference to an existing practice, or in what has been described by many as an 'incremental' fashion.[50] This pattern of piecemeal policy change is the stuff of 'normal' policy-making.

A second pattern of policy change is more dramatic, though infrequent, and represents a major reconceptualization and restructuring of policy. This type of policy change is often described as 'paradigmatic.'[51] The primary differences between the two relate to the fact that incremental change involves non-innovative changes at the margin of existing policies utilizing existing policy processes, institutions, and regimes. Non-incremental, 'paradigmatic,' change involves new policies that represent a sharp break from how policies were developed, conceived, and implemented in the past.[52] Frequently cited examples of paradigmatic changes include shifts in fiscal and monetary policy in most Western countries from a balanced-budget orthodoxy to Keynesian principles and practices in the 1930s and 1940s and a subsequent shift away from Keynesianism to forms of monetarism in the 1970s and 1980s;[53] and similar shifts in resource policy from pure exploitation to conservation in the nineteenth century and then from conservation to sustainable management in the twentieth.[54] While incremental change is usually thought of as a process of more-or-less linear evolutionary change, paradigmatic change is usually seen as involving periods of stability and incremental adaptations interspersed by periods of revolutionary upheaval or what has often been referred to as a 'punctuated equilibrium' pattern of policy change.[55]

A useful way to look at these different typical patterns of policy change has been suggested by Durrant and Diehl.[56] Analogizing from work in palaeobiology, they have argued that policy change has two components. Policies can vary not only in terms of the mode of change – between the normal pattern of piecemeal incremental change and the pattern of paradigmatic change mentioned above – but also in terms of the tempo or speed of change (see table 8.2).

As this model demonstrates, paradigmatic change, although infrequent, can be either rapid or slow. This is somewhat different from the usual conception of paradigmatic change cited in the literature, which has emphasized its often rapid nature. However, empirical evidence of such gradual processes has been generated in diverse areas such as fiscal policy, agricultural policy, aboriginal policy, and forestry policy, among others.[57] The same is true for the more common pattern of incremental change that can occur at either tempo, despite the fact that

TABLE 8.2
Basic patterns of policy change

	Speed of change	
Mode of change	Fast	Slow
Paradigmatic	Rapid paradigmatic	Gradual paradigmatic
Normal or intra-paradigmatic	Rapid incremental	Gradual incremental

Source: Adapted from R.F. Durrant and P.F. Diehl, 'Agendas, Alternatives and Public Policy: Lessons from the U.S. Foreign Policy Arena,' *Journal of Public Policy* 9, no. 2 (1989): 179–205.

TABLE 8.3
The effects of changes in actors and ideas on policy change

	Introduction of new actors	
Introduction of new ideas	Yes	No
Yes	Rapid paradigmatic	Slow paradigmatic
No	Rapid incremental	Slow incremental

Source: Adapted from M. Howlett and M. Ramesh, 'Policy Subsystem Configurations and Policy Change: Operationalizing the Postpositivist Analysis of the Politics of the Policy Process,' *Policy Studies Journal* 26, no. 3 (1998): 466–82.

the literature has tended to focus on the gradual nature of many incremental policy processes.[58]

Linking these typical patterns of change to the central variables identified in the previous section is a critical first step in any effort to understand, and manage, a sectoral, or any other, policy process. That is, the previous section identified the presence or absence of new actors and new ideas as crucial variables related to the presence or absence of specific change and stability processes identified in the policy literature. Table 8.3 outlines the central relationship expected to apply between the major patterns of policy change discussed above and the central variables affecting change outlined in the previous section.

This analysis suggests that there can be no paradigmatic change without the introduction of new ideas, but that even with the introduction of such ideas the speed of change will be affected by whether the

TABLE 8.4
Stability and change processes and associated patterns of policy change

	Involves presence of new actors	
	Yes Subsystem spillovers Systemic perturbations	*No* Closed subsystems Hard issues
Involves presence of new ideas		
Yes Policy-learning Venue change	Rapid paradigmatic	Gradual paradigmatic
No Non-decisions Path dependency	Rapid incremental	Gradual incremental

ideas are generated by new or old actors. This, in turn, suggests that certain change and stability processes can be linked with certain typical patterns of policy change (see Table 8.4 above). Since both the typical general patterns of policy change and the specific processes outlined in the previous section involved a different emphasis on the presence or absence of new policy actors and policy ideas, it follows that the different change and stability processes can be combined to generate a propensity towards typical general patterns of change.

That is, each of the change and stability processes fundamentally involves the introduction, or the prevention of the introduction, of either new actors or new ideas into a policy process. Each, however, can be involved with other processes that also affect these two central variables. Thus, for example, while policy-learning and venue change are primarily about the introduction of new ideas, they can be combined with processes, such as subsystem spillovers or systemic perturbations, that can introduce new actors into the policy system or subsystem. Understanding the relationships between the two central change variables, and the eight specific change and stability processes they influence, is an essential part of the identification and analysis of typical patterns of policy change. Such an understanding, therefore, is a basic requirement for the analysis of future trends in specific policy sectors, and moreover, for the design of effective governmental responses to such trends.[59] In the following section, the ability of governmental procedural policy tools to facilitate or impede policy change through the manipulation of the introduction of new ideas and actors into policy processes will be discussed.

4. Managing Policy Change: Tools for Complex Network Management

As will be apparent from the above discussion, some of the policy processes that promote or facilitate policy change or stability can be subjected to manipulation by governments including venue-shifting, policy-learning, and non-decision-making, among others. Others, such as systemic perturbations, cannot be directly manipulated, although governments can prepare themselves for their occurrence. A variety of tools can be used by governments to promote, or prevent, specific types of change *by altering the distribution of new ideas and actors involved in the policy process*, and hence altering the propensity for specific types of policy change. That is, policy effects can be designed into policy processes by contemporary governments that can influence these patterns through various kinds of network-management activities.[60] This can be done for a variety of reasons and general policy aims, such as 'getting out in front of an issue' in order to retain some steering capacity in the face of change, or attempting to restrain the impact of change in order to minimize turbulence and any resulting policy instability.[61]

Although a complete discussion of the possible means for enhancing policy change is beyond the scope of this paper,[62] it should be noted that Bressers and Klok, Schneider and Ingram, and others have identified a number of policy instruments that can be used to alter the ideas and actors involved in policy subsystems.[63] These include education, training, institution creation, the provision of information, 'labeling,' propaganda, exhortation, formal evaluations, hearings and institutional reform.[64]

Research into the tools and mechanisms used in intergovernmental regulatory and government organizational design has also identified several other instruments such as 'treaties' and a variety of 'political agreements' that can affect target-group recognition of government intentions and vice versa.[65] Other research into interest-group behaviour and activities has highlighted the existence of tools related to group creation and manipulation, including the role played by private- or public-sector patrons in aiding the formation and activities of such groups,[66] and their selective representation on government advisory bodies.[67]

Still other research into contemporary policy-making has highlighted the use of techniques such as focus groups,[68] research funding for, and access to, investigative hearings and tribunals,[69] and the awarding of various powers to inquiries and hearings such as the ability to subpoena witnesses or enforce orders.[70] Finally, some researchers have also emphasized the manner in which tools can be used to negatively affect the behaviour of interest groups and other actors. Such 'negative' procedural instruments include suppression of information, misleading the public, withholding information, deception, obfuscation, and other forms of administrative delay.[71]

This latter point emphasizes the fact that procedural tools can be used in a variety of ways to enhance or diminish change and stability processes.[72] As table 8.5 shows, in the abstract, tools can be used to promote either incremental or paradigmatic change, or to increase the speed or tempo of either mode of change.

While the effects of the use of such tools should not be exaggerated, neither should their impact be discounted. Although these instruments remain for the most part indirect, limited in scope, and often largely invisible, or only partially visible, they are an important, and increasingly significant, element of the tool kit of government in the contemporary period.[73]

5. Environmental Trends and Their Likely Effect on Canadian Policy Outcomes with and without Government Action

Utilizing the concepts, variables, and relationships set out above, this section examines the most likely consequences of several currently identifiable political, economic, socio-cultural, and ecological trends for Canadian environmental policy. There are numerous such trends apparent in the contemporary era and only several of the most significant of these will be examined below in terms of their likely effect on Canadian policy-making. In the next subsection, the impact of those trends on policy-making in the absence of the concerted use of procedural policy tools will be assessed. The manner in which such tools can be used to mediate the impact of these trends will be discussed in the subsequent subsection.

General Environmental Trends and Canadian Government Environmental Policy

Among the most significant trends affecting the contours and contents of Canadian environmental policy-making are the political consequences of the internationalization of environmental issues; continued

TABLE 8.5
Policy tools for managing policy change

General aim	General strategy	Specific mechanisms	Examples of relevant policy tools
Promote gradual incremental change	Enhance: Stability processes	Encourage: Non-decisions Hard issues Path dependency Closed networks	• Eliminate public debate and partici- pation • Bureaucratize processes and administration • Restrict membership in advisory bodies • Lock in programs
	Discourage: Change processes	Discourage: Policy-learning Venue change Systemic perturbations Sub-system spillovers	• Censorship • Restrictions on judicial review • Build absorptive capacity • Isolate policy sectors
Promote rapid incremental change	Enhance: Idea-based stability and Actor-based change processes	Encourage: Non-decisions Path dependency Systemic perturbations Subsystem spillovers	• Re-organize adminis- tration • Create technical advisory groups • Lock in programs
	Discourage: Actor-based stability and Idea-based change processes	Discourage: Closed networks Hard issues Policy-learning Venue change	• Disseminate informa- tion to public • Discourage judicial or administrative reviews
Promote gradual paradigmatic change	Enhance: Actor-based stability and Idea-based change processes	Encourage: Closed networks Hard issues Policy-learning Venue change	• Discourage public participation • Facilitate judicial or administrative reviews • Encourage inter- national linkages
	Discourage: Idea-based stability and Actor-based change processes	Discourage: Non-decisions Path dependency Systemic perturbations Subsystem spillovers	• Enhance technical or legal capacity of Administration advisory committees • Sunset clauses

TABLE 8.5
(*concluded*)

General aim	General strategy	Specific mechanisms	Examples of relevant policy tools
Promote rapid paradigmatic change	Enhance: Change processes	Encourage: Policy-learning Venue change Systemic perturbations Subsystem spillovers	• Fund interest groups • Create royal commissions • Provide new program funds • Enhance judicial review
	Discourage: Stability processes	Discourage: Non-decisions Hard issues Path dependency Closed networks	• Enhance public participation • Provide public information campaigns and advertising • Sunset clauses • Create cross-sectoral advisory committees

geophysical and ecological problems related to resource depletion and environmental degradation; and a range of economic problems related to shifts in economic activity away from resource-intensive development and towards service industries and less resource-intensive manufacturing processes.[74] In addition, the propensity for spillovers from on-going policy development in other areas, such as the continuing struggle to expand human and aboriginal rights, and demands for enhanced public participation by increasingly well-educated and informed citizens in larger numbers of democratically organized polities promises to affect environmental policy-making in Canada and elsewhere.[75]

Internationalization

Several key trends relate to the internationalization of environmental politics. The spread of environmental politics beyond national borders is partially related to the scale and trans-boundary nature of many environmental issues.[76] However, it is also closely linked to the improvements in transportation and communications technologies that have facilitated international and transnational contacts among activists, experts, officials, and others involved in a variety of policy areas, including the environment.[77] The development of stable and effective international ENGOs such as Greenpeace and many other less well-known organizations, is a manifestation of this process,[78] as is the increasingly frequent and more closely integrated meetings of experts and politicians on environmental subjects,[79] and the establishment of many new international treaties and conventions on environmental subjects.[80]

All of these developments affect Canadian policy-making as internationalization (1) undermines existing policy networks with a virtually exclusive domestic base,[81] (2) facilitates cross-national learning and policy transfer,[82] and (3) provides alternative venues for policy actors blocked at the domestic level in pursuing their interests.[83]

A variety of non–environmentally specific trends are also associated with internationalization that can have, and have had, spillover effects on activities and development in this sector. For example, fiscal issues related to international investment flows have affected governments' capacity to deal with environmental issues, as occurred in the 1990s when budget cuts occasioned by government deficit concerns in an era of mobile capital cut into the resources and capacities of environmental-protection agencies in many countries.[84]

Hence, internationalization is a potent trend favouring policy change. Three of the change-enhancing processes identified above are influenced by this trend. Moreover, while augmenting the potential for venue-shifting, spillovers, and policy-learning, internationalization also affects path dependence, closed networks, and non-decisions by undermining the established institutions, actors, and ideas present in this sector.

Ecological Crises

Probably the most highly publicized trend, of course, relates to an apparent increase in the various environmental crises that occur from time to time.[85] It is important to note, however, that these crises are of different types and have different effects on policy-making. That is, crises vary according to their duration and geographical specificity. At one extreme are crises that have specific spatial and temporal effects, such as oil or toxic spills and accidents. At the other extreme are those that are more general and long-term in nature, such as those related to alterations in weather patterns and pollution-related disasters such as global warming or acid precipitation. In between fall a variety of other crises of varying duration and coverage, such as a short-term but widespread decline in a fish stock or the localized but long-term problems associated with the commissioning and decommissioning of nuclear generating facilities.

While all of these crises can be classified as potential systemic perturbations, upsetting various routines and procedures common to policy systems, the potential for such crises to effect policy change varies directly with the type of crisis that occurs. That is, localized, short-term accidents can act as 'focussing events' and open windows for policy reform, but are unlikely in themselves to result in policy change unless accompanied by substantial pre-existing support for change.[86] More widespread, short-term crises can reveal gaps and inconsistencies in planning and policy systems and effect limited types of procedural policy change.[87] However, longer-term problems, be they local or more general in nature, can lead to the creation of interest groups and other organized forms of public involvement that can open up previously closed policy networks and re-frame hard issues into less-technical ones relating to, for example, community, public, or individual health and safety.[88]

Canada, of course, has had its share of all these different types of such crises, and there is no reason to expect their number to diminish. In fact, as human beings continue to put pressure on ecological systems in numerous different ways and as public information media continue to expand and develop, it is likely that an increase in the number and prominence of both short- and long-term crises will occur. Hence, although with different potential effects, the number of systemic perturbations in this sector is likely to increase.

Post-Staples Economic Adjustment

A third major trend with significant potential impact on environmental policy-making in Canada is socio-economic in nature. It has involved the continual progression of most of Canada towards a 'post-staples' economy in which the country's historical emphasis and reliance on natural-resource-based economic activity is lessened by a shift towards service-sector and other less resource-intensive forms of economic activity. Although it is important not to exaggerate this trend, since many regions of Canada may still be characterized as 'resource dependent,' there is little doubt that the economy as a whole is more diffused and diversified than in the past.[89] The development of significant new non-resource-based information and other technologies[90] has accompanied severe pressures on older critical resource sectors such as the fishery and forest industries, and has involved substantial changes in much of Canada's social, cultural, and demographic landscape.

Rapid sectoral shifts in the structure of the Canadian economy, including a shift to services, rapid tertiarization, and significant industrial expansion in regional centres has led to an internal 'reconfiguration' of growth and development, with a significant increase in metropolitan shares of population and employment, the emergence of regional economic centres, and the decline of smaller resource-dependent communities.[91] Among the ecological aspects of these changes has been a shift from resource-intensive production processes to more environmentally benign ones – even in resource-based industries such as eco-tourism.[92]

The economic restructuring of Canada's political economy in a post-staples direction has been associated with changes in the movements of capital, global competition, and technological innovation in the resource sector, all of which have resulted in the 'downsizing' of the resource-based workforce and extensive job loss in rural areas. The loss of existing jobs, and the inadequate creation of new jobs in the resource sector has become increasingly problematic in many regions that now face decline and depopulation. The growth of the tertiary sector, by contrast, is largely urban-based and involves the creation of more jobs with proportionally less direct resource reliance and negative impact.[93]

The combined effect of changes in industrial structure and labour markets has altered the level of popular support and interest in environmental issues among the Canadian public. In resource-based rural areas, support for basic values such as wilderness protection has dropped, as these are seen as contributing to the decline of the traditional resource industries. In urban areas, by contrast, there is less opposition to activities such as wilderness-park creation in rural areas, although individuals are less likely to rank environmental issues as high in terms of political salience.[94]

Thus, economic restructuring and associated population movements and settlements patterns in Canada have had a somewhat paradoxical impact on public opinion and activism in the environmental sector. That is, overall, given the general decline of rural areas and the increase in urban populations over the past decades, diffuse general support for environmental issues has increased at the same time that opposition to specific projects and proposals in non-urban areas has intensified.

In terms of the change and stability processes outlined above, post-staples economic adjustment has raised the potential for spillovers from a variety of economic activities into environmental policy-making and has enhanced the number of venues available to activists through, for example, the institutionalization of various kinds of regional-development and land-use boards and agencies. More significantly, restructuring undermines an important stability process – path dependency – by altering the value and significance of traditional resource industries, thereby changing the cost implications of shifts in traditional land- and resource-use patterns of activity.

Political and Cultural Change

Environmental policy-making is also affected by the general trends visible in the enhanced democratization and fragmentation of Canadian civil society. Although the exact parameters of these changes are somewhat unclear, the mobilization of previously quiescent portions of the population to embrace various forms of political action and involvement – including that regarding the environment[95] – has potent implications for environmental policy-making.

Although Canada has so far eschewed the development of an exhaustively litigious form of citizen-led policy-making,[96] there has been a manifest increase in the willingness of individual companies and citizens to redefine many conflicts as rights-related and to challenge government regulatory actions through judicial and quasi-judicial venues.[97] While the direct impact of this movement on the environment has been limited,[98] in many areas courts have created new sets of rights and entitlements that have spilled over into environmental areas. This is especially the case with the First Nations of Canada, which have benefited from a series of Supreme Court rulings that have created new land-use and land-management rights forcing the inclusion of aboriginal groups in resource and environmental policy-making both on treaty and non-treaty lands.[99] It is also the case with litigation and activism surrounding the free-trade agreements, which have resulted in the establishment of new forms of investment rights that have undermined government latitude in regulatory matters.[100]

This trend, therefore, has augmented the potential for environmentally relevant policy spillovers and has provided new venues for policy deliberations through the promotion of a loosely defined but justiciable 'rights' agenda.

The Likely Effects of Unmediated Environmental Trends on Canadian Government Environmental Policy

The preceding analysis of three major international, ecological, and socio-political trends suggests that, taken together, they have undermined all the major stability processes present in the Canadian environmental sector and augmented the potential of all the change-oriented ones. That is, stability processes such as non-decisions are being overcome by the introduction of ideas from the international and transnational sphere, such as biodiversity and bioregionalism, which have been in circulation for some time, but have only recently begun to emerge as the guiding principles behind environmental treaties and resource-management efforts.[101] These ideas help to alter the frames of policy discourse in the sector. Similarly, stability-enhancing factors such as hard issues and closed networks are being undermined by the emergence of new policy actors such as international ENGOs and by the redefinition of environmental issues in terms of frames related to community health and individual or group rights. Finally, the nature of path dependencies in this sector is also being altered as new institutions are created in the new international environmental order and the political economy of Canada restructures.

Policy-change processes are also being enhanced by these trends. The number and type of systemic perturbations is likely to increase in frequency as populations place increasing pressure on ecosystems and existing infrastructure ages, making the occurrence of various types of ecological crises more and more likely. Similarly, the emergence of new international institutions and the development of a more-activist Canadian judiciary enhances the number of judicial and other administrative and public venues for policy deliberations. Globalization and increasing international integration, generally, also increases the potential for policy-learning. Finally, developments in Canadian social and political culture that promote individual activism and the linkage of various subsystems in areas such as health and aboriginal affairs, to name only two, redefine 'hard issues' into more publicly digestible forms.

Overall, following the model of policy change set out in table 8.4

TABLE 8.6

Effects of unmanaged environmental trends on change and stability processes in Canadian environmental policy-making

	Environmental trend	Direction of effect
Change processes		
Learning	Internationalization	Encourages cross-national transfers through elite networking
Venue change	Internationalization Political/social and cultural change	Provides alternative policy venues
Spillover	Environmental complexity Economic restructuring Political/social and cultural change	Crosses traditional sectoral and geographic policy boundaries
Systemic perturbations	Ecological crises	Introduces new actors, undermines existing institutions and policy processes
Stability process		
Hard issues	Ecological crises Economic adjustment Socio-political change	Redefines issues from the technological to the public realms
Non-decisions	Internationalization	Discouraged by rapid dissemination of ideas
Closed subsystems	Internationalization Socio-political change	Adds multiple new domestic and international actors to existing policy subsystems
Path dependency	Internationalization Economic restructuring	Creates new institutional structures and treaties and undermines resource dependence of the economy and sunk costs

above, this analysis suggests that the likely impact of unmediated environmental trends on Canadian environmental policy is towards rapid paradigmatic change. That is, the trends identified above serve to enhance policy-change processes and reduce policy-stability ones.[102] By ensuring that both new actors and new ideas will be present in this policy sector, they are likely to lead to significant changes not only in the mode of policy-making, but also in its tempo. These general observations are set out in table 8.6.

The Potential for Procedural Policy Tools to Mediate the Impact of Environmental Trends on Canadian Government Environmental Policies

Some of the effects of these processes can already be seen in the shifts that have been occurring in Canada away from the old implementation style of regulation by bilateral negotiation towards more open, and less predictable, multi-stakeholder policy processes, many of which were forced upon recalcitrant Canadian governments by new policy actors.[103] However, while rapid paradigmatic change is one possible outcome of current environmental trends, it is by no means certain that this will occur.

As was suggested above, contemporary governments have a wide range of procedural tools at their disposal that can serve to either speed up or slow down the tempo of policy change, or alter its general nature.[104] In order to enhance the potential for learning, for example, Canadian governments could undertake a variety of capacity-building activities related to the dissemination of information, the provision of funding and access for subsystem members, and the inclusion of net-work members in formal policy deliberations.[105] These could be incorporated into policy design in order to encourage learning and prepare governments to deal with the results of the change processes outlined above.[106] Alternatively, governments could attempt to slow change or prevent it from occurring through, for example, the withdrawal of funding from interest groups or the elimination of advisory groups.[107]

However, while the effects and impact of future environmental crises remain somewhat unpredictable, it is highly unlikely that the process of the internationalization of policy-making or the restructuring of the Canadian economy will be reversed and Canada adopt a more autarchous form of socio-economic, political, and cultural development.[108] Similarly, it is difficult to imagine Canadian society moving in a less democratic direction than has been the case over the past decade.

As a result, the continued presence of, and positive reception provided to, new ideas in this sector, again following the logic of the model set out in table 8.4, preclude a return to any form of incremental policy-making. Rather, *the choice before Canadian policy-makers in the environmental sector is largely restricted to altering or attempting to alter the tempo of policy change, rather than its fundamental nature.* Table 8.7 sets out the general situation and the potential of procedural instrument used by Canadian governments to slow down the process of non-

TABLE 8.7
Policy tools for managing paradigmatic environmental policy change in Canada

General options	Change factor	General prognosis	General strategy	Specific tactics	Examples of policy tools
Promote gradual incremental change	Undermined by new ideas	Unlikely to be attained due to impact of inter-nationalization and economic restructuring			
Promote rapid incremental change	Undermined by new ideas	Unlikely to be attained due to impact of inter-nationalization			
Promote gradual paradigmatic change	Likely due to presence of new ideas, but undermined by presence of new actors	Can be attained by restricting entrance of new actors into policy processes	Enhance actor-based stability and discourage actor-based change processes	Encourage: Closed networks Hard issues Discourage: Systemic perturbations Subsystem spillovers	• Discourage public participation • Restrict judicial or administrative reviews • Enhance technical or legal capacity of administration • Restrict multi-sectoral advisory committees
Promote rapid paradigmatic change	Enhanced by presence of new ideas and new actors	Default position			

incremental, or paradigmatic, policy change that is likely to occur in this sector.

That is, given the configuration of change and stability factors outlined in this chapter, it is likely that some form of non-incremental or paradigmatic change will occur in the Canadian environmental sector over the short to medium term. Because of closer international integration, firm government action to prevent the flow of new ideas is highly unlikely. Thus, some form of paradigmatic change is the most probable change outcome in the near future. The central question, then, is whether this change will occur at a rapid pace (the default position) or whether Canadian governments will act to slow down the tempo of change by implementing various forms of network-management activities aimed at promoting a shift towards gradual rather than rapid paradigmatic change. While it would be difficult to attempt to block change entirely given the strength of the change processes under way, the speed or tempo of change could be reduced through enhancement of actor-based stability processes and the reduction of the potential for actor-based policy change. This would allow existing actors to deal with new ideas, limiting the speed, but not the mode, of policy change.

6. Conclusion: Consequences of Environmental Trends for Canadian Governance

This discussion has shown that different patterns of policy change exist, linked to different change and stability processes, and centered on the presence or absence of new actors and new ideas in sectoral policy processes. As this chapter has argued, governments can manipulate both change and stability processes through the use of policy tools that can affect the range of ideas and actors present in policy deliberations. A critical question for anyone concerned with future trends in Canadian environmental policy-making is, therefore, which particular processes are present and whether and how these processes can be affected or otherwise manipulated by governments. Although the extent to which either process can be manipulated will vary according to the exact specification of the change and stability processes involved, several conclusions can be reached in the case of Canadian environmental policy:

1 As in all other policy areas, both sets of policy change forces and processes exist; that is, both policy-change and stability-enhancing processes are present in the environmental area.

2 Current trends such as internationalization, ecological crises, economic restructuring, and social, cultural, and political change are enhancing change processes and undermining stability processes in this sector.
3 Left unmediated by the use of government procedural policy tools, the conjuncture or vector of such forces is leading in the direction of rapid paradigmatic change as new actors and new ideas are introduced into this sector.
4 Any attempt to shift environmental policy change onto an incremental basis would require Canadian government actions to curtail the flow of knowledge and new ideas circulating in to the policy process. This outcome would appear to be very difficult to achieve given current trends towards internationalization, even in the unlikely event that a Canadian government would actually wish to do so.
5 While restricting the entrance of new policy ideas in this sector would be extremely difficult in present circumstances, governments in Canada could use specific policy tools to offset the introduction of new actors into the policy process, hence slowing down the process of paradigmatic policy change.

NOTES

1 I would like to thank Harry Swain, Tsuyoshi Kawasaki, Jeremy Rayner, George Hoberg, Ben Cashore, Allen Sutherland, and Edward Parson for comments on earlier drafts of this paper.
2 On the paradox of enhanced state capacity and reduced state autonomy in the era of globalization see P.G. Cerny, 'International Finance and the Erosion of State Policy Capacity,' in P. Gummett, ed., *Globalization and Public Policy* (Cheltenham, UK: Edward Elgar, 1996), 83–104, and W.H. Reinicke, *Global Public Policy: Governing without Government?* (Washington: Brookings Institution, 1998).
3 See L. Dobuzinskis, *The Self-Organizing Polity: An Epistemological Analysis of Political Life* (Boulder: Westview, 1987); G. Lehmbruch, 'The Organization of Society, Administrative Strategies, and Policy Networks,' in R.M. Czada and A. Windhoff-Heritier, eds, *Political Choice: Institutions, Rules, and the Limits of Rationality* (Boulder: Westview, 1991), 121–55; and R. Mayntz, 'Modernization and the Logic of Interorganizational Networks,' in J. Child, M. Crozier, and R. Mayntz, eds, *Societal Change between Market and Organization* (Aldershot, UK: Avebury, 1993), 3–18.
4 K. Hawkins and J.M. Thomas, 'Making Policy in Regulatory Bureaucracies,'

in K. Hawkins and J.M. Thomas, eds, *Making Regulatory Policy* (Pittsburgh: University of Pittsburgh Press, 1989), 3–30; K. Woodside, 'The Political Economy of Policy Instruments: Tax Expenditures and Subsidies in Canada,' in M. Atkinson and M. Chandler, eds, *The Politics of Canadian Public Policy* (Toronto: University of Toronto Press, 1983), 173–97; J.A. Weiss and M. Tschirhart, 'Public Information Campaigns as Policy Instruments,' *Journal of Policy Analysis and Management* 13, no. 1 (1994): 82–119; and M. Howlett and M. Ramesh, 'Patterns of Policy Instrument Choice: Policy Styles, Policy Learning, and the Privatization Experience,' *Policy Studies Review* 12, no. 1 (1993): 3–24. On these trends in public administration more generally see C. Hood, 'A Public Management for All Seasons?' *Public Administration* 69 (Spring 1991): 3–19 and G.B. Doern and S. Wilks, eds, *Changing Regulatory Institutions in Britain and North America* (Toronto: University of Toronto Press, 1998).

5 T.R. La Porte, ed., *Organized Social Complexity: Challenge to Politics and Policy* (Princeton: Princeton University Press, 1975); H.B. Milward, K.G. Provan, and B.A. Else, 'What Does the "Hollow State" Look Like?' in B. Bozeman, ed., *Public Management: The State of the Art* (San Francisco: Jossey-Bass, 1993), 309–23; and B.G. Peters and J. Pierre, 'Governance without Government? Rethinking Public Administration,' *Journal of Public Administration Research and Theory* 8, no. 2 (1998): 223–44.

6 On 'traditional' substantive policy tools see K. Woodside, 'Policy Instruments and the Study of Public Policy,' *Canadian Journal of Political Science* 19, no. 4 (1986): 775–93 and L.M. Salamon, ed., *Beyond Privatization: The Tools of Government Action* (Washington: Urban Institute, 1989). On 'procedural' instruments see M. Howlett 'Legitimacy and Governance: Re-Discovering Procedural Policy Instruments,' paper presented to annual meeting of British Columbia Political Studies Association, Vancouver: 1996 and R.J. in't Veld, 'The Dynamics of Instruments,' in B.G. Peters and F.K.M. Van Nispen, eds, *Public Policy Instruments: Evaluating the Tools of Public Administration* (New York: Edward Elgar, 1998), 153–62.

7 See B.G. Peters, *The Future of Governing: Four Emerging Models* (Lawrence, KA: University Press of Kansas, 1996) and M.A. Emmert, M. Crow, and R.F. Shangraw Jr, 'Public Management in the Future: Post-Orthodoxy and Organization Design,' in B. Bozeman, ed., *Public Management: The State of the Art* (San Francisco: Jossey-Bass, 1993), 345–60.

8 See E.-H. Klijn, 'Analyzing and Managing Policy Processes in Complex Networks: A Theoretical Examination of the Concept Policy Network and Its Problems,' *Administration and Society* 28, no. 1 (1996): 90–119; J.A. de Bruijn and E.F. ten Heuvelhof, 'Policy Networks and Governance,' in D.L.

Weimer, ed., *Institutional Design* (Boston: Kluwer Academic Publishers, 1995, 161–79; and J.A. de Bruijn and E.F. ten Heuvelhof, 'Instruments for Network Management,' in W.J.M. Kickert, E.-H. Klijn, and J.F.M. Koppenjan, eds, *Managing Complex Networks: Strategies for the Public Sector* (London: Sage, 1997), 119–36.

9 See P.A. Hall, 'Policy Paradigms, Social Learning and the State: The Case of Economic Policy Making in Britain,' *Comparative Politics* 25, no. 3 (1993): 275–96.

10 See G. Hernes, 'Structural Change in Social Processes,' *American Journal of Sociology* 82, no. 3 (1976): 513–47.

11 On the multidimensional aspects of policy instruments and the interrelationship of means and ends see S.H. Linder and B.G. Peters, 'Instruments of Government: Perceptions and Contexts,' *Journal of Public Policy* 9, no. 1 (1989): 35–58; C. Hood, *The Tools of Government* (London: Chatham House, 1986) and G. Majone, *Evidence, Argument, and Persuasion in the Policy Process* (New Haven: Yale University Press, 1989).

12 It is important to note here that policy change can occur at different levels, ranging from the broad parameters of a political system to the sub-sectoral or issue area. In this discussion the focus is upon the meso or sectoral level. For examples of analyses focusing on different levels of policy-making see C. Daugbjerg and D. Marsh, 'Explaining Policy Outcomes: Integrating the Policy Network Approach with Macro-Level and Micro-Level Analysis,' in D. Marsh, ed., *Comparing Policy Networks* (Buckingham, UK: Open University Press, 1998), 52–71; M. Cavanagh, D. Marsh, and M. Smith, 'The Relationship between Policy Networks at the Sectoral and Sub-Sectoral Levels: A Response to Jordan, Maloney and McLaughlin,' *Public Administration* 73, Winter (1995): 627–9; and M.A. Eisner, 'Discovering Patterns in Regulatory History: Continuity, Change and Regulatory Regimes,' *Journal of Policy History* 6, no. 2 (1994): 157–87.

13 See H. Heclo, 'Ideas, Interests and Institutions,' in L.C. Dodd and C. Jillson, eds, *The Dynamics of American Politics: Approaches and Interpretations* (San Francisco: Westview, 1994), 366–92, and H. Heclo, 'Conclusion: Policy Dynamics,' in R. Rose, ed., *The Dynamics of Public Policy: A Comparative Analysis* (London: Sage, 1976), 237–66.

14 L.G. Zucker, 'Where Do Institutional Patterns Come from? Organizations as Actors in Social Systems,' in L.G. Zucker, ed., *Institutional Patterns and Organizations: Culture and Environment* (Cambridge, MA: Ballinger, 1988), 23–49.

15 See J.D. Starling, 'The Use of Systems Constructs in Simplifying Organized Social Complexity,' in T.R. La Porte, ed., *Organized Social Complexity: Challenge to Politics and Policy* (Princeton: Princeton University Press, 1975),

131–72, and R. Aminzade, 'Historical Sociology and Time,' *Sociological Methods and Research* 20, no. 4 (1992): 456–80.

16 See J. Douglas, 'Review Article: The Overloaded Crown,' *British Journal of Political Science* 6 (1975): 488–500, and R. Simeon, 'The "Overload Thesis" and Canadian Government,' *Canadian Public Policy* 2, no. 4 (1976): 541–52.

17 For examples of the recent use of similar models see D.J. Savoie, *Governing from the Centre: The Concentration of Power in Canadian Politics* (Toronto: University of Toronto Press, 1999) and B.D. Jones, *Reconceiving ⁿecision-Making in Democratic Politics: Attention, Choice and Public Policy* (Chicago: University of Chicago Press, 1994).

18 See G.A. Daneke, 'Back to the Future: Misplaced Elements of Political Inquiry and the Advanced Systems Agenda,' in W.N. Dunn and R.M. Kelly, eds, *Advances in Policy Studies since 1950* (New Brunswick, NJ: Transaction Press, 1992), 267–90, and R. Jervis, *System Effects: Complexity in Political and Social Life* (Princeton: Princeton University Press, 1997). On the origins of these models see W. Buckley, 'Society as a Complex Adaptive System,' in W. Buckley, ed., *Modern System Research for the Behavioural Scientist* (Chicago: Aldine Publishing Co., 1968), 490–513.

19 See C.J. Bennett and M. Howlett, 'The Lessons of Learning: Reconciling Theories of Policy Learning and Policy Change,' *Policy Sciences* 25, no. 3 (1992): 275–94.

20 A.D. Meyer, 'Adapting to Environmental Jolts,' *Administrative Science Quarterly* 27 (1982): 515–37.

21 P.A. Sabatier, 'An Advocacy Coalition Framework of Policy Change and the Role of Policy-oriented Learning Therein,' *Policy Sciences* 21, no. 2/3 (1988): 129–68; P.A. Sabatier, 'Knowledge, Policy-oriented Learning, and Policy Change,' *Knowledge: Creation, Diffusion, Utilization* 8, no. 4 (1987): 649–92; and P.A. Sabatier and H.C. Jenkins-Smith, eds, *Policy Change and Learning: An Advocacy Coalition Approach* (Boulder: Westview, 1993).

22 On the first uses of this concept see E.E. Schattschneider, *The Semisovereign People: A Realist's View of Democracy in America* (New York: Holt, Rinehart and Winston, 1960).

23 F.R. Baumgartner and B.D. Jones, *Agendas and Instability in American Politics* (Chicago: University of Chicago Press, 1993), 26 and 239–41.

24 On the distinction between policy communities and networks see S. Wilks and M. Wright, 'Conclusion: Comparing Government-Industry Relations: States, Sectors, and Networks,' in S. Wilks and M. Wright, eds, *Comparative Government-Industry Relations: Western Europe, the United States, and Japan* (Oxford: Clarendon Press, 1987), 274–313, and M. Howlett and M. Ramesh, *Studying Public Policy: Policy Cycles and Policy Subsystems* (Toronto: Oxford

University Press, 1995). For an example of its application see M. Howlett and J. Rayner, 'Do Ideas Matter? Policy Subsystem Configurations and the Continuing Conflict over Canadian Forest Policy,' *Canadian Public Administration* 38, no. 3 (1995): 382–410.

25 Other examples of venue-shifting behaviour can be found in G. Jordan, 'Indirect Causes and Effects in Policy Change: Shell, Greenpeace and the Brent Spar,' paper presented to annual meeting of the American Political Science Association, Boston, 1998; G. Hoberg, 'Distinguishing Learning from Other Sources of Policy Change: The Case of Forestry in the Pacific Northwest,' paper presented to annual meeting of American Political Science Association, Boston, 1998; and J. Richardson, 'Interest Groups, Multi-Arena Politics and Policy Change,' in S.S. Nagel, ed., *The Policy Process* (Commack, NY: Nova Science Publishers, 1999), 65–100.

26 H. Heclo, *Modern Social Politics in Britain and Sweden: From Relief to Income Maintenance* (New Haven: Yale University Press, 1974).

27 Cf. R. Rose, *Lesson-Drawing in Public Policy: A Guide to Learning across Time and Space* (Chatham, NJ: Chatham House Publishing, 1993); R. Rose, 'What Is Lesson-Drawing,' *Journal of Public Policy* 11, no. 1 (1991): 3–30; and J.P. Olsen and B.G. Peters, eds, *Lessons from Experience: Experiential Learning in Administrative Reforms in Eight Democracies* (Oslo: Scandinavian University Press, 1996).

28 See P. Pierson, 'When Effect Becomes Cause: Policy Feedback and Political Change,' *World Politics* 45, no. 595–628 (1993) and P. Knoepfel and I. Kissling-Naf, 'Social Learning in Policy Networks,' *Policy and Politics* 26, no. 3 (1998): 343–67.

29 On the different types of learning see C.J. Bennett and M. Howlett, 'The Lessons of Learning: Reconciling Theories of Policy Learning and Policy Change,' *Policy Sciences* 25, no. 3 (1992): 275–94, and P.J. May, 'Policy Learning and Failure,' *Journal of Public Policy* 12, no. 4 (1992): 331–54.

30 D. Dery, 'Policy by the Way: When Policy Is Incidental to Making Other Policies,' *Journal of Public Policy* 18, no. 2 (1999): 163–76. On earlier uses of the term to explain the process of European integration see E.B. Haas, *The Uniting of Europe: Political, Social and Economical Forces 1950–1957* (London: Stevens and Sons, 1958) and R.O. Keohane and S. Hoffman, 'Institutional Change in Europe in the 1980s,' in R.O. Keohane and S. Hoffman, eds, *The New European Community: Decision-Making and Institutional Change* (Boulder: Westview, 1991), 1–40.

31 See G. Hoberg and E. Morawaski, 'Policy Change through Sector Intersection: Forest and Aboriginal Policy in Clayoquot Sound,' *Canadian Public Administration* 40, no. 3 (1997): 387–414, and W. Grant and A. MacNamara,

'When Policy Communities Intersect: The Cases of Agriculture and Banking,' *Political Studies* 43 (1995): 509–15. On system and subsystem linkages, more generally, see R. Marion, *The Edge of Organization: Chaos and Complexity Theories of Formal Social Systems* (London: Sage, 1999).

32 See P. Bachrach and M.S. Baratz, 'Decisions and Nondecisions: An Analytical Framework,' *American Political Science Review* 56, no. 2 (1962): 632–42, and F.W. Frey, 'Comment: On Issues and Nonissues in the Study of Power,' *American Political Science Review* 65 (1971): 1081–1101.

33 See P. Bachrach and M.S. Baratz, *Power and Poverty: Theory and Practice* (New York: Oxford University Press, 1970), esp. chap. 3.

34 See S. Phillips, 'Discourse, Identity, and Voice: Feminist Contributions to Policy Studies,' in L. Dobuzinskis, M. Howlett, and D. Laycock, eds, *Policy Studies in Canada: The State of the Art* (Toronto: University of Toronto Press, 1996), 242–65.

35 See E. Goffman, *Frame Analysis: An Essay on the Organization of Experience* (Cambridge, MA: Harvard University Press, 1974); D.A. Schon and M. Rein, *Frame Reflection: Towards the Resolution of Intractable Policy Controversies* (New York: Basic Books, 1994); and esp. J.L. Campbell, 'Institutional Analysis and the Role of Ideas in Political Economy,' *Theory and Society* 27, no. 5 (1998): 377–409.

36 Earlier studies sometimes referred to these as 'wicked' problems. See H.W.J. Rittel and M.M. Webber, 'Dilemmas in a General Theory of Planning,' *Policy Sciences* 4 (1973): 155–69, and J.F. Martin, *Reorienting a Nation: Consultants and Australian Public Policy* (Aldershot, UK: Ashgate, 1998).

37 See R.W. Cobb and C.D. Elder, *Participation in American Politics: The Dynamics of Agenda-Building* (Boston: Allyn and Bacon, 1972); and R. Cobb, J.K. Ross, and M.H. Ross, 'Agenda Building as a Comparative Political Process,' *American Political Science Review* 70, no. 1 (1976): 126–38.

38 See P.H. Pollock, S.A. Lilie, and M.E. Vittes, 'Hard Issues, Core Values and Vertical Constraint: The Case of Nuclear Power,' *British Journal of Political Science* 23, no. 1 (1989): 29–50; and P.J. May, 'Reconsidering Policy Design: Policies and Publics,' *Journal of Public Policy* 11, no. 2 (1991): 187–206.

39 A.C. Keller, 'Innovation and Influence: Scientists as Advocates in Environmental Policy Change,' paper presented to annual meeting of the Western Political Science Association, Seattle, 1999.

40 See M. Weir, 'Ideas and the Politics of Bounded Innovation,' in S. Steinmo, K. Thelen, and F. Longstreth, eds, *Structuring Politics: Historical Institutionalism in Comparative Analysis* (Cambridge: Cambridge University Press, 1992), 188–216; P.A. David, 'Clio and the Economics of QWERTY,' *American Economic Review* 75, no. 2 (1985): 332–7; and R. Rose, 'Inheritance before Choice

in Public Policy,' *Journal of Theoretical Politics* 2, no. 3 (1990): 263–91.

41 See D. Wilsford, 'The *Conjoncture* of Ideas and Interests,' *Comparative Political Studies* 18, no. 3 (1985): 357–72; D. Wilsford, 'Path Dependency, or Why History Makes It Difficult but Not Impossible to Reform Health Care Systems in a Big Way,' *Journal of Public Policy* 14, no. 3 (1994): 251–84; and A. Rona-Tas, 'Path Dependence and Capital Theory: Sociology of the Post-Communist Economic Transformation,' *East European Politics and Societies* 12, no. 1 (1998): 107–31.

42 See Weir, 'Ideas'; J.G. March and J.P. Olsen, *Rediscovering Institutions: The Organizational Basis of Politics* (New York: Free Press, 1989), 52. See also J. Haydu, 'Making Use of the Past: Time Periods as Cases to Compare and as Sequences of Problem Solving,' *American Journal of Sociology* 104, no. 2 (1998): 339–71; and M.J.W. van Twist and C.J.A.M. Termeer, 'Introduction to Configuration Approach: A Process for Societal Steering,' in R. in't Veld et al., eds, *Autopoiesis and Configuration Theory: New Approaches to Societal Steering* (Dordrecht: Kluwer, 1991), 19–30.

43 See W.P. Browne, 'Organized Interests and Their Issue Niches: A Search for Pluralism in a Policy Domain,' *Journal of Politics* 52, no. 2 (1990): 477–509, and W.P. Browne, 'Issue Niches and the Limits of Interest Group Influence,' in A.J. Cigler and B.A. Loomis, eds, *Interest Group Politics* (Washington: CQ Press, 1991), 345–70.

44 R.A.W. Rhodes, *Understanding Governance: Policy Networks, Governance, Reflexivity, and Accountability* (Buckingham, UK: Open University Press, 1997). See also L. Schaap and M.J.W. van Twist, 'The Dynamics of Closedness in Networks,' in W.J.M. Kickert, E.-H. Klijn, and J.F.M. Koppenjan, eds, *Managing Complex Networks: Strategies for the Public Sector*, 3rd ed. (London: Sage, 1997), 62–78; and F.R. Baumgartner and B.D. Jones, 'Agenda Dynamics and Policy Subsystems,' *Journal of Politics* 53, no. 4 (1991): 1044–74.

45 See P. Pross, *Group Politics and Public Policy*, 2nd ed. (Toronto: Oxford University Press, 1992); G. Parker and A. Wragg, 'Networks, Agency and (De)stabilization: The Issue of Navigation on the River Wye, UK,' *Journal of Environmental Planning and Management* 42, no. 4 (1999): 471–87; and D. Knoke, *Political Networks: The Structural Perspective* (Cambridge: Cambridge University Press, 1987).

46 J.L. Campbell, 'Institutional Analysis and the Role of Ideas in Political Economy,' *Theory and Society* 27, no. 5 (1998): 377–409. More generally, see M.M. Blyth, '"Any More Bright Ideas?" The Ideational Turn of Comparative Political Economy,' *Comparative Politics* 29 (1997): 229–50; J.A. Hall, 'Ideas and the Social Sciences,' in J. Goldstein and R.O. Keohane, eds, *Ideas and Foreign Policy: Beliefs, Institutions and Political Change* (Ithaca: Cornell

University Press, 1993), 31–56; and J.K. Jacobsen, 'Much Ado about Ideas: The Cognitive Factor in Economic Policy,' *World Politics* 47 (1995): 283–310.

47 See G.B. Thomas, 'External Shocks, Conflict and Learning as Interactive Sources of Change in U.S. Security Policy,' *Journal of Pubic Policy* 19, no. 2 (1999): 209–31. More generally, see R. Nisbet, 'Introduction: The Problem of Social Change,' in R. Nisbet, ed., *Social Change* (New York: Harper and Row, 1972), 1–45.

48 This 'vector' approach to policy dynamics shares some similarities with the 'field' approach to group dynamics developed in the organizational-psychology literature of the early 1950s. See K. Lewin, 'Frontiers in Group Dynamics,' in D. Cartwright, ed., *Field Theory in Social Science* (New York: Harper, 1951), 188–237, and, more recently, D.C. Wilson, *A Strategy of Change: Concepts and Controversies in the Management of Change* (London: Routledge, 1992). See also T.H. Hammond and C.K. Butler, 'Some Complex Answers to the Simple Question, 'Do Institutions Matter?': Aggregation Rules, Preference Profiles, and Policy Equilibria in Presidential and Parliamentary Systems' (Detroit: Michigan State University PIPC Working Paper 96-02, 1996).

49 N.W. Polsby, ed., *Political Innovation in America: The Politics of Policy Initiation* (New Haven: Yale University Press, 1984).

50 See C.E. Lindblom, 'The Science of Muddling Through,' *Public Administration Review* 19, no. 2 (1959): 79–88. More generally, see M.T. Hayes, *Incrementalism and Public Policy* (New York: Longmans, 1992).

51 Peter Hall defines a policy paradigm as establishing 'the broad goals behind policy, the related problems or puzzles that policy-makers have to solve to get there, and, in large measure, the kind of instruments that can be used to attain these goals.' P.A. Hall, 'Policy Paradigms, Social Learning and the State: The Case of Economic Policy Making in Britain,' *Comparative Politics* 25, no. 3 (1993): 275–96.

52 See W.T. Berry, 'The Confusing Case of Budgetary Incrementalism: Too Many Meanings for a Single Concept,' *Journal of Politics* 52 (1990): 167–96, and R.H. Cox, 'Can Welfare States Grow in Leaps and Bounds? Non-Incremental Policymaking in the Netherlands,' *Governance* 5, no. 1 (1992): 68–87.

53 See P.A. Hall, ed., *The Political Power of Economic Ideas: Keynesianism across Nations* (Princeton: Princeton University Press, 1989) and P.A. Hall, 'The Change from Keynesianism to Monetarism: Institutional Analysis and British Economic Policy in the 1970s,' in S. Steinmo, K. Thelen, and F. Longstreth, eds, *Structuring Politics: Historical Institutionalism in Comparative Analysis* (Cambridge: Cambridge University Press, 1992), 90–114.

54 See S.P. Hays, *Conservation and the Gospel of Efficiency: The Progressive Conservation Movement, 1890–1920* (Cambridge, MA: Harvard University Press, 1959) and S.P. Hays, *Beauty, Health, and Permanence: Environmental Politics in the United States, 1955–1985* (New York: Cambridge University Press, 1987).

55 See C.J.G. Gersick, 'Revolutionary Change Theories: A Multilevel Exploration of the Punctuated Equilibrium Paradigm,' *Academy of Management Review* 16, no. 1 (1991): 10–36, and N. Eldredge and S.J. Gould, 'Punctuated Equilibria: An Alternative to Phyletic Gradualism,' in T.J.M. Schopf, ed., *Paleobiology* (San Francisco: Freeman, Cooper, 1972), 82–115.

56 See R.F. Durrant and P.F. Diehl, 'Agendas, Alternatives and Public Policy: Lessons from the U.S. Foreign Policy Arena,' *Journal of Public Policy* 9, no. 2 (1989): 179–205, and A.D. Meyer, G.R. Brooks, and J.B. Goes, 'Environmental Jolts and Industry Revolutions: Organizational Responses to Discontinuous Change,' *Strategic Management Journal* 11 (1990): 93–110.

57 For examples of rapid paradigmatic change, see P.A. Hall, 'Policy Paradigms, Social Learning and the State: The Case of Economic Policy Making in Britain,' *Comparative Politics* 25, no. 3 (1993): 275–96. On gradual paradigmatic change see M. Howlett, 'Policy Paradigms and Policy Change: Lessons from the Old and New Canadian Policies towards Aboriginal Peoples,' *Policy Studies Journal* 22, no. 4 (1994): 631–51; and W.D. Coleman, G.D. Skogstad, and M. Atkinson, 'Paradigm Shifts and Policy Networks: Cumulative Change in Agriculture,' *Journal of Public Policy* 16, no. 3 (1996): 273–302.

58 See, e.g., M.T. Hayes, *Incrementalism and Public Policy* (New York: Longmans, 1992). The originator of the concept, Charles Lindblom, of course, had noted that incremental change can occur at both speeds. See C.E. Lindblom, 'Still Muddling, Not Yet Through,' *Public Administration Review* 39, no. 6 (1979): 517–26.

59 A.P. Cortell and S. Peterson, 'Altered States: Explaining Domestic Institutional Change,' *British Journal of Political Science* 29 (1999): 177–203; N. Zahariadis and C.S. Allen, 'Ideas, Networks, and Policy Streams: Privatization in Britain and Germany,' *Policy Studies Review* 14, no. 1/2 (1995): 71–98; and H. Bressers and M. Honigh, 'A Comparative Approach to the Explanation of Policy Effects,' *International Social Science Journal* 108 (1986): 267–88.

60 See A. Heritier, 'Policy-Making by Subterfuge: Interest Accommodation, Innovation and Substitute Democratic Legitimation in Europe – Perspectives from Distinctive Policy Areas,' *Journal of European Public Policy* 4, no. 2 (1997): 171–89; J.A. de Bruijn and E.F. ten Heuvelhof, 'Policy Networks and Governance,' in D.L. Weimer, ed., *Institutional Design* (Boston: Kluwer Aca-

demic Publishers, 1995), 161–79; B.G. Peters and J. Pierre, 'Governance without Government? Rethinking Public Administration,' *Journal of Public Administration Research and Theory* 8, no. 2 (1998): 223–44; and H.Th.A. Bressers, 'The Choice of Policy Instruments in Policy Networks,' in B.G. Peters and F.K.M. Van Nispen, eds, *Public Policy Instruments: Evaluating the Tools of Public Administration* (New York: Edward Elgar, 1998), 85–105.

61 L.A. Pal, *Beyond Policy Analysis: Public Issue Management in Turbulent Times* (Toronto: ITP Nelson, 1997).

62 A good overview is provided in J.A. de Bruijn and E.F. ten Heuvelhof, 'Policy Instruments for Steering Autopoietic Actors,' in R. in't Veld et al., eds, *Autopoiesis and Configuration Theory: New Approaches to Societal Steering* (Dordrecht: Kluwer, 1991), 161–70.

63 See H. Bressers and P.-J. Klok, 'Fundamentals for a Theory of Policy Instruments,' *International Journal of Social Economics* 15, no. 3/4 (1988): 22–41, and A.L. Schneider and H. Ingram, 'Behavioural Assumptions of Policy Tools,' *Journal of Politics* 52, no. 2 (1990): 511–29.

64 On specific tools see J.A. Weiss and M. Tschirhart, 'Public Information Campaigns as Policy Instruments,' *Journal of Policy Analysis and Management* 13, no. 1 (1994): 82–119; R. Bellehumeur, 'Review: An Instrument of Change,' *Optimum* 27, no. 1 (1997): 37–42; M. Saward, *Co-Optive Politics and State Legitimacy* (Aldershot, UK: Dartmouth, 1992); and J. Rose, 'Government Advertising in a Crisis: The Quebec Referendum Precedent,' *Canadian Journal of Communication* 18 (1993): 173–96.

65 See S.J. Bulmer, 'The Governance of the European Union: A New Institutionalist Approach,' *Journal of Public Policy* 13, no. 4 (1993): 351–80; B.G. Peters, 'Government Reorganization: A Theoretical Analysis,' *International Political Science Review* 13, no. 2 (1992): 199–218; and M.J. Hollander and M.J. Prince, 'Analytical Units in Federal and Provincial Governments: Origins, Functions and Suggestions for Effectiveness,' *Canadian Public Administration* 36, no. 2 (1993): 190–224.

66 On the U.S. situation of private-sector patronage see A. Nownes and G. Neeley, 'Toward an Explanation for Public Interest Group Formation and Proliferation: "Seed Money," Disturbances, Entrepreneurship, and Patronage,' *Policy Studies Journal* 24, no. 1 (1996): 74–92. On the Canadian situation of public-sector patronage see L.A. Pal, *Interests of State: The Politics of Language, Multiculturalism, and Feminism in Canada* (Montreal: McGill-Queen's University Press, 1993); S. Burt, 'Canadian Women's Groups in the 1980s: Organizational Development and Policy Influence,' *Canadian Public Policy* 16, no. 1 (1990): 17–28; and P. Finkle et al., *Federal Government Relations with Interest Groups: A Reconsideration* (Ottawa: Privy Council Office, 1994).

67 D.S. Brown, 'The Management of Advisory Committees: An Assignment for the '70's,' *Public Administration Review* 32 (1972): 334–42; T.B. Smith, 'Advisory Committees in the Public Policy Process,' *International Review of Administrative Sciences* 43, no. 2 (1977): 153–66; and C.L. Brown-John, 'Advisory Agencies in Canada: An Introduction,' *Canadian Public Administration* 22, no. 1 (1979): 72–91.

68 See S.R. Furlong, 'Reinventing Regulatory Development at the Environmental Protection Agency,' *Policy Studies Journal* 23, no. 3 (1995): 466–82.

69 See J. Jenson, 'Commissioning Ideas: Representation and Royal Commissions,' in S.D. Phillips, ed., *How Ottawa Spends 1994–95: Making Change*, (Ottawa: Carleton University Press, 1994), 39–69; A.C. Cairns, 'Reflections on Commission Research,' in I. Christie, J.A. Yogis, and A.P. Pross, ed., *Commissions of Inquiry* (Toronto: Carswell, 1990), 87–110; K.C. Wheare, *Government by Committee* (Oxford: Clarendon Press, 1955); L. Dion, 'The Politics of Consultation,' *Government and Opposition* 8, no. 3 (1973): 332–53; and R.E. Wraith and G.B. Lamb, *Public Inquiries as an Instrument of Government* (London: George Allen and Unwin, 1971).

70 See, e.g., L. Salter and D. Slaco, *Public Inquiries in Canada* (Ottawa: Science Council of Canada, 1981) and B. Schwartz, 'Public Inquiries,' *Canadian Public Administration* 40, no. 1 (1997): 72–85.

71 See C. Mueller, *The Politics of Communication: A Study in the Political Sociology of Language, Socialization and Legitimation* (New York: Oxford University Press, 1973).

72 See T.N. Gilmore and J. Krantz, 'Innovation in the Public Sector: Dilemmas in the Use of Ad Hoc Processes,' *Journal of Policy Analysis and Management* 10, no. 3 (1991): 455–68.

73 See H. Aldrich, 'Visionaries and Villains: The Politics of Designing Interorganizational Relations,' in E.H. Burack and A.R. Negandhi, eds, *Organization Design: Theoretical Perspectives and Empirical Findings* (Kent, OH: Kent State University Press, 1977), 23–40; E.A. Nordlinger, *On the Autonomy of the Democratic State* (Cambridge, MA: Harvard University Press, 1981); and D.L. Weimer, 'The Craft of Policy Design: Can It Be More than Art?' *Policy Studies Review* 11, no. 3/4 (1992): 370–88.

74 A similar list has been used by the U.S.-Canada International Joint Commission in assessing its likely future role in this sector. See IJC, *The IJC and the 21st Century: Response of the IJC to a Request by the Governments of Canada and the United States on How to Best Assist Them to Meet the Environmental Challenges of the 21st century* (Washington: IJC, 1999). On these trends, generally, see M. Hessing and M. Howlett, *Canadian Natural Resource and Environmental Policy: Political Economy and Public Policy* (Vancouver: UBC Press,

1997); T. Fleming, ed., *The Environment and Canadian Society* (Toronto: ITP Nelson, 1997); and U. Collier, *Deregulation in the European Union: Environmental Perspectives* (London: Routledge, 1998).

75 On these overall, non-environmentally specific, socio-political trends see W.L. Bennett, 'The Uncivic Culture: Communication, Identity and the Rise of Lifestyle Politics,' *PS: Political Science and Politics* 31, no. 4 (1998): 741–62, and, in Canada, N. Nevitte, *The Decline of Deference: Canadian Value Change in Cross-National Perspective* (Peterborough, ON: Broadview Press, 1996).

76 See N. Brenner, 'Beyond State-Centrism? Space, Territoriality, and Geographical Scale in Globalization Studies,' *Theory and Society* 28 (1999): 39–78, and O.R. Young, 'The Problem of Scale in Human/Environment Relationships,' *Journal of Theoretical Politics* 6, no. 4 (1994): 429–47.

77 See, generally, T. Risse-Kappen, *Bringing Transnational Relations Back In: Non-State Actors, Domestic Structures and International Institutions* (Cambridge: Cambridge University Press, 1995) and M.E. Keck and K. Sikkink, eds, *Activists beyond Borders: Advocacy Networks in International Politics* (Ithaca: Cornell University Press, 1998), esp. chap. 4.

78 M. Zurn, 'The Rise of International Environmental Politics: A Review of Current Research,' *World Politics* 50, no. 4 (1998): 617–49, and J. Galtung, 'The Green Movement: A Socio-Historical Exploration,' *International Sociology* 1, no. 1 (1986): 75–90.

79 P.M. Haas, 'Introduction: Epistemic Communities and International Policy Coordination,' *International Organization* 46, no. 1 (1992): 1–36.

80 N. Choucri, ed., *Global Accord: Environmental Challenges and International Responses* (Boston: MIT Press, 1993); A. Hurrell and B. Kingsbury, eds, *The International Politics of the Environment* (Oxford: Clarendon Press, 1992); P.M. Johnson and A. Beaulieu, *The Environment and NAFTA: Understanding and Implementing the New Continental Law* (Washington: Island Press, 1996); L.C. Reif, 'International Environmental Law,' in G. Thompson, M.L. McConnell, and L.B. Huestis, eds, *Environmental Law and Business in Canada* (Aurora, ON: Canada Law Book, 1993), 71–103; and J. Kirton, 'The Commission for Environmental Cooperation and Canada-U.S. Environmental Governance in the NAFTA Era,' *American Review of Canadian Studies* 27, no. 3 (1997): 459–86.

81 See H.R. Alker and P.M. Haas, 'The Rise of Global Ecopolitics,' in N. Choucri, ed., *Global Accord: Environmental Challenges and International Responses*, (Boston: MIT Press, 1993), 205–54.

82 See C.J. Bennett, 'Understanding Ripple Effects: The Cross-National Adoption of Policy Instruments for Bureaucratic Accountability,' *Governance*, 10, no. 3 (1997): 213–33, and, more generally, C.J. Bennett, 'What Is Policy

Convergence and What Causes It?' *British Journal of Political Science* 21, no. 2 (1991): 215–33.

83 See M. Kahler, *International Institutions and the Political Economy of Integration* (Washington: Brookings Institution, 1995). The actual effect, of course, varies according to the type of internationalization process at work. On the various types of effects – such as the use of global markets by business, adherence to international rules and regulations by governments, changes in international discourses on the part of policy experts and others, and infiltration of domestic policy processes by non-domestic actors – see S. Bernstein and B. Cashore, 'Globalization, Four Paths of Internationalization, and Domestic Policy Change: The Case of Eco-Forest in British Columbia,' *Canadian Journal of Political Science* 33, no. 1 (2000): 67–100, and R.O. Keohane and H.V. Milner, eds, *Internationalization and Domestic Politics* (New York: Cambridge University Press, 1996).

84 See, generally, P.G. Cerny, 'International Finance and the Erosion of State Policy Capacity,' in P. Gummett, ed., *Globalization and Public Policy* (Cheltenham: Edward Elgar, 1996), 83–104. On the impact in Canada see G. Toner and T. Conway, 'Environmental Policy,' in G.B. Doern, L.A. Pal, and B.W. Tomlin, eds, *Border Crossings: The Internationalization of Canadian Public Policy* (Toronto: Oxford University Press, 1996), 108–42; M. Howlett, 'Sustainable Development: Environmental Policy,' in A. Johnson and A. Stritch, eds, *Canadian Public Policy: Globalization and Political Parties* (Toronto: Copp Clark Longman, 1996), 47–64; and K. Harrison, *Passing the Buck: Federalism and Canadian Environmental Policy* (Vancouver: UBC Press, 1996).

85 See M. Paterson, *Global Warming and Global Politics* (London: Routledge, 1996) and Government of Canada, *The State of Canada's Environment* (Ottawa: Minister of Supply and Services, 1991).

86 On the role of accidents in opening policy windows and their limited effects, see J.W. Kingdon, *Agendas, Alternatives and Public Policies* (Boston: Little, Brown and Co., 1984); T.A. Birkland, *After Disaster: Agenda Setting, Public Policy and Focusing Events* (Washington: Georgetown University Press, 1997); and M. Howlett, 'Predictable and Unpredictable Policy Windows: Issue, Institutional and Exogenous Correlates of Canadian Federal Agenda-Setting,' *Canadian Journal of Political Science* 31, no. 3 (1998).

87 On these dimensions see P. Gray and P. 't Hart, *Public Policy Disasters in Western Europe* (London: Routledge, 1998).

88 See F.W. Scharpf, 'Policy Failure and Institutional Reform: Why Should Form Follow Function?' *International Social Science Journal* 108 (1986): 179–90.

89 See M. Hessing and M. Howlett, *Canadian Natural Resource and Environmental Policy: Political Economy and Public Policy* (Vancouver: UBC Press, 1997)

and J.N.H. Britton et al., 'Technological Change and Innovation: Policy Issues,' in J.N.H. Britton, ed., *Canada and the Global Economy: The Geography of Structural and Technological Change* (Montreal: McGill-Queen's University Press, 1996), 241–87.

90 See D. Wolfe, 'Technology and Trade,' in S. Rosenblum and P. Findlay, eds, *Debating Canada's Future: Views from the Left* (Toronto: James Lorimer, 1991), 106–27, and R. Anderson et al., eds, *Innovation Systems in a Global Context: The North American Experience* (Montreal: McGill-Queen's University Press, 1998).

91 For a discussion of the implications of such transitions for a regional/provincial political economy see M. Howlett and K. Brownsey, 'From Timber to Tourism: The Political Economy of British Columbia,' in R.K. Carty, ed., *Politics, Policy and Government in British Columbia* (Vancouver: UBC Press, 1996), 18–31.

92 See M. Janicke, H. Monch, and M. Binder, 'Ecological Aspects of Structural Change,' *Intereconomics* 28, no. 4 (1993): 159–69, and T.A. Hutton, *Visions of a 'Post-Staples' Economy: Structural Change and Adjustment Issues in British Columbia* (Vancouver: UBC Centre for Human Settlements, 1994).

93 L. Osberg, F. Wien, and J. Grude, *Vanishing Jobs: Canada's Changing Workplaces* (Toronto: James Lorimer and Co., 1995).

94 P. Dearden and R. Rollins, eds, *Parks and Protected Areas in Canada: Planning and Management* (Toronto: Oxford University Press, 1993).

95 R. Paehlke, 'Green Politics and the Rise of the Environmental Movement,' in T. Fleming, ed., *The Environment and Canadian Society* (Toronto: ITP Nelson, 1997), 251–74.

96 On this pattern see R.A. Kagan, 'Adversarial Legalism and American Government,' *Journal of Policy Analysis and Management* 10, no. 3 (1991): 369–406; R.A. Kagan, 'Should Europe Worry about Adversarial Legalism?' *Oxford Journal of Legal Studies* 17, no. 2 (1997): 165–83; and R.A. Kagan and L. Axelrad, 'Adversarial Legalism: An International Perspective,' in P.S. Nivola, ed., *Comparative Disadvantages? Social Regulations and the Global Economy* (Washington: Brookings Institution Press, 1997), 146–202.

97 C. Manfredi, 'The Judicialization of Politics: Rights and Public Policy in Canada and the United States,' in K. Banting, G. Hoberg, and R. Simeon, eds, *Degrees of Freedom: Canada and the United States in a Changing World* (Montreal: McGill-Queen's University Press, 1997), 152–85, and D. Schneiderman and K. Sutherland, eds, *Charting the Consequences: The Impact of Charter Rights on Canadian Law and Politics* (Toronto: University of Toronto Press, 1997).

98 See S. Elgie, 'Environmental Groups and the Courts: 1970–1992,' in G.

Thompson, M.L. McConnell, and L.B. Huestis, eds, *Environmental Law and Business in Canada* (Aurora, ON: Canada Law Book, 1993), 185–224, and M. Howlett, 'The Judicialization of Canadian Environmental Policy 1980–1990 – A Test of the Canada-U.S. Convergence Hypothesis,' *Canadian Journal of Political Science* 27, no. 1 (1994).

99 See, generally, Royal Commission on Aboriginal Peoples, *Treaty Making in the Spirit of Co-Existence: An Alternative to Extinguishment* (Ottawa: Minister of Supply and Services, 1994) and M. Asch, ed., *Aboriginal and Treaty Rights in Canada: Essays on Law, Equity and Respect for Difference* (Vancouver: UBC Press, 1997). More specifically, see G. Hoberg and E. Morawaski, 'Policy Change through Sector Intersection: Forest and Aboriginal Policy in Clayoquot Sound,' *Canadian Public Administration* 40, no. 3 (1997): 387–414.

100 See H. Scofield, 'Nafta trio warned of corporate lawsuits: Plug loophole to avoid claims, think-tank says,' *Globe and Mail*, 23 June 1999: A7; J. Kirton, 'The Commission for Environmental Cooperation and Canada-U.S. Environmental Governance in the NAFTA Era,' *American Review of Canadian Studies* 27, no. 3 (1997): 459–86, and J.M. Ayres, *Defying Conventional Wisdom: Political Movements and Popular Contention against North American Free Trade* (Toronto: University of Toronto Press, 1998).

101 D. Alexander, 'Bioregionalism: Science or Sensibility?' *Environmental Ethics* 12 (1990): 161–73. See also R. Haeuber, 'Setting the Environmental Policy Agenda: The Case of Ecosystem Management,' *Natural Resources Journal* 36, no. 1 (1996): 1–27, and J. Rayner, 'Evaluating National Forest Programmes: Lessons from Biodiversity Policies in Canada,' in P. Gluck et al., eds, *Formulation and Implementation of National Forest Programmes: Volume 1 – Theoretical Aspects* (Joensuu, Fin.: European Forest Institute, 1999), 229–36.

102 A. Jordan, R. Brouwer, and E. Noble, 'Innovative and Responsive? A Longitudinal Analysis of the Speed of EU Environmental Policy-Making, 1967–97,' *Journal of European Public Policy* 6, no. 3 (1999): 376–98, and A.P. Cortell and J.W. Davis, 'How Do International Institutions Matter? The Domestic Impact of International Rules and Norms,' *International Studies Quarterly* 40 (1996): 451–78.

103 See J.M. Simmons, 'The Canada-wide Accord on Environmental Harmonization and Value Change within the Department of the Environment,' paper presented to annual meeting of the Canadian Political Science Association, Sherbrooke, 1999; L. Stefanick, 'Organization, Administration, and the Environment: Will a Facelift Suffice or Does the Patient Need Radical Surgery,' *Canadian Public Administration* 41, no. 1 (1998): 99–146; and B.G. Rabe, 'The Politics of Sustainable Development: Impediments to Pollution Prevention and Policy Integration in Canada,' *Canadian Public Administra-*

tion 40, no. 3 (1997): 415–35. More generally, see M. Howlett, 'Beyond Legalism? Policy Instruments, Implementation Styles and Convergence in Canadian and U.S. Environmental Policy,' paper presented to annual meeting of the Western Economics Association, San Diego, 1999.

104 See E.A. Lindquist, 'Public Managers and Policy Communities: Learning to Meet New Challenges,' *Canadian Public Administration* 35, no. 2 (1992): 127–59; R. Agranoff and M. McGuire, 'Managing in Network Settings,' *Policy Studies Review* 16, no. 1 (1999): 18–41; and R. Mayntz, 'Public Bureaucracies and Policy Implementation,' *International Social Science Journal* 31, no. 4 (1979): 633–45.

105 See chapter 4 of J.G. March and J.P. Olsen, *Rediscovering Institutions: The Organizational Basis of Politics* (New York: Free Press, 1989); and V.W. Ruttan, 'Designing Institutions for Sustainability,' in E.T. Loehman and D.M. Kilgour, eds, *Designing Institutions for Environmental and Resource Management* (Cheltenham, UK: Edward Elgar, 1998), 142–64.

106 See M. Janicke and H. Weidner, *National Environmental Policies: A Comparative Study of Capacity Building* (Berlin: Springer, 1997); M. Janicke and H. Jorgens, *National Environmental Policy Plans and Long-Term Sustainable Development Strategies: Learning from International Experiences* (Berlin: Freie Universitate Berlin Forschungsstelle für Umweltpolitik Paper 96-5, 1997); and M. Janicke et al., 'Structural Change and Environmental Impact,' *Intereconomics* 24, no. 1, January/February (1989): 24–35. See also P. Glasbergen, 'Learning to Manage the Environment,' in W.M. Lafferty and J. Meadowcroft, eds, *Democracy and the Environment: Problems and Prospects* (Cheltenham, UK: Edward Elgar, 1996), 175–93.

107 S.D. Phillips, 'How Ottawa Blends: Shifting Government Relationships with Interest Groups,' in F. Abele, ed., *How Ottawa Spends 1991–92: The Politics of Fragmentation* (Ottawa: Carleton University Press, 1991), 183–228, and M.M. Atkinson and C.W. Pervin, 'Sector Councils and Sectoral Corporatism: Viable? Desirable?' in M. Gunderson and A. Sharpe, ed., *Forging Business-Labour Partnerships: The Emergence of Sector Councils in Canada* (Toronto: University of Toronto Press, 1998), 271–94. See also L.A. Pal, *Interests of State: The Politics of Language, Multiculturalism, and Feminism in Canada* (Montreal: McGill-Queen's University Press, 1993).

108 See G.B. Doern, L. Pal, and B.W. Tomlin, eds, *Border Crossings: The Internationalization of Canadian Public Policy* (Toronto: Oxford University Press, 1996) and A. Johnson and A. Stritch, eds, *Canadian Public Policy: Globalization and Political Parties* (Toronto: Copp Clark, 1997). More generally, see A. Hammond, *Which World? Scenarios for the 21st Century* (Washington: Island Press, 1998).

9. Persistent Challenges, Uncertain Innovations: A Synthesis

Edward A. Parson

The papers collected in this volume have discussed a set of fundamental challenges that confront the governance of environmental issues in Canada over the coming few decades: their dependence on uncertain and evolving scientific knowledge; their complex linkages across multiple scales of distance and authority; their vulnerability and present subordination to the drive for economic globalization; and their evocation of deep differences in values. While these challenges are not new, they are increasing in severity as environmental stresses from human activities worldwide are growing sharper. Moreover, this increase in severity is occurring at a time of general worldwide diminution of states' capacity and willingness to control the behaviour of private actors through coercive regulation.

The authors have also considered several innovative approaches to environmental governance that have been proposed as broad means to address its unique challenges. Like the challenges we have considered, these proposed innovations are not new, but have been proposed, discussed, and occasionally attempted in various jurisdictions for a few decades. But they are increasing in maturity, accumulated knowledge, and prominence on policy agendas. The innovations discussed here do not, for the most part, concern specific policy instruments, but rather involve various redefinitions, divisions, and sharing of responsibility for environmental governance between various actors – between governments and scientific advisory processes; between international, national, and subnational governments; between institutions responsible for environmental and economic policy; or between the state and non-state actors, including firms, industry, or citizens' associations, First Nations, and individual citizens.

This synthesis essay considers the major questions of environmental governance and sustainable development that are discussed in the volume. What guidelines can be articulated for more effective integration of scientific knowledge and environmental governance, to advance the goal of adaptive management? What guidelines can be stated for the most promising sharing of environmental authority among government institutions, and between governments and other actors? What are the likely promise and limitations of the specific governance innovations discussed? And how does the pursuit of sustainable development complement, or compete with, other large-scale social trends and aspirations such as economic globalization and liberalization, world development, and alleviation of poverty?

More broadly, how serious a challenge to present forms of governance do environmental stresses pose? Do the seemingly modest innovations discussed here measure up to the task? Or, alternatively, does managing the environment or pursuing sustainable development require fundamental political or social transformation? And if so, transformation of what kinds and at what scales? Alternatively, do environmental trends make such transformation likely – that is, will necessity be the mother of invention in this respect? Finally, to the extent that these questions cannot be answered, what are the broad directions of research or of policy that appear most likely to move us closer to an ability to answer them, and to cope with continuing environmental change?

Science, Assessment, and Policy Decisions

In bread terms, the challenges discussed in this volume define some of the most basic requirements for effective governance of the environment, governance that moves society toward the diffuse goal of sustainable development. For example, although the conditions necessary for sustainable development are not fully known, they must surely include adequate knowledge of the properties of the natural systems on which society depends, and the means to apply available knowledge to guide development decisions. The knowledge that must be generated, synthesized, and applied may be specific or general: from the particularities of stock assessment to manage a fishery to the broad knowledge of regional or global systems necessary to provide early warning of risks or provide help in identifying technological, behavioural, or policy responses.

A useful and legitimate synthesis of expert knowledge with democratically accountable deliberation and decision-making poses grave challenges, both conceptual and practical, to the design of policy processes and institutions. At a conceptual level, the domains of science and of democratic politics have different goals, standards of merit, norms of participation, and procedures for reaching agreement and resolving conflicts. At a practical level, desired knowledge is often unavailable and available relevant knowledge is often not adequately used.

For many aspects of the environment, the available knowledge is often inadequate to give high confidence in the consequences of decisions, and decisions often cannot be delayed until high confidence is attained. Uncertainty is thus unavoidable and pervasive in environmental governance, with two consequences of fundamental importance.

First, costly decisions to avert an environmental risk must sometimes be made without strong confidence in the magnitude and character of the risk. This insight is increasingly recognized, and expressed as the 'precautionary principle': that precautionary measures should be taken against likely but unconfirmed risks. Although this principle seems to evoke a rational process of decision analysis, by which the likelihood and severity of a risk would be weighed against the cost of action to avoid it, the principle's operational meaning is scarcely more precise than that of 'sustainable development.' It does, however, clearly reject one view of the burden and standard of proof needed to impose protective measures, which was once dominant – at least in rhetoric, if not always in practice. According to this view, inappropriately drawn from criminal law, activities and materials (e.g., chemicals) are presumed to be environmentally benign until demonstrated harmful beyond a reasonable doubt. The precautionary principle is the slogan for the long-developing realization that sometimes activities should be restricted in the absence of decisive demonstration of harm. The opposing extreme view, that activities are 'guilty when charged' with any environmental harm, is of course equally insupportable. Thus, ample room is left for both discretion and dissent over what the precautionary principle requires in any particular case.

The second consequence of pervasive uncertainty is less widely recognized: that decisions carry unavoidable risk of error. Any environmental decision may, with more information or better understanding, be revealed as too stringent, too weak, or simply misconceived. Rational environmental governance thus requires some way to adapt policies and decisions to advancing knowledge, a goal widely described as 'Adaptive management.' As for many abstract environmental desiderata, the concrete meaning of adaptive management has never been fully specified, but a few of its basic requirements are evident.

First, resources must be invested in learning. Monitoring and research must continue, not cease, when initial management decisions are made. Moreover, monitoring and research programs must be designed not just to advance general understanding, but for their relevance to informing potential future decisions. Often, a powerful way to advance understanding is to design policies to be *informative*, in addition to their other goals. What this requires will vary, but will certainly include the goal that decisions should perturb environmental systems strongly enough to generate a signal, and be sustained for long enough to observe a response.[1] Loose federal systems like Canada's routinely generate potentially informative variation in management, as different jurisdictions take different paths. But this potential for learning is seldom realized. It requires unbiased, consistent monitoring and evaluation and, ideally, some way to coordinate policy 'experiments' as to their form, time of enactment, and duration.

In addition, policy institutions need both the capacity to assimilate new knowledge and the flexibility to respond to it appropriately. While the other conditions for adaptive management have proved challenging, this one is the hardest to achieve. It requires that systems of governance be able to distinguish between three types of supposed new knowledge: new information that shows prior decisions were so bad as to be worth bearing the cost of changing them; new information that does not meet this threshold; and supposed new information advanced as a rear-guard action by the initial decision's opponents, which a competent and impartial observer would judge to have no merit. To draw such distinctions requires that pluralistic and partisan governance processes have access to objective high-quality scientific advice, including non-partisan expert judgments that weigh the importance of new findings, synthesize multiple competing claims, and assess their merits. Moreover, the ability to act appropriately on new information requires a governance process, and individuals within it, capable of acknowledging error – or, more plausibly, requires that the political or bureaucratic cost of acknowledging error be reduced, without sacrificing adequate standards of professional competency.

The implications of a commitment to adaptive management in public policy are not confined to government. Because regulatory decisions affect the permissible uses and commercial value of private-property, a commitment to adaptive management would necessarily reduce the security of private property rights. If all decisions are subject to revision, the risk of future restrictions hangs over every activity and property. Government cannot even promise when imposing restrictions that the same activity or property will not be subject to stricter or different restrictions in the future.[2] This conflict remains nascent in Canada for now, but is already fully engaged in the United States. Following a promise by Interior Secretary Bruce Babbitt that there would be 'no surprises' in endangered-species policy, many western property owners have negotiated agreements with the EPA over the Endangered Species Act that effectively thwart any attempt to manage adaptively by excluding any future restrictions in return for present accommodations.[3] In contrast, in U.S. regulation of alternatives for the ozone-depleting chemicals restricted by the Montreal Protocol, industry sought – and the EPA refused – firm commercial lifetimes for chemicals once their introduction had been approved.

The preceding conditions appear to be essential requirements of governance systems that advance understanding and act on it, but they are a tall order. Schrecker discusses several conspicuous failures to obtain or appropriately use essential information in Canadian policy. His cautionary tales reveal how difficult it is for government to support good, independent, policy-relevant research, and to act on it. How do Schrecker's three prescriptions for better science-based policy measure up to the task?

His first proposal is for 'firewalls,' organizational barriers strong enough to protect publicly employed or funded scientists from suppression of their results or professional retaliation when their results offend their superiors. Some such barriers appear to be essential if policy-relevant research, data, and conclusions that are politically uncomfortable are to be conducted and made publicly available. But there is a potential cost. Since professional incentives in many fields of scientific research do not value policy-relevant research highly, there must be enough managerial control over researchers to ensure they are addressing important policy-relevant questions. The detailed design of such barriers to adequately ensure that publicly supported research addresses the most important questions, but to prevent control of its content for political ends, would be a delicate matter.

Schrecker's other two proposals both call for more transparency in government decision-making processes. Responsible officials would have to reveal both the evidence on which particular decisions are based and the general guidelines they follow (assuming they know and can articulate them) in weighing evidence and deciding what and whom to believe. These proposals are more risky than the first one. Such transparency is clearly attractive in principle, but what might its consequences be?

Public actors often have a strong interest in the opposite goal, obscuring the actual criteria and trade-offs that guide their decisions. Indeed, it can be politically advantageous to maintain the discretion to act while being able to demonstrate, at will, that compelling argument or overwhelming force left only one conceivable choice. The *force majeure* so invoked may be an international obligation, a classic strategy of Canadian bureaucrats to overcome domestic blockage, even when they have been instrumental in creating the international commitments;[4] it may be the risk of capital leaving, or not coming; or it may be science. Any of these can seem to bind decision-makers' hands, forcing upon them the action that they in fact wish to take. In many cases, this is simple deception: power is only seemingly lost, or is voluntarily given up and can be readily reclaimed. In some cases, however, enough delay in taking required action can lead to real compulsion: a fishing moratorium may be imposed 'by the fish.'

When science is the pretext used in this charade, however, the cost can be high. If scientific advice is made to compel policy choice, then political debate and discretion are likely to be pushed back into the processes of developing the scientific advice. Accountability is likely to be lost if the decisive political debate is moved into closed and non-representative fora. High-quality objective scientific advice is likely to be lost if an advisory body's output is manipulated to appear to support the decision adopted. Paradoxically, pursuit of greater transparency in political decision-making may jeopardize both the quality of advice and the accountability of decisions.

Several other approaches have been proposed to ensure that scientific advice is high in quality, independence, and relevance. Sometimes merely avoiding explicit policy conclusions may protect advisory bodies from political interference, even if such conclusions are plainly implied. But this is a balancing act: avoiding recommendations may be essential, but failing to state policy implications can be a large step toward irrelevance. Moreover, advisory bodies speak to multiple audiences, and what is obvious to some is not to all. Conversely, unexplicated policy implications, or even pure statements of scientific theory or data, can sometimes be embarrassing enough to provoke attempted suppression or disavowal.

Another approach, practised with some success since 1990, has been to move scientific and technical assessments to the international arena. For several global issues, including both ozone depletion and climate change, international assessments have gained ever-greater participation and have largely supplanted national assessments. While the substantive rationale for international assessment of global issues like these is compelling, there are also political advantages. The extreme diversity of political interests, and the reduced likelihood of control by any faction or perspective, can facilitate assessments that attain both high quality and relevance. These advantages may explain the increasing internationalization since 1990 of some issues that actually have much smaller scales, such as biodiversity and desertification. Even when understanding the issue requires local knowledge, international bodies can still specify standards for national assessments or national contributions to an international assessment.

Scales of Environmental Authority

While moving governance to the international level may not be feasible or appropriate for all environmental issues, it can be an effective approach even for issues whose apparent spatial scale is smaller. Relative to other policy domains, the environment is extreme in the extent of overlapping and shared authority between governments, and between state, non-state, and inter-state actors. Such overlap arises from the complex spatial structure of environmental processes, which link scales ranging from local to global, and because effective environmental governance depends on the behaviour and knowledge of many diverse actors, which the state lacks the knowledge and authority to specify. Moreover, in Canada and most federal states, the environment is distributed among multiple related constitutional powers, some of which are held at each level of government. Several authors in the volume have examined various aspects of this sharing of authority.

Because of environmental issues' complex mixture of local, regional, and global-scale dynamics, one cannot simply match the primary scale of a problem with the primary scale of authority to manage it. The appropriate division of small-scale and large-scale environmental authority has been debated with particular vigour in Canada.[5] Here, decision-making is simultaneously pulled outward toward international management and inward toward greater provincial authority. Paehlke examines the challenges these complex spatial linkages pose for an effective sharing of authority between subnational, national, and international levels of governance.

An enduring theme in this debate is the bioregionalist aspiration for political authority to reside in local communities organized on ecosystem boundaries. Paehlke rejects this aspiration for three reasons. First, ecosystems do not possess clear, coherent boundaries along which to divide such communities; rather, they comprise multiple, interlinked systems whose boundaries are diffuse and do not coincide. Second, sovereign local authority can and often does violate basic democratic norms. Third and most important, the political and economic forces that dominate modern society are increasingly organized globally, so even local autarkies would be unable to manage their economies and resources in isolation from them.

Turning to the division of environmental authority between existing levels of government, Paehlke assumes a constitutional blank slate and argues for the inherent preferability of national supremacy in matters relating to the environment – while noting that nearly the opposite is occurring in Canada, as environmental authority is being ceded at once downward to the provinces and upward to an increasingly dense web of international treaties and institutions. Three factors favour federal predominance, which are offset – but in Paehlke's view, only partially – by the greater knowledge and concern that smaller jurisdictions are likely to have for their own environment and resources.

First, national governments have the resources and legal standing to act in the international domain, where the crucial balancing of environmental with economic authority must occur. To participate credibly at this level, a state needs the authority to deliver on its commitments. National governments are also better than subnational governments at resisting two structural forces that systematically favour too-weak environmental protection: the race to the bottom in fiscal and regulatory policy, as jurisdictions compete to attract and keep investment, and the greater sectoral concentration of smaller economies.

These claims are controversial, particularly in the recent Canadian climate of provincial assertiveness and federal diffidence, but they carry some force. The first is correct as a matter of law, and appears to be supported by diplomatic experience; the other two are empirical claims, and are at least plausible. The argument from the sectoral concentration of small economies in particular is supported by Canadian experience, where provincial governments have consistently been highly solicitous of dominant local industry and resource sectors.

The race-to-the-bottom claim, while also theoretically plausible and observed in some policy domains,[6] is more complex and the evidence around it more ambiguous. Two parts of the claim must be distinguished, one concerning how firms make location decisions and one concerning how governments try to influence those decisions. Location decisions by firms must consider a host of factors, including transport costs, quality and cost of workforce, political and currency risk, and many dimensions of government fiscal and regulatory policy. The cost of meeting environmental standards must surely enter into these decisions, but as one factor among many. Empirical studies in the 1980s found that environmental standards were a strong location factor only for a few extremely dirty industries. While these studies are now out of date, and have been criticized for counting environmental costs too narrowly, more recent studies of factors driving location decisions reach the same broad conclusion: other factors nearly always overwhelm environmental standards. In those infrequent cases where they do not, the capital that goes elsewhere may well be capital that a rich, environmentally concerned nation would rather not have. To observe that capital rarely leaves (or fails to come) due to environmental regulations does not, however, mean that firms rarely *threaten* to do so; abundant narrative evidence suggests that such threats are made frequently.

Do officials believe them? Governments do sometimes relax environmental standards, grant exceptions to them, or fail to enforce them. Such decisions sometimes target a particular firm, sometimes in response to a threat, but are often broadly targeted, as in the early Harris government years in Ontario. When offered, the public justifications for such decisions are often the need to protect jobs or attract new investment, but not always. It would appear that politicians and officials, at least some of the time, do believe that strong environmental standards, effectively enforced, risk loss of investment, despite studies that show the risk to be small.

Why? Only three explanations appear plausible. Perhaps government officials are bad poker players, easily misled or intimidated; perhaps the empirical studies understate the true risk of capital flight; or perhaps officials use the threat of lost jobs and investment as a pretext, which 'forces' them to do what they in fact wish to do for other reasons – whether those other reasons are a sincere belief that the standard in question was too strict, an ideological opposition to regulation in general, or a desire to favour their friends and supporters. Determining the actual patterns of bargaining between firms and officials over environmental standards, and the mix of interests that motivate each side, involves empirical, potentially researchable questions of great importance, though the difficulties of obtaining reliable evidence are likely to be severe.

In aggregate, Paehlke contends that appropriate environmental protection is systematically more likely to be blocked at smaller scales of government authority than larger ones. But the evidence, of several kinds, is mixed. In Canada, the federal government has by no means always led the way on the environment, even considering the constitutional limits on its authority. Indeed, Harrison's paper identifies several occasions when the federal government had to be compelled, reluctantly, to exercise environmental regulatory authority that it clearly did possess.

There are other bodies of evidence that appear to favour local authority, although their applicability to questions of the division of authority between levels of government in a federal system are questionable. For example, both theory and empirical evidence suggest that the most successful management of common-property resources is at the most local levels, when at most a few hundred agents must develop means of mutual restraint.[7] Where competent and legitimate governments are in place, however, few environmental problems have the structure of a commons. Similarly, municipalities have shown substantial interest in global environmental issues, but their concrete actions have typically been symbolic and very low in cost, or have brought local benefits sufficient to justify their costs, so they provide only weak evidence of local willingness to contribute to global environmental goals. Finally, the hypothesis that there may exist a 'race to the top,' by which jurisdictions seek competitive advantage in advanced clean technologies by adopting stringent environmental regulations, appears to be of extremely restricted validity.[8]

A more persuasive basis for favouring substantial environmental authority at subnational levels is suggested, however, by the preceding discussion of adaptive management. Locating authority at smaller scales allows for diverse standards and approaches. While such diversity is most often advocated as a response to variation in local conditions and preferences, it can also allow jurisdictions to experiment with diverse and innovative approaches. Such diversity could greatly promote learning about the effects and effectiveness of alternative responses if sufficiently controlled that the variation is informative and if programs and results are adequately monitored. The diversity would also carry real costs, such as allowing local jurisdictions to choose weaker standards than are supported by a national or international consensus, and enduring the risk of failed policy experiments. Moreover, as in all pursuit of adaptive management, the political challenges would be substantial. The approach would require an institutional capacity to admit ignorance, admit error, and revise policies revealed to be inadequate, even after they have accreted constituencies with stakes in their continuance.

A promising direction for resolving competing claims of environmental authority at multiple scales would be to construct cross-scale networks of shared authority and negotiated joint decisions that mirror the complex cross-scale structure of environmental issues. Canada's loose federal structure may facilitate such an approach, or indeed compel it if redrawing the lines of formal environmental authority is out of the question. In fact, Canada did experience several years of such effective collaboration under the Canadian Council of Ministers of the Environment (CCME), following a series of decisions in the late 1980s that strengthened its role. Benefiting from a strong commitment from several key ministers and deputy ministers, and from careful attention to institutional design, CCME contributed to coherent and effective national environmental policy in several ways. It helped build technical capacity in smaller jurisdictions; it invested provincial and territorial officials with a national perspective when they held the rotating chair; and it provided key research and analysis to address technically challenging problems shared by multiple jurisdictions. CCME's subsequent decline reflected a weakened commitment from several key jurisdictions, for both fiscal and ideological reasons. The decline also followed an attempt to harmonize all responsibilities for environmental protection across jurisdictions, an attempt that no doubt was encouraged by earlier successes, but which in retrospect clearly overreached, and ended in embarrassing failure. The richly instructive experience of CCME remains to be mined, and likely holds valuable lessons about the scope, limits, and conditions for environmental-policy coordination and harmonization, both in Canada and in the international arena.

International Economic Regimes and Environmental Protection

While the future path of domestic sharing of environmental authority is quite obscure, the international path is substantially clearer. We are in the midst of a powerful shift of economic activity and its regulation toward global integration. Not only is economic activity becoming more global; international institutions are also becoming more economic, in that the most powerful global institutions are increasingly those dedicated to the economic goals of income growth through the free movement of goods and services, capital, and labour.

But international economic regimes affect other social and political domains, including the environment. They must often, for example, resolve disputes, many of which concern environmental or conservation measures. Economic regimes are thereby called on to judge the acceptability of environmental measures, both domestic and international, as regards their intent (i.e., are they disguised trade protection?) and their effect (i.e., does their harm to trade outweigh their environmental benefits?). In so doing, economic regimes render far-reaching judgments on the relative weighting, and the reconciliation, of liberal economic goals and environmental goals.

Juillet points out that different economic regimes conduct this reconciliation differently, both in their dominant ideologies and in their institutional frameworks. Most lack expertise or sympathy for environmental goals, and make liberal trade goals supreme. Moreover, many make these high-stakes judgments without democratic accountability, rendering their decisions in closed and non-representative proceedings or deferring to standards developed by private bodies. Still, some do better than others. Juillet argues that the EU better balances economic and environmental values than does either NAFTA or the WTO. NAFTA's Chapter 11 is particularly egregious in this regard, providing expedited secret procedures through which firms can attack national environmental regulations.

More fundamentally, Juillet argues that seemingly reasonable principles to guide such decisions may severely and inappropriately constrain national authority over the level of environmental standards, the form of policy instruments used, or the manner of implementation, thereby directly threatening national pursuit of sustainable development. For example, the widely endorsed principle that environmental controls must have a 'scientific basis' has been frequently interpreted, simplistically, to require high levels of confidence in the severity of a risk before allowing a regulatory response. This stance effectively reverses the hard-won twenty-year shift toward more precautionary management of the environment. Similarly, the 'risk assessment' principle and the product-process distinction might both, depending on details of interpretation, restrict the scope of permissible environmental controls. The 'risk assessment' principle, that an environmental measure's economic costs must be balanced against the risk of environmental harm (or, more narrowly, the direct harm to people) that it avoids, might exclude reasonable environmental measures because their clearly demonstrable contribution to specific risk reduction, narrowly defined and held to an unreasonably high standard of proof, is less than their more readily measurable economic burdens. The product-process distinction, which says that when products themselves are identical, those made by environmentally preferable processes may not command any regulatory advantage in international trade, would clearly exclude measures to reduce the environmental burden of foreign production, even when the resources being harmed are of international consequence or concern.

So what way forward? Attempting to protect the environment by fighting the economic forces of globalization is clearly futile. Rather, the present imbalance between liberal trade principles and environmental principles must be redressed at the international level. This is an essential component of the vision of an environmentally benign globalism that Juillet and Paehlke share, although their specific proposals differ. For environmental issues of global significance, the path forward appears fairly clear. One essential component would be explicit acknowledgment by economic institutions of the legitimacy of multilateral environmental commitments, at least as regards their core environmental protection provisions. The inclusion of trade restrictions within environmental agreements would require more careful negotiation, whose details would likely differ between the case of trade restrictions that are essential means of effecting the treaty's environmental goals, as with the Convention on International Trade in Endangered Species (CITES) and the Basel Convention on trade in hazardous wastes, and the case of targeted trade restrictions whose purpose is to give states incentives to join and comply with the treaty, as with the Montreal Protocol. While universal deference of trade regimes to environmental ones is no more likely to be an acceptable outcome than the present, nearly opposite situation, it is likely that both these kinds of environmental treaty-based trade restrictions could, under certain restrictions, be acceptable to a liberal international economic system and be granted a conditional presumption of deference.

A second condition would likely be the need to construct countervailing institutional strength and expertise on environmental issues at the international level, and to ensure the reciprocal consideration of primary environmental and economic principles in setting and evaluating policies in each domain. While in principle it might be desirable to graft the new environmental mandate and expertise onto existing international economic institutions, this path would not likely succeed. Trade agreements confer on their parties valuable property rights, which are extremely rigid once enacted and do not readily admit of modification to incorporate additional concerns. The lamentable experience thus far of the attempt to infuse environmental concerns into the WTO and the World Bank, and indeed the limited clout of the environmental agreements and institutions belatedly grafted onto NAFTA, all speak to the difficulty of this task. The construction of parallel international environmental institutional capacity, while also a tall order, is, with sufficient initial political resolve, less clearly doomed. Paehlke describes the need as 'globaliz[ing] environmental protection at least as much as we have globalized economic activity,' and argues that this ambitious goal can be achieved if governments make it the price of further movement toward economic globalization, for instance, through the proposed Multilateral Agreement on Investment (MAI).

For national or local environmental concerns, the path is even murkier. Even on global issues, leading nations often wish to enact national measures stronger than their treaty obligations require, since treaties most often reflect a middle-of-the-road or lower level of concern. For issues that predominantly lie within national borders, or that evoke predominantly national (or idiosyncratically national) concerns, international treaties may be neither feasible nor appropriate. Here, it is not clear how to protect national discretion in environmental governance, or even how much discretion should be protected. Paehlke's advocacy of global environmental authority can be read as rejecting national or subnational divergence in environmental protection – regardless of diverse local conditions or the spatial scale of the issue – as the price of raising the global political status and force of environmental protection to equal that of economic growth.

The present situation is indeed hostile to divergent or idiosyncratic national measures. The dominant presumptions are that a single level and form of environmental protection is appropriate for all jurisdictions; that stringency of protection should be harmonized at that level, and implemented through least-trade-restrictive policy instruments; and that the appropriate level can be determined through universally accepted processes of scientific reasoning and assessment. As Juillet argues, the EU offers a partial exception to this pattern, able to sustain greater international diversity in part because of its dense network of institutions and commitments that permits complex trades on many dimensions. In other economic regimes, the forces favouring such levelling now largely prevail.

But some jurisdictions may not want to harmonize their standards. They may want to protect more strongly, or with more precaution, than an international consensus can support; to protect unique national resources or values; to protect against certain risks for expressive or cultural reasons that lack a well-substantiated scientific foundation; or to implement environmental protection through idiosyncratic policy instruments that fail the 'least trade-restrictive' test. Alternatively, in order to gain a broad enough political coalition to protect a sincerely held environmental value, a jurisdiction might have to ally with protectionist groups and implement the measure in such a way as to advance their interests. While any of these decisions might be legitimate, the emerging principles of international economic regimes would forbid them all. And indeed, any of these would be hard to distinguish from disingenuous measures, primarily motivated by protectionism but construed as environmental measures. Drawing these distinctions would require some fair dispute-resolution process that grants sincere pursuit of environmental protection equivalent standing to liberal trade principles.

These possibilities suggest that environmental measures might be understood in part as expressions of local or national cultural diversity. On that basis, perhaps they should be permitted; or permitted when judged by a neutral body to be sincere; or permitted with a requirement of compensation, in order to increase the likelihood that they are enacted only when sincere. Consider Canada's decision to ban the gasoline additive MMT. Two hypothetical descriptions of the basis for the Cabinet decision have been advanced: first, that advisers judged MMT likely to cause substantial environmental harm, while acknowledging that the scientific evidence remained ambiguous; second, that a political decision was made to favour the automobile industry, which supported the ban, over the oil industry, which opposed it. The ban might be judged acceptable in either case – simply because the oil industry prevailed over the auto industry in the United States, it is not obvious that it should be allowed to use international trade regimes to make its victory global – but the ban would surely appear more acceptable, and MMT's U.S. manufacturer less entitled to compensation, if the first reason predominated. Similarly, should Europeans be allowed to decide they do not want to eat hormone-fed beef or genetically modified foods, despite the weak present evidence of health risk, simply because it scares them or they find it offensive? Labelling products would obviously mitigate such conflicts in some cases, such as food production; the fact that producers have opposed labelling suggests they have other concerns than mere market access. Labelling would not, however, resolve conflicts such as that over MMT, because the needed coordination of changes to fuel and vehicles can only be acomplished by a centralized system-wide decision, not by individual consumer choice.

Although protecting national discretion in such matters has much to commend it in principle, it would clearly create a serious moral hazard. A promising approach to resolving the tension might involve two elements. First, some dimensions of environmental authority would be shifted to international bodies, even for issues of predominantly local or national effect, to counterbalance the economic bias of present global institutions. Such an international authority need not imply complete rejection of diverse standards and approaches across jurisdictions, but would clearly require the power to delimit their acceptable scope, or to judge the acceptability of particular measures case by case. The basic difference from the present regime would be that such an authority would make these decisions from a basis of primary concern for the environment rather than for liberal trade. The second element would combine neutral international expert assessment of measures in dispute, and graduated compensation to parties that the measures harm. Compensation would be scaled according to neutral judgments of the measure's trade effects, its motivation, and the gravity and basis of the environmental value it seeks (or purports) to protect.

The Public-Private Interface: Regulation, Voluntarism, and Environmental Governance

As Canadian institutions are challenged by federal sharing of authority, and by erosion of national environmental authority in the face of international economic regimes, they are also following a widespread trend toward intentionally devolving some aspects of their environmental authority to non-state actors. Harrison, Doyle-Bedwell and Cohen, and Dorcey and McDaniels all consider different aspects of this devolution.

Harrison examines voluntary programs that devolve some authority over defining, implementing, or even enforcing environmental measures to private actors, replacing coercive state regulation. While general limits to state power and knowledge inevitably imply *some* sharing of effective authority with non-state actors, she provides several grounds for caution in endorsing a major shift toward explicit reliance on voluntary measures.

She reviews present experience to ask why such measures are adopted, and how well they work. She argues that such measures may be adopted for various reasons, of greater or lesser legitimacy. On the one hand, firms have better access to, and information about, their operations than regulators do, so delegating implementation to them could realize environmental goals with greater efficiency and reduced burden. On the other hand, such delegation may simply be regulators' response to political or organizational weakness; or, worse still, a way to appear to tackle an environmental problem without commitment, burden on firms, or hope of success. In the first case, the policies are adopted because they work better, in the second because they work worse; which of these is the case in any particular instance depends on the details.

Turning to the effectiveness of voluntary measures, Harrison argues that inflated claims are rampant, and that even serious attempts to assess effectiveness accurately are often obstructed by confounding factors, implementation lags, and lack of reliable information. The programs' design often exacerbates these problems, in that they typically lack clear targets, reporting requirements, or provisions for independent performance audits. Finally, she expresses concern that a major purpose – and effect – of voluntary measures may be to thwart democratic accountability, by shifting important decisions on environmental protection into closed bargaining sessions.

As Harrison points out, the term 'voluntary measures' embraces so diverse a collection of approaches as to foster widespread confusion. In particular it is often used, rather misleadingly, for approaches in which the state requires firms to do *different things* than under conventional regulation, imposing environmentally relevant requirements but granting flexibility in deciding how best to attain them. Examples include shifting from technology standards to performance standards; shifting from command-and-control regulation to market-based mechanisms such as tradable emission permits; and substituting information disclosure and reporting requirements for standards.

The essence of these approaches is not that they reduce state coercion; any of them could equally well be agreed upon through voluntary negotiations, imposed through binding regulatory or legal measures, or agreed upon through negotiations and implemented through binding measures. Rather, they seek a more efficient division of responsibility, in which the state attends to environmental ends and the non-state regulatory targets attend to means. By giving firms the flexibility to decide how to meet a performance standard; by extending that same flexibility to groups of firms, allowing them to meet an environmental target jointly rather than separately; or by requiring only that firms publicly disclose their environmental behaviour, choosing for themselves how to deal with the pressure that markets or civil society impose on them once this information is widely distributed – the state allows firms' greater knowledge of technical possibilities, and more detailed influence over internal behaviour, to yield better and cheaper ways of meeting environmental goals.

These approaches have analogies, albeit imperfect ones, to the sharing of authority in many other domains – between international regimes and states, federal and provincial governments, and even firms and employees.[9] In each case, a central actor seeks to influence the behaviour of multiple decentralized actors to pursue a shared goal, while harnessing the benefits of their specific knowledge and ability. In each case, there is an initial attraction to predominantly central authority over ends, but substantially decentralized authority over means. But such neat division of responsibility is somewhat too simplistic. When the world is messy enough – and a perennial characteristic of environmental issues is their messiness – it cannot be effectively managed by advance agreement on precise division of responsibilities. Ambiguity of authority and role confusion are inevitable – not least because what is a means and what is an end are ambiguous and depend on context – posing substantial personal and organizational challenges.

Because the state possesses clear authority, however, the state/ non-state case is somewhat less messy than the others, and some clear guidelines for government responsibility can be sketched. A possible list of government responsibilities might include defining specific, environmentally relevant objectives; ensuring credible monitoring and verification of performance; disseminating results widely; ensuring appropriate consequences for failure to meet objectives; and requiring continuing improvement. These requirements appear to be both consistent with successful environmental performance and within the authority of government. In their inclusion of 'continuous improvement,' they also appear consistent with the requirements of adaptive management. They are, however, seldom realized, perhaps reflecting the previously noted reluctance of regulatory bodies to set clear targets for themselves, through fear of the consequences of failing to meet them.

Harrison considers a different class of voluntary instruments, which reflect this reluctance and which more clearly merit the title 'voluntary.' She considers measures that relax, to at least some extent, any direct use of the state's coercive authority. These remain a highly diverse set on many dimensions, including both the degree of effective coercion they retain for practical purposes, and its source. Few are *entirely* voluntary, in the sense of relying entirely on sincere environmental concern as the basis for behaviour change without *any* externally applied incentives. Rather, the great majority involve the manipulation of incentives in three ways: through varying non-zero degrees use of actual state power; through varying degrees of saliency of the *threat* of coercive state action as an alternative to negotiated agreement; and through varying degrees of coercion by non-state actors acting in lieu of the state.

First, the state has abundant resources to influence behaviour without invoking its legal authority to coerce compliance. It can offer resources, expedited processing of other business, exhortation, public praise for achievements, and public censure for failure. Even such limited use of state authority can elicit changes in target behaviour, altering both incentives and capacity.

Second, voluntary measures are often the outcome of negotiations between the state and regulatory targets. As in all negotiations, however, the agreements reached depend in part on each party's alternatives to a negotiated agreement. For firms and the state, a clearly present alternative to agreement is unilateral imposition of regulation by the state. Though exercising this authority may be costly and difficult for the state as well as for the targets, the threat of using it – if credible – can encourage targets to agree 'voluntarily' to substantial behaviour changes to avoid the risk of its imposition. The threat succeeds although – or rather, because – it is not carried out.[10] Moreover, as in mediated rather than court settlement of disputes, the state and firms may reach a more nuanced, cheaper agreement that both prefer to the blunter outcome they would likely obtain through adversarial regulatory proceedings.

One way to implement such a nuanced agreement, widely employed and discussed by Harrison, is to delegate authority for the more coercive aspects of the agreement, such as monitoring, verification, and reporting, to non-state bodies who act in lieu of the state. This approach can offer several important advantages. Non-state monitors can be chosen for their relevant knowledge and the respect in which the targets hold them; and also for their seeing the threat of the regulatory alternative more clearly than do some of the targets. For example, the monitor might be an industry association, often allied with the largest or most technically advanced firms, which can solve their collective-action problem by disciplining small bad actors that besmirch the industry's reputation and harm all firms. Moreover, non-state actors may gain access and discretion that government officials doing the same job could never have – in part precisely because they are not backed by the blunt coercive authority of the state, and in part because targets of regulation, like all of us, prefer to be told what to do by people they know and like, rather than by people they do not know and do not like.

Some programs may appear to be entirely voluntary, in that they include no binding provisions and no threat of regulation is imminent. Though the state must not and cannot fully renounce its legitimate authority to act in the public interest to protect the environment, some governments attempt (or pretend) to do so out of general ideological opposition to regulation. Alternatively, conditions of political or organizational weakness sometimes render governments unable even credibly to threaten regulation. Under these circumstances, the incentives that states can apply to target behaviour are modest, and exclusively in the positive direction. These may still change behaviour, under certain conditions: they may increase targets' capacity to undertake environmental measures they were willing but unable to take; or they may, through learning, exhortation, or modelling, change firms' preferences for good environmental conduct. But the lack of even the threat of regulatory action surely limits what such programs can accomplish.

A potential offsetting advantage of voluntary programs is provided by the psychological theory of cognitive dissonance, which finds that when people find themselves acting contrary to their preferences or beliefs, they are likely to adjust their preferences or beliefs to be more consistent with their behaviour. The adjustment is stronger, the less the external pressure applied to induce the behaviour. Consequently, applying the minimum coercive pressure to gain a desired behaviour change is likely to yield the greatest change in attitudes, and hence in likely future behaviour. If a similar process operates in organizations, for example through changing internal organizational values and routines, subsequent external incentives may become increasingly irrelevant, an outcome that would confer an important advantage on voluntary programs.

First Nations and Environmental Governance

Doyle-Bedwell and Cohen discuss a related dimension of shifting authority that is of great historical importance: the increasing recognition in Canadian law and policy of First Nations' aboriginal and treaty rights, which raises the possibility of the transfer to them from the Crown of ownership and authority over large quantities of land and resources. Doyle-Bedwell and Cohen argue that this process will transform relationships between First Nations, government policy-makers, and other citizens, in ways that are certain to challenge all three but whose shape is not yet clear. While this transformation will affect many domains of society and governance, its effects on natural-resource management and environmental protection will be particularly profound. In Howlett's terms, a new set of actors, with greatly increased resources and authority and a distinctive set of ideas, are now at the table. This transformation calls for the development of novel systems for sharing access to resources, and authority over their conservation and management. Reactions to the 1999 *Marshall* decision of the Supreme Court have revealed just how little prepared policy-makers, and others dependent on natural resources, are for the regime shift that is already under way.[11]

Resource conservation occupies a prominent role in current policy debates over these new regimes. On the one hand, resource conservation has been identified as one example of a compelling justification for which aboriginal and treaty rights may be curtailed; on the other hand, many First Nations leaders are concerned, with some basis, that fabricated conservation concerns may be used as a pretext to weaken their legitimate rights. Thus, arguments over whether First Nations as resource managers are likely to be more or less competent, and more or less conservationist, than present regimes have become a high-stakes side battle in a conflict that is principally about competing claims to exploit and control resources. Charges of plundering, and other extreme characterizations, have been exchanged in both directions. Though the history of natural resource management in Canada does not grant Canadians much authority to denounce First Nations as potential plunderers, some have done just that in the heated aftermath of the *Marshall* decision.

On the other hand, one also hears romantic characterizations of First Nations as simple Arcadians, whose profound identification with and knowledge of the land promise the salvation of the environment, indeed of Western industrial society. As Doyle-Bedwell and Cohen have argued, many First Nations societies do have deeply held principles of respect for the earth and its resources, restraint, and obligation. But a naively romantic view of First Nations is surely as demeaning as viewing them as plunderers. Like this other view, the romantic image may also threaten, albeit more subtly, to deny First Nations rights that the constitution and courts have affirmed, and to obstruct their ability to earn livelihoods, develop their communities, and participate equally in governance. This threat arises in holding First Nations to an impossible standard of restraint and skill in resource management, one that industrial societies have never approached and that neglects the profound challenges they face in developing their communities and putting their traditional principles into practice in the modern world.

Even as we reject both these rhetorical extremes, however, the practical question of how First Nations will operate as resource managers in Canada remains one of substantial importance, and little information is available on which to base projections. Traditional teachings, while providing one powerful rhetorical and moral basis (among others) for reclaiming authority over lands and resources, cannot provide precise predictions of how resources will subsequently be managed. Predicting a people's behaviour from the teachings of its wisest elders is likely to lead to serious error, certainly for the predominant Canadian society and likely for First Nations as well. Moreover, the evidence from First Nations' management of resources where they have gained control over them, notably in the United States, has been highly variable. American tribes' resource management has ranged from sophisticated and judicious development within strict conservation standards to rapid and destructive exploitation; faced with opportunities for commercial development of sacred sites, some tribes have chosen to do so, others not; while tribes in New Mexico, Montana, and Idaho have used the courts to force strict environmental protection on their neighbours (including the city of Albuquerque), the Goshute of Utah have attempted to promote their lands for nationwide storage of toxic and nuclear wastes. The factors determining these extremely disparate choices are not well understood.[12]

In speculating on the likely environmental consequences of the regime shift now under way in Canada, Doyle-Bedwell and Cohen find mostly opportunity. While properly noting the need for caution, they argue that First Nations' traditional principles and practices concerning people's relationship with and responsibilities to the land may form the basis of management regimes that are more conservationist and more long-viewed than present ones.

Several challenges stand in the way of realizing this vision. Acting as resource managers, First Nations will face many of the same problems as other governments, including finding means to control the exploitative ambitions of individuals. Traditional teachings and practices, as well as social pressures available within tight-knit communities, may help to provide the required incentives. So too may evolving ways of developing norms and sanctions within communities, such as the authors describe in their discussion of the Nuxalk fishery.

A related challenge will be learning how to apply traditional teachings of connection to the natural world, restraint, and obligation to guide concrete management decisions in the modern world. As Doyle-Bedwell and Cohen point out, citing Borrows, what worked under particular past conditions – typically, small homogeneous communities with strong social networks and pre-industrial technology – cannot necessarily be applied successfully under the vastly different conditions of the present crowded, technological, and heterogeneous world.[13] Translating the ethical and prudential content of traditional teachings into guidance for management and action in the twenty-first century will require a demanding exercise of reconstructing them from their essential moral foundations.[14]

Finally, the attempt to marry traditional ecological knowledge with scientific knowledge in guiding resource-management decisions will represent a further challenge. Court decisions have required consultation to realize such a synthesis, and each approach in principle has much to gain from the other. Realizing this promise, however, will require developing mutually acceptable bases for verification and means for resolving differences of view when they arise. Early experiments in co-management provide useful models, but much work remains to be done.[15] As in all attempts to communicate, collaborate, and agree on joint action across large differences in world view and epistemology, the challenges will be substantial, perhaps especially when resource-management decisions carry external effects. As with other dimensions of sharing authority, participants will have to learn to tolerate substantial role ambiguity.

Despite these challenges, the increasing role of First Nations may hold substantial opportunities for environmental and resource management in Canada. Whatever the degree of historical accuracy of the image of First Nations as restrained, wise conservationists, the power this image holds for many people, First Nations and others, makes it a potentially useful vision for animating new approaches to protecting the environment. The vision needs to be developed, through articulating and elaborating traditional principles into specific practices and strategies that can be applied under modern conditions – ideally, ones that can be understood and applied as well by people and institutions that do not share the First Nations' cultural heritage. This is not to ask First Nations to save the world, but only to acknowledge that others might benefit from whatever applicable insights or wisdom might be derived from their traditions. Realizing such an optimistic vision of the broader influence of First Nations in environmental governance would impose demanding requirements on all parties. Principally, they must sincerely attempt to manage resources wisely, and not hold conservation decisions hostage to allocation conflicts.

Environmental Governance through Direct Citizen Involvement

Dorcey and McDaniels examine a further trend that is shifting relationships of authority between state and non-state actors: the increasing use of processes of Citizen Involvement (CI) to engage citizens directly in deliberations or decision-making on matters of traditional state authority. They identify two historical waves of enthusiasm for such processes in Canadian environmental governance, in the early 1970s and the early 1990s. Both waves receded due to a combination of over-promising and consequent disappointment with results, lack of clarity regarding mandate and responsibilities, and – at least in the second wave – overload and diffusion of attention from pursuing too many such processes simultaneously. The authors predict, and endorse, a third wave, in which CI approaches will be used selectively, with mandate and process tailored to specific issues where their chances of contributing are greatest; in which evaluation of CI processes will be undertaken routinely and systematically; and in which progressive development of a tested body of professional knowledge will clarify the appropriate conditions under which to use different CI processes, and will enable better evaluation of and training for that crucial input, the facilitator's skill. To realize this potential, they caution, sponsors must be more explicit than they typically have been regarding the mandate of CI processes, particularly on the extent to which processes are advisory or authoritative.

They do not propose CI as a return to an idealized direct democracy, but as a selectively employed augmentation to representative government. CI may serve certain functions of public decision-making more effectively than do representative or bureaucratic institutions; for example, by helping to define questions, clarify relevant values, objectives, and trade-offs, and marshal knowledge – including local knowledge – from diverse sources. CI processes can be particularly useful at explicating values, particularly when conducted using some of the devices the authors propose for structured decision-making. CI may thus offer a practical counter-balance to the widely noted tendency for representative bodies to resist clear and explicit articulation of objectives and priorities. It may even help bring more explicit consideration of ethical perspectives into public decision-making. CI processes may also carry intrinsic benefits, independent of their effect on decisions, by either enhancing perceived legitimacy or empowering citizens through meaningful participation in their communities.[16]

The clarification of goals in a diverse polity is not without risks, however. If the obstacle to decision-making is that goals are obscure, then deliberative processes may help to clarify and elaborate them; but if the problem is that goals are deeply contested, or parties' interests are recalcitrantly opposed, such elaboration may exacerbate rather than mute conflict. Sometimes it is easier to agree on actions than on goals.

The authors identify three central challenges to an expanded use of CI: articulating a legitimate basis for participation; the risk of reducing the broad public interest into bargaining among stakeholders; and ensuring the responsible use of available scientific and technical information in CI-based decision processes.

The question of which citizens participate and by what criteria they are chosen is a tension that runs through many discussions of CI. Participants might self-select for any number of reasons; they might be invited because the decision affects them, or because they represent a class of affected people; or they might be invited because their participation is expected to improve the quality of the decisions.[17] Each criterion is likely to yield a different set of participants, and managing participation so that CI processes are widely perceived as legitimate may well pose extreme challenges. These are likely to be most difficult for decisions with high stakes and acute conflicts, in which cases CI processes may have to be limited to advisory roles.

A closely related tension concerns the responsibility of government in using CI processes. All citizens have an interest in the kind of nation they inhabit and in the conduct of their government, but not all citizens are stakeholders – in the usual sense of having a direct material interest – in any particular decision. To divert public decision processes to an exclusive focus on stakeholders can risk losing accountability for the broader public welfare and the ethics of state conduct. Government has the responsibility to seek, support, and when necessary arbitrate the public interest. It can no more escape this responsibility than it can escape its ultimate coercive authority in implementing laws and policies. The use of CI processes must not allow officials or legislators to evade this responsibility by declaring themselves only mediators among stakeholder groups, or bankers who bring public funds to the table to facilitate agreement.

Dorcey and McDaniels take due note of each of these concerns, and propose a few potential fixes. To mitigate the risk that participation will not be sufficiently legitimate, they argue, facilitators must be alert to the tendency for the most acutely interested and the powerful to be overrepresented, and must take special measures to ensure that important interests not participating are nevertheless effectively represented. To mitigate the risk of loss of government accountability, they contend, all CI processes must have clear mandates and lines of accountability, including an explicit statement of whether its results will be advisory or authoritative. On the issue of the risk of neglecting, or inadequately using, scientific and technical information, they note that conventional public decision processes also often succumb to this risk, and propose that it can be mitigated by facilitators being substantively expert in the material under consideration.

These suggestions all promise some amelioration of the risks in practical terms, but have evident limitations. To make facilitators responsible for substantive expert knowledge, and for discerning and voicing inadequately represented interests, is to give them an enormous job and to rely heavily on their expertise and integrity. Clear mandates are surely advantageous, but unlikely to relieve all concerns about illegitimate delegation of government authority. Where authority is explicitly delegated for decisions with primarily local implications, as in resource co-management arrangements with local communities, sufficiently broad community participation with government oversight of the process may suffice. But for decisions with larger-scale implications, even officially advisory processes can raise concerns about illegitimate delegation because how much actual influence the CI process exercises over subsequent government decisions may be impossible to determine. Moreover, achieving enough of both legitimacy and technical adequacy, properly integrating expertise and participation, analysis and deliberation, will surely be more difficult in CI than in conventional governance processes, with their greater reliance on the impartial authority of experts operating within democratically delimited bounds.[18]

Finally, to the authors' list of challenges might be added a fourth: understanding the contribution and limits of CI in the increasingly international context for environmental policy-making. Although there is no super-national state to authorize CI processes internationally, some involvement and consultation with various kinds of non-governmental bodies has become the norm in international environmental policy since the 1992 Earth Summit. Questions on the mandate, legitimacy, technical adequacy, and effects of CI arise even more sharply here than in national arenas. Determining the basis for legitimacy of participation in a vast and diverse world is much more difficult than in a single nation. Participation biases toward the wealthy and powerful operate even more strongly in the global arena, while a proliferation of diverse and specialized actors may make it even more difficult to reach consensus on important matters. If the mobilization of international non-governmental participants continues to increase and broaden, this complexity will only increase; some such participants have resources that exceed those of many states, and have amply demonstrated their ability to subvert small states to their ends.[19]

Moreover, in several international bodies,[20] states are now counter-attacking the proliferation of non–state actor involvement in international decision processes. This may be a reminder of the ultimate power and authority of states, and of their inclination to resist infringements on that power, which may impose strict limits on the diffusion of CI processes and the authority invested in them.

As Harrison argues for voluntary measures, Dorcey and McDaniels note that evaluations of CI processes have thus far been woefully inadequate. A body of professional knowledge of best practices is beginning to emerge, but is not shared widely enough and many areas of dissent or ignorance remain. For these reasons, they advocate an 'adaptive approach' to CI, a procedural analogue to the adaptive management discussed for substantive environmental decisions. CI processes should be carefully monitored and their results assessed in order to revise and improve them and contribute to the accumulation of professional knowledge and skill.

Environmental Pressure and Paradigmatic Policy Change

The increasing use of both the voluntarism in implementation and consultative processes in policy formation represents a reduction in the exclusivity of state authority for environmental governance. Howlett argues that a broader diminution of state authority is making traditional coercive policy instruments less viable in general, and indirect, procedural instruments more prevalent. In this context, he examines the prospects for major change in Canadian environmental policy, proposing a theoretical scheme by which the rate and character of policy change is determined by the presence or absence of new actors and new ideas. The presence of new actors determines whether change is slow or fast; the presence of new ideas determines whether its character is 'incremental' or 'paradigmatic.'

In the domain of the environment, he argues that the current prominence of both new actors and new ideas predicts rapid, paradigmatic policy change. In the face of these forces government can only marginally perturb change, slowing or speeding its pace, modestly altering its direction or character, or making it slightly more orderly. The instruments available for such fine-tuning are those that regulate the access of new actors and new ideas to policy-making. These include, for example, greater or lesser standing and support for NGOs, broader or narrower availability of information, and greater or lesser independence, resources, and participation in advisory bodies.

New ideas clearly do matter in political and social change, and clearly there are new ideas around in environmental policy – or at least new forms of old ideas, or ideas that are only a few decades old. Candidates for important 'new' environmental ideas might include global limits (1970s); bio-geochemical cycles (1930s, revived in the 1970s); geo-engineering to manage the earth system actively (1960s); the tragedy of the commons (1840s, then 1970s); the commodification of environmental insult through such instruments as tradable emission permits, the modern analog of the enclosure of the commons (1970s);

the precautionary principle (1980s); sustainable development (1980s); and adaptive management (1980s).[21] New actors are clearly also present, such as environmental NGOs, especially ones of international scope; and, in Canada, increasingly organized and legally empowered First Nations' groups.

For the most part, however, these ideas and actors are not very new. Nor are claims that environmental stresses are about to transform society. Projections of rapid change must consequently be weighed cautiously against the record of similar, erroneous past predictions, asking what has changed, or what cumulative factors are now building to a breaking point.

Citizen concern for the environment has been persistently mixed, labile, and ambiguous, only infrequently reaching and holding the intensity required to provoke major policy change. Moreover, citizens' declared concern for the environment often exceeds the evidence of concern discernible in their major consumption choices such as those relating to residence and transport. Thus, governments most often treat environmental protection as a secondary priority, and occasionally with active hostility. While periodic short-term environmental crises (e.g., the 1988 PCB warehouse fire at St-Basile-le-Grand, Quebec,[22] or the 1990 tire fire in Hagersville, Ontario)[23] can be expected to occur, these provoke specific, narrowly targeted responses, not a broad reorientation of policy and behaviour.

In contrast, some have argued that the required (as opposed to the likely) scope of changes of behaviour is enormous, and that the modest policy initiatives now on the agenda are vastly inadequate to bring such changes about.[24] Hostility toward the idea of commodifying environmental insult, and the implementation of this idea in policy measures that create private, transferable property rights in permission to impose environmental burdens, is particularly strong. This is not principally because such approaches are suspected of being ineffective: although the empirical question of their effectiveness remains open, the present weight of evidence suggests they are quite effective. Rather, it is because privatizing the environment acknowledges the inability of the public domain to manage adequately the prior state of environmental abundance and free access.

That new environmental ideas have not yet brought fundamental change in governance does not mean that they cannot. Perhaps their effect occurs over decades, not years. But if they cannot, two kinds of historical events, it is widely proposed, might well be needed to bring about the required changes. The first would be a major environmental scare – not a catastrophe, but an event like the Antarctic ozone hole that vividly illustrates the possibility of sudden, major environmental transformation without imposing costs so severe that they hinder society's ability to respond. The second 'event', equally beyond the reach of calculated pursuit, would be a widespread transformation of people's ethical or religious world view toward the environment. The longing for such a transformation may partly explain the hopes (and projections), perhaps excessive and unfair, that some environmentalists continue to vest in First Nations.

But such invocation of historical transformations may set the standard too high, or seek solutions in the wrong place. Major social change does happen, but outside revolutionary times it happens on a scale of decades or longer. Moreover, as Howlett suggests for the environment, such change is not driven exclusively, or perhaps even primarily, by government policy. Government can participate and help, but cannot force social change through its exclusive efforts; rather, many causal forces interact. Moreover, many distinct types of change also interact, so changes seemingly inadequate for the problem on their own can add up. In particular, the transformative power of cumulative technological change is not to be casually dismissed. Technological change interacts with policy and ideas, is usually industry-driven, and has already relieved a host of environmental stresses this century, at least in the rich world. The remaining contribution toward easing global environmental stresses from this source, while unlikely to be sufficient in itself, is likely to be substantial.

Key Knowledge Needs for Better Environmental Governance

The environmental trends project has elaborated three sharply drawn challenges for environmental governance in pursuing the grail of sustainable development, as well as a set of priority knowledge needs for improving environmental governance over the coming decades. A first theme concerns the need for adaptive management, and the difficulties involved in achieving it. This need will impose demanding conditions both on the institutions that advance scientific knowledge and synthesis and on those responsible for public and private decision-making. More effective methods are needed to conduct scientific and technical assessments, and to define their boundaries with policy processes, in order to ensure relevance while protecting against partisan control. Prospective assessment, to identify emerging stresses, will likely require new and different methods.

A second theme concerns the need for increased institutional capacity for environmental protection at the international level to balance the present predominance of the principles of liberal trade. This further shift of environmental authority to the international level must, however, allow for some diversity in environmental standards and measures, and in the specific aspects of the environment chosen for protection. A third theme concerns the need to construct networks of shared authority and continuing negotiation to reconcile inevitable areas of overlapping capacity and authority between levels of government, and between state and non-state actors. Managing the environment over the coming decades will involve enough uncertainty and complexity that precise and static division of responsibilities is unlikely to be viable.

Priority knowledge needs for environmental governance can be grouped into five areas. The first concerns the problem of uncertain global limits. Questions of the existence and character of global limits, and of the conditions under which they can be probed or anticipated, have remained unresolved for decades but still urgently require continuing attention. Priority research areas include integrated modelling and assessment of simultaneous human perturbations of multiple environmental systems and biogeochemical cycles; identifying characteristic modes of system behaviour as major thresholds are approached, to help understand how long in advance we might hope to anticipate major environmental changes; and assessing potential technical and policy interventions, such as active geo-engineering, that might allow rapid reductions of specific human material or energy flows, should these come to be necessary.

Further research into governance under uncertainty is a related high-priority need. Though researchers have continually noted the need for effective means of managing and making decisions under uncertainty, few institutions have successfully developed these. Key research areas include empirical studies of the use of scientific consensus and uncertainty in environmental policy debates and further specification of the requirements for better implementation of adaptive management, as well as identification of important associated pitfalls and obstacles.

A third area for inquiry concerns the resolution of coordination problems, under conditions of shared and overlapping authority, between different levels of government and between private and public actors. Detailed empirical studies are needed of how these conditions are managed in different institutional settings and on different issues, in order to identify the conditions associated with more and less effective linkage of decisions, information, and authority across spatial scales. A detailed examination of the successes and failures of the CCME and similar coordination vehicles, identifying their capabilities and limits and the conditions associated with success, would be of particular value. Good empirical studies are also needed of the competitive dynamics among jurisdictions (municipal, provincial, and national) seeking to attract and retain investment. Such studies would complement the growing literature on firm location decisions by examining the public side of the associated bargaining. How and under what conditions do firms bargain for favourable regulatory treatment on environmental issues? How and under what conditions do officials and politicians grant or withhold such treatment? How do environmental issues fit into broader patterns of accommodations that firms seek and jurisdictions make to attract them? Related studies would examine salient influences between environmental and economic policies and outcomes at the domestic and international levels. These should include the effects of short-term financial flows as well as of trade and direct investment, and the potential effects, scope, and limits of international market-like policy instruments such as tradable emission permits.

A fourth area of investigation concerns the evaluation of particular innovations of environmental governance that have been attempted and proposed. The discussions of both citizen involvement and voluntary measures have revealed that very little is known of the conditions and scope of their effectiveness, principally because they have almost never been adequately evaluated. Further experimentation with such programs, in various forms, with thorough, systematic, independent monitoring and evaluation, will be essential to correct this deficiency. Such studies might also illuminate broader questions of the conditions for effective sharing of authority between public and private bodies, between levels of government, and between representative processes and direct consultations.

More broadly, study is needed of how currently proposed innovations stand up relative to the behaviour changes needed to manage environmental stresses and pursue the grail of sustainable development. Both sides of this question are difficult. The cryptic concept of sustainable development directs us toward deep questions on one side, but gives little guidance on how to address them. How much, in what ways, and with what substitution possibilities does human welfare depend on the natural environment – relative to both marginal changes and large ones? What social and political factors shape human development or its stagnation?

On the other side, the innovations discussed here – voluntary measures and citizen involvement – may appear feeble relative to expansive views of the changes required. Indeed, since these approaches both involve renouncing certain aspects of state authority, they might appear to be movements in the wrong direction. Although market-based environmental measures have not been discussed here, their adequacy to effect similarly large-scale behavioural change also remains undemonstrated. In contrast, there is a near-unanimous consensus that conventional command-and-control regulation is an inadequate response to present environmental challenges, for several basic reasons. It is too short-term; it provides inadequate incentives for innovation; and, because it carries higher costs than other approaches, it is unlikely to be politically sustainable. The view that procedural innovations such as those discussed here are too feeble may understate their cumulative influence over several decades, particularly in conjunction with other measures and technological change. If they are judged fundamentally inadequate, however, it is not clear what kind of responses would be both feasible and adequate.

The magnitude of the challenge that environmental change poses to governance remains deeply uncertain. Looking forward even a few decades, neither extreme view – that modest incremental changes in policy, technology, and behaviour are adequate, or that fundamental realignment of human societies is necessary to avert global catastrophe – can be confidently rejected from the available evidence. The enormity of this uncertainty underlines how imperative it is to learn more effective ways of governing our use of the environment under uncertainty, and of responding adaptively to incremental advances in knowledge.

NOTES

1 K.N. Lee, *Compass and Gyroscope: Integrating Science and Politics for the Environment* (Washington: Island Press, 1993).

2 I am indebted to Rod Dobell's comments in the workshop for this observation.

3 Reichhardt, T. 'Endangered Species Bill Faces Battle against Property Lobby.' *Nature* 388 (1997): 506.

4 E.A. Parson, 'Leading While Keeping in Step: Management of Global Atmospheric Issues in Canada,' with A.R. Dobell et al. in The Social Learning Group, *Learning to Manage Global Environmental Risks: A Comparative History of Social Responses to Climate Change, Ozone Depletion, and Acid Rain*, ed. W.C. Clark et al. (Cambridge, MA: MIT Press, 2001, forthcoming).

5 G. Skogstad and P. Kopas, 'Environmental Policy in a Federal System: Ottawa and the Provinces,' in R. Boardman, ed., *Canadian Environmental Policy: Ecosystems, Politics, and Process*, 43–59. Toronto: University of Toronto Press, 1992.

6 P.E. Peterson, *The Price of Federalism* (Washington: Brookings Institution, Twentieth Century Fund, 1995).

7 E. Ostrom, *Governing the Commons: the Evolution of Institutions for Collective Action* (Cambridge: Cambridge University Press, 1990).

8 See, e.g., M.E. Porter and C. van der Linde, 'Toward a New Conception of the Environment-Competitiveness Relationship,' *Journal of Economic Perspectives* 9, no. 4 (Fall 1995): 97–118; and K. Palmer, W.E. Oates, and P.R. Portney, 'Tightening Environmental Standards: The Benefit-Cost or the No-Cost Paradigm?' *Journal of Economic Perspectives* 9, no. 4 (Fall 1995): 119–32.

9 The analogy to management and employees, and the list of appropriate jobs for government that follows, are drawn from Linda Coady's discussant comments in the workshop.

10 T.C. Schelling, *The Strategy of Conflict* (Cambridge, MA: Harvard University Press, 1960).

11 *R. v. Marshall*, Supreme Court of Canada, File no. 26014, 17 Sept. 1999. Appeal from a judgment of the Nova Scotia Court of Appeal (1997), 159 N.S.R. (2d) 186, 468 A.P.R. 186, 146 D.L.R. (4th) 257, [1997] 3 C.N.L.R. 209, [1997] N.S.J. No. 131 (QL), affirming [1996] N.S.J. No. 246 (QL).

12 See, e.g., Stephen Cornell and Joseph Kalt, 'Sovereignty and Nation-Building: The Development Challenge in Indian Country Today,' *American Indian Culture and Research Journal* 22, no. 3 (1998): 187–214; S. Cornell and J.P. Kalt, 'Cultural Evolution and Constitutional Public Choice: Institutional Diversity and Economic Performance on American Indian Reservations,' Report 95-2, Harvard Project on American Indian Economic Development, 1995; M.B. Krepps, 'Can Tribes Manage Their Own Resources? A Study of American Indian Forestry and the 638 Program,' Report 91-04, Harvard Project

on American Indian Economic Development, 1991; M.L. Wald, 'Tribe in Utah fights for nuclear waste dump,' *New York Times*, 18 April 1999: 1; J.J. Fialka, 'Goshute Indians' plan to store nuclear waste for eight utilities is opposed by Utah governor,' *Wall Street Journal*, 26 August 1998: 1.

13 J. Borrows, 'Living between Water and Rocks: First Nations, Environmental Planning, and Democracy,' *University of Toronto Law Journal* 47 (Fall 1997): 418–67.

14 Trosper sketches a such possible set of modern applications of traditional principles: R.G. Trosper, 'Traditional American Indian Economic Policy,' *American Indian Culture and Research Journal* 19, no. 1 (1995): 65–95.

15 F. Berkes and K. Folke, eds, *Linking Social and Ecological Systems: Management Practices and Social Mechanisms for Building Resilience* (Cambridge: Cambridge University Press, 1998).

16 O. Renn, T. Webler, and P. Wiedemann, *Fairness and Competence in Citizen Participation* (Dordrecht: Kluwer, 1995).

17 The discussion of this point draws on comments of Jeremy Rayner in the workshop.

18 United States, National Research Council, *Understanding Risk: Informing Decisions in a Democratic Society* (Washington: National Academy Press, 1996).

19 See, e.g., M.J. Peterson, 'Whalers, Cetologists, Environmentalists, and the International Management of Whaling,' *International Organization* 46, no. 1 (1992): 147–86; E. Masood, 'Companies Cool to Tactics of Global Warming Lobby,' *Nature* 383 (1986): 470.

20 See, e.g., Z. Young, 'NGOs and the Global Environmental Facility: Friendly Foes?' *Environmental Politics* 8, no. 1 (Spring 1999): 243–67; A.A. Clark 'The Sovereign Limits of Global Civil Society: A Comparison of NGO Participation in UN World Conferences on the Environment, Human Rights, and Women,' *World Politics* 51, no. 1 (October 1998): 1–35.

21 For early presentations of these ideas, see D.H. Meadows et al., *The Limits to Growth* (New York: Universe Books, 1972); V.I. Vernadsky, 'The Biosphere and the Noosphere,' *American Scientist* 33, no. 1 (January 1945): 1–12; C. Marchetti, 'On Geoengineering and the CO_2 Problem,' *Climatic Change* 1, no. 1 (1977): 59–68; G. Hardin, 'The Tragedy of the Commons,' *Science* 162, no. 3859 (13 December 1968): 1243–8; J. Dales, *Pollution, Property, and Prices* (Toronto: University of Toronto Press, 1968); World Commission on Environment and Development, *Our Common Future* (New York: Oxford University Press, 1987); and C.S.Holling, ed., *Adaptive Environmental Assessment and Management* (Chichester: Wiley, 1978).

22 'Toxic fire forces 3,000 from homes,' *Globe and Mail*, 25 August 1988.

23 'Stigma of disaster clings to region affected by tire fire,' *Globe and Mail,*
   5 March 1990.
24 The discussion of this paragraph is principally drawn from comments of
   William Rees in the workshop discussion.

Bibliography

Abbott, Frederick M. 'The NAFTA Environmental Dispute Settlement System as Prototype for Regional Integration Arrangements.' In G. Handl, ed., *Yearbook of International Environmental Law 1995*, 3–29. Oxford: Clarendon Press, 1996.

Aboriginal Fisheries Commission of British Columbia. 'Framework: Co-Management.' www.afcbc.or.

Abrahams, Mark, et al. (640 signers in all). 'Endangered Species Protection.' Letter to Rt. Hon. Jean Chrétien, Prime Minister of Canada, 24 February 1999. http://www.bcendangeredspecies.org/inforesources/scientists. html

Agawal, A. 'Community in Conservation: Beyond Enchantment and Disenchantment, Discussion Paper.' Gainesville, FL: CDF, 1997.

Aglukark, B. 'Inuit and the Land as One.' Nunavut Handbook, www.nunavut.com/nunavut99/english/inuit_land.htm.

Agranoff, Robert, and Michael McGuire. 'Managing in Network Settings.' *Policy Studies Review* 16, no. 1 (1999): 18–41.

Alberta-Pacific Environmental Impact Assessment Review Board. 'The Proposed Alberta-Pacific Pulp Mill: Report of the EIA Review Board.' Edmonton: Alberta Environment, March 1990.

Aldrich, Howard. 'Visionaries and Villains: The Politics of Designing Interorganizational Relations.' In E.H. Burack and A.R. Negandhi, eds, *Organization Design: Theoretical Perspectives and Empirical Findings*, 23–40. Kent, OH: Kent State University Press, 1977.

Alexander, Donald. 'Bioregionalism: Science or Sensibility?' *Environmental Ethics* 12 (1990): 161–73.

Alfred, G.R. *Heeding the Voices of Our Ancestors: Kahnawake Mohawk Politics and the Rise of Native Nationalism*. Toronto: Oxford University Press, 1995.

Algemene Rekenkamer. 'Convenanten van het Rijk met bedrijven en instellingen.' Tweede Kamer, vergaderjaar 1995–1996, 24 480, nos. 1–2. November 1995.

Alker, Hayward R., and Peter M. Haas, 'The Rise of Global Ecopolitics.' In Nazli Choucri, ed., *Global Accord: Environmental Challenges and International Responses*, 205–54. Boston: MIT Press, 1993.

Aminzade, Ronald. 'Historical Sociology and Time.' *Sociological Methods and Research* 20, no. 4 (1992): 456–80.

Amy, Douglas J. *The Politics of Environmental Mediation*. New York: Columbia University Press, 1987.

Anderson, E. *Ecologies of the Heart: Emotion, Belief and the Environment*. New York: Oxford University Press, 1996.

Anderson, Robert, et al., editors. *Innovation Systems in a Global Context: The North American Experience*. Montreal: McGill-Queen's University Press, 1998.

Anderson, Roger N. 'Oil Production in the 21st Century.' *Scientific American* 278, no. 3 (March 1999): 86–91.

Andersson, Thomas, Carl Folke, and Stefan Nyström. *Trading with the Environment*. London: Earthscan, 1995.

Andrews, Richard N.L. 'Environmental Regulation and Business "Self-Regulation."' *Policy Sciences* 31 (1998): 177–97.

ARET. *Environmental Leaders 2: Update*. Ottawa: ARET, January 1998.

– *Environmental Leaders 3: Voluntary Action on Toxic Substances*. Ottawa: ARET, 1999.

Arnstein, Sherry R. 'A Ladder of Citizen Participation.' *Journal of the American Institute of Planners* 35 (1969): 216–24.

Arora, S., and T.N. Cason. 'Why Do Firms Volunteer to Exceed Environmental Regulations? Understanding Participation in EPA's 33/50 Program.' *Land Economics* 72, no. 4 (1996): 413–32.

Asad, T. *Anthropology and the Colonial Encounter*. London: Ithaca Press, 1975.

Asch, Michael, editor. *Aboriginal and Treaty Rights in Canada: Essays on Law, Equity and Respect for Difference*. Vancouver: University of British Columbia Press, 1997.

Atkinson, Michael M., and Cassandra W. Pervin. 'Sector Councils and Sectoral Corporatism: Viable? Desirable?' In Morley Gunderson and Andrew Sharpe, eds, *Forging Business-Labour Partnerships: The Emergence of Sector Councils in Canada*, 271–94. Toronto: University of Toronto Press, 1998.

Atlantic Policy Congress of First Nations Chiefs Secretariat. 'Atlantic First Nations Sustainable Development Consultation Report.' 1997. www.apcfnc.ca.

Ayres, I., and J. Braithwaite. *Responsive Regulation: Transcending the Deregulation Debate*. New York: Oxford University Press, 1992.

Ayres, Jeffrey M. *Defying Conventional Wisdom: Political Movements and Popular Contention against North American Free Trade.* Toronto: University of Toronto Press, 1998.

Bachrach, Peter and Morton S. Baratz. 'Decisions and Nondecisions: An Analytical Framework.' *American Political Science Review* 56, no. 2 (1962): 632–42.

– *Power and Poverty: Theory and Practice.* New York: Oxford University Press, 1970.

Baggott, Rob. 'By Voluntary Agreement: The Politics of Instrument Selection.' *Public Administration* 64 (1986): 51–67.

– 'The BSE Crisis: Public Health and the "Risk Society."' In P. Gray and P. 't Hart, eds, *Public Policy Disasters in Western Europe*, 61–78. London: Routledge, 1998.

Baker Fox, Annette. 'Environment and Trade: The NAFTA Case.' *Political Science Quarterly* 110, no. 1 (1995): 49–68.

Barber, Benjamin. *Strong Democracy: Participatory Politics for a New Age.* Berkeley: University of California Press, 1984.

– *A Place for Us: How to Make Society Civil and Democracy Strong.* New York: Hill and Wang, 1998.

Barney, Darin. *Prometheus Wired: Hope for Democracy in the Age of Network Technology.* Chicago: University of Chicago Press, 2000.

Barsh, R. 'The Illusion of Religious Freedom for Indigenous Americans.' *Oregon Law Review* 65 (1986): 365.

Bartlett, R. *Resource Development and Aboriginal Land Rights.* Calgary: Canadian Institute of Resources Law, 1991.

Bastmeijer, K. 'The Covenant as an Instrument of Environmental Policy: A Case Study from the Netherlands.' In *Cooperative Approaches to Regulation.* Paris: OECD Public Management Occasional Papers no. 18, 1997.

Battiste, M., editor. *Reclaiming Indigenous Voice and Vision.* Vancouver: University of British Columbia Press, 2000.

Baumgartner, Frank R., and Bryan D. Jones. 'Agenda Dynamics and Policy Subsystems.' *Journal of Politics* 53, no. 4 (1991): 1044–74.

– *Agendas and Instability in American Politics.* Chicago: University of Chicago Press, 1993.

Beakhust, Grahame. 'The Berger Inquiry.' In Barry Sadler, ed., *Involvement and the Environment.* Volume 2. Edmonton: Environment Council of Alberta, 1979.

Beardsley, D., *Incentives for Environmental Improvement: An Assessment of Selected Innovative Programs in the States and Europe.* Washington: Global Environmental Management Initiative, 1996.

Beardsley, D., T. Davies, and R. Hersh. 'Improving Environmental Management.' *Environment* 39, no. 7 (1997): 6.

Beierle, Thomas. 'Public Participation in Environmental Decisions: An Evaluative Framework Using Social Goals.' Discussion paper 99-06. Washington:
Resources for the Future, 1998.

Bella, David A. 'The Pressures of Organizations and the Responsibilities of
University Professors.' *BioScience* 46 (1996): 772–8.

Bellehumeur, Robert. 'Review: An Instrument of Change.' *Optimum* 27, no. 1
(1997): 37–42.

Bennett, Colin J. 'What Is Policy Convergence and What Causes It?' *British
Journal of Political Science* 21, no. 2 (1991): 215–33.

– 'Understanding Ripple Effects: The Cross-National Adoption of Policy
Instruments for Bureaucratic Accountability.' *Governance* 10, no. 3 (1997):
213–33.

Bennett, Colin J., and Michael Howlett. 'The Lessons of Learning: Reconciling
Theories of Policy Learning and Policy Change.' *Policy Sciences* 25, no. 3
(1992): 275–94.

Bennett, W. Lance. 'The Uncivic Culture: Communication, Identity and the Rise
of Lifestyle Politics.' *PS: Political Science and Politics* 31, no. 4 (1998): 741–62.

Berger, T. *Northern Frontier, Northern Homeland: The Report of the Mackenzie
Valley Pipeline Inquiry.* Toronto: J. Lorimer, 1977.

– 'Native Rights and Self-Determination: An Address to the Conference on the
Voices of Native People on September 25, 1983.' *University of Western Ontario
Law Review* 22 (1984).

– *A Long and Terrible Shadow: White Values, Native Rights in the Americas.*
Vancouver: Douglas and McIntyre, 1991.

Berkes, Fikret. 'Co-management: Bridging the Two Solitudes.' *Northern Perspectives* 22, no. 2–3 (1994): 18–20.

– *Sacred Ecology: Traditional Ecological Knowledge and Resource Management.*
Philadelphia: Taylor and Francis, 1999.

Berkes, F., editor. *Common Property Resources: Ecology and Community Based
Sustainable Development.* London: Bellhaven, 1989.

Berkes, Fikret, and Karl Folke, editors. *Linking Social and Ecological Systems:
Management Practices and Social Mechanisms for Building Resilience.* Cambridge: Cambridge University Press, 1998.

Berkes, F., P. George, and R.J. Preston. 'Co-management: The Evolution in
Theory and Practice of the Joint Administration of Living Resources.' *Alternatives* 18 (1991): 12–17.

Berneshawi, S. 'Resource Management and the Mi'kmaq Nation.' *Canadian
Journal of Native Studies* 17, no. 1 (1997): 118.

Bernstein, Steven, and Benjamin Cashore. 'Globalization, Four Paths of Internationalization, and Domestic Policy Change: The Case of Examining Eco-Forestry in British Columbia.' *Canadian Journal of Political Science* 33, no. 1 (2000): 67–100 (2000, forthcoming).

Berry, William T. 'The Confusing Case of Budgetary Incrementalism: Too Many Meanings for a Single Concept.' *Journal of Politics* 52 (1990): 167–96.

Bhagwati, Jagdish. 'Trade and the Environment: The False Conflict?' In D. Zaelke, P. Orbuch, and R. Housman, eds, *Trade and the Environment*, 159–90. Washington: Island Press.

Biekart, J.W. 'Environmental Covenants between Government and Industry: A Dutch NGO's Experience.' *Review of European Community and International Environmental Law* 4, no. 2 (1995): 141–9.

Birkland, Thomas A. *After Disaster: Agenda Setting, Public Policy and Focusing Events.* Washington: Georgetown University Press, 1997.

Birnie, Patricia W. 'Fisheries Conservation.' In *Conservation and Environmentalism: An Encyclopedia.* Robert Paehlke, ed., New York: Garland, 1995.

Black, Dorothy. 'International Trade v. Environmental Protection: The Case of the U.S. Embargo on Mexican Tuna.' *Law and Policy in International Business* 24 (1992): 123–56.

Blyth, Mark M. '"Any More Bright Ideas?" The Ideational Turn of Comparative Political Economy.' *Comparative Politics* 29 (1997): 229–50.

Bookchin, Murray. *Post-Scarcity Anarchism.* Berkeley, CA: Ramparts Press, 1971.

Börkey, Peter, and François Lévêsque. *Voluntary Approaches for Environmental Protection in the European Union.* Paris: OECD, 1998.

Borrows, J. 'Living between Water and Rocks – First Nations, Environmental Planning, and Democracy.' *University of Toronto Law Journal* 47 (1997): 418–67.

Boston, Tim. 'Greenwashing in America: An Ideological Analysis of Corporate Front Groups.' Paper presented to Environmental Studies Association of Canada, Ottawa, June 1998.

Brams, Steven, and Peter Fishburn. *Approval Voting.* Boston: Birkhauser, 1983.

Brenner, Neil. 'Beyond State-Centrism? Space, Territoriality, and Geographical Scale in Globalization Studies.' *Theory and Society* 28 (1999): 39–78.

Bressers, Hans Th.A. 'The Choice of Policy Instruments in Policy Networks.' In B. Guy Peters and F.K.M. Van Nispen, eds, *Public Policy Instruments: Evaluating the Tools of Public Administration*, 85–105. New York: Edward Elgar, 1998.

Bressers, Hans, and Mac Honigh. 'A Comparative Approach to the Explanation of Policy Effects.' *International Social Science Journal* 108 (1986): 267–88.

Bressers, Hans, and Pieter-Jan Klok. 'Fundamentals for a Theory of Policy Instruments.' *International Journal of Social Economics* 15, no. 3/4 (1988): 22–41.

Brinkhorst, L.J., and A. Van Buitenen. *Focus on Environment and Trade*. The Hague: Europa Institute, 1994.

British Columbia, Ministry of Environment, Lands and Parks. *Environmental Trends in British Columbia 2000*. Victoria: Ministry of Environment, 2000. http://www.elp.gov.bc.ca/sppl/soerpt.

- Round Table on the Environment and the Economy. *Reaching Agreement: Implementing Consensus Processes in British Columbia*. Volume 2. Victoria: BC Round Table, 1991.

- Round Table on the Environment and the Economy and Commission on Resources and Environment. *Local Round Tables: Realizing Their Full Potential*. Vancouver: Fraser Basin Management Board, 1994.

Britton, John N.H., et al. 'Technological Change and Innovation: Policy Issues.' In John N.H. Britton, ed., *Canada and the Global Economy: The Geography of Structural and Technological Change*, 241–87. Montreal: McGill-Queen's University Press, 1996.

Bromley, Daniel W. *Making the Commons Work: Theory, Practice and Policy*. San Francisco: Institute for Contemporary Studies Press, 1992.

Brown, David S. 'The Management of Advisory Committees: An Assignment for the '70's.' *Public Administration Review* 32 (1972): 334–42.

Browne, William P. 'Organized Interests and Their Issue Niches: A Search for Pluralism in a Policy Domain.' *Journal of Politics* 52, no. 2 (1990): 477–509.

- 'Issue Niches and the Limits of Interest Group Influence.' In Allan J. Cigler and Burdett A. Loomis, eds, *Interest Group Politics*, 345–70. Washington: CQ Press, 1991.

Brown-John, C. Lloyd. 'Advisory Agencies in Canada: An Introduction.' *Canadian Public Administration* 22, no. 1 (1979): 72–91.

Brule, Bernard, et al. *An Evaluation of the River Basin Planning and Implementation Programs*. Inland Waters Directorate, Environmental Conservation Service, Planning and Evaluation Directorate, Corporate Planning Group. Ottawa: Environment Canada, 1981.

Brunk, Conrad, Lawrence Haworth, and Brenda Lee. *Value Assumptions in Risk Assessment: A Case Study of the Alachlor Controversy*. Waterloo, ON: Wilfrid Laurier University Press, 1991.

Buckley, Walter. 'Society as a Complex Adaptive System.' In W. Buckley, ed., *Modern System Research for the Behavioural Scientist*, 490–513. Chicago: Aldine Publishing Co., 1968.

Bulmer, Simon J. 'The Governance of the European Union: A New Institutionalist Approach.' *Journal of Public Policy* 13, no. 4 (1993): 351–80.

Burbidge, John. *Beyond Prince and Merchant: Citizen Participation and the Rise of Civil Society*. New York: Pact Publications, 1997.

Burby, R.J., and R.G. Paterson. 'Improving Compliance with State Environmental Regulations.' *Journal of Policy Analysis and Management* 12, no. 4 (1993): 753–72.

Burda, C., R. Collier, and B. Evans. 'The Gitxsan Model: An Alternative to the Destruction of Forests, Salmon and the Gitxsan Land.' Victoria, BC: Eco-Research Chair of Environmental Law and Policy, University of Victoria, 1999.

Burt, Sandra. 'Canadian Women's Groups in the 1980s: Organizational Development and Policy Influence.' *Canadian Public Policy* 16, no. 1 (1990): 17–28.

Bush, Robert A. B., and Joseph P. Folger. *The Promise of Mediation: Responding to Conflict through Empowerment and Recognition*. San Francisco: Jossey-Bass, 1994.

Cairns, Alan C. 'Reflections on Commission Research.' In Innis Christie, John A. Yogis, and A. Paul Pross, eds, *Commissions of Inquiry*, 87–110. Toronto: Carswell, 1990.

Calder v. Attorney-General of British Columbia, [1973] S.C.R. 313, [1973] 4 W.W.R. 1, 34 D.L.R. (3d) 145, 7 C.N.L.C. 91.

Caldwell, Lynton K. *Between Two Worlds: Science, the Environmental Movement, and Policy Choice*. Cambridge: Cambridge University Press, 1990.

Campbell, Colin J., and Jean H. Laherrère. 'The End of Cheap Oil.' *Scientific American* 278, no. 3 (March 1999): 78–83.

Campbell, John L. 'Institutional Analysis and the Role of Ideas in Political Economy.' *Theory and Society* 27, no. 5 (1998): 377–409.

Canada. Department of Fisheries and Oceans. 'Federal Aboriginal Fisheries Strategy.' Ottawa, 1995.

– Department of Indian and Northern Affairs. 'The Western Arctic Claim: The Inuvialuit Final Agreement.' Ottawa, 1984.

– Dept. of Indian and Northern Affairs. 'Federal Policy for the Settlement of Native Claims.' Ottawa, 1993.

– Treasury Board Secretariat, Office of Consumer Affairs and Regulatory Affairs Division. *Voluntary Codes: A Guide for Their Development and Use*. Ottawa: Government of Canada, 1998.

Canadian Chemical Producers Association. 'Does Responsible Care Pay?: A Primer on the Unexpected Benefits of the Initiative.' www.ccpa.ca.

Canadian Endangered Species Coalition. 'Federal Endangered Species Legislation – Background.' [Handout.] Ottawa, 8 August 1997.

Canadian Environmental Assessment Agency. *Military Flying Activities in Labrador and Quebec: Report of the Environmental Assessment Panel*. Ottawa: Minister of Supply and Services, 1995.

Carley, Michael, and Philippe Spapens. *Sharing the World*. London: Earthscan, 1998.

Carpenter, Richard A. 1996. 'Uncertainty in Managing Ecosystems Sustain-
ably.' In J. Lemons, ed., *Scientific Uncertainty and Environmental Problem
Solving*, 118–59. Cambridge, MA: Blackwell Science, 1996.

Carpenter, Susan L., and W.J.D. Kennedy. *Managing Public Disputes: A Practical
Guide to Handling Conflict and Reaching Agreement*. San Francisco: Jossey-Bass,
1988.

Carroll, John E. 'International Joint Commission.' In Robert Paehlke, ed., *Conservation and Environmentalism: An Encyclopedia*, 367. New York: Garland,
1995.

Castrilli, Joseph F., and C. Clifford Lax. 'Environmental Regulation-Making in
Canada: Towards a More Open Process.' In John Swaigen, ed., *Environmental
Rights in Canada*, 334–95. Toronto: Butterworth, 1981.

Cavanagh, Michael, David Marsh, and Martin Smith. 'The Relationship
between Policy Networks at the Sectoral and Sub-Sectoral Levels: A
Response to Jordan, Maloney and McLaughlin.' *Public Administration* 73,
Winter (1995): 627–9.

Cerny, Philip G. 'International Finance and the Erosion of State Policy Capacity.' In Philip Gummett, ed., *Globalization and Public Policy*, 83–104. Cheltenham, UK: Edward Elgar, 1996.

Chang, E., D. MacDonald, and J. Wolfson. 'Who Killed CIPSI?' *Alternatives* 24,
no. 2 (1998): 21–5.

Charih, Mohammed, and Arthur Daniels. *New Public Management and Public
Administration in Canada*. Toronto: Institute of Public Administration in
Canada, 1997.

Charnovitz, Steve. 'The Environment vs. Trade Rules: Defogging the Debate.'
Environmental Law 23 (1994): 475–518.

– 'The North American Free Trade Agreement: Green Law or Green Spin?' *Law
and Policy in International Business* 26 (1994): 1–77.

Chess, Caron, and Kristen Purcell. 'Public Participation and the Environment:
Do We Know What Works?' *Environmental Science and Technology* 33, no. 16
(1998).

Choucri, Nazli, editor. *Global Accord: Environmental Challenges and International
Responses*. Boston: MIT Press, 1993.

Christensen, Bev. *Too Good to Be True: Alcan's Kemano Completion Project*.
Vancouver: Talonbooks, 1995.

Clancy, P. 'Political Devolution and Wildlife Management.' In G. Dacks, ed.,
Devolution and Constitutional Development in the Canadian North, 87. Ottawa:
Carleton University Press, 1990.

Clapp, Jennifer. 'The Privatization of Global Environmental Governance: ISO
14000 and the Developing World.' *Global Governance* 4, no. 3 (1998): 295–316.

– 'Foreign Direct Investment in Hazardous Industries in Developing Countries: Rethinking the Debate.' *Environmental Politics* 7, no. 4 (1998): 92–113.
– 'The Illicit Trade in Hazardous Wastes and CFCs: International Responses to Environmental "Bads."' In R. Friman and P. Andreas, eds, *The Illicit Global Economy and State Power*, 91–123. Lanham, MD: Rowman & Littlefield, 1999.
Clark, Ann Marie. 'The Sovereign Limits of Global Civil Society: A Comparison of NGO Participation in UN World Conferences on the Environment, Human Rights, and Women.' *World Politics* 51, no. 1 (October 1998): 1–35.
Clark, K. *The Use of Voluntary Pollution Prevention Agreements in Canada: An Analysis and Commentary.* Toronto: Canadian Institute for Environmental Law and Policy, 1995.
Clark, William C. 'Sustainable Development of the Biosphere: Themes for a Research Program.' In William C. Clark and R.E. Munn, eds, *Sustainable Development of the Biosphere.* Cambridge: Cambridge University Press, 1986.
Clarkson, L., Y. Morrissette, and G. Regallet. *Our Responsibility to the Seventh Generation: Indigenous Peoples and Sustainable Development.* Winnipeg: International Institute for Sustainable Development, 1992.
Cobb, R., J.K. Ross, and M.H. Ross. 'Agenda Building as a Comparative Political Process.' *American Political Science Review* 70, no. 1 (1976): 126–38.
Cobb, Roger W., and Charles D. Elder. *Participation in American Politics: The Dynamics of Agenda-Building.* Boston: Allyn and Bacon, 1972.
Cohen, F.G. 'Treaty Indian Tribes and Washington State: The Evolution of Tribal Involvement in Fisheries Management in the U.S. Pacific Northwest.' In E. Pinkerton, ed., *Co-operative Management of Local Fisheries: New Directions for Improved Management and Community Development*, 37–48. Vancouver: University of British Columbia Press, 1989.
Cohen, F., and Hanson, A.J. 'Community-based Resource Management in Canada: An Inventory of Research and Projects.' Ottawa: Canadian Commission for UNESCO, 1989.
Cohen, F.G., A. Luttermann, and A. Bergen. 'Comparative Perspectives on Indigenous Rights to Marine Resources in Canada and Australia.' In L.K. Kriwoken et al., *Oceans Law and Policy in the Post-UNCED Era: Australian and Canadian Perspectives.* London: Kluwer, 1996.
Cohen, Joel E. *How Many People Can the Earth Support?* New York: Norton, 1995.
Cohen, Stewart, David Demeritt, John Robinson, and Dale Rothman. 'Climate Change and Sustainable Development: Towards Dialogue.' *Global Environmental Change* 8 (1998): 341–71.
Colborn, Thea, D. Dumanoski, and J.P. Myers. *Our Stolen Future: Are We Threatening Our Fertility, Intelligence, and Survival?* New York: Dutton, 1996.
Coleman, William D., Grace D. Skogstad, and Michael Atkinson. 'Paradigm

Shifts and Policy Networks: Cumulative Change in Agriculture.' *Journal of Public Policy* 16, no. 3 (1996): 273–302.

Collier, Ute. *Deregulation in the European Union: Environmental Perspectives.* London: Routledge, 1998.

Columbia River Intertribal Fish Commission. www.critfc.org/index.html.

Commission of the European Communities. 'Le défi de l'élargissement: Avis de la Commission sur la demande d'adhésion de la Suède.' Brussels: Commission des Communautés européennes, 1992.

– 'Communication from the Commission to the Council and the European Parliament on Trade and the Environment.' Brussels, 1996.

– 'Communication from the Commission to the Council and the European Parliament on Environmental Agreements.' COM(96) 561. Brussels, 1996.

– (DG-3). 'Study on Voluntary Agreements Concluded between Industry and Public Authorities in the Field of the Environment: Final Report.' Brussels, January 1997.

Commission for Environmental Cooperation. *Voluntary Measures to Ensure Environmental Compliance.* Montreal: CEC, 1998.

Commission on Resources and Environment. *A Sustainability Act for British Columbia–Provincial Land Use Strategy.* Volume 1. Victoria: Commission on Resources and Environment, 1994.

– *Public Participation – Provincial Land Use Strategy.* Volume 3. Victoria: CORE, 1994.

– *Dispute Resolution – Provincial Land Use Strategy.* Volume 4. Victoria: CORE, 1994.

– *Strategic Land Use Planning Source Book.* Victoria: CORE, 1996.

Commissioner of the Environment and Sustainable Development. *Report to the House of Commons.* Ottawa: Public Works and Government Services Canada, 1999.

Committee on the Status of Endangered Wildlife in Canada (COSEWIC). 'A Brief History.' Ottawa, 2000. www.cosewic.gc.ca/cosewic/history.cfm.

– 'Frequently Asked Questions.' Ottawa, 2000. www.cosewic.gc.ca/cosewic/faq_e.htm.

Constitution Act 1982, being Schedule B to the Canada Act 1982 (U.K.).

Coover, Virginia, et al. *Resource Manual for a Living Revolution: A Handbook of Skills and Tools for Social Change Activists.* Philadelphia: New Society Publishers, 1977.

Cornell, Stephen, and Joseph P. Kalt. 'Cultural Evolution and Constitutional Public Choice: Institutional Diversity and Economic Performance on American Indian Reservations.' Report 95-2, Harvard Project on American Indian Economic Development, 1995.

- 'Sovereignty and Nation-Building: The Development Challenge in Indian Country Today.' *American Indian Culture and Research Journal* 22, no. 3 (1998): 187–214.

Cortell, Andrew P., and James W. Davis, 'How Do International Institutions Matter? The Domestic Impact of International Rules and Norms.' *International Studies Quarterly* 40 (1996): 451–78.

Cortell, Andrew P., and Susan Peterson. 'Altered States: Explaining Domestic Institutional Change.' *British Journal of Political Science* 29 (1999): 177–203.

Costanza, Robert, et al. 'The Value of the World's Ecosystem Services and Natural Capital.' *Nature* 387, no. 6630 (1997): 253–60.

Council of Science and Technology Advisors. *Building Excellence in Science and Technology (BEST): The Federal Roles in Performing Science and Technology.* Ottawa: Industry Canada, 1999.

- *Science Advice for Government Effectiveness (SAGE).* Ottawa: Industry Canada, 1999.

Cox, Robert H. 'Can Welfare States Grow in Leaps and Bounds? Non-Incremental Policymaking in the Netherlands.' *Governance* 5, no. 1 (1992): 68–87.

Crisp, Thomas M., et al. 'Environmental Endocrine Disruption: An Effects Assessment and Analysis.' *Environmental Health Perspectives* 106 (Supplement 1, 1998): 11–56.

Crocker, Thomas D. 'Scientific Truths and Policy Truths in Acid Deposition Research.' In T. Crocker, ed., *Economic Perspectives on Acid Deposition Control.* Ann Arbor Science Acid Precipitation Series, 8: 65–79. Boston: Butterworth, 1984.

Cronon, William, editor. *Uncommon Ground: Toward Reinventing Nature.* New York: Norton, 1995.

Cruikshank, J. *The Social Life of Stories: Narrative and Knowledge in the Yukon Territory.* Lincoln: University of Nebraska Press, 1998.

Cruikshank, J., in collaboration with A. Sidney, K. Smith, and A. Ned. *Lives Lived Like a Story: Life Stories of Three Yukon Native Elders.* Lincoln: University of Nebraska Press, 1990.

Dacks, G. *Nunavut: Aboriginal Self-Determination through Public Government.* Prepared for the Royal Comission on Aboriginal Peoples, 1996.

Dacks, G., ed. *Devolution and Constitutional Development in the Canadian North.* Ottawa: Carleton University Press, 1990.

Dahl, Robert A. *A Preface to Democratic Theory.* Chicago: University of Chicago Press, 1956.

Dales, John. *Pollution, Property, and Prices.* Toronto: University of Toronto Press, 1968.

Dalhousie Law Journal 23, no. 1, Spring 2000 (issue on *Marshall* decision).

Daly, Herman E., and John B. Cobb, Jr. *For the Common Good*. Boston: Beacon Press, 1989.

Daneke, Gregory A. 'Back to the Future: Misplaced Elements of Political Inquiry and the Advanced Systems Agenda.' In William N. Dunn and Rita Mae Kelly, eds, *Advances in Policy Studies since 1950*, 267–90. New Brunswick, NJ: Transaction Press, 1992.

Darby, W. 'An Example of Decision-Making on Environmental Carcinogens: The Delaney Clause.' *Journal of Environmental Systems* 9 (1979): 109–17.

Daugbjerg, Carsten, and David Marsh. 'Explaining Policy Outcomes: Integrating the Policy Network Approach with Macro-Level and Micro-Level Analysis.' In David Marsh, ed., *Comparing Policy Networks*, 52–71.Buckingham, UK: Open University Press, 1998.

David, Paul A. 'Clio and the Economics of QWERTY.' *American Economic Review* 75, no. 2 (1985): 332–7.

Davies, J.C., and J. Mazurek. *Industry Incentives for Environmental Improvement: Evaluation of US Federal Initiatives*. Washington: Global Environmental Initiative, 1996.

Davis, Devra Lee, et al. 'Rethinking Breast Cancer Risk and the Environment: The Case for the Precautionary Principle.' *Environmental Health Perspectives* 106 (September 1998): 523–9.

Dearden, Philip, and Rick Rollins, editors. *Parks and Protected Areas in Canada: Planning and Management*. Toronto: Oxford University Press, 1993.

de Bruijn, Johan A., and Ernst F. ten Heuvelhof. 'Policy Instruments for Steering Autopoietic Actors.' In Roeland in't Veld et al., eds, *Autopoiesis and Configuration Theory: New Approaches to Societal Steering*, 161–70. Dordrecht: Kluwer, 1991.

– 'Policy Networks and Governance.' In David L. Weimer, ed., *Institutional Design*, 161–79. Boston: Kluwer Academic Publishers, 1995.

– 'Instruments for Network Management.' In W.J.M. Kickert, E.-H. Klijn, and J.F.M. Koppenjan, eds, *Managing Complex Networks: Strategies for the Public Sector*, 119–36. London: Sage, 1997.

De Haes, H.U. 'Slow Progress in Ecolabelling: Technical or Institutional Impediments,' *Journal of Industrial Ecology* 1, no. 1 (1997): 4–6.

Dehousse, Franklin. 'Le projet de taxe communautaire sur l'énergie: Un révélateur des faiblesses structurelles de la politique européenne de l'environnement.' *Actualités du droit* 4 (1992): 523–41.

Dehousse, Renaud. 'Integration v. Regulation? On the Dynamics of Regulation in the European Community,' *Journal of Common Market Studies* 30, no. 4 (1992): 383–402.

Delgamuukw v. British Columbia, [1997] 3 S.C.R 1010.

Deloria, B., K. Foehner, and S. Seinta, eds. *Spirit and Reason: The Vine Deloria Jr. Reader.* Golden, CO.: Fulcrum Publishing, 1999.

Deloria, V., Jr. *God Is Red.* New York: Grossett and Dunlap, 1973.

– *Red Earth White Lies: Native Americans and the Myth of Scientific Fact.* New York: Scribner, 1999.

DeMarco, Jerry V., Anne C. Bell, and Stewart Elgie. 'The Bear Necessities.' *Alternatives: Environmental Thought, Policy and Action* 23, no. 4 (Fall 1997), 22–7.

De Rosa, Christopher, et al. 'Environmental Exposures That Affect the Endocrine System: Public Health Implications.' *Journal of Toxicology and Environmental Health, Part B* 1 (1998): 3–26.

Dery, David. 'Policy by the Way: When Policy Is Incidental to Making Other Policies.' *Journal of Public Policy* 18, no. 2 (1999): 163–76.

Diebert, Ron. *Parchment, Printing, and Hypertext.* New York: Columbia University Press, 1998.

Dion, Leon. 'The Politics of Consultation.' *Government and Opposition* 8, no. 3 (1973): 332–53.

Dobbin, Murray. *The Myth of the Good Corporate Citizen: Democracy under the Rule of Big Business.* Toronto: Stoddart, 1998.

Dobuzinskis, Laurent. *The Self-Organizing Polity: An Epistemological Analysis of Political Life.* Boulder: Westview, 1987.

Doern, G. Bruce. *The Peripheral Nature of Scientific and Technological Controversy in Federal Policy Formulation*, Background Study no. 46. Ottawa: Science Council of Canada, 1981.

– *Green Diplomacy: How Environmental Policy Decisions Are Made.* Policy Study 16. Toronto: C.D. Howe Institute, 1993.

– '"Patient Science" versus "Science on Demand": The Stretching of Green Science at Environment Canada.' Paper prepared for Conference on Science, Government and Global Markets. Ottawa: Carleton Research Unit on Innovation, Science and Environment (CRUISE), 20 September 1998.

– 'Science and Scientists in Federal Policy and Decision Making.' Paper prepared for Policy Research Secretariat, Government of Canada. Ottawa: Carleton Research Unit on Innovation, Science and Environment (CRUISE), 1999.

Doern, G. Bruce, and Thomas Conway. *The Greening of Canada.* Toronto: University of Toronto Press, 1994.

Doern, G.B., L. Pal, and B.W. Tomlin, editors. *Border Crossings: The Internationalization of Canadian Public Policy.* Toronto: Oxford University Press, 1996.

Doern, G.B., and R.W. Phidd. *Canadian Public Policy: Ideas, Structure, Process.* 2nd ed. Scarborough, ON: Nelson Canada, 1992.

Doern, G. Bruce, and Stephen Wilks, editors. *Changing Regulatory Institutions in Britain and North America.* Toronto: University of Toronto Press, 1998.

Dorcey, Anthony H.J. 'Research for Water Resources Management: The Rise and Fall of Great Expectations.' In Michael C. Healey and R.R. Wallace, eds, *Canadian Aquatic Resources.* Canadian Bulletin of Fisheries and Aquatic Sciences 215. Ottawa: Fisheries and Oceans Canada, 1987.

– 'Perspectives on Sustainable Development in Water Management: Towards Agreement in the Fraser River Basin.' Vancouver: Westwater Research Centre, UBC, 1991.

– 'Collaborating towards Sustainability Together: The Fraser Basin Management Board and Program.' In Dan Shrubsole and Bruce Mitchell, eds, *Practising Sustainable Water Management: Canadian and International Experiences.* Cambridge, ON: Canadian Water Resources Association, 1997.

Dorcey, Anthony H.J., Lee Doney, and Harriet Rueggeberg. *Public Involvement in Government Decision-Making: Choosing the Right Model.* Victoria: BC Round Table on the Environment and the Economy, 1994.

Dorcey, Anthony H.J., and Riek, Christine L. 'Negotiation-based approaches to the settlement of environmental disputes in Canada.' In *The Place of Negotiation in Environmental Assessment.* Ottawa: Canadian Environmental Assessment Research Council, 1987.

Doubleday, William G., D.B. Atkinson, and J. Baird. 'Comment: Scientific Inquiry and Fish Stock Assessment in the Canadian Department of Fisheries and Oceans.' *Canadian Journal of Fisheries and Aquatic Sciences* 54 (1997): 1422–6.

Douglas, James. 'Review Article: The Overloaded Crown.' *British Journal of Political Science* 6 (1975): 488–500.

Douglas, Mary, and Aaron Wildavsky. *Risk and Culture: An Essay on the Selection of Technological and Environmental Dangers.* Los Angeles: University of California Press, 1982.

Draper, James A. 'Evolution of Citizen Participation in Canada.' In B. Sadler, ed., *Involvement and the Environment.* Volume 1. Edmonton: Environment Council of Alberta, 1978.

Druckrey, Frauke. 'How to Make Business Ethics Operational: Responsible Care – An Example of Successful Self-Regulation?' *Journal of Business Ethics* 17 (1998): 979–85.

Duffy, Dorli, et al. *Improving the Shared Decision-Making Model: An Evaluation of Public Participation in Land and Resource Management Planning (LRMP) in British Columbia.* Volumes 1 and 2. Vancouver: Department of Geography and School of Resource and Environmental Management, Simon Fraser University, 1998.

Dukes, E. Franklin. *Resolving Public Conflict: Transforming Community and Governance*. Manchester: Manchester University Press, 1996.

Dunoff, Jeffrey L. 'From Green to Global: Toward the Transformation of International Environmental Law.' *Harvard Environmental Law Review* 19 (1995): 241–301.

Durrant, Robert F., and Paul F. Diehl. 'Agendas, Alternatives and Public Policy: Lessons from the U.S. Foreign Policy Arena.' *Journal of Public Policy* 9, no. 2 (1989): 179–205.

Eadie, Alexandra. 'On the grid: Net balances for Canada's exports and imports.' *Globe and Mail*, 17 September 1998: B15.

Earll, R.C. 'Commonsense and the Precautionary Principle – An Environmentalist's Viewpoint.' *Marine Pollution Bulletin* 24 (1992): 182–6.

Economic Council of Canada. *Reforming Regulation*. Ottawa: Supply and Services Canada, 1981.

Ehrlich, Paul R., and John P. Holdren. 'Impact of Population Growth.' *Science* 171 (1971): 1212–17.

Eisner, Marc Allen. 'Discovering Patterns in Regulatory History: Continuity, Change and Regulatory Regimes.' *Journal of Policy History* 6, no. 2 (1994): 157–87.

Eldredge, Niles, and Stephen Jay Gould. 'Punctuated Equilibria: An Alternative to Phyletic Gradualism.' In Thomas J.M. Schopf, *Paleobiology*, 82–115. San Francisco: Freeman, Cooper, 1972.

Elgie, Stewart. 'Environmental Groups and the Courts: 1970–1992.' In Geoffrey Thompson, Moira L. McConnell, and Lynne B. Huestis, eds, *Environmental Law and Business in Canada*, 185–224. Aurora, ON: Canada Law Book, 1993.

Elliott, Lorraine. *The Global Politics of the Environment*. New York: New York University Press, 1998.

Elster, Jon. *Ulysses and the Sirens: Studies in Rationality and Irrationality*. Cambridge: Cambridge University Press, 1984.

– *Deliberative Democracy*. Cambridge: Cambridge University Press, 1998.

Emmert, Mark A., Michael Crow, and R.F. Shangraw, Jr. 'Public Management in the Future: Post-Orthodoxy and Organization Design.' In Barry Bozeman, ed., *Public Management: The State of the Art*, 345–60. San Francisco: Jossey-Bass, 1993.

Emond, Paul. 'Environmental Case Law: Canada.' In R. Paehlke, *Conservation and Environmentalism: An Encyclopedia*. New York: Garland, 1995.

Enman, Charles. 'DFO officials threaten to sue Citizen.' *Ottawa Citizen*, 3 July 1997: A1, A2.

– '36 scientists: End the suppression.' *Ottawa Citizen*, 4 July 1997: A1, A4.

Environment Canada. *The State of Canada's Environment 1996*. Ottawa: Environ-

ment Canada, 1996. Tables 14.3, 14.11. http://www1.ncr.ec.gc.ca/~soer/
SOE.
- *Canada Country Study: Climate Impacts and Adaptation*, 8 vols. Downsview,
ON: Atmospheric Environment Service, Environment Canada, 1997.
www.ec.gc.ca/climate/ccs/.
- 'Municipal Population Served by Wastewater Treatment.' National Environ-
mental Indicator Series, Spring 1998. http://www3.ec.gc.ca.
- 'Ozone-Depleting Chemicals.' National Environmental Indicator Series,
Spring 1998. www3.ec.gc.ca/ind/english/ozone/bulleting/stind1_e.cfm.
- Science and Technology Advisory Board. *Achievements to Date, Recommenda-
tions for Future Action*. Ottawa: Environment Canada, October 1999.
Estrin, David, and John Swaigen, editors. *Environment on Trial*. 3rd ed. Toronto:
Emond & Montgomery, 1993.
Esty, Daniel C., and Damien Geradin. 'Market Access, Competitiveness, and
Harmonization: Environmental Protection in Regional Trade Agreements.'
Harvard Environmental Law Review 21 (1997): 265–336.
- 'Environmental Protection and International Competitiveness: A Conceptual
Framework.' *Journal of World Trade* 32, no. 3 (1998): 5–46.
European Environment Agency. *Environmental Agreements: Environmental
Effectiveness*. Copenhagen: EEA, 1997.
Falk, Richard. 'Regional Experiences and International Environmental Order.'
In G. Handl, ed., *Yearbook of International Environmental Law 1992*, 1–46.
Oxford: Clarendon Press, 1993.
Feest, C., editor. *Indians and Europe: An Interdisciplinary Collection of Essays*.
Aachen: Alano, 1989.
Feit, H. 'Waswanipi Realities and Adaptation: Resource Management and
Cognitive Structure.' Ph.D. thesis, McGill University, 1973.
Fellegi, Ivan (chair). *Strengthening Our Policy Capacity: Task Force Report*.
Ottawa: Privy Council Office, December 1996.
Feschuk, Scott. 'Only one big processor ready for cod clobbering.' *Globe and
Mail*, 3 July 1992.
Fialka, John J. 'Goshute Indians' plan to store nuclear waste for eight utilities is
opposed by Utah governor.' *Wall Street Journal*, 26 August 1998: 1.
Finkle, Peter, et al. 'Federal Government Relations with Interest Groups: A
Reconsideration.' Ottawa: Privy Council Office, 1994.
Fischhoff, B., P. Slovic, and S. Lichtenstein. 'Knowing What You Want: Measur-
ing Labile Values.' In T. Wallsten, ed., *Cognitive Processes in Choice and Deci-
sion Behavior*. Hillsdale, NJ: Erlbaum, 1979.
Fisher, Roger, and William Ury. *Getting to Yes: Reaching Agreement without
Giving In*. Boston: Houghton Mifflin, 1981.

Fleming, Thomas, editor, *The Environment and Canadian Society.* Toronto: ITP Nelson, 1997.

Forester, John. *Planning in the Face of Power.* Berkeley: University of California Press, 1989.

Fouda, Safaa A. 'Liquid Fuels from Natural Gas.' *Scientific American* 278, no. 3 (March 1999): 92–5.

Frey, Frederick W. 'Comment: On Issues and Nonissues in the Study of Power.' *American Political Science Review* 65 (1971): 1081–1101.

Friends of the Earth. *A Superficial Attraction: The Voluntary Approach and Sustainable Development.* London: Friends of the Earth Trust, 1997.

Furlong, Scott R. 'Reinventing Regulatory Development at the Environmental Protection Agency.' *Policy Studies Journal* 23, no. 3 (1995): 466–82.

Gallon, G., 'Accuracy Is Optional in Reporting Voluntary Success.' *Alternatives* 24 (1998): 12.

Galtung, Johan. 'The Green Movement: A Socio-Historical Exploration.' *International Sociology* 1, no. 1 (1986): 75–90.

Gardner, Julia E. 'Environmental Non-Government Organisations and the Management of the Aquatic Environment for Sustainable Development.' In Anthony H.J. Dorcey, ed., *Perspectives on Sustainable Development in Water Management: Towards Agreement in the Fraser River Basin.* Vancouver: Westwater Research Centre, UBC, 1991.

GATT. 'Trade and Environment – News and Views from the GATT.' No. 93-0461, Geneva: Gatt, 1993.

– Information and Media Relations Division. 'Trade and Environment – News and Views from the GATT.' No. TE 005, Geneva: GATT, 17 February 1994.

Georg, Susse. 'Regulating the Environment: Changing from Constraint to Gentle Coercion.' *Business Strategy and the Environment* 3, no. 2 (1994): 11–20.

George, Richard L. 'Mining for Oil.' *Scientific American* 278, no. 3 (March 1999): 84–5.

Gersick, Connie J.G. 'Revolutionary Change Theories: A Multilevel Exploration of the Punctuated Equilibrium Paradigm.' *Academy of Management Review* 16, no. 1 (1991): 10–36.

Gibson, Robert B, editor. *Voluntary Initiatives: The New Politics of Corporate Greening.* Peterborough, ON: Broadview, 1999.

Gilmore, Thomas N., and James Krantz. 'Innovation in the Public Sector: Dilemmas in the Use of Ad Hoc Processes.' *Journal of Policy Analysis and Management* 10, no. 3 (1991): 455–68.

Glachant, M. 'The Setting of Voluntary Agreements between Industry and Government: Bargaining and Efficiency.' *Business Strategy and the Environment* 3, no. 2 (1994): 43–9.

Glasbergen, Peter. 'Learning to Manage the Environment.' In William M. Lafferty and James Meadowcroft, eds, *Democracy and the Environment: Problems and Prospects*, 175–93. Cheltenham: Edward Elgar, 1996.

Globe and Mail. 'Toxic fire forces 3,000 from homes.' 25 August 1988.

– 'Stigma of disaster clings to region affected by tire fire.' 5 March 1990.

Goffman, Erving. *Frame Analysis: An Essay on the Organization of Experience*. Cambridge, MA: Harvard University Press, 1974.

Goldsmith, James. *The Trap*. London: Macmillan, 1994.

Golub, Jonathan. 'State Power and Institutional Influence in European Integration: Lessons from the Packaging Waste Directive.' *Journal of Common Market Studies* 34, no. 3 (1996): 313–39.

– 'Global Competition and EU Environmental Policy.' In J. Golub, ed., *Global Competition and EU Environmental Policy*, 1–33. London: Routledge, 1998.

Gouvernement du Québec. 'The James Bay and Northern Quebec Agreement.' Quebec: Éditeur Officiel du Québec, 1975.

Government of Canada. *The State of Canada's Environment*. Ottawa: Minister of Supply and Services, 1991.

Grant, Wyn, and Anne MacNamara. 'When Policy Communities Intersect: The Cases of Agriculture and Banking.' *Political Studies* 43 (1995): 509–15.

Gray, Barbara. *Collaborating: Finding Common Ground for Multiparty Problems*. San Francisco: Jossey-Bass, 1989.

Gray, Pat, and Paul 't Hart. *Public Policy Disasters in Western Europe*. London: Routledge, 1998.

Great Lakes Indian Fish and Wildlife Commission. www.glifwc.org.

Greaves, T., editor. *Intellectual Property Rights for Indigenous Peoples: A Source Book*. Oklahoma City: Society for Applied Anthropology, 1994.

Gregory, Robin, Sarah Lichtenstein, and Paul Slovic. 'Valuing Environmental Resources: A Constructive Approach.' *Journal of Risk and Uncertainty* 7 (1993): 177–97.

Greider, William. *One World, Ready or Not*. New York: Simon & Schuster, 1997.

Gunningham, Neil, and Peter Grabosky. *Smart Regulation: Designing Environmental Policy*. New York: Oxford, 1998.

Haas, Ernst B. *The Uniting of Europe: Political, Social and Economical Forces 1950–1957*. London: Stevens and Sons, 1958.

Haas, Peter M. 'Introduction: Epistemic Communities and International Policy Coordination.' *International Organization* 46, no. 1 (1992): 1–36.

Habermas, Jürgen. *The Theory of Communicative Action*. Trans. T. McCarthy. Boston: Beacon Press, 1984.

Haeuber, Richard. 'Setting the Environmental Policy Agenda: The Case of Ecosystem Management.' *Natural Resources Journal* 36, no. 1 (1996): 1–27.

Hall, John A. 'Ideas and the Social Sciences.' In Judith Goldstein and Robert O. Keohane, eds, *Ideas and Foreign Policy: Beliefs, Institutions and Political Change*, 31–56. Ithaca: Cornell University Press, 1993.

Hall, Peter A. 'The Change from Keynesianism to Monetarism: Institutional Analysis and British Economic Policy in the 1970s.' In Sven Steinmo, Kathleen Thelen, and Frank Longstreth, eds, *Structuring Politics: Historical Institutionalism in Comparative Analysis*, 90–114. Cambridge: Cambridge University Press, 1992.

– 'Policy Paradigms, Social Learning and the State: The Case of Economic Policy Making in Britain.' *Comparative Politics* 25, no. 3 (1993): 275–96.

Hall, Peter A., editor, *The Political Power of Economic Ideas: Keynesianism across Nations*. Princeton: Princeton University Press, 1989.

Halliwell, Janet E., and William Smith. 'Scientific Advice in Government Decision-Making: The Canadian Experience.' Report to Council of Science and Technology Advisors. Gloucester, ON: JEH Associates Inc., March 1999.

Hammond, Allen. *Which World? Scenarios for the 21st Century*. Washington: Island Press, 1998.

Hammond, Thomas H., and Christopher K. Butler. 'Some Complex Answers to the Simple Question, "Do Institutions Matter?": Aggregation Rules, Preference Profiles, and Policy Equilibria in Presidential and Parliamentary Systems.' Detroit: Michigan State University, PIPC Working Paper 96-02, 1996.

Hardin, Garrett. 'The Tragedy of the Commons.' *Science* 162, no. 3859 (13 December 1968): 1243–8.

Harrison, Kathryn. 'Is Cooperation the Answer? Canadian Environmental Enforcement in Comparative Context.' *Journal of Policy Analysis and Management* 14 (1995): 221–44.

– 'Federalism and Environmental Protection: Canada.' In R. Paehlke, ed., *Conservation and Environmentalism: An Encyclopedia*. New York: Garland, 1995.

– *Passing the Buck: Federalism and Canadian Environmental Policy*. Vancouver: University of British Columbia Press, 1996.

– 'Talking with the Donkey: Cooperative Approaches to Environmental Protection.' *Journal of Industrial Ecology* 2 (1998): 51–72.

– 'Racing to the Top or Bottom? Industry Resistance to Ecolabelling of Paper Products in Three Jurisdictions.' *Environmental Politics* 8 (1999): 110–36.

Harrison, K., and G. Hoberg. 1994. *Risk, Science and Politics: Regulating Toxic Substances in Canada and the United States*. Montreal: McGill-Queen's University Press, 1994.

Hart, Michael. 'Globalization and Governance.' *Policy Options* 16, no. 5 (1995): 49–53.

Hartig, John. *Under RAPs: Towards Grassroots Ecological Democracy in the Great Lakes Basin.* Ann Arbor: University of Michigan Press, 1993.

Hartman, Cathy L., and Edwin R. Stafford. 'Green Alliances: Building New Business with Environmental Groups.' *Long Range Planning* 30 (1997): 184–96.

Hawkins, Keith, and John M. Thomas. 'Making Policy in Regulatory Bureaucracies.' In Keith Hawkins and John M. Thomas, eds, *Making Regulatory Policy,* 3–30. Pittsburgh: University of Pittsburgh Press, 1989.

Haydu, Jeffrey. 'Making Use of the Past: Time Periods as Cases to Compare and as Sequences of Problem Solving.' *American Journal of Sociology* 104, no. 2 (1998): 339–71.

Hayes, Michael T. *Incrementalism and Public Policy.* New York: Longmans, 1992.

Hays, Samuel P. *Conservation and the Gospel of Efficiency: The Progressive Conservation Movement, 1890–1920.* Cambridge, MA: Harvard University Press, 1959.

– *Beauty, Health, and Permanence: Environmental Politics in the United States, 1955–1985.* New York: Cambridge University Press, 1987.

Health Canada. Science Advisory Board. 'Terms of Reference.' Ottawa: Health Canada, 1998. www.hc-sc.gc.ca/hpb/science/mandat.html.

– 'Meeting Report, January 19–20, 1999.' Ottawa: Health Canada, 1999. www.hc.-sc.gc.ca/hpb/science/jan99.html.

Heclo, Hugh. *Modern Social Politics in Britain and Sweden: From Relief to Income Maintenance.* New Haven: Yale University Press, 1974.

– 'Conclusion: Policy Dynamics.' In Richard Rose, ed., *The Dynamics of Public Policy: A Comparative Analysis,* 237–66. London: Sage, 1976.

– 'Ideas, Interests and Institutions.' In Lawrence C. Dodd and Calvin Jillson, eds, *The Dynamics of American Politics: Approaches and Interpretations,* 366–92. San Francisco: Westview, 1994.

Heinz Center, 1999. 'Designing a Report on the State of the Nation's Ecosystems.' H. John Heinz III Center, Washington. www.us-ecosystems.org.

Hempel, Lamont. *Environmental Governance: The Global Challenge.* Washington: Island Press, 1996.

Henderson, James. 'Aboriginal Rights in Western Legal Tradition.' In M. Boldt and J. Anthony Long, eds, *The Quest for Justice: Aboriginal People and Aboriginal Rights.* Toronto: University of Toronto Press 1985.

– 'Empowering Treaty Federalism.' *Saskatchewan Law Review* 58 (1994): 241.

– *The Mi'kmaq Concordant.* Halifax: Fernwood Publishing, 1997.

Henderson, Laurie. 'Forging a Link: Two Approaches to Integrating Trade and Environment.' *Alternatives* 20, no. 1 (1993): 30–6.

Henderson, M. 'Mikmaw Tenure in Atlantic Canada.' *Dalhousie Law Journal* 18 (1995): 239.

Heritier, Adrienne. 'Policy-Making by Subterfuge: Interest Accommodation, Innovation and Substitute Democratic Legitimation in Europe – Perspectives from Distinctive Policy Areas.' *Journal of European Public Policy* 4, no. 2 (1997): 171–89.

Hernes, Gudmund. 'Structural Change in Social Processes.' *American Journal of Sociology* 82, no. 3 (1976): 513–47.

Hessing, Melody, and Michael Howlett. *Canadian Natural Resource and Environmental Policy: Political Economy and Public Policy.* Vancouver: University of British Columbia Press, 1997.

Hickling Corporation. 'Evaluation of the Environmental Choice Program: Final Report.' Prepared for Environment Canada, 29 November 1993.

Hoberg, G., and K. Harrison. 'It's Not Easy Being Green: The Politics of Canada's Green Plan.' *Canadian Public Policy* 20 (1994): 119–37.

Hoberg, G., and E. Morawaski. 'Policy Change through Sector Intersection: Forest and Aboriginal Policy in Clayoquot Sound.' *Canadian Public Administration* 40, no. 3 (1997): 387–414.

Hoberg, George. 'Comparing Canadian Performance in Environmental Policy.' In R. Boardman, ed., *Canadian Environmental Policy: Ecosystems, Politics and Process*, 246–62. Toronto: Oxford University Press, 1992.

– 'Environmental Policy: Alternative Styles.' In M. Atkinson, ed., *Governing Canada: Institutions and Public Policy.* Toronto: Harcourt Brace Jovanovich, 1993.

– 'Governing the Environment: Comparing Canada and the United States.' In K. Banting, G. Hoberg, and R. Simeon, eds, *Degrees of Freedom: Canada and the United States in a Changing World*, 341–85. Montreal: McGill-Queen's University Press, 1997.

– 'Distinguishing Learning from Other Sources of Policy Change: The Case of Forestry in the Pacific Northwest.' Paper presented to annual meeting of the American Political Science Association, Boston, 1998.

Holgate, M.W. 'Pathways to Sustainability: The Evolving Role of Transnational Institutions.' *Environment* 37, no. 9 (November 1995): 16–42.

Hollander, Marcus J., and Michael J. Prince. 'Analytical Units in Federal and Provincial Governments: Origins, Functions and Suggestions for Effectiveness.' *Canadian Public Administration* 36, no. 2 (1993): 190–224.

Holling, C.S. 'An Ecologist's View of the Malthusian Conflict.' Paper presented at Population-Environment-Development Lecture Series. Stockholm: Royal Swedish Academy of Sciences, 1993.

Holling, C.S., editor. *Adaptive Environmental Assessment and Management.* Chichester: Wiley, 1978.

Holtzinger, Brenda E. 'Rethinking American Public Policy: The Environment,

Federalism, States, and Supranational Influences.' *Policy Studies Journal* 26, no. 3 (Autumn 1998): 499–511.

Hood, Christopher. *The Tools of Government.* London: Chatham House, 1986.

– 'A Public Management for All Seasons?' *Public Administration* 69, no. 1, (Spring 1991): 3–19.

Hornung, Robert. 'The VCR Is Broken.' In R. Gibson, ed., *Voluntary Initiatives: The New Politics of Corporate Greening.* Peterborough, ON: Broadview, 1999.

Hougton, J.T., et al., editors. *Climate Change 1995: The Science of Climbate Change.* Cambridge: Cambrdige University Press, 1995.

Housman, Robert F., and Durwood J. Zaelke. 'Making Trade and Environmental Policies Mutually Reinforcing: Forging Competitive Sustainability.' *Environmental Law* 23 (1993): 545–73.

Howlett, Michael. 'The Round Table Experience: Representation and Legitimacy in Canadian Environmental Policy-Making.' *Queen's Quarterly* 97, no. 4 (1990): 580–601.

– 'Policy Paradigms and Policy Change: Lessons from the Old and New Canadian Policies towards Aboriginal Peoples.' *Policy Studies Journal* 22, no. 4 (1994): 631–51.

– 'The Judicialization of Canadian Environmental Policy 1980–1990 – A Test of the Canada-U.S. Convergence Hypothesis.' *Canadian Journal of Political Science* 27, no. 1 (1994).

– 'Legitimacy and Governance: Re-Discovering Procedural Policy Instruments.' Paper presented to annual meeting of the British Columbia Political Studies Association, Vancouver 1996.

– 'Sustainable Development: Environmental Policy.' In A. Johnson and A. Stritch, eds, *Canadian Public Policy: Globalization and Political Parties*, 47–64. Toronto: Copp Clark Longman, 1996.

– 'Predictable and Unpredictable Policy Windows: Issue, Institutional and Exogenous Correlates of Canadian Federal Agenda-Setting.' *Canadian Journal of Political Science* 31, no. 3 (1998).

– 'Beyond Legalism? Policy Instruments, Implementation Styles and Convergence in Canadian and U.S. Environmental Policy.' Paper presented to the Western Economics Association, San Diego, 1999.

Howlett, Michael, and Keith Brownsey. 'From Timber to Tourism: The Political Economy of British Columbia.' In R.K. Karty, ed., *Politics, Policy and Government in British Columbia*, 18–31. Vancouver: UBC Press, 1996.

Howlett, M., and M. Ramesh. 'Patterns of Policy Instrument Choice: Policy Styles, Policy Learning, and the Privatization Experience.' *Policy Studies Review* 12, no. 1 (1993): 3–24.

– *Studying Public Policy: Policy Cycles and Policy Subsystems.* Toronto: Oxford University Press, 1995.

Howlett, Michael, and Jeremy Rayner. 'Do Ideas Matter? Policy Subsystem Configurations and the Continuing Conflict over Canadian Forest Policy.' *Canadian Public Administration* 38, no. 3 (1995): 382–410.

Hudson, Stewart. 'The NAFTA-NACE Relationship.' In S. Richardson, ed., *North American Free Trade Agreement and the North American Commission on the Environment – Report of a Workshop on NAFTA and NACE, 16–20.* Ottawa: National Round Table on the Environment and the Economy, 1992.

Huffman, J. 'An Exploratory Essay on Native Americans and Environmentalism.' *University of Colorado Law Review* 63 (1992): 901.

Hulkrantz, A. *Belief and Worship in Native North America.* Syracuse, NY: Syracuse University Press, 1981.

Hurrell, Andrew, and Benedict Kingsbury, editors. *The International Politics of the Environment.* Oxford: Clarendon, 1992.

Hutchings, Jeffrey A. 1999. 'The Biological Collapse of Newfoundland's Northern Cod.' In Dianne Newell and Rosemary E. Ommer, eds, *Fishing Places, Fishing People: Traditions and Issues in Canadian Small-Scale Fisheries*, 260–75. Toronto: University of Toronto Press, 1999.

Hutchings, Jeffrey A., and Ransom A. Myers. 'What Can Be Learned from the Collapse of a Renewable Resource? Atlantic Cod, *Gadus morhua*, of Newfoundland and Labrador.' *Canadian Journal of Fisheries and Aquatic Sciences* 51 (1994): 2126–46.

Hutchings, Jeffrey A., Carl Walters, and Richard L. Haedrich. 'Is Scientific Inquiry Incompatible with Government Information Control?' *Canadian Journal of Fisheries and Aquatic Sciences* 54 (1997): 1198–1210.

Hutton, Thomas A. 'Visions of a "Post-Staples" Economy: Structural Change and Adjustment Issues in British Columbia.' Vancouver: UBC Centre for Human Settlements, 1994.

Impact Group. 'The Roles of the Federal Government in Performing Science and Technology: The Canadian Context and Major Forces.' Report prepared for Council of Science and Technology Advisors. Ottawa: Industry Canada, 1999.

Industry Canada. *The Power of Partnerships: Industry and Government Working Together for Economic Growth and a Cleaner Environment.* Ottawa: Industry Canada. 1998.

INFORM. *Toxics Watch 1995.* New York: INFORM, 1995.

Inglehart, Ronald. *Culture Shift in Advanced Industrial Society.* Princeton, NJ: Princeton University Press, 1990.

Innes, Judith E. 'Planning Theory's Emerging Paradigm: Communication

Action and Interactive Practice.' *Journal of Planning Education and Research* 14, no. 3 (1995): 183–9.

Innes, Judith E., and David E. Booher. 'Consensus Building as Role Playing and Bricolage: Towards a Theory of Collaborative Planning.' *Journal of the American Planning Association* 65, no. 1 (1999): 9–26.

International Institute for Sustainable Development. 'The World Trade Organization and Sustainable Development: An Independent Assessment.' Winnipeg: IISD, 1996.

International Joint Commission. 'The IJC and the 21st Century: Response of the IJC to a Request by the Governments of Canada and the United States on How to Best Assist Them to Meet the Environmental Challenges of the 21st Century.' Washington: IJC, 1999.

in't Veld, Roeland J. 'The Dynamics of Instruments.' In B. Guy Peters and F.K M. Van Nispen, eds, *Public Policy Instruments: Evaluating the Tools of Public Administration*, 153–62. New York: Edward Elgar, 1998.

Jackson, John H. 'World Trade Rules and Environmental Policies: Congruence or Conflict?' In D. Zaelke, P. Orbuch, and R. Housman, eds, *Trade and the Environment*, 219–36. Washington: Island Press, 1993.

Jacobsen, John Kurt. 'Much Ado about Ideas: The Cognitive Factor in Economic Policy.' *World Politics* 47 (1995): 283–310.

Janicke, Martin, and Helge Jorgens. 'National Environmental Policy Plans and Long-Term Sustainable Development Strategies: Learning from International Experiences.' Berlin: Freie Universitate Berlin Forschungsstelle für Umweltpolitik Paper 96-5, 1997.

Janicke, Martin, Harald Monch, and Manfred Binder. 'Ecological Aspects of Structural Change.' *Intereconomics* 28, no. 4 (1993): 159–69.

Janicke, M., and H. Weidner. *National Environmental Policies: A Comparative Study of Capacity Building.* Berlin: Springer, 1997.

Janicke, M., et al. 'Structural Change and Environmental Impact.' *Intereconomics* 24, no. 1 (1989): 29–35.

Janis, Irving, and Leon Mann. *Decision Making: A Psychological Analysis of Conflict, Choice, and Commitment.* New York: Free Press, 1977.

Jasanoff, Sheila. 'Acceptable Evidence in a Pluralistic Society.' In Deborah G. Mayo and Rachelle D. Hollander, eds, *Acceptable Evidence: Science and Values in Risk Management*, 29–47. New York: Oxford University Press, 1991.

Jeanrenaud, C. editor. *Environmental Policy: Between Regulation and Market.* Basel: Birkhäuser, 1997.

Jellinek, Steven D. 'On the Inevitability of Being Wrong.' *Annals of the New York Academy of Science* 363 (1981): 43–8.

Jenson, Jane. 'Commissioning Ideas: Representation and Royal Commissions.'

In Susan D. Phillips, ed., *How Ottawa Spends 1994–95: Making Change*, 39–69. Ottawa: Carleton University Press, 1994.

Jervis, Robert. *System Effects: Complexity in Political and Social Life.* Princeton: Princeton University Press, 1997.

Jessop, Bob. 'The Schumpeterian Workfare State.' *Studies in Political Economy* no. 40 (1993): 7–39.

Jochem, Eberhard, and Wolfgang Eichhammer. 'Voluntary Agreements as an Instrument to Substitute Regulating and Economic Instruments. Lessons from the German Voluntary Agreements on CO_2 Reduction.' In Carlo Carraro and François Levesque, eds, *Voluntary Approaches in Environmental Policy.* Boston: Kluwer Academic Publishers, 1999.

Johnson, Andrew, and Andrew Stritch, editors. *Canadian Public Policy: Globalization and Political Parties.* Toronto: Copp Clark, 1997.

Johnson, M., editor. *Lore: Capturing Traditional Ecological Knowledge.* Hay River, NWT, and Ottawa: Dene Cultural Institute and International Development Research Centre, 1992.

Johnson, Pierre Marc, and André Beaulieu. *The Environment and NAFTA: Understanding and Implementing the New Continental Law.* Washington: Island Press, 1996.

Jones, Bryan D. *Reconceiving Decision-Making in Democratic Politics: Attention, Choice and Public Policy.* Chicago: University of Chicago Press, 1994.

Jordan, Andrew. 'The Construction of a Multilevel Environmental Governance System.' *Environment and Planning C: Government and Policy* 17 (1999): 1–17.

– 'The Implementation of EU Environmental Policy: A Policy Problem without a Political Solution?' *Environment and Planning C: Government and Policy* 17 (1999): 69–90.

Jordan, Andrew, Roy Brouwer, and Emma Noble. 'Innovative and Responsive? A Longitudinal Analysis of the Speed of EU Environmental Policy-Making, 1967–97.' *Journal of European Public Policy* 6, no. 3 (1999): 376–98.

Jordan, Grant. 'Indirect Causes and Effects in Policy Change: Shell, Greenpeace and the Brent Spar.' Paper presented to annual meeting of the American Political Science Association, Boston, 1998.

Joseph, Tamara L. 'Preaching Heresy: Permitting Member States to Enforce Stricter Environmental Laws than the European Community.' *Yale Journal of International Law* 20, no. 2 (1995): 227–71.

Judge, David. '"Predestined to Save the Earth": The Environment Committee of the European Parliament.' *Environmental Politics* 1, no. 4 (1992): 186–212.

Juillet, Luc. 'Les politiques environnementales canadiennes.' In Manon Tremblay, ed., *Les politiques publiques canadiennes*, 161–205. Ste-Foy: Les Presses de l'Université Laval, 1998.

Juillet, Luc, Jeffrey Roy, and Francesca Scala. 'Sustainable Agriculture and Global Institutions: Emerging Institutions and Mixed Incentives.' *Society and Natural Resources* 10 (1997): 309–18.

Kagan, Robert A. 'Adversarial Legalism and American Government.' *Journal of Policy Analysis and Management* 10, no. 3 (1991): 369–406.

– 'Should Europe Worry about Adversarial Legalism?' *Oxford Journal of Legal Studies* 17, no. 2 (1997): 165–83.

Kagan, Robert A., and Lee Axelrad. 'Adversarial Legalism: An International Perspective.' In Pietro S. Nivola, ed., *Comparative Disadvantages? Social Regulations and the Global Economy*, 146–202. Washington: Brookings Institution, 1997.

Kahler, Miles. *International Institutions and the Political Economy of Integration.* Washington: Brookings Institution, 1995.

Kahneman, Daniel, Paul Slovic, and Amos Tversky. *Judgment under Uncertainty: Heuristics and Biases.* New York: Cambridge University Press, 1982.

Kaner, Sam, et al. *Facilitator's Guide to Participatory Decision-Making.* Gabriola Island, BC: New Society Publishers, 1996.

Kapashit, R., and M. Klippenstein. 'Aboriginal Group Rights and Environmental Protection.' *McGill Law Journal* 36 (1991): 925.

Kazis, Richard, and Richard Grossman. *Fear at Work: Job Blackmail, Labor, and the Environment.* New York: Pilgrim Press, 1982.

Keck, Margaret E., and Kathryn Sikkink, editors. *Activists beyond Borders: Advocacy Networks in International Politics.* Ithaca: Cornell University Press, 1998.

Keeney, Ralph. *Value-focused Thinking: A Path to Creative Decisionmaking.* Cambridge: Harvard University Press, 1992.

Keller, Ann C. 'Innovation and Influence: Scientists as Advocates in Environmental Policy Change.' Paper presented to the Western Political Science Association, Seattle, 1999.

Kelman, Steven. 'Cost-Benefit Analysis: An Ethical Critique.' *Regulation* 5, no. 1 (1981): 33–40.

Keohane, Robert O., and Stanley Hoffman. 'Institutional Change in Europe in the 1980s.' In Robert O. Keohane and Stanley Hoffman, eds, *The New European Community: Decision-Making and Institutional Change*, 1–40. Boulder: Westview, 1991.

Keohane, Robert O., and Helen V. Milner, editors. *Internationalization and Domestic Politics.* New York: Cambridge University Press, 1996.

Kerr, Robert, Aaron Cosbey, and Ron Yachnin. *Beyond Regulation: Exporters and Voluntary Environmental Measures.* Winnipeg: International Institute for Sustainable Development, 1998.

King, Richard J. 'Regional Trade and the Environment: European Lessons for North America.' *Journal of Environmental Law* 14 (1996): 209–45.

Kingdon, John W. *Agendas, Alternatives and Public Policies*. Boston: Little, Brown and Co., 1984.

Kingsbury, Benedict. 'The Tuna-Dolphin Controversy, the World Trade Organization, and the Liberal Project to Reconceptualize International Law.' In G. Handl, ed., *Yearbook of International Environmental Law 1994*, 1–40. Oxford: Clarendon, 1995.

Kirton, John. 'The Commission for Environmental Cooperation and Canada-U.S. Environmental Governance in the NAFTA Era.' *American Review of Canadian Studies* 27, no. 3 (1997): 459–86.

Kirton, John, and Rafael Fernandez de Castro. 'NAFTA's Institutions: The Environmental Potential and Performance of the NAFTA Free Trade Commission and Related Bodies.' Montreal: North American Commission for Environmental Cooperation, 1997.

Kiy, Richard, and John D. Wirth, editor. *Environmental Management on North America's Borders*. College Station: Texas A & M University Press, 1998.

Klein, Naomi. 'The Real APEC Scandal.' *Saturday Night*, February 1999: 42–9.

Klijn, Erik-Hans. 'Analyzing and Managing Policy Processes in Complex Networks: A Theoretical Examination of the Concept Policy Network and Its Problems.' *Administration and Society* 28, no. 1 (1996): 90–119.

Knoepfel, Peter, and Ingrid Kissling-Naf. 'Social Learning in Policy Networks.' *Policy and Politics* 26, no. 3 (1998): 343–67.

Knoke, David. *Political Networks: The Structural Perspective*. Cambridge: Cambridge University Press, 1987.

Knox, Paul, and Barrie McKenna. 'NAFTA partners' environmental deal at risk, groups say.' *Globe and Mail*, 27 April 2000: A9.

Kolb, Deborah M. *When Talk Works: Profiles of Mediators*. San Francisco: Jossey-Bass, 1994.

KPMG. 'Canadian Environmental Management Survey.' Toronto: KPMG, 1994.

Kraft, Michael E. *Environmental Politics and Policy*. New York: HarperCollins, 1996.

Krepps, Matthew B., 'Can Tribes Manage Their Own Resources? A Study of American Indian Forestry and the 638 Program.' Report 91-04, Harvard Project on American Indian Economic Development, 1991.

Kretch, S., II, editor. *Indians, Animals and the Fur Trade: A Critique of Keepers of the Game*. Athens: University of Georgia Press, 1981.

Krever, Mr Justice Horace. *Commission of Inquiry on the Blood System in Canada: Final Report*. 3 vols. Ottawa: Public Works and Government Services Canada, 1997.

Laird, F.N. 'Participatory Analysis, Democracy and Technological Decision Making.' *Science, Technology and Human Values* 18, no. 3 (1993).

La Porte, Todd R., editor. *Organized Social Complexity: Challenge to Politics and Policy.* Princeton: Princeton University Press, 1975.

Lash, Harry. 'Planning in a Human Way: Personal Reflections on the Regional Planning Experience in Greater Vancouver.' Ministry of State for Urban Affairs, Ottawa, 1976.

Lawrence, J. 'Green Marketing Jobs Wilt at Big Companies.' *Advertising Age* 27 (1993): 54.

Lax, D.A., and J.K. Sebenius. *The Manager as Negotiator.* New York: Free Press, 1986.

Lee, Kai N. *Compass and Gyroscope: Integrating Science and Politics for the Environment.* Washington: Island Press, 1993.

Lehmbruch, Gerhard. 'The Organization of Society, Administrative Strategies, and Policy Networks.' In Roland M. Czada and Adrienne Windhoff-Heritier, eds, *Political Choice: Institutions, Rules, and the Limits of Rationality,* 121–55. Boulder: Westview, 1991.

Leiss, William. *Governance and the Environment.* Working Paper Series 96-1, Environmental Policy Unit, School of Policy Studies, Queen's University, 1996.

– 'The Trouble with Science: Public Controversy over Genetically-Modified Foods.' Paper presented at eastern regional meetings of the Canadian Society of Plant Physiologists, Queen's University, 12 December 1999. www.ucalgary/ca/~wleiss/news/trouble_with_science.htm.

– 'Between Expertise and Bureaucracy: Risk Management Trapped at the Science/Policy Interface.' In G. Bruce Doern and Ted Reed, eds, *Risky Business: Canada's Changing Science-Based Policy and Regulatory Regime.* Toronto: University of Toronto Press, 2000.

Leiss, W., and Associates. 'Lessons Learned from ARET: A Qualitative Survey of Perceptions of Stakeholders, Final Report.' Working Paper Series 96-4, Environmental Policy Unit, School of Policy Studies, Queen's University, June 1996.

Leiss, William, and Christina Chociolko. *Risk and Responsibility.* Montreal: McGill-Queen's University Press, 1994.

Lemons, John. 'The Conservation of Biodiversity: Scientific Uncertainty and the Burden of Proof.' In John Lemons, *Scientific Uncertainty and Environmental Problem Solving,* 206–32. Cambridge, MA: Blackwell Science, 1996.

Lester, James. 'A New Federalism? Environmental Policy in the States.' In N. Vig and M. Kraft, eds, *Environmental Policy in the 1990s (2nd ed.),* 51–68. Washington: Congressional Quarterly Press, 1994.

Lévêque, François. 'Externalities, Collective Goods and the Requirements of a State's Intervention in Pollution Abatement.' Fondazione Eni Enrico Mattei, Working paper 20.97, February 1997.

Lewin, Kurt. 'Frontiers in Group Dynamics.' In Dorwin Cartwright, ed., *Field Theory in Social Science*, 188–237. New York: Harper, 1951.

Lindblom, Charles E. 'The Science of Muddling Through.' *Public Administration Review* 19, no. 2 (1959): 79–88.

– *Politics and Markets*. New York: Basic Books, 1977.

– 'Still Muddling, Not Yet Through.' *Public Administration Review* 39, no. 6 (1979): 517–26.

Linder, Stephen H., and B. Guy Peters. 'Instruments of Government: Perceptions and Contexts.' *Journal of Public Policy* 9, no. 1 (1989): 35–58.

Lindquist, Evert A. 'Public Managers and Policy Communities: Learning to Meet New Challenges.' *Canadian Public Administration* 35, no. 2 (1992): 127–59.

London, Caroline. 'Droit communautaire de l'environnement.' *Revue trimestrielle de droit européen* 30, no. 2 (1994): 291–325.

Longino, Helen. *Science as Social Knowledge: Values and Objectivity in Scientific Inquiry*. Princeton: Princeton University Press, 1990.

Lovins, Amory. *Soft Energy Paths*. Cambridge, MA: Ballinger, 1977.

Lowe, M. *Premature Bonanza: Standoff at Voisey's Bay*. Toronto: Between the Lines, 1998.

Lucas, A.R. 'Fundamental Prerequisites for Citizen Participation.' In Barry Sadler, ed., *Involvement and the Environment*. Volume 1. Edmonton: Environment Council of Alberta, 1978.

Lukasik, Lynda. 'The Dofasco Deal.' In R. Gibson, ed., *Voluntary Initiatives: The New Politics of Corporate Greening*. Peterborough, ON: Broadview, 1999.

Lyons, O. 'Spirituality, Equality and Natural Law.' In M. Boldt, J.A. Long, and L. Little Bear, et al., *The Quest for Justice: Aboriginal People and Aboriginal Rights*. Toronto: University of Toronto Press, 1985.

Macklem, P. 'First Nations Self-Government and the Borders of the Canadian Legal Imagination.' *McGill Law Journal* 36, no. 383 (1991): 447.

MacLean, Douglas. 'Risk and Consent: Philosophical Issues for Centralized Decisions.' *Risk Analysis* 2, no. 2 (1982): 59–67.

MacNeill, James, Pieter Winsemius, and Tazio Yakushiji. *Beyond Interdependence*. New York: Oxford University Press, 1991.

Mahon, Rianne. 'Canadian Public Policy: The Unequal Structure of Representation.' In Leo Pantich, ed., *The Canadian State: Political Economy and Political Power*, 165–98. Toronto: University of Toronto Press, 1977.

Maienschein, Jane, James P. Collins, and Daniel S. Strouse. 'Biology and Law:

Challenges of Adjudicating Competing Claims in a Democracy.' *Jurimetrics Journal* 38 (1998): 151–81.

Majone, Giandomenico. *Evidence, Argument, and Persuasion in the Policy Process.* New Haven: Yale University Press, 1989.

Mathus, Thomas Robert. *An Essay on the Principle of Population and a Summary View of the Principle of Population.* Ed. and intro. Antony Flew; reprint, 1798. Harmondsworth, Middlesex: Penguin, 1970.

Mander, D., and P. Perkins. 'Trade Disputes and Environmental "Regulatory Chill": The Case of Ontario's Environmental Levy.' *World Competition* 18, no. 2 (1994): 57–76.

Mander, Jerry, and Edward Goldsmith, editors. *The Case against the Global Economy and for a Turn toward the Local.* San Francisco: Sierra Club Books, 1996.

Manfredi, Christopher. 'The Judicialization of Politics, Rights and Public Policy in Canada and the United States.' In K. Banting, G. Hoberg, and R. Simeon, eds, *Degrees of Freedom, Canada and the United States in a Changing World,* 152–85. Montreal: McGill-Queen's University Press, 1997.

Mann, Howard, and Konrad von Moltke. 'NAFTA's Chapter 11 and the Environment: Addressing the Impacts of the Investor-State Process on the Environment.' Winnipeg: International Institute for Sustainable Development, 1999.

March, James. 'Bounded Rationality, Ambiguity, and the Engineering of Choice.' *Bell Journal of Economics* 9, no. 4 (1978): 587–608.

March, James G., and Johan P. Olsen. *Rediscovering Institutions: The Organizational Basis of Politics.* New York: Free Press, 1989.

Marchak, Patricia. *Logging the Globe.* Montreal: McGill-Queen's University Press, 1995.

Marchetti, Cesare. 'On Geoengineering and the CO_2 Problem.' *Climatic Change* 1, no. 1 (1977): 59–68.

– '10^{12}: A Check on the Earth Carrying Capacity for Man.' *Energy* 4 (1979): 1107–17

Marion, Russ. *The Edge of Organization: Chaos and Complexity Theories of Formal Social Systems.* London: Sage, 1999.

Markusen, James R., Edward R. Morey, and Nancy Olewiler. 1995. 'Competition in Regional Environmental Policies When Plant Locations Are Endogenous.' *Journal of Public Economics* 56, no. 1 (1995): 55–78.

Marshall, M. 'Values, Customs and Traditions of the Mi'kmaq Nation.' In L. Choyce and R. Joe, eds, *The Mi'kmaq Anthology.* Lawrencetown Beach, NS: Pottersfield Press, 1997.

Martin, C. *Keepers of the Game.* Berkeley: University of Georgia Press, 1981.

Martin, Hans-Peter, and Harald Schumann. *The Global Trap*. Montreal: Black Rose Books, 1997.

Martin, John F. *Reorienting a Nation: Consultants and Australian Public Policy* Aldershot, UK: Ashgate, 1998.

Masood, E. 'Companies Cool to Tactics of Global Warming Lobby.' *Nature* 383 (1986): 470.

Mattson, David J. 'Ethics and Science in Natural Resource Agencies.' *BioScience* 46 (1996): 767–71.

May, Peter J. 'Reconsidering Policy Design: Policies and Publics.' *Journal of Public Policy* 11, No. 2 (1991): 187–206.

– 'Policy Learning and Failure.' *Journal of Public Policy* 12, no. 4 (1992): 331–54.

Mayntz, Renate. 'Public Bureaucracies and Policy Implementation.' *International Social Science Journal* 31, no. 4 (1979): 633–45.

– 'Modernization and the Logic of Interorganizational Networks.' In J. Child, M. Crozier, and R. Mayntz, eds, *Societal Change between Market and Organization*, 3–18. Aldershot, UK: Avebury, 1993.

Mazurek, Janice, 'The Use of Unilateral Agreements in the United States: The Responsible Care Initiative.' ENV/EPOC/GEEI(98)25/FINAL. Paris: OECD, 1998.

– 'The Use of Unilateral Agreements in the United States: An Initial Survey.' ENV/EPOC/GEEI(98)27/FINAL. Paris: OECD, 1998.

McAfee, Ann. 'When Theory Meets Practice – Citizen Participation in Planning.' *Plan Canada* 37, no. 3 (1997): 18–22.

McAndrew, Brian, 'Water pollution violations ignored.' *Toronto Star*, 1 March 1999: A1, A13.

– 'Politicians flout deal on lakes, report says.' *Toronto Star*, 8 March 1999: A6.

McCloskey, Michael. 'The Limits of Collaboration.' *Harper's Magazine*, November 1996: 34–6.

McCormick, John. 'International Nongovernmental Organizations: Prospects for a Global Environmental Movement.' In Sheldon Kamieniecki, ed., *Environmental Politics in the International Arena*, 131–44. Albany: SUNY Press, 1993.

McDaniels, Timothy, Michael Healey, and Richard Paisley. 'Cooperative Fisheries Management Involving First Nations in British Columbia: An Adaptive Approach to Strategy Design.' *Canadian Journal of Fisheries and Aquatic Science* 51, no. 9 (1994): 2115–25.

McDaniels, Timothy, and Karen Thomas. 'Eliciting Public Preferences for Local Land Use Alternatives: A Structured Referendum with Approval Voting.' *Journal of Policy Analysis and Management* 18, no. 2 (1999): 264–80.

McGarity, Thomas O. 'Substantive and Procedural Discretion in Administrative Resolution of Science Policy Questions.' *Georgetown Law Journal* 67: 729–810.

M'Gonigle, R. Michael, et al. 'Taking Uncertainty Seriously: From Permissive Regulation to Preventive Design in Environmental Decision Making.' *Osgoode Hall Law Journal* 32 (1994): 99–169.

McIlroy, Anne. 'Wildlife panel scientists to get vote, Stuart says.' *Globe and Mail*, 23 March 1999: A2.

McIlwraith, T.F. *The Bella Coola Indians*. 2 vols. Toronto: University of Toronto Press, 1948, 1992.

Meadows, Donella H., Dennis L. Meadows, Jorgen Randers, and William H. Behrens III. *The Limits to Growth*, a report for the Club of Rome's project on the predicament of mankind. New York: Universe Books, 1972.

Meadows, Donella H., Dennis L. Meadows, and Jorgen Randers. *Beyond the Limits: Confronting Global Collapse, Envisioning a Sustainable Future*. Post Mills, VT: Chelsea Green Publishing, 1992.

Mellon, Margaret. *The Regulation of Toxic and Oxidant Air Pollution in North America*. Don Mills, ON: CCH Canadian, 1996.

Mercredi, O. 'Address to the United Nations.' In A. Ewen, ed., *Voice of Indigenous Peoples*. Santa Fe: Clear Light Publishers, 1994.

Mercredi, O., and M.E. Turpel. *In the Rapids: Navigating the Future of First Nations*. Toronto: Viking, 1993.

Meyer, Alan D. 'Adapting to Environmental Jolts.' *Administrative Science Quarterly* 27 (1982): 515–37.

Meyer, Alan D., Geoffrey R. Brooks, and James B. Goes. 'Environmental Jolts and Industry Revolutions: Organizational Responses to Discontinuous Change.' *Strategic Management Journal* 11 (1990): 93–110.

Milward, H. Brinton, Keith G. Provan, and Barbara A. Else. 'What Does the "Hollow State" Look Like?' In Barry Bozeman, ed., *Public Management: The State of the Art*, 309–23. San Francisco: Jossey-Bass, 1993.

Mishan, E.J. *The Costs of Economic Growth*. London: Staples Press, 1967.

Mitchell, Robert, and Richard Carson. *Using Surveys to Value Public Goods: The Contingent Valuation Method*. Washington: Resources for the Future, 1989.

Moffet, John, and François Bregha. 'The Canadian Chemical Producers' Association's Responsible Care Program.' In Kernaghan Webb and David Cohen, eds, *Voluntary Codes: Private Governance, the Public Interest and Innovation*. Ottawa: Carlton University, forthcoming.

Montreal Protocol Science Assessment Panel. *Scientific Assessment of Ozone Depletion: 1998*. Geneva: World Meteorological Organization, 1999.

Montreal Protocol Technology and Economics Assessment Panel. *1998 Assessment*. Nairobi: UN Environment Programme, 1999.

Moore, Christopher W. *The Mediation Process: Practical Strategies for Resolving Conflicts*. 2nd edition. San Francisco: Jossey-Bass, 1996.

Morgan, J.P., and J.D. Henry. 'Hunting Grounds: Making Co-operative Wildlife Management Work.' *Alternatives* 22 (1996): 24–30.

Mueller, Claus. *The Politics of Communication: A Study in the Political Sociology of Language, Socialization and Legitimation*. New York: Oxford University Press, 1973.

Nakashima, D.J. *Application of Native Knowledge in EIA: Inuit, Eiders and Hudson Bay Oil*. Ottawa: Canadian Environmental Assessment Research Council, 1999.

Nash, J., and J. Ehrenfeld. 'Codes of Environmental Management Practice: Assessing Their Potential as a Tool for Change.' *Annual Review of Energy and Environment* 22 (1997): 487–535.

Nash, Roderick. *Wilderness and the American Mind*. New Haven: Yale University Press, 1973.

National Round Table on the Environment and the Economy. 'Building Consensus for a Sustainable Future: Guiding Principles.' Ottawa: National Round Table, 1993.

– 'Building Consensus for a Sustainable Future: Putting Principles into Practice.' Ottawa: NRT, 1996.

– 'Sustainable Strategies for Oceans: A Co-Management Guide.' Ottawa: NRT, 1998.

Native Council of Nova Scotia. *Mi'kmaq Fisheries: Netukulimk – Toward a Better Understanding*. Truro, NS, 1993.

Natural Resources Canada. 'Canada's Emissions Outlook: An Update.' Analysis and Modelling Group. Ottawa: Natural Resources Canada, 1999. www.nrcan.gc.ca/es/ceo/update.htm.

Nelkin, Dorothy, and Michael Pollak. 'Public Participation in Technological Decisions: Reality or Grand Illusion?' *Technology Review* 82 (August/September 1979): 55–64.

Netherlands, *Ministry of Housing, Spatial Planning and the Environment. Towards a Sustainable Netherlands*. The Hague: Ministry, 1997.

Nevitte, Neil. *The Decline of Deference: Canadian Value Change in Cross-National Perspective*. Peterborough, ON: Broadview Press, 1996.

Nichols, Will. 'Masters of Conquest.' *The Nation* 1 (February 1994): 10.

Nisbet, Robert, editor. *Social Change*. New York: Harper and Row, 1972.

Noonan, P. 'Mining Desecration and the Protection of Indian Sacred Sites: A Lesson in First Amendment Hurdling.' *University of Pittsburgh Law Review* 50 (Summer 1989): 1131–52.

Nordlinger, Eric A. *On the Autonomy of the Democratic State*. Cambridge, MA: Harvard University Press, 1981.

North American Commission for Environmental Cooperation. 'Annual Workplan 1998.' Montreal, 1998.

Northwest Indian Fisheries Commission. www.nwifc.wa.gov.

Notze, C. *Aboriginal Peoples and Natural Resources in Canada*. North York, ON: Captus Press, 1994.

Nownes, Anthony, and Grant Neeley. 'Toward an Explanation for Public Interest Group Formation and Proliferation: "Seed Money," Disturbances, Entrepreneurship, and Patronage.' *Policy Studies Journal* 24, no. 1 (1996): 74–92.

Nunavut Land Claims Agreement Act, chapters N-28.6, N-28.7 (1993, c. 28). 'An Act to establish a territory to be known as Nunavut and to provide for its government and to amend certain Acts in consequence thereof.'

Oberthur, Sebastien. *Production and Consumption of Ozone-Depleting Substances, 1986–1996: The Data Reporting System under the Montreal Protocol*. Eschborn, FRG: Deutsche Gesellschaft für Technische Zusammenarbeit, 1998.

Offe, Claus. *Contradictions of the Welfare State*. Cambridge, MA: MIT Press, 1984.

Ohmae, Kenichi. *The End of the Nation State*. New York: Free Press, 1995.

Olsen, Johan P., and B. Guy Peters, editors. *Lessons from Experience: Experiential Learning in Administrative Reforms in Eight Democracies*. Oslo: Scandinavian University Press, 1996.

Olson, Mancur. *The Logic of Collective Action: Public Goods and the Theory of Groups*. Cambridge, MA: Harvard University Press, 1965.

Ommer, Rosemary. 'Deep Water Fisheries, Policy and Management Issues, and the Sustainability of Fishing Communities.' In Alan G. Hopper, ed., *Deep Water Fisheries of the North Atlantic Slope*, Proceedings of the NATO Advanced Research Workshop, 307–22. Dordrecht: Kluwer, 1995.

Organisation for Economic Co-operation and Development. *Environmental Labelling in OECD Countries*. Paris: OECD, 1991.

– *Eco-Labelling: Actual Effects of Selected Programmes*. Paris: OECD, 1997.

– *Extended Producer Responsibility: Case Study on the Dutch Packaging Covenant*. Paris: OECD, 1997.

– *Voluntary Approaches for Environmental Policy: An Assessment*. Paris: OECD, 1999.

– Trade Directorate. Joint Session of Trade and Environment Experts: Draft 1995 Report to Ministers. Paris: OECD, April 1995.

O'Riordan, Timothy, editor. *Ecotaxation*. London: Earthscan, 1997.

O'Riordan, T., and H. Voisey, editors. *The Transition to Sustainability: The Politics of Agenda 21 in Europe*. London: Earthscan, 1998.

Osberg, Lars, Fred Wien, and Jan Grude. *Vanishing Jobs: Canada's Changing Workplaces*. Toronto: James Lorimer and Co., 1995.

Ostrom, Elinor. *Governing the Commons: The Evolution of Institutions for Collective Action*. New York: Cambridge University Press, 1990.

Paehlke, Robert. *Environmentalism and the Future of Progressive Politics*. New Haven: Yale University Press, 1989.

– 'Eco-History: Two Waves in the Evolution of Environmentalism.' *Alternatives* 19, no. 1 (September/October 1992): 18–23.

– 'Green Politics and the Rise of the Environmental Movement.' In Thomas Fleming, ed., *The Environment and Canadian Society*, 251–74. Toronto: ITP Nelson, 1997.

Page, Talbot. 'A Generic View of Toxic Chemicals and Similar Risks.' *Ecology Law Quarterly* 7 (1978): 207–44.

– 'A Framework for Unreasonable Risk in the Toxic Substances Control Act (TSCA).' *Annals of the New York Academy of Sciences* 363 (1981): 145–66.

Paigen, Beverly. 'Controversy at Love Canal.' *Hastings Center Report* 12 (June 1982): 29–37.

Pal, Leslie A. *Interests of State: The Politics of Language, Multiculturalism, and Feminism in Canada*. Montreal: McGill-Queen's University Press, 1993.

– *Beyond Policy Analysis: Public Issue Management in Turbulent Times*. Toronto: ITP Nelson, 1997.

Palmer, K., W.E. Oates, and P.R. Portney. 'Tightening Environmental Standards: The Benefit-Cost or the No-Cost Paradigm?' *Journal of Economic Perspectives* 9, no. 4 (Fall 1995): 119–32.

Paquet, Gilles. 'Tectonic Changes in Canadian Governance.' In Leslie A. Pal, ed., *How Ottawa Spends, 1999–2000: Shape Shifting – Canadian Governance toward the 21st Century*, 75–112. Toronto: Oxford University Press, 1999.

Parker, Gavin, and Amanda Wragg. 'Networks, Agency and (De)stabilization: The Issue of Navigation on the River Wye, UK.' *Journal of Environmental Planning and Management* 42, no. 4 (1999): 471–87.

Parson, Edward A., with A.R. Dobell, Adam Fenech, Don Munton, and Heather Smith. 'Leading While Keeping in Step: Management of Global Atmospheric Issues in Canada.' In The Social Learning Group, *Learning to Manage Global Environmental Risks: A Comparative History of Social Responses to Climate Change, Ozone Depletion, and Acid Rain*, ed. William C. Clark et al. Cambridge, MA: MIT Press, forthcoming 2001.

Paté, M. Elisabeth. 'Acceptable Decision Processes and Acceptable Risks in Public Sector Regulation.' *IEEE Transactions on Systems, Man, and Cybernetics* 13 (March/April 1983): 113–24.

Paterson, Matthew. *Global Warming and Global Politics*. London: Routledge, 1996.

Payer, Cheryl. *The World Bank: A Critical Analysis*. New York: Monthly Review Press, 1982.

Payne, John, James Bettman, and Eric Johnson. 'Behavioural Decision
    Research: A Constructive Processing Perspective.' *Annual Review of Psychol-
    ogy* 43 (1992): 87–132.
Perkins, Ellie. 'Trade Agreements and Environmental Policy: Ontario
    Examples.' Unpublished paper presented at Swedish-Canadian Academic
    Foundation 3rd annual conference, 'Environmental Issues in Canada and
    Sweden: The Challenge of Sustainability,' York University, Toronto, May
    1996.
Persky, S. *Delgamuukw: The Supreme Court of Canada's Decision on Aboriginal
    Title*. Vancouver: Greystone Books, 1998.
Peterman, Randall M., and Michael M'Gonigle. 'Statistical Power Analysis and
    the Precautionary Principle.' *Marine Pollution Bulletin* 24 (1982): 231–4.
Peters, B. Guy. 'Government Reorganization: A Theoretical Analysis.' *Interna-
    tional Political Science Review* 13, no. 2 (1992): 199–218.
– *The Future of Governing: Four Emerging Models*. Lawrence, KA: University
    Press of Kansas, 1996.
Peters, B. Guy, and Jon Pierre. 'Governance without Government? Rethinking
    Public Administration.' *Journal of Public Administration Research and Theory* 8,
    no. 2 (1998): 223–44.
Peterson, David L., and V. Thomas Parker, editors. *Ecological Scale*. New York:
    Columbia University Press, 1998.
Peterson, M.J. 'Whalers, Cetologists, Environmentalists, and the International
    Management of Whaling.' *International Organization* 46, no. 1 (1992): 147–86.
Peterson, Paul E. *The Price of Federalism*. Washington: Brookings Institution
    (Twentieth Century Fund), 1995.
Phillips, Susan D. 'How Ottawa Blends: Shifting Government Relationships
    with Interest Groups.' In Frances Abele, ed., *How Ottawa Spends 1991–92: The
    Politics of Fragmentation*, 183–228. Ottawa: Carleton University Press, 1991.
– 'Discourse, Identity, and Voice: Feminist Contributions to Policy Studies.' In
    L. Dobuzinskis, M. Howlett, and D. Laycock, eds, *Policy Studies in Canada:
    The State of the Art*, 242–65. Toronto: University of Toronto Press, 1996.
Pierson, Paul. 'When Effect Becomes Cause: Policy Feedback and Political
    Change.' *World Politics* 45, no. 595–628 (1993).
Pinkerton, E. *Cooperative Management of Local Fisheries: New Directions for
    Improved Management and Community Development*. Vancouver: University of
    British Columbia Press, 1989.
– 'Local Fisheries Co-Management: A Review of International Experiences
    and Their Implications for Salmon Management in British Columbia.'
    Canadian Journal of Fisheries and Aquatic Sciences 51 (1994): 2363.
Pollock, Philip H., Stuart A. Lilie, and M. Elliot Vittes. 'Hard Issues, Core

Values and Vertical Constraint: The Case of Nuclear Power.' *British Journal of Political Science* 23, no. 1 (1989): 29–50.

Polsby, Nelson W., editor. *Political Innovation in America: The Politics of Policy Initiation.* New Haven: Yale University Press, 1984.

Porter, M.E., and C. van der Linde. 'Toward a New Conception of the Environment-Competitiveness Relationship.' *Journal of Economic Perspectives* 9, no. 4 (Fall 1995): 97–118.

Pratt, Larry, and Ian Urquhart. *The Last Great Forest: Japanese Multinationals and Alberta's Northern Forests.* Edmonton: NeWest Press, 1994.

Presidential/Congressional Commission on Risk Assessment and Risk Management. *Framework for Environmental Health Risk Management. Final Report.* Vol. 1. Washington, 1997.

Projet de Société. 'Planning for a Sustainable Future: Canadian Choices for Transitions to Sustainability.' Ottawa: National Round Table on Environment and Economy, 1995.

Pross, A. Paul. *Group Politics and Public Policy.* 2nd edition. Toronto: Oxford University Press, 1992.

Prudencio, Roberto J., and Stewart J. Hudson. 'The Road from Marrakesh.' Unpublished paper presented at GATT Symposium on Trade, Environment and Sustainable Development, TE 009, June 1994.

Putnam, Robert. 'Bowling Alone: America's Declining Social Capital.' *Journal of Democracy* 6, no. 1 (1995): 65.

R. v. Badger [1996] 1 S.C.R. 771, [1996] 2 C.N.L.R. 77.

R. v. Guerin [1984] 2 S.C.R. 335, 13 D.L.R. (4th) 321, [1985] 1 C.N.L.R. 120 [1999].

R. v. Marshall [1999] 3 S.C.R. 456, 159 N.S.R. (2d) 186, 468 A.P.R. 186, 146 D.L.R. (4th) 257, [1997] 3 C.N.L.R. 209, [1997] N.S.J. No. 131 (QL), affirming [1996] N.S.J. No. 246 (QL).

R. v. Marshall [1999] 3 S.C.R. 533.

R. v. Sparrow, (1990) 3 C.N.L.R. 98, [1990] 1 S.C.R. 1075, 56 C.C.C. (3d) 263, 46 B.C.L.R (2d) 1, [1990] 4 W.W. R. 410, 70 D.L.R. (4th) 385, 11 N.R. 241, [1990] 3 C.N.L.R. 160.

R. v. Van der Peet [996] 2 S.C.R. 507.

Rabe, Barry G. 'The Politics of Sustainable Development: Impediments to Pollution Prevention and Policy Integration in Canada.' *Canadian Public Administration* 40, no. 3 (1997): 415–35.

– 'State Policy Innovations as Models for Sustainable Development.' Mimeo., 1998, forthcoming. (Author: brabe@umich.edu.)

Raiffa, Howard. *The Art and Science of Negotiation.* Cambridge, MA: Harvard University Press, 1982.

Rankin, Murray. 1981. 'Information and the Environment: The Struggle for

Access.' In John Swaigen, ed., *Environmental Rights in Canada*, 285–333. Toronto: Butterworth, 1981.

Raustiala, Kal. 'The Political Implications of the Enforcement Provisions of the NAFTA Environmental Side Agreement.' *Environmental Law* 25 (1995): 31–56.

Rayner, Jeremy. 'Evaluating National Forest Programmes: Lessons from Biodiversity Policies in Canada.' In P. Gluck et al., eds, *Formulation and Implementation of National Forest Programmes: Volume 1 – Theoretical Aspects*, 229–36. Joensuu, Fin.: European Forest Institute, 1999.

Reed, M.G. 'Environmental Assessment and Aboriginal Claims: Implementation of the Inuvialuit Final Agreement.' Ottawa: Canadian Environmental Assessment Research Council, 1990.

Rees, William E. 'Environmental Assessment and Planning Process in Canada.' In S.D. Clarke, ed., *Environmental Assessment in Australia and Canada*. Vancouver: Westwater Research Centre, UBC, 1981.

Regier, Henry A. 'Great Lakes.' In R. Paehlke, ed., *Conservation and Environmentalism: An Encyclopedia*. New York: Garland, 1995.

Regier, Henry, and G.L. Baskerville. 'Sustainable Redevelopment of Regional Ecosystems Degraded by Exploitive Development.' In W. Clark and R.E. Munn, eds, *Sustainable Development of the Biosphere*, 75–100. Cambridge: Cambridge University Press, 1986.

Reichhardt, T. 'Endangered Species Bill Faces Battle against Property Lobby.' *Nature* 388 (1997): 506.

Reif, Linda C. 'International Environmental Law.' In G. Thompson, M.L. McConnell, and L.B. Huestis, eds, *Environmental Law and Business in Canada*, 71–103. Aurora, ON: Canada Law Book, 1993.

Reinicke, Wolfgang H. *Global Public Policy: Governing without Government?* Washington: Brookings Institution, 1998.

Renn, Ortren, Thomas Webler, and Peter Wiedemann. *Fairness and Competence in Citizen Participation*. Dordrecht: Kluwer Academic Press, 1995.

Rennings, K., Ludwig Brockmann, and H. Bergmann. 'Voluntary Agreements in Environmental Protection: Experiences in Germany and Future Perspectives.' *Business Strategy and the Environment* 6 (1997): 245–63.

Report of the Royal Commission on Aboriginal Peoples. 5 volumes. Ottawa: Supply and Services Canada, 1996.

Revesz, Richard L. 'Rehabilitating Interstate Competition: Rethinking the "Race-to-the-Bottom" Rationale for Federal Environmental Regulation.' *New York University Law Review* 67, no. 4 (December 1992): 1210–54.

– 'The Race to the Bottom and Federal Environmental Regulation: A Response to Critics.' *Minnesota Law Review* 82, no. 2 (December 1997): 535–64.

Rhodes, R.A.W. *Understanding Governance: Policy Networks, Governance, Reflexivity, and Accountability*. Buckingham, UK: Open University Press, 1997.

Richardson, B. *People of Terra Nullius: Betrayal and Rebirth in Aboriginal Canada*. Toronto: Douglas and McIntyre, 1993.

Richardson, Jeremy. 'Interest Groups, Multi-Arena Politics and Policy Change.' In Stuart S. Nagel, ed., *The Policy Process*, 65–100. Commack, NY: Nova Science Publishers, 1999.

Risse-Kappen, Thomas. *Bringing Transnational Relations Back In: Non-State Actors, Domestic Structures and International Institutions*. Cambridge: Cambridge University Press, 1995.

Rittel, Horst W.J., and Melvin M. Webber. 'Dilemmas in a General Theory of Planning.' *Policy Sciences* 4 (1973): 155–69.

Robinson, Allan. 'Ottawa, NWT to pay for Giant cleanup.' *Globe and Mail*, 28 August 1999.

Rocha, Elizabeth M. 'A Ladder of Empowerment.' *Journal of Planning Education and Research* 17 (1997): 31–44.

Rock, Paul. *A View from the Shadows: The Ministry of the Solicitor General of Canada and the Making of the Justice for Victims of Crime Initiative*. Oxford: Clarendon Press, 1986.

Rogers, Raymond A. *Solving History: The Challenge of Environmental Activism*. Montreal: Black Rose Books, 1998.

Rona-Tas, Akos. 'Path Dependence and Capital Theory: Sociology of the Post-Communist Economic Transformation.' *East European Politics and Societies* 12, no. 1 (1998): 107–31.

Roodman, David Malin. *Paying the Piper: Subsidies, Politics, and the Environment*. Washington: Worldwatch, 1996.

Rose, Jonathan. 'Government Advertising in a Crisis: The Quebec Referendum Precedent.' *Canadian Journal of Communication* 18 (1993): 173–96.

Rose, Richard. 'Inheritance before Choice in Public Policy.' *Journal of Theoretical Politics* 2, no. 3 (1990): 263–91.

– 'What Is Lesson-Drawing.' *Journal of Public Policy* 11, no. 1 (1991): 3–30.

– *Lesson-Drawing in Public Policy: A Guide to Learning across Time and Space*. Chatham, NJ: Chatham House Publishers, 1993.

Roseland, Mark. *Eco-city Dimensions: Healthy Communities, Healthy Planet*. Gabriola Island, BC: New Society Books, 1997.

Rosenberg, David M., et al. 'Recent Trends in Environmental Impact Assessment.' *Canadian Journal of Fisheries and Aquatic Sciences* 38 (1981): 591–624.

Rosener, J.B. 'User Oriented Evaluation: A New Way to View Citizen Participation.' In Daneke, Gregory A., Margot W. Garcia, and Jerome Delli Priscolli, eds, *Public Involvement and Social Impact Assessment*, 45–60. Boulder: Westview Press, 1983

Roszak, Theodore. *Where the Wasteland Ends*. Garden City, NJ: Doubleday, 1973.

Royal Commission on Aboriginal Peoples. *Treaty Making in the Spirit of Co-Existence: An Alternative to Extinguishment*. Ottawa: Minister of Supply and Services, 1994.

Rugman, Alan M., John Kirton, and Julie Soloway. 'NAFTA, Environmental Regulations, and Canadian Competitiveness.' *Journal of World Trade* 31, no. 4 (1997): 129–44.

Runge, C. Ford. *Freer Trade, Protected Environment: Balancing Trade Liberalization and Environmental Interests*. New York: Council on Foreign Relations Press, 1994.

Ruttan, Vernon W. 'Designing Institutions for Sustainability.' In Edna Tusak Loehman and D. Marc Kilgour, eds, *Designing Institutions for Environmental and Resource Management*, 142–64. Cheltenham: Edward Elgar, 1998.

Rykiel, Edward, Jr. 'Relationships of Scale to Policy and Decision Making.' In David L. Peterson and V. Thomas Parker, eds, *Ecological Scale*, 485–97. New York: Columbia University Press, 1998.

Sabatier, Paul A. 'Knowledge, Policy-oriented Learning, and Policy Change.' *Knowledge: Creation, Diffusion, Utilization* 8, no. 4 (1987): 649–92.

– 'An Advocacy Coalition Framework of Policy Change and the Role of Policy-oriented Learning Therein.' *Policy Sciences* 21, no. 2/3 (1988): 129–68.

Sabatier, Paul A., and Hank C. Jenkins-Smith, editors. *Policy Change and Learning: An Advocacy Coalition Approach*. Boulder: Westview, 1993.

St. Catherine's Milling and Lumber Co. v. The Queen (1888), 14 A.C. 56 (AC.).

Salamon, Lester M., editor. *Beyond Privatization: The Tools of Government Action*. Washington: Urban Institute, 1989.

Sale, Kirkpatrick. *Human Scale*. New York: Coward, McCann & Geoghegan, 1980.

Salter, Liora, and Debra Slaco. *Public Inquiries in Canada*. Ottawa: Science Council of Canada, 1981.

Salzman, J. 'Informing the Green Consumer: The Debate over the Use and Abuse of Environmental Labels.' *Journal of Industrial Ecology* 1 (1997): 11–21.

Saunders, D.E. 'The Indian Lobby and the Canadian Constitution, 1978–82.' In Noel Dyke, ed., *Indigenous Peoples and the Nation State: Fourth World Politics in Canada, Australia and Norway*. St John's: Memorial University Institute of Social and Economic Research, 1985.

Savoie, Donald J. *Governing from the Centre: The Concentration of Power in Canadian Politics*. Toronto: University of Toronto Press, 1999.

Saward, Michael. *Co-Optive Politics and State Legitimacy*. Aldershot, UK: Dartmouth, 1992.

Sbragia, Alberta. 'Environmental Policy: The "Push-Pull" of Policy-Making.' In Hellen Wallace and William Wallace, eds, *Policy-Making in the European Union*, 235–56. 3rd ed. Oxford: Oxford University Press, 1996.

Schaap, L., and M.J.W. van Twist. 'The Dynamics of Closedness in Networks.' In W.J.M. Kickert, E.-H. Klijn, and J.F.M. Koppenjan, eds, *Managing Complex Networks: Strategies for the Public Sector, the European Union*, 62–78. London: Sage, 1997.

Scharpf, Fritz W. 'Policy Failure and Institutional Reform: Why Should Form Follow Function?' *International Social Science Journal* 108 (1986): 179–90.

Schattschneider, E.E. *The Semisovereign People: A Realist's View of Democracy in America*. New York: Holt, Rinehart and Winston, 1960; Hinsdale, IL: Dryden Press, 1975.

Schelling, Thomas C. *The Strategy of Conflict*. Cambridge, MA: Harvard University Press, 1960.

Schneider, Anne L., and Helen Ingram. 'Behavioural Assumptions of Policy Tools.' *Journal of Politics* 52, no. 2 (1990): 511–29.

Schneiderman, David, and Kate Sutherland, editors. *Charting the Consequences: The Impact of Charter Rights on Canadian Law and Politics*. Toronto: University of Toronto Press, 1997.

Schoenbaum, Thomas J. 'Free International Trade and Protection of the Environment: Irreconcilable Conflict?' *American Journal of International Law* 86 (1992): 700–27.

– 'International Trade and Protection of the Environment: The Continuing Search for Reconciliation.' *American Journal of International Law* 91 (1997): 268–313.

Scholz, J.T. 'Cooperative Regulatory Enforcement and the Politics of Administrative Effectiveness.' *American Political Science Review* 85 (1991): 115–36.

Schon, Donald A., and Martin Rein. *Frame Reflection: Towards the Resolution of Intractable Policy Controversies*. New York: Basic Books, 1994.

Schon, Donald A., Bish Sanyal, and William J. Mitchell, *High Technology and Low-Income Communities: Prospects for the Positive Use of Advanced Information Technology*. Chicago: University of Chicago Press, 1999.

Schrecker, Ted. *Political Economy of Environmental Hazards*, Study paper, Protection of Life, Health and the Environment Project. Ottawa: Law Reform Commission of Canada, 1984.

– 'Resisting Environmental Regulation: The Cryptic Pattern of Business-Government Relations.' In R. Paehlke and D. Torgorson, eds, *Managing Leviathan: Environmental Politics and the Administrative State*, 165–99. Peterborough, ON: Broadview, 1989.

– 'Of Invisible Beasts and the Public Interest: Environmental Cases and the

Judicial System.' In R. Boardman, ed., *Canadian Environmental Policy*, 83–105, 284–92. Toronto: Oxford University Press Canada, 1992.

– 'Environmental Law and the Greening of Government: A Cynical Guide.' In G. Thompson, M. McConnell, and L. Huestis, eds, *Environmental Law and Business in Canada*, 161–83. Aurora, ON: Canada Law Book, 1993.

– (editor). *Surviving Globalization: The Social and Environmental Challenges*. London: Macmillan, 1997.

Schrecker, Ted, et al. 'Biotechnology, Ethics and Government: Report to the Interdepartmental Working Group on Ethics in Biotechnology.' In *Renewal of the Canadian Biotechnology Strategy, Resource document 3.4.1: Ethics*, 135–261. Ottawa: Industry Canada, 1998. http://strategis.ic.gc.ca/bh/bioteche.pdf.

Schumacher, E.F. *Small Is Beautiful*. New York: Harper & Row, 1973.

Schwartz, Bryan. 'Public Inquiries.' *Canadian Public Administration* 40, no. 1 (1997): 72–85.

Schwartz, Roger M. *The Skilled Facilitator: Practical Wisdom for Developing Effective Groups*. San Francisco: Jossey-Bass, 1994.

Scientific Inquiry. Princeton: Princeton University Press, 1990.

Scofield, Heather. 'NAFTA trio warned of corporate lawsuits: Plug loophole to avoid claims, think-tank says.' *Globe and Mail*, 23 June 1999: A7.

Seelig, Michael, and Julie Seelig. 'CityPlan: Participation or Abdication?' *Plan Canada* 37, no. 3 (1997): 18–22.

Segerson, Kathleen, and Thomas J. Miceli. 'Voluntary Approaches to Environmental Protection: The Role of Legislative Threats.' In Carlo Carraro and François Lévêsque, eds, *Voluntary Approaches in Environmental Policy*. Boston: Kluwer Academic Publishers, 1999.

Sewell, W.R. Derrick. 'Public Involvement.' In *Monograph on Comprehensive River Basin Planning*. Ottawa: Environment Canada, 1975.

Shrader-Frechette, Kristin S. *Risk and Rationality: Philosophical Foundations for Populist Reforms*. Berkeley: University of California Press, 1991.

Shrader-Frechette, Kristin S., and Earl D. McCoy. *Method in Ecology: Strategies for Conservation*. Cambridge: Cambridge University Press, 1993.

Sierra Club of Canada. 'Action Alert! SARA Is Weak and Ineffective.' Toronto: Sierra Club of Canada, 2000. www.sierraclub.ca/national/es.

Silbergeld, Ellen. 'Risk Assessment and Risk Management: An Uneasy Divorce.' In Deborah G. Mayo and Rachelle D. Hollander, eds, *Acceptable Evidence: Science and Values in Risk Management*, 99–114. New York: Oxford University Press, 1991.

Sillitoe, P. 'The Development of Indigenous Knowledge: A New Applied Anthropology.' *Current Anthropology* 39 (1994): 223.

Simeon, Richard. 'The "Overload Thesis" and Canadian Government.'
Canadian Public Policy 2, no. 4 (1976): 541–52.

Simmons, Julie M. 'The Canada-Wide Accord on Environmental Harmonization and Value Change within the Department of the Environment.'
Paper presented at the Canadian Political Science Association, Sherbrooke, 1999.

Simon, Herbert. 'Invariants of Human Behaviour.' *Annual Review of Psychology*
41 (1990): 1–19.

Simon v. The Queen [1985] 2 S.C.R. 387.

Simonelli, R. 'Sustainable Science: A Look at Science through Historic Eyes and
through the Eyes of Indigenous Peoples.' *Bulletin of the Science and Technology
society* 24 (1994): 1.

Singleton, S. *Constructing Co-operation: The Evolution of Institutions of Co-
Management*. Ann Arbor: University of Michigan Press, 1998.

Sjolander, Claire Turenne. 'International Trade as Foreign Policy: "Anything for
a Buck."' In Gene Swimmer, ed., *Seeing Red: How Ottawa Spends, 1997–98*,
111–34. Ottawa: School of Public Administration, Carleton University, 1997.

Skogstad, Grace, and Paul Kopas. 'Environmental Policy in a Federal System:
Ottawa and the Provinces.' In Robert Boardman, ed., *Canadian Environmental
Policy: Ecosystems, Politics, and Process*, 43–59. Toronto: Oxford University
Press, 1992.

Slattery, B. 'Understanding Aboriginal Rights.' *Canadian Bar Review* 66 (1987):
711–53.

Slovic, Paul, Baruch Fischhoff, and Sarah Lichtenstein. 'Behavioural Decision
Theory.' *Annual Review of Psychology* 28 (1977): 1–39.

Smith, David. *Monitoring Report on the Public Participation Program of the GVRD*.
Vancouver: Greater Vancouver Regional District and Ministry of State for
Urban Affairs, October 1974.

Smith, Thomas B. 'Advisory Committees in the Public Policy Process.' *International Review of Administrative Sciences* 43, no. 2 (1977): 153–66.

Smith, William, and Janet Halliwell. *Principles and Practices for Using Scientific
Advice in Government Decision Making: International Best Practices*. Report to
Science and Technology Strategy Directorate, Industry Canada. Ottawa:
Industry Canada, January 1999.

Socolow, Robert, 'Nitrogen Management and the Future of Food.' *Proceedings of
the National Academy of Sciences* 96 (May 1999): 6001–8.

Somerville, Margaret A., and Norbert Gilmore. 'From Trust to Tragedy: HIV /
AIDS and the Canadian Blood System.' In Eric A. Feldman and Ronald
Bayer, eds, *Blood Feuds: AIDS, Blood, and the Politics of Medical Disaster*,
127–59. New York: Oxford University Press, 1999.

Soros, George. 'The Capitalist Threat.' *The Atlantic Monthly* 279, no. 2 (Februrary 1997): 45–58.

Staffin, Elliot B. 'Trade Barrier or Trade Boon? A Critical Evaluation of Environmental Labelling and Its Role in the "Greening" of World Trade.' *Columbia Journal of Environmental Law* 21, no. 2 (1996): 205–86.

Starling, Jay D. 'The Use of Systems Constructs in Simplifying Organized Social Complexity.' In Todd R. Laporte, ed., *Organized Social Complexity: Challenge to Politics and Policy,* 131–72. Princeton: Princeton University Press, 1975.

Statistics Canada. Population statistics at http://www.statcan.ca/english/pgdb/people/population/demo02. htm.

Stearman, A.M. 'Revisiting the Myth of the Ecologically Noble Savage in Amazonia: Implications for Indigenous Land Rights.' *Culture and Agriculture* 49 (1994): 2.

Stefanick, L. 'Organization, Administration, and the Environment: Will a Facelift Suffice or Does the Patient Need Radical Surgery?' *Canadian Public Administration* 41, no. 1 (1998): 99–146.

Steinberg, Paul F. 'Setting Global Conservation Priorities: The Political Economy of Noah's Ark.' *Society and Natural Resources,* July 1996.

Steinberg, Richard H. 'Trade-Environment Negotiations in the EU, NAFTA, and WTO: Regional Trajectories of Rule Development.' *American Journal of International Law* 91 (1997): 231–67.

Stoddard, J.L., et al. 'Regional Trends in Aquatic Recovery from Acidification in North America and Europe.' *Nature* 401, no. 6753 (7 October 1999): 571.

Storey, M. 'Demand-Side Efficiency: Voluntary Agreements with Industry.' Annex I Expert Group on the UN FCCC, supported by the OECD and IEA. December 1996.

Stevens, Daniel J., and Oral History Five. mrc.uccb.ns.ca/oralhis.html#4.

Strange, Susan. *States and Markets*. London: Pinter, 1988.

Susskind, Lawrence, and Jeffery Cruikshank. *Breaking the Impasse: Consensual Approaches to Resolving Disputes*. New York: Basic Books, 1987.

Susskind, Lawrence, Sarah McKearnan, and Jennifer Thomas-Larmer. *The Consensus Building Handbook: A Comprehensive Guide to Reaching Agreement*. Thousand Oaks, CA: Sage, 1999.

Svensson, Sven. 'Swedes Vote Yes to Membership in the EU.' Stockholm: The Swedish Institute, 1994.

Swagerty, W.R., editor. *Scholars and the Indian Experience: Critical Reviews of Recent Writing in the Social Sciences*. Bloomington: University of Indiana Press, 1984.

Tapper, Richard. 'Voluntary Agreements for Environmental Performance

Improvement: Perspectives on the Chemical Industry's Responsible Care Program.' *Business Strategy and the Environment* 6 (1997): 287–92.

Task Force on Incomes and Adjustment in the Atlantic Fishery. *Charting a New Course: Towards the Fishery of the Future.* Ottawa: Department of Fisheries and Oceans, 1993.

Taylor, Barbara L., and Tim Gerrodette. 'The Uses of Statistical Power in Conservation Biology: The Vaquita and Northern Spotted Owl.' *Conservation Biology* 7 (1993): 489–500.

Tester, Frank J. 'Reflections on Tin Wis: Environmentalism and the Evolution of Public Participation in Canada.' *Alternatives* 19, no. 1 (1992): 34–41.

Thieffry, Patrick. 'Les nouveaux instruments juridiques de la politique communautaire de l'environnement.' *Revue trimestrielle de droit européen* 28, no. 4 (1992): 669–85.

Thomas, Christopher, and Gregory A. Tereposky. 'The NAFTA and the Side Agreement on Environmental Co-operation.' *Journal of World Trade* 27, no. 6 (1993): 5–34.

Thomas, Gerald B. 'External Shocks, Conflict and Learning as Interactive Sources of Change in U.S. Security Policy.' *Journal of Public Policy* 19, no. 2 (1999): 209–31.

Thomas, John C. *Public Participation in Public Decisions: New Skills and Strategies for Public Managers.* San Francisco: Jossey-Bass, 1995.

Thompson, Andrew. *Canadian Environmental Regulation.* Vancouver: Westwater Research Centre, UBC, 1980.

Thompson, Andrew, et al. 'Rivers Defence Coalition Final Argument, Phase V, Kemano Completion Project Review.' British Columbia Utilities Commission. Vancouver, mimeo, 1993 (on file with West Coast Environmental Law Association).

Toner, Glen. 'Environment Canada's Continuing Roller Coaster Ride.' In Gene Swimmer, ed., *How Ottawa Spends, 1996–97: Life under the Knife.* Ottawa: Carleton University Press, 1996.

Toner, Glen, and Tom Conway. 'Environmental Policy.' In G. Bruce Doern, Leslie A. Pal, and Brian W. Tomlin, eds, *Border Crossings: The Internationalization of Canadian Public Policy,* 108–42. Toronto: Oxford University Press, 1996.

Toughill, Kelly. 'Pesticide levels dropping in Arctic.' *Toronto Star,* 5 March 1999: A6.

Trebilcock, Michael. *The Political Economy of Economic Adjustment: The Case of Declining Sectors.* Royal Commission on the Economic Union and Development Prospects for Canada, Collected Research Studies Series vol. 8. Toronto: University of Toronto Press, 1986.

Trebilcock, Michael, et al. *The Political Economy of Business Bailouts.* Toronto: Ontario Economic Council, 1985.

Trombelti, Orland, and Kenneth Cos. 'Land Law and Wildlife Conservation: Easements and Covenants in Canada.' Reference Paper no. 3, Wildlife Habitat Canada, November 1990.

Trosper, Ronald G. 'Traditional American Indian Economic Policy.' *American Indian Culture and Research Journal* 19, no. 1 (1995): 65–95.

Turner, N.J., and J.T. Jones. 'Occupying the Land: Traditional Paters of Land and Resource Ownership among First Peoples of British Columbia.' Presented at 'Constituting the Commons,' 8th annual conference of the International Association for the Study of Common Property, June 2000. www.indiana.edu/~isascp2000.htm.

United Nations. Conference on Environment and Development (UNCED). 'Agenda 21.' In Joyce Quarrie, ed., *Earth Summit '92,* 46–240. London: Regency Press, 1992.

– Department of Policy Coordination and Sustainable Development. *Critical Trends: Global Change and Sustainable Development.* New York: UN, 1997.

– Economic Commision for Europe. Convention on Long-Range Transboundary Air Pollution. LRTAP Emissions Data and Ratification Status. http://www.unece.org.2000.

– World Commission on Environment and Development. *Our Common Future.* New York: Oxford University Press, 1987.

United Nations Development Programme. UNDP, *Human Development Indicators 1999.* New York: 1999.

United Nations Environment Programme. *Voluntary Industry Codes of Conduct for the Environment.* Technical Report no. 40. Paris: UNEP Industry and Environment, 1998.

United States, National Research Council. *Fostering Industry-Initiated Environmental Protection Efforts.* Washington: National Academy Press, 1997.

– Committee on Hormonally Active Agents in the Environment. *Hormonally Active Agents in the Environment.* Washington: National Academy Press, 1999.

– Committee on Risk Characterization. *Understanding Risk: Informing Decisions in a Democratic Society.* Washington: National Academy Press, 1996.

Usher, P. 'Some Implications of the Sparrow Judgement for Resource Conservation and Management.' *Alternatives* 18 (1991): 20–1.

– 'Contemporary Aboriginal Land, Resource and Environmental Regimes: Origins, Problems and Prospects.' Report prepared for Royal Commission on Aboriginal Peoples, 1996.

VanderZwaag, David, and Linda Duncan. 'Canada and Environmental Protection: Confident Political Faces, Uncertain Legal Hands.' In Robert Boardman, ed., *Canadian Environmental Policy: Ecosystems, Politics, and Process*, 5–23. Toronto: Oxford University Press, 1992.

Van Nijnatten, D.L. 'The Day the NGOS Walked Out.' *Alternatives* 24, no. 2 (1998): 10–15.

van Twist, M.J.W., and C.J.A.M. Termeer. 'Introduction to Configuration Approach: A Process for Societal Steering.' In Roeland in't Veld et al., eds, *Autopoiesis and Configuration Theory: New Approaches to Societal Steering*. Dordrecht: Kluwer, 1991.

Van Zijst, H. 'A Change in the Culture.' *Environmental Forum*, May/June 1993: 12–17.

Vedung, Evert. 'Policy Instruments: Typologies and Theories.' In Marie-Louise Bemelmans-Videc, Ray C. Rist, and Evert Vedung, eds, *Carrots, Sticks and Sermons: Policy Instruments and Their Evaluation*. New Brunswick, NJ: Transaction, 1998.

Vernadsky, V.I. 'The Biosphere and the Noosphere.' *American Scientist* 33, no. 1 (January 1945): 1–12.

Versteeg, Hajo, editor. 'Workshop Proceedings: Environmental Canada Workshop to Obtain Advice on Essential Elements for Federal Endangered Species Legislation.' Ottawa: Environment Canada, 1998. www1.ec.gc.ca/ ~cws/endangered/work10/eng/index.html.

Vidich, Arthur, and Joseph Bensman. *Small Town in Mass Society*. Garden City, NJ: Doubleday, 1960.

Vitousek, P.M., P.R. Ehrlich, et al. 'Human Appropriation of the Products of Photosynthesis.' *Bioscience* 36 (6 June 1986): 368.

Vitousek, P.M., H.A. Mooney, et al. 'Human Domination of Earth's Ecosystems.' *Science* 277, no. 5325 (25 July 1997): 494–9.

Vogel, David. 'EU Environmental Policy and the GATT/WTO.' In Jonathan Golub, ed., *Global Competition and EU Environmental Policy*, 142–60. London: Routledge, 1998.

Von Moltke, Konrad. 'A European Perspective on Trade and the Environment.' In Durwood Zaelke, Paul Orbuch, and Robert Housman, eds, *Trade and the Environment*, 93–108. Washington: Island Press, 1993.

– 'The Last Round: The General Agreement on Tariffs and Trade in Light of the Earth Summit.' *Environmental Law* 23 (1993): 519–31.

von Weizsäcker, Ernst, Amory B. Lovins, and L. Hunter Lovins. *Factor Four: Doubling Wealth, Halving Resource Use*. London: Earthscan, 1998.

von Winterfeldt, Detlov, and Ward Edwards. *Decision Analysis and Behavioral Research*. Cambridge: Cambridge University Press, 1986.

Vroom, Victor H., and Arthur G. Jago. *The New Leadership: Managing Participation in Organizations*. Englewood Cliffs, NJ: Prentice-Hall, 1988.

Vroom, Victor H., and P. Yetton. *Leadership and Decision Making*. Pittsburgh: University of Pittsburgh Press, 1973.

Wald, Matthew L. 'Tribe in Utah fights for nuclear waste dump.' *New York Times*, 18 April 1999: 1.

Walker, Vern R. 'Keeping the WTO from Becoming the "World Trans-science Organization": Scientific Uncertainty, Science Policy, and Factfinding in the Growth Hormones Dispute.' *Cornell International Law Journal* 31 (1998): 251–320.

Wallis, W.D., and R.S. Wallace. *The Micmac Indians of Eastern Canada*. Minneapolis: University of Minnesota Press, 1955.

Walters, Carl. *Adaptive Management of Renewable Resources*. New York: Wiley, 1986.

Washington, R.O., and Denise Strong. 'A Model for Teaching Environmental Justice in a Planning Curriculum.' *Journal of Planning Education and Research* 16 (1997): 280–90.

Weale, Albert. 'European Environmental Policy by Stealth: The Dysfunctionality of Functionalism.' *Environment and Planning C: Government and Policy* 17 (1999): 37–51.

Webb, Kernaghan. 'Between Rocks and Hard Places: Bureaucrats, Law and Pollution Control.' In R. Paehlke and D. Torgerson, eds, *Managing Leviathan: Environmental Policy and the Administrative State*, 201–28. Peterborough, ON: Broadview, 1989.

– 'Voluntary Initiatives and the Law.' In Robert Gibson, ed., *Voluntary Initiatives: The New Politics of Corporate Greening*. Peterborough, ON: Broadview, 1999.

Weimer, David L. 'The Craft of Policy Design: Can It Be More than Art?' *Policy Studies Review* 11, no. 3/4 (1992): 370–88.

Weir, Margaret. 'Ideas and the Politics of Bounded Innovation.' In Sven Steinmo, Kathleen Thelen, and Frank Longstreth, eds, *Structuring Politics: Historical Institutionalism in Comparative Analysis*, 188–216. Cambridge: Cambridge University Press, 1992.

Weis, Judith S. 'Scientific Uncertainty and Environmental Policy: Four Pollution Case Studies.' In John Lemons, ed., *Scientific Uncertainty and Environmental Problem Solving*, 160–87. Cambridge, MA: Blackwell Science, 1996.

Weiss, Janet A., and Mary Tschirhart. 'Public Information Campaigns as Policy Instruments.' *Journal of Policy Analysis and Management* 13, no. 1 (1994): 82–119.

Weller, G.A., and M. Lange, editors. 'Impacts of Global Change in the Arctic Regions.' Report from a workshop, 25–6 April 1999. Tromso, Norway: International Arctic Science Committee, 1999.

Westbrook, David A. 'Environmental Policy in the European Community: Observations on the European Environment Agency.' *Harvard Environmental Law Review* 15 (1991): 257–73.

Westell, D. 'New rules to cut toxic wastes 47%.' *Globe and Mail*, 14 September 1994: B2.

Whalley, John. *The Trading System after the Uruguay Round*. Washington: Institute for International Economics, 1996.

Wheare, K.C. *Government by Committee*. Oxford: Clarendon Press, 1955.

White, R. 'Native Americans and the Environment.' In W.R. Swagerty, *Scholars and the Indian Experience: Critical Reviews of Recent Writings in the Social Sciences*, 179–204. Bloomington: University of Indiana Press, 1984.

Wiktorowicz, Mary. 'Shifting Priorities at the Health Protection Branch: Challenges to the Regulatory Process.' *Canadian Public Administration* 43, no. 1 (2000): 1–22.

Wilks, Stephen, and Maurice Wright. 'Conclusion: Comparing Government-Industry Relations: States, Sectors, and Networks.' In Stephen Wilks and Maurice Wright, eds, *Comparative Government-Industry Relations: Western Europe, the United States, and Japan*, 274–313. Oxford: Clarendon Press, 1987.

Williams, Bruce A., and Albert R. Matheny. *Democracy, Dialogue and Environmental Disputes: The Contested Language of Social Regulation*. New Haven: Yale University Press, 1995.

Wilsford, David. 'The *Conjuncture* of Ideas and Interests.' *Comparative Political Studies* 18, no. 3 (1985): 357–72.

– 'Path Dependency, or Why History Makes It Difficult but not Impossible to Reform Health Care Systems in a Big Way.' *Journal of Public Policy* 14, no. 3 (1994): 251–84.

Wilson, David C. *A Strategy of Change: Concepts and Controversies in the Management of Change*. London: Routledge, 1992.

Wilson, Jeremy. *Talk and Log: Wilderness Politics in British Columbia*. Vancouver: University of British Columbia Press, 1998.

Winbourne, J.L. 'Meeting Needs: A Consideration of the Aboriginal Fisheries Strategy and the Future of First Nations Food Fisheries.' In *Abstracts: Crossing Boundaries*, 297–8. 7th conference of the International Association for the Study of Common Property, Vancouver, June 1998.

– 'Taking Care of Salmon: Significance, Sharing, and Stewardship in a Nuxhalk Food Fishery.' Master of Environmental Studies thesis, Dalhousie University, Halifax, 1998.

Wirth, Timothy E., and John Heinz. *Project 88, Round 2. Incentives for Action: Designing Market-Based Strategies*. Washington: 1991.

Wolfe, David. 'Technology and Trade.' In Simon Rosenblum and Peter Findlay, eds, *Debating Canada's Future: Views from the Left*, 106–27. Toronto: James Lorimer, 1991.

Woodside, K. 'The Political Economy of Policy Instruments: Tax Expenditures and Subsidies in Canada.' In M. Atkinson and M. Chandler, eds, *The Politics of Canadian Public Policy*, 173–97. Toronto: University of Toronto Press, 1983.

– 'Policy Instruments and the Study of Public Policy.' *Canadian Journal of Political Science* 19, no. 4 (1986): 775–93.

World Bank. *The World Bank Participation Sourcebook*. Washington: The World Bank, 1996.

World Health Organization. 'Improving child Health.' http://www.sho.int/chd/publications/cdd/meded/1med.htm.

Wraith, R.E., and G.B. Lamb. *Public Inquiries as an Instrument of Government*. London: George Allen and Unwin, 1971.

York, G., and L. Pindera. *People of the Pines: The Warriors and the Legacy of Oka*. Toronto: Little, Brown, 1991.

Yosie, Terry F., and Timothy D. Herbst. *Using Stakeholder Processes in Environmental Decisionmaking: An Evaluation of Lessons Learned, Key Issues, and Future Challenges*. Washington: Ruder Finn and ICF Inc., 1998.

Young, Oran R. 'The Problem of Scale in Human/Environment Relationships.' *Journal of Theoretical Politics* 6, no. 4 (1994): 429–47.

Young, Zoe. 'NGOs and the Global Environmental Facility: Friendly Foes?' *Environmental Politics* 8, no. 1 (Spring 1999): 243–67.

Zahariadis, Nikoloas, and Christopher S. Allen. 'Ideas, Networks, and Policy Streams: Privatization in Britain and Germany.' *Policy Studies Review* 14, no. 1/2 (1995): 71–98.

Zinsser, J. *A New Partnership: Indigenous Peoples and the United Nations System*. Paris: UNESCO, 1994.

Zito, A. R. 'Task Expansion: A Theoretical Overview.' *Environment and Planning C: Government and Policy* 17 (1999): 19–35.

Zucker, Lynne G. 'Where Do Institutional Patterns Come from? Organizations as Actors in Social Systems.' In Lynne G. Zucker, ed., *Institutional Patterns and Organizations, Culture and Environment*, 23–49. Cambridge, MA: Ballinger, 1988.

Zurn, Michael. 'The Rise of International Environmental Politics: A Review of Current Research.' *World Politics* 50, no. 4 (1998): 617–49.